SPREADING THE WORD

PREVIOUS TITLES IN THE SERIES

Edited by Robin Myers & Michael Harris

Development of the English Book Trade 1700–1899. OPP, 1981

Sale and Distribution of Books from 1700. OPP, 1982

Author-Publisher Relations in the Eighteenth and Nineteenth Centuries.
  OPP, 1983

Maps and Prints: Aspects of the English Booktrade. OPP, 1984

Economics of the British Booktrade 1605–1939. Chadwyck–Healey, 1985

Bibliophily. Chadwyck–Healey, 1986

Aspects of Printing from 1600. OPP, 1987

Pioneers in Bibliography. St Paul's Bibliographies, 1988

Fakes and Frauds. Varieties of deception in print and manuscript.
  St Paul's Bibliographies, 1989

SPREADING THE WORD

THE DISTRIBUTION NETWORKS
OF PRINT 1550–1850

Edited by
Robin Myers and Michael Harris

ST PAUL'S BIBLIOGRAPHIES
WINCHESTER

OAK KNOLL PRESS
New Castle, Delaware
1998

© 1990 The Contributors

First Published 1990 by
St Paul's Bibliographies,
West End House,
1 Step Terrace,
Winchester,
Hampshire SO22 5BW

and reprinted in
1998 with Oak Knoll Press,
414 Delaware Street,
New Castle. DE 19720

British Library Cataloguing in Publication Data
Spreading the word: the distribution networks of print,
1550–1850.
1. Great Britain. Publishing, History
I. Myers, Robin   II. Harris, Michael, *1938*–
070. 50941

ISBN 0 906795 87 7 (UK)
ISBN 1 884718 54 X (USA)

Typeset in Monophoto Garamond by
August Filmsetting, Haydock, St Helens
Printed in England on long-life ∞ paper by
St Edmundsbury Press Ltd., Bury St Edmunds, Suffolk

RODNEY TRIUMPHANT,
AND
FRANCE HUMBLED.

YE failors that fail on the ocean fo wide,
  Right valiant, courageous and bold,
Now is the time for yourfelves to provide,
  And line all your pockets with gold.
Let us never be fearful to enter, brave boys,
  Since Rodney commands on the main;
For wherever he goes, he gives fatal blows
  To the fleets of proud France and of Spain.

When that our thundering cannons do roar,
  And trumpets and drums make a noife,
Our valiant commander, brave Rodney, does cry,
  Stand firm for your honour, brave boys,
And you fhall have ftore of bright dollars, my lads,
  As foon as the victory's gain'd.
Then our cannons we fire at Rodney's defire,
  And conquer the French dogs again.

Come venture, brave boys, for now is the time
  Your honour and courage to fhew,
All thofe who defire their fortune to make,
  Along with brave Rodney muft go,
For in the Weft Indies he's taken De Graffe,
  With eight of his fhips of the line,
And now he is gone the Spaniards to meet,
  And conquer the Dons once again.

Kind heaven he pleas'd to protect all our fleets,
  And fill each Britifh tar with delight,
And enfure them fuccefs, whene'er on the fea
  For Old England's wel are they fight.
May the church and the crown ftand ever on earth,
  Which to us a bleffing muft prove,
May George our king, all his enemies fling,
  Grant this, all ye powers above.

So here is a health unto George our king,
  And to Rodney and Hood here's the fame,
Hughes, Kempenfelt, Howe, Barrington and Rofs,
  Prince William, and Digby all fam'd.
May each bold commander on fea or on land,
  While bravely oppofing the foe,
Put thoufands to flight, for Old England's right,
  And conquer wherever they go.

EXON: Printed by T. BRICE, Goldfmiths'
Street.

The Maid's Lamentation for
Lofs of her Shepherd.

DOWN to the Woods, down to the
    Groves,
There I faw Phillis quite alone.
  There, &c.
Where little Fifhes do fport and play,
She for her Shepherd did make her Moan
  She, &c.

How cou'd young Strephon be fo fevere,
To flight a Girl that lov'd him dear?
Where I fhall wander, where I fhall go,
To find my Shepherd, I do not know.
  To, &c.

How can my True Love be fo unkind,
To go and leave me in Grief behind?
I'll fearch the Hills, the Vales and Rocks
But I'll bring my Shepherd to his Flocks.
  But, &c.

But fince that he has been fo unkind,
To go and leave me here behind,
I'll tend his Flock, I'll feed his Sheep,
Till Death does clofe my Eyes in Sleep.
  Till, &c.

Farewell, my Love, fince he is gone,
I like a Turtle for him will mourn.
True Love is like the raging Seas,
Toft up and down I take no Eafe.
  Toft, &c.

But if my Strephon fhould change his
    Mind,
Return to his True Love he left behind,
But if not fo, I do wifh him well,
But what I fuffer no Tongue can tell.
  But, &c.

Preface

THE ESSAYS in this collection are concerned with the history of publishing in its most precise sense, that is with the physical distribution of printed material and with the ways in which the networks linking different sectors of the market were constructed. How did printed material in Britain get from producer to reader? What were the mechanics of supply by which individuals from very varied social backgrounds came into contact with the print culture? These are hard questions lying at the heart of what is sometimes called the new bibliography. Distribution is a particularly complex line of book trade history because it leads out of the self-contained area of the printing office and bookshop, into the often baffling regions of redistribution and consumption. London, with its ever-increasing output of books, pamphlets, newspapers, ballads and ephemera, has always been the dominant influence on the market; but the contributors to this volume are almost all concerned with the local trade, and, by providing a series of detailed investigations into the distribution networks which supplemented or meshed in with those based on the capital, they are able to provide a fresh view of the developing relationship between print and society.

The way that the distribution of print was organised through the regional centres of population in Scotland, Ireland and Wales is only now beginning to be the subject of research. Eiluned Rees, the leading authority on the Welsh trade before 1800, describes how 'the Welsh language and cultural tradition gave the book world a unique flavour which influenced the London-Welsh tradition'. She identifies three 'distinct phases'; the first, up to 1718, when Welsh book-production was mainly centred on London; the second, in the mid-18th Century when it was augmented by printing in Wales and the Border towns; and the third, from 1762, when Welsh printers, by now thoroughly professional, forged highly organised trade links with London firms. She shows how personal the Welsh trade was, its development depending throughout on the involvement of a limited number of individuals. Warren McDougall's pioneering study of the 18th-Century trade between London and America via Scotland describes a well-planned and flourishing export network. This is a new aspect of the export book trade which was described by Giles Barber in an earlier volume in this series. McDougall's list of the materials which crossed the Atlantic in these years, the fruit of many years' research, is startling in its extent. Charles Benson's view of the Dublin book trade complements the essays of Warren McDougall and Eiluned Rees and provides a valuable supplement to the recent Lyell lectures of Mary Pollard which examined the Dublin trade from 1550 to 1800. Benson indicates the importance of the copyright law, introduced under the Act of Union in 1801, and the economic slump of the 1840s. He suggests in his analysis that there was less of an organised network of distribution, 1800–1850, than in the 18th Century when reprints, both legitimate and piratical, of English authors provided the Dublin trade with its staple.

The production and distribution of print in English provincial towns and cities included a growing proportion of books and pamphlets aimed at the middling and upper levels of society. The contribution of imprint information to an understanding of the way that distribution and marketing was organised forms part of John Feather's summarising essay. He makes the point that the 18th-Century provincial book trade was, in the main, distributive rather than productive, and local printers derived most of their work from jobbing and the printing of ephemera rather than from the production of books. This could suggest a local trade which was both sluggish and unproductive. However, Ian Maxted shows that this was far from the case. In his dynamic investigation into the single-sheet output of Exeter he indicates how important the activity of local printers was in sustaining a regional system of communication. In a survey which ranges from printed bills to political squibs and dying speeches he identifies a massive and almost entirely submerged stratum of print circulating through a highly active local community.

Local printing was distributed over a wide area. The itinerant hawker or flying stationer, selling his own or other people's material across large swathes of the country, was a familiar figure until well into the 19th century. Yet his crucial presence as the prime mover of the street traffic in print, extending into the most obscure districts and to the humblest social levels, has never been fully integrated with other sectors of the book trade. This may partly be because these individuals merged with the highly miscellaneous community of the road which, during the 18th Century, included actors, musicians, artists and bell-founders as well as pedlars, gypsies and beggars. The long historical pedigree of the itinerant seller of print is indicated by Tessa Watt who describes the changing nature of the broadside trade distributed by pedlars and pot-poets in the period 1550–1640. Michael Harris picks up this theme at the point that Tessa Watt leaves off, and using the previously neglected autobiography of David Love, flying stationer, suggests how these individuals organised their lives and related to the formal structure of the shop-based trade.

Central to any account of the local distribution networks of print from the late 17th Century is the newspaper. Originating in London this form of printed material had a particular force in a local setting. By creating a regular circuit which linked producer, distributor and reader in a system of mutual interest the newspaper became not only a vehicle for information and comment but a means of sustaining a wide variety of commercial relationships. Christine Ferdinand, using the unique records of a Hampshire weekly, is able for the first time to show in detail the way in which the distribution of such publications was organised and how they were used to construct networks of contacts over a considerable area. Michael Perkin, on the other hand, looks at one local newspaper a generation later, and suggests how it fitted into the business of an established printer, albeit a highly individual and colourful personality who we may doubt was typical of local newspaper printing in the 19th century.

These essays, as well as pinpointing some of the structural characteristics of distribution over three centuries, also provide a contribution to the debate on the relationship between 'high' and 'popular' culture. To some extent the division appears sharp. The single sheets sold and sometimes written by the local printer and the home-made verses of the flying stationer seem to belong to a different world from that of the specialist, shop-based bookseller. On the other hand, even the most derelict of the sellers of print was linked to the high-flying members of the commercial elite through an interest in the common medium as well as through the organisational structures of the trade. The issue is one which will continue to be the subject of research and analysis. Meanwhile, the contributors to this volume have opened up some of the most interesting and useful lines of enquiry into book and newspaper distribution as well as into the lives and experiences of some of those engaged in spreading the printed word.

This volume is based on the papers given at the eleventh annual conference on book trade history held at the Centre for Extra-Mural Studies, Birkbeck College (University of London). The discussion session was chaired by John Feather, with support from Charles Benson, the other papers were chaired by Robin Myers. Discussion was brisk and some of the material introduced and comments made have been integrated into the texts.

Robin Myers and Michael Harris
London
March 1990

Contributors

CHARLES BENSON is keeper of Early Printed Books at Trinity College, Dublin. He is currently compiling a dictionary of the Dublin book trade between 1801 and 1850.

JOHN FEATHER is Professor of Library and Information Studies at Loughborough University. He has written extensively on the history of the book trade and is author of *The Provincial Book Trade in Eighteenth Century England* (1985).

CHRISTINE FERDINAND is engaged in research at Wolfson College, Oxford. She is editor of the printing and bibliography section of the annual listing of current eighteenth-century studies and has written major articles on the early history of the *Salisbury Journal* and its printer Benjamin Collins.

MICHAEL HARRIS lectures in history at the Centre for Extra-Mural Studies, Birkbeck College. As well as acting as joint-editor of the conference papers he has written extensively on areas of book trade history. He is General Editor of the *Journal of Newspaper and Periodical History*.

WARREN MCDOUGALL teaches English in Edinburgh. His special field of interest is Hamilton and Balfour, and the Edinburgh book trade in the 18th century.

IAN MAXTED is Librarian at the Westcountry Studies Library, Exeter. Although 'isolated in the far western reaches of the world' he continues to produce invaluable bibliographical material through his series *Exeter Working Papers in British Book Trade History*.

MICHAEL PERKIN was formerly Curator of Special Collections at the University of Liverpool. He edited the two volumes, published as part of the Book Trade in the North West Project, which contain a directory of the Liverpool trade before 1850.

EILUNED REES is Conservation Co-ordinator in the National Library of Wales. In 1987 she published a catalogue of pre-1820 Welsh books under the title *Libri Walliae*.

TESSA WATT was formerly Research Fellow at Pembroke College, Cambridge. She recently completed a study of the relationship of cheap print and religion during the 16th and 17th centuries.

List of those attending the Conference

Jean Archibald
Librarian

Patricia Anderson
Historian

Paul Baines
Research Fellow

T.A. Birrell
Retired teacher

Richard Burleigh

Jackie Canning
Student

Dorothy Collin
University teacher

Andrew Cook
Archivist

Karen Cook
Map librarian

Robert Cross
Publisher

Ian Grant
Bookseller

David Hall
Librarian

J.F. Hewish
Librarian

Paul Hopkins
Historian

A.W. Huish
Librarian

Arnold Hunt
Student

Peter Isaac
Retired teacher

Mervyn Jannetta
Librarian

Graham Jefcoate
Librarian

Adrian Johns
Research Student

J. Knight
Curator

Brian Lake
Bookseller

Sheila Lambert

Colin Lee

Elizabeth Leedham-Green
Archivist

Giles Mandelbrote

D.F. McKenzie
Book historian

Rosamond McGuiness
University lecturer

Charles Parry
Librarian

John Palmer
Librarian

Margaret Payne
Librarian

Esther Potter
Librarian

Maurice Rickards
Editor: The Ephemerist

Charles Rivington
Retired

Alison Shell
Postgraduate student

R.M. Sparks
Writer

Peter Stockham
Bookseller

David Stoker
University lecturer

Katherine Swift
Library consultant

Tony Watts
Printer and Publisher

Ian Willison
Book historian

Janice Wilson
Research Assistant

P.K.J. Wright
Lecturer

Mr Zachs

Barbara Eifle
Costume historian

✠To my louing Friende ᴍaiſter Humfrey Toy.

SEEING THAT heretofore ſtanding nothing in the lyke poſsibilitie and good hope of profiting the ſimple and vnlearned of my Countrey, as I doe at this preſent, and haue yet than publiſhed thys litle treatiſe, now can I not iuſtly at your requeſt, deare Friende, who doeth ſo good a turne for all my Countrey, denye you to pervſe the ſame, being partly perſwaded that there maye come hereby ſo much vtilitie, as ſhall countervayle either my paines, your charges, & his ſpéding of tyme, that hath good cauſe to reade it. The matter I acknowledge to be but baſe, the tongue to be but obſcure(ſuch is the force of Tyme, or rather the prouidéce of the Almightie)though in times paſſed (as the names of the moſt famous Cities, auncient Boroughes, Territories, Countries, Riuers, and other notable places ouer all thys whole Iſle of Britain to ſuche as be ſkilfull in the tongue, do beare moſt euident wytnes euen to this day) it was ſo renowmed, and they that ſpake it, ſo puiſſant and valyant, that euen the mighty Emperor *Iulius Ceſar* him ſelfe wyth all hys prowes, in the tyme of their encounter, thought it the ſureſt ſafegard for themſelues to recoyle and turne their backs, as declareth (maugre the head of froward Myſtres *Inuidia*) their own country Poet *Lucanus*, writing thus,

Territa queſitis oſtendunt terga Britannis.

The ignorãt malignant, & contemptuous cauſed thys digreſſion.

A.ij. Vnto

Fig. 1   W. Salesbury,
A Playne and a familiar introduction, teaching how to pronounce the letters in the Brytishe tongue (Imprinted at London by Henry Denham, for Humfrey Toy, 1567.)
Reproduced by kind permission of the National Library of Wales.

Wales and the London book trade before 1820

EILUNED REES

[IN 1987, the National Library of Wales published *Libri Walliae: a catalogue of Welsh books and books printed in Wales, 1546–1820*. I was responsible for compiling the work and I duly wrote an accompanying essay entitled 'The Welsh book trade before 1820', which was subsequently issued as a separate publication. People who have read the essay will recognise in this article many references. Although I do not like re-using material in print, I found I could not avoid doing so without giving a distorted picture of the relationship between Wales and the London book trade. I plead with those who wanted the thrill of the new to view the old in a new context, as I did.]

Welshmen seeking fame and fortune have tended, like Dick Whittington, to go to London. In medieval times, they found careers as soldiers, doctors or lawyers. The Tudor dynasty owed its existence to the charm of a Welsh soldier, Owen Tudor, who won the heart of King Henry V's widow. When their grandson ascended the throne as King Henry VII, he recognised his debt to his fellow-Welshmen; able Welshmen received unprecedented opportunities for advancement. His patronage of the Welsh was emulated by his successors and the presence in London of an élite body of Welsh intellectuals was an important factor in the development of the Welsh book trade.

The relationship between Wales and the London book trade has many features in common with the relationship between the English provincial towns and London. Where scholarly publications were concerned, Welsh antiquaries were indistinguishable from their English counterparts in their publishing activities. However, the Welsh language and the Welsh cultural tradition gave the book-world a unique flavour which influenced the London-Welsh association. The relationship did not remain static and there are three distinct phases:

(1) *1546–1718*, the period during which Welsh book-production was centred mainly in London.

(2) *1718–1762*, a period when Welsh book-production in London was augmented by printing within Wales itself and by Welsh printing in the Border towns.

(3)   *1762–1820*, a period which saw a dramatic leap from amateurishness to professionalism amongst Welsh printers and which led to well-organised trade links with London firms.

If there is one strand which runs through these phases, it is the personal element. People, individuals, have shaped the history of the Welsh book trade and it is the personal element which lends charm to the tale. Some of the characters have reached the pages of biographical dictionaries but there are others who have remained in obscurity, who would have been gratified to learn that in pursuing their daily tasks they were influencing the cultural heritage of their country.

1546–1718

One man who does appear in biographical dictionaries is Sir John Price. Educated at Oxford and the Middle Temple, he rose through the household of Thomas Cromwell to prominence in the court of King Henry VIII. As Notary Public and the King's Principal Registrar in causes ecclesiastical, he was closely involved in the Dissolution of the Monasteries. He also became Secretary of the Council of Wales and the Marches. Sir John, like other scholars of the age, was imbued with the spirit of the Renaissance and it was as a Renaissance scholar that he gloried in his nation's ancient history. When the Welsh monasteries were dissolved, he rescued what he could of the manuscripts in their libraries, an inestimable service. He wrote historical works, in Latin, for they were a contribution to European scholarship. It would be tempting to see him merely as an ambitious civil servant, amassing a fine antiquarian library in the tradition of contemporary antiquaries, but he published the first book in the Welsh language and his motives for publishing the book reveal him to be a Protestant of conviction, deeply concerned about the spiritual welfare of his countrymen. The book is usually known by its opening words, *Yny lhyvyr hwnn*, (In this book), and it was printed in London by Edward Whitchurch in 1546. Sir John outlines his aim, which was to give the monoglot Welshmen selections from the Scriptures in their own tongue, the Creed, the Lord's Prayer and the Ten Commandments, knowledge of which was vital to their souls. A nondescript little book, it would hardly be recognised by the casual observer as the herald of a new era in Welsh culture.

Features associated with Welsh printing were already in evidence: the aesthetics of printing were not accorded high priority, the contents of the books were what mattered and the cheaper the production costs the better; religion was the driving force behind publishing and the cost had to be borne by those who could afford it rather than by the people for whose benefit the works were published; the language posed problems.

In the irreligious climate of the 20th century, it is difficult to appreciate the impact of the Reformation on the medieval world. Also, surrounded as we are by printed material, it is difficult for us fully to appreciate the implications of the invention of printing by movable type. Sir John Price was but one Welshman who realised how important it was that the vacuum left in the spiritual lives of ordinary people when the familiar images and paintings in their churches were destroyed be filled. Access to the Scriptures was vital to the Protestant cause and a Welsh Bible was needed. In 1563, Queen Elizabeth decreed that the Bible and the Book of Common Prayer be translated into Welsh. Letters Patent bestowed upon William Salesbury and John Waley for a period of seven years the sole right to print the Bible, the Book of Common Prayer and the Administration of the Sacraments and the Book of Homilies 'or any other book of godly doctrine in the British tongue, provided it be allowed by the Bishops of Hereford, St Davids, Asaph, Bangor and Llandaff, or any two of them who know Welsh'.[1]

William Salesbury was a Renaissance scholar with a special interest in the Welsh language. Amongst the earliest publications in the language are his dictionaries.[2] Unfortunately, his interest in linguistics marred his translations of the New Testament and the Book of Common Prayer, both printed in 1567; he chose to spell words in a way that would indicate their derivation. His collaborator in the translating of the Bible into Welsh was Richard Davies, Bishop of St Davids, but the men quarrelled and the task fell upon William Morgan, subsequently appointed Bishop of Llandaff and then St Asaph. His translation was printed in 1588.

Salesbury's translations were printed not by John Waley but by Henry Denham 'at the costes and charges of Humphrey Toy', at whose house Salesbury was staying. Toy's father Robert had a Welsh mother and a Welsh wife. William Morgan's Bible was printed by the Deputies of Christopher Barker, the King's Printer, who held the Bible Patent. Morgan spent a year in London, his expenses being borne by Gabriel Goodman, Dean of Westminster. Goodman was a Ruthin man, who had been in the service of William Cecil, Lord Burghley, another Welshman favoured by the Tudors. The 1588 Bible was a folio Bible, intended for use in churches, and it is believed that about 1,000 copies were printed.

The printing of the 1588 Bible proved crucial not only for Protestantism but also for the Welsh language. Although in the 16th century there was an accepted literary language which had evolved in the poetry and prose writing of the Middle Ages, it was the language of an educated minority, available only to those who had access to Welsh manuscripts. People normally conversed in the dialects of their districts, which at extreme points of Wales were mutually incomprehensible. The Bible provided the Welsh people with a standard language, which could co-exist with the dialects, and it provided the book trade with an accessible reference tool for proof-reading. When Stephen Hughes in 1672 was trying to get support for a cheap, pocket-sized Welsh Bible, he specified that a Church Bible should be offered as a copy in preference to a small Bible as the compositors would find it easier to read.[3]

Proof-reading was a problem. Welsh was a foreign language where the London compositors were concerned and complaints about misprints abound; Richard Davies in his introduction to the 1567 New Testament apologises for the printing errors, adding that the printers have never known one word of the language. There was an added complication, the language itself. In Welsh, y and w are both vowels and consonants and there are letters not found in the English alphabet, such as dd, ll, ff, ch, ph, th. The customary fount of type was found inadequate for the needs of the Welsh alphabet and various devices were tried to cope with the problem. Sir John Price's solution was to print dd as đ and ll as lh. Similar solutions appeared in the ensuing decades; dd was printed as d:, đ or dh. Incidentally, Welsh Catholic refugees on the Continent were encountering the same difficulties. The grammarian Gruffydd Robert, based in Italy, advised Welsh authors to adopt the Hebrew practice of doubling a letter by putting a full point beneath it.

Attempts were made in London to cut special founts of type for Welsh. In 1592 Thomas Orwin printed John David Rhys's *Cambrobrytannicae Cymraecaeve linguae institutiones et rudimenta*. The work is of interest to historians of typography because of the extensive use made of Hebrew type but historians of the Welsh book trade are interested in the specially cut w and y which were used in addition to the conventional forms, pronunciation being the guide to usage. The expense of cutting the additional letters must have added considerably to the printing costs, which were borne, predictably, by a member of the Welsh gentry, in this case Sir Edward Stradling of St Donat's. Even more letters were specially cut for Henry Salesbury's *Grammatica Britannica*, which was published a year later by Thomas Salisbury and which may have been printed at the Eliot's Court Press: y, w, ll, th, ng, dd and f. The y and w are not the same as those cut for Rhys's book. In 1595 yet another fount entered the lists, when John Danter printed Henry Perry's edition of William Salesbury's *Egluryn Phraethineb*. At least some of these special letters were re-used in later works, which was not the case with the previous attempts at Welsh letter-forms.

Recurrent complaints by Welsh authors that printers were unfamiliar with the language is a little odd as records indicate that Welshmen had infiltrated the book trade as they had other London trades. Humphrey Toy's Welsh connections have already been referred to. His forebears were from South Wales, whereas Thomas Salisbury, bookseller, hailed from North Wales. Salisbury, who was admitted freeman of the Stationers' Company in 1588, may be described as a scholar-publisher; he published two translations of the Psalms and Henry Salesbury's *Grammatica Britannica*.[4] About 50 Welshmen were apprenticed to the trade between 1605 and 1640 and yet their names rarely appear in imprints. An exception is Peter Bodvell, a Caernarvonshire man. He was apprenticed to Thomas Brewster, after which he became a bookseller, first in London and then in Chester. He is found in the imprint to the Welsh Book of Common Prayer of 1664,[5] when he was in London, and in the imprint to an edition of the Psalms and New Testament in 1672, when he had moved to Chester.[6]

Printing Welsh books was hardly lucrative and authors uttered bitter comments at the reluctance of London printers to take on Welsh books. The King's Printer, whose privilege it was to print the Bible, complained with matching bitterness at the heavy losses incurred in printing the 1620 edition of the Welsh Bible.[7] The market for Welsh books was limited, the scope for making profit negligible. Patronage was essential.

London-based philanthropists helped to subsidise the earliest Welsh publications on a personal basis but inevitably a more formal method of subsidy would be required. In 1674 Thomas Gouge set up the Welsh Trust. Gentry and clergy, not necessarily Welsh, of all denominations, undertook to set up schools in Wales and to publish and distribute edifying literature in the vernacular. Stephen Hughes, an Independent minister from Carmarthenshire, contributed much in the way of translating and editing texts and he realised his dream of a cheap edition of the Bible in Welsh. He was responsible for editing for publication the poems of Rees Prichard, Vicar of Llandovery, which gained immense popularity under a later title *Canwyll y Cymry*. The poems were homely verses in the Llandovery dialect, which conveyed the precepts of Christian life in easily memorised verses in everyday language. Hughes had to add glosses for the benefit of North Walian readers.

The work of the Welsh Trust had far-reaching implications for the book trade. By setting up schools, it was promoting literacy; by establishing libraries, it was promoting the sale of books; by formulating a publishing policy, it was gaining the confidence of the London printers; by organising a network of contacts throughout Wales, it was encouraging a formal book-distribution system. When the Trust came to an end, its functions were taken over by the Society for Promoting Christian Knowledge, a Church of England Society which was founded in 1698 and which catered for England as well as Wales.

Once the habit of reading has been established, readers do not necessarily confine their reading material to recommended texts. An enterprising Welsh tailor in London, Thomas Jones, decided to take advantage of the situation. In 1679, he embarked on a career as publisher of Welsh books as a commercial venture rather than as a philanthropic gesture. It was a courageous thing to do. He was taking financial risks and he had to tread carefully through a mine-field of restrictive practices governing the London book trade. What was the significance, for example, of Thomas Dawkes, who was in business c.1674–96, calling himself 'His Majesty's British Printer'? There were all sorts of complications with copyrights of Welsh books as so many of them were translations. One case which can be used as an example is that of a Welsh translation of Alexander Nowell's *Least Catechism* in 1578. Richard Jones wanted to print it but John Day held the privilege for catechisms. The decision of the Court of the Stationers' Company was that Jones should print the work only 'in the name of . . . Iohn Day and as assignee with him' but that he should hold the copyright as if he had printed it in his own name.[8]

The poems of Rees Prichard were so popular that they were reprinted several times during the latter half of the 17th century. No copy survives of the first edition. The second and third editions of parts one and two of the Works were published in 1659 under the imprint of Thomas Brewster. The first entry in the Stationers' Registers is for the fourth edition, entered by Anna Brewster in 1672. She sold the two parts in the same year to John Darby, who was probably responsible for the third part, a fragment of which survives. Darby published all three parts, also in 1672, together with a fourth part, the property of Samuel Gellibrand.[9]

Thomas Jones was not deterred. He embarked on a publishing programme which aimed to provide books which people wanted to read rather than books which they ought to read. Amongst the publications was his own pocket-sized Welsh dictionary, *The British language in its lustre*,[10] a dictionary which differed from its predecessors by being less concerned with scholarship than with the need of the common man to link English and Welsh in everyday life. The dictionary had two title-pages and the Welsh one translates the addresses of the two booksellers literally: Lawrence Baskerville's premises, 'At the Red Lion in Aldermanbury' becomes 'Tan Lun y Llew Coch yn yr henadur-Rewl' while John Marsh's premises 'at the Red Lion in Cateaton Street' becomes 'tan Lun y Llew Coch yn rhewl Cathfwytaad'. There were precedents for translating addresses into Welsh in imprints. In fact, in an imprint of 1629 [1630], even the personal names were translated, with comical effect: the book was *Pregeth dduwiol*, Robert Llwyd's translation of a sermon by Arthur Dent, printed by Nicholas Okes for Michael Sparkes, which became 'Printiedig gan Nicholas Dderwen dros Mihangel Wreichionen'.

Thomas Jones rightly surmised that a literate Welshman would welcome an almanack. In January 1679 he secured from the King a 'Letter Patent, for the Sole Liberty and Lisence of writing, Printing and Publishing an Almanack in the British Language'.[11] Two months later, he received in Articles of Agreement with the Stationers' Company 'the full and Sole Liberty Lisence and Priviledge of Writing, Printing, and putting to Sale yearly from hence-forth dureing his naturall life, All and as many Almanacks for each year in the Welsh Tongue, with Prognostications and Observations therein or without as he or they shall find cause for, and to alter and change the fform and method thereof, Yearly as he or they shall see good'.[11] No copy survives of his first almanack but it must have appeared in 1680 because in 1681 he was offering a reward of 20 shillings for information about a rival Welsh almanack and disposing of the services of John Braynton and John Jackson of Cateaton Street because 'I was forced to sue to an Execution before I could recover my Money for the parcels of my first Almanacks which they had of me to furnish their Country Customers'.[12]

Thomas Jones's volatile temperament has been a boon to the historian of the Welsh book trade. He had few inhibitions about proclaiming his indignation to the world and from his complaints can be gleaned information about current trade practices. He complained about everyone, including the printers of his diction-ary.[13] One wonders how the compositors reacted as they set the complaints against them, for they were bilingual. The Welsh Trust had made use of mercers as book-sellers back in Wales and Jones did the same, initially at least. Several distributors are known by name and one of the most illustrious was Dawkin Gove, Mayor of Carmarthen in 1648 and 1677. An inventory drawn up on his death in 1692 indi-cates the growth of the local trade; his stock of books formed a third of his total estate. He was obviously dealing wholesale as there were as many as 74 copies of one title.[14]

In his almanack for 1685, Jones announced that it was inconvenient to deal with everyone who sold books in Wales, it was not worth the trouble. In his almanack for 1688, he went a stage further and declared that he had left off dealing with the country; 'Those Country Chapmen that desire to have of my books or Oyntments, if they please to write to their Correspondents in London, that furnish them with other goods, and give them directions (in English) to send to my House (for the Books, &c.) which is by the End of Long-Alley in Moor-Fields'. He named John Marsh as his London agent. In the 1691 almanack, he was complaining that the shopkeepers and pedlars in Wales were selling books at twice the price. One of the culprits was Evan Lloyd of Haverfordwest, who appears in another context as an agent for Bromfield's anti-scurvy pills.[15]

When the Licensing Act lapsed in 1695, Thomas Jones moved to Shrewsbury, a town which served as the main trading centre for North Wales. Here, he set up as a printer, specialising in Welsh books and railing at all who threatened his livelihood. The demand for Welsh books was increasing steadily and the supply of Books of Common Prayer, for example, was not fulfilling the expectations of the newly literate public. Thomas Jones had published an unauthorised edition in 1687 and it sold well enough to encourage him to print further editions in Shrewsbury. He was characteristically irate that the Society for Promoting Christian Knowledge pro-posed publishing an octavo edition of the Book of Common Prayer in 1709, to be offered to subscribers at 18 shillings a dozen: 'Notwithstanding the fair proposals (or promises) made you by the Londoners for a small Common-Prayer in Welsh; you'l find your old Servant still kinder than they to you. for he hath already begun an Impression of the Common Prayer book in the ancient British Language, in a small volume, fit for the Pocket; with as good a Letter and on better Paper than they propose; and will sell them much cheaper than they offer; And besides, the Carriage from London will be saved you; and the Book will be finished and some bound for Sale by Wrexham Fair in March next, viz. 1707. And when the Book is ready, you will not be ty'd to buy a 100 50 or 25 of them together, but shall be welcome to buy one or more at a Reasonable Rate than they offer them by the hundred'.[16]

In Jones's diatribe lies the key to the relationship between Wales and the London book trade for the next half-century. London printers would continue to print subsidised publications, while in Shrewsbury and, after 1718, in Wales itself, books were printed according to local demand, usually by subscription. With London would be associated a wholesale trade as editions would run to thousands, while locally an edition of 500 would be considered ambitious and the closest approximation to bulk-buying would be an itinerant bookseller's order of a dozen copies.

1718–1762

In 1718 Isaac Carter set up a press in the village of Trefhedyn on the outskirts of Newcastle-Emlyn, just within the borders of Cardiganshire. In 1721, Nicholas Thomas issued the first book from his press in Carmarthen. It is assumed that both men had acquired their limited printing skills in Shrewsbury. Printing was established in Wales, albeit in a somewhat amateurish way. It has already been intimated that most books were published by subscription. The onus for publication usually lay with the author or translator and it thus follows that Welsh printers had one thing in common with their London counterparts; they were not taking any risks with their own capital.

Welsh printers printed books in English as well as in Welsh but obviously it was cheaper to import popular non-Welsh books and the book trade flourished. New and second-hand books, in English, Latin, Greek and Hebrew, on a variety of subjects, were being advertised by booksellers in sizable towns like Wrexham and Carmarthen. The cheapest way of despatching books from London was by sea, to the ports in South Wales via Bristol and to North Wales ports via Liverpool. Carriers were extensively used. Itinerant booksellers toured fairs and markets, usually on foot; a horse was a luxury.

The Welsh book trade in London was dominated during this period by societies. The Society for Promoting Christian Knowledge generously supported schools and libraries in Wales and continued to supply cheap Bibles, Prayer Books and devotional works. Amongst the most devoted labourers for the cause were Moses Williams, scholar, cleric and a Fellow of the Royal Society, who was closely involved with the publishing programme, and John Vaughan, squire of Derllys in Carmarthenshire, whose regular correspondence with the Society's headquarters ensured that the needs of the Welsh people would not be overlooked and who distributed thousands of books amongst the poor of his locality. His friend, Sir John Philipps of Picton Castle in neighbouring Pembrokeshire, was a philanthropist in the same mould. Sir John's protegé and later, brother-in-law, was a cleric, Griffith Jones, who gave literacy a dramatic boost with his Circulating Schools. The Circulating Schools were an early and eminently successful experiment in adult education. The demand for edifying literature became more pressing. Translators were recruited and once again the problems of proof-reading Welsh had to be faced. Thomas Williams of Denbigh was one of the translators and he offered in a letter dated 15 November 1709 to correct the proofs of his translation of William Assheton's Book on the Sacrament as they came off the press if they could be franked to him in the country.[17] Incidentally, Joseph Downing and John Oliver were the London printers whose names appeared most frequently in publications associated with the S.P.C.K., the former being a specialist dealer in theological books and the latter being the Society's official printer.

Moses Williams's literary activities ranged beyond the bounds of the Society. He was a regular customer of William Bowyer, the King's Printer, and his accounts are recorded in the Bowyer Ledgers. The most interesting entry appears on 2 April 1725, when he was paying by instalments his account for the printing of William Baxter's *Reliquiae Baxterianae*, which he edited. He paid ten guineas in cash and 'By a quantity of Ale from Wales amounting to £1. 3s. 6d.'

The Welsh are a gregarious people and those who were based in London gathered together to celebrate St David's Day. Maybe they had to show solidarity to combat the signs of unpopularity represented by the annual baking of ginger-bread *Taffies* in the shape of skewered Welshman![18] In 1715, the Honourable and Loyal Society of Antient Britons was formed, with the Princess of Wales, Caroline of Anspach, as patron, her qualifications for the honour being the good fortune to have been born on 1 March. Part of the St David's Day celebrations was a sermon preached in Welsh, the text of which was printed. 4,000 copies of George Lewis's sermon were issued in 1715.[19] A Welsh school was mooted and duly instituted in 1718. While not as lucrative for the London book trade as the S.P.C.K., the Society of Antient Britons was providing an identifiable market for Welsh books.

In 1751, a Welsh Society was founded which included the provision of books as part of its constitution. Part of Clause XIV of the Constitution of the Honourable Society of Cymmrodorion decreed that 'the Society are also to print and publish all scarce and valuable ancient British Manuscripts that they shall become possessed of, with Notes Critical and Explanatory – The Copies of all Books published by the Society shall vest in them; and the Profits arising from the Sale thereof, shall be appropriated to defray the Charge of such other Publications as the Society shall deem useful and necessary for promoting Knowledge and Virtue: And the better to carry on such Publications, a Printer and Bookseller to the Society shall be chosen yearly, at the Time appointed for electing principal Officers'.[20] The publishing aspirations of the Society may not have been fully realised but the Society exercised considerable influence on book-production. Unlike the societies already mentioned, the Cymmrodorion Society was neither primarily philanthropic nor charitable; it was patriotic. Its active members were drawn mainly from the gentry and professional classes, with the Morris brothers from Anglesey, notably Lewis, as its inspiration. Richard was the only one of the four brothers who was permanently resident in London and he was very much the focal point of its activities, Lewis being engaged most of the time in safeguarding the King's interests in the mines of Cardiganshire. There is no doubt that Richard was exploited; even cynical Lewis recognised the fact and wrote to William, the brother who stayed in Anglesey, saying that Richard 'loves his country to excess, and for that reason his country-men, who all impose upon him'.[21] His services as proof-reader, distributor and general factotum were taken for granted. Remuneration was sparse enough to keep him in a state of constant penury. He saw through press the 1746 and 1752 S.P.C.K. editions of the Welsh Bible and Book of Common Prayer.

The first work to carry a Cymmrodorion imprint is Thomas Pennant's *British Zoology*, 1766: 'Published under the inspection of the Cymmrodorion Society' and 'sold for the benefit of the British Charity-School'. Unfortunately, the imprint is a device by Pennant for hiding his identity as an author from a disapproving family and he later admitted that he was considerably out of pocket after paying for the handsome volume. His accounts survive, showing his payments to the artists and engravers. Also noted are payments to Benjamin White in 1763 and 1764: 'Allowed White for selling 5 sets £1. 6s. 3d', 'Do for advertising 4 times 14/- od', 'To Mr White for selling 20 sets £5. 5s. od'.[22]

The only printer who called himself 'Printiwr y Gymdeithas' was the Welshman William Roberts. He printed registers of members in 1759 and 1762.[23] He under-took the printing of the poet Hugh Jones's anthology *Diddanwch Teuluaidd* (1763), with Richard Morris doing the proof-reading, but the poet defaulted on payment and the printer went bankrupt.

Members of the Cymmrodorion were avid supporters of Welsh publishing, their names in subscription lists sometimes being distinguished by asterisks. Their support extended to Welsh books printed outside London, even when they de-plored the low standards of book-production. Country members built up their libraries with the help of the London friends, who were well placed to comb bookshops and attend sales on their behalf. The correspondence of the Morrisses has been published and it abounds in requests to poor Richard on the lines of the following from Lewis in 1761: 'I wish you would enquire into the price of Dr. Brooke's *Introduction to Physic and Surgery*, containing ten heads and articles, printed for J. Newberry at the Bible and Sun, Paul's Churchyard. If the price is moderate I would buy it. I am also told there is an English translation of Linnaeus, or some part of his works, by some hand near London; enquire about it, and by all means let me have the Copenhagen book mentioned by Pegge.'[24]

The range of Welsh books had expanded considerably by the end of this period. From subscription lists it is evident that literacy was widespread; all trades and professions are represented among the subscribers. The proportion of books 'inflicted' on the populace by well-meaning philanthropists was being matched by the books published by popular request, a factor easily assessed by the response to proposals circulated when publication was mooted. Poetry, ballads, chapbooks, almanacks, craft handbooks, sectarian tracts and hymnals became familiar features of humble households. They were of little aesthetic value, unlike the books that graced the walls of gentlemen's libraries, but they were cherished by their owners,

who had now acquired the habit of book-buying; the Welsh book trade was ripe
for expansion.

1762–1820

1762 may seem as strange a date to start a new phase of publishing history as was
1718. 1718 marks the advent of commercial printing in Wales; 1762 is significant
in that it marks the advent of professional printing. John Ross came to Carmarthen, a Scotsman who had been apprenticed to the trade, who had worked in a
London printing-house for seven years, who was obtaining new types and a
printing-press from London, who by 1764 had already got an overseer for the
Welsh work.[25] The days of amateur printers, using second-hand equipment, paying scant attention to presswork and relying mainly on personal contact for
distribution, were over. John Ross took on John Daniel as one of his apprentices,
and he, after gaining further experience as compositor to the King's Printers in
London, returned to Carmarthen in 1784 to set up his own business. In 1795,
John Evans set up business in Carmarthen. There was ample work for all three
printers; their output was prodigious. Meanwhile, printing-houses were mush-
rooming throughout Wales, all run by men who had served formal apprentice-
ships, who were regarding their ventures as commercial propositions and who,
therefore, had to establish links with their fellows in the book-world throughout
Wales and east of Offa's Dyke. The links within Wales were a development of
what was already happening: printers and booksellers responded to printing-
proposals with their subscriptions, allowing trade discounts; they exchanged
publications; they cooperated with the itinerant booksellers and ballad-mongers
and they kept in close touch with their clients.

Their clientèle was expanding. With the improvement in quality of book-
production came commissions from clergy, gentry, schoolmasters and littera-
teurs; Welsh imprints appeared increasingly in non-Welsh-language books.
Booksellers stocked an increasing quantity and range of books, no longer advertising them in the odd page at the end of a book but issuing catalogues. They
set up subscription reading rooms and circulating libraries, the success of which
depended on a supply of newspapers and new publications. Trade links with
London had to be well organised.

The trade links were reciprocal; London firms sold books printed in Wales
(South Wales in most cases), their names appearing in imprints. Lackington,
Allen & Co. appears in certain imprints of books printed by John Evans in
Carmarthen, William Williams in Merthyr Tydfil, Mark Willett in Chepstow,
John White in Carmarthen and Thomas Jenkins in Swansea. The firm subscribed
to Thomas Heywood's *Life of Merlin*, printed in Carmarthen by John Evans in
1812, ordering 100 copies. The following year, the copies were issued with a new
title-page bearing the imprint 'Printed for Lackington, Allen & Co., 1813'. The

most striking involvement of the firm with Wales, however, must be the publication of William Turton's multi-volumed translation of Linnaeus. Turton was living in Swansea, which explains why the volumes were actually printed in the town, by Zecharias Bevan Morris, John Voss and David Williams.[26] *The Cambrian* newspaper was printed in Swansea and the number for 6 August 1808 carries an advertisement for Lackington, Allen & Co.'s Catalogue for 1808–9, costing 4 shillings.

The firm of Cadell and Davies is another which had links with the Welsh book trade, the links being perfectly logical when one learns that William Davies was the son of a Welshpool clergyman. He was greatly respected by his contemporaries: 'Those who knew him best never witnessed in him anything but the most liberal conduct as a friend, and a straightforward man of business, in which he was assiduous and attentive, always giving most valuable advice, and acting with the utmost fairness and liberality in the position in which his good conduct had placed him.'[27]

The same respect was accorded to Owen Rees, a partner in the firm of Longman.[28] He had been apprenticed in Bristol and he joined Longmans in 1797. John Britton, who had known him for 40 years paid a warm tribute to him: 'Never was there a man who more fully and truly acted the character of "Harmony" on the great stage of the world . . . In an extensive intercourse with authors and artists, with booksellers and other tradesmen, indeed, with all classes of society, he was bland, courteous, candid, and sincere'.[29] Rees died in 1837, when he was making arrangements for his retirement in his old home, Gelli-gron, Glamorgan. A farewell party had been given in his honour when he was leaving Longmans, which must have been a memorable one as it is mentioned in most of his obituaries.

Longmans had trade links with printers in all major towns in South Wales and the evidence of the links is easily traced in imprints. A service to Welsh culture less easily assessed but probably of greater import is its fostering of personal links between the literati, the antiquaries and the book trade. In 1803, William Owen Pughe, a key figure in Welsh studies at this time, wrote to Edward Williams, 'Iolo Morganwg', (the Welsh counterpart of Chatterton and Macpherson), to tell him that 'Longman and Rees have established a converzatione every Saturday evening at their house; where when you make your appearance in London, you will meet with all sorts of curious gossip. This is an example for you by individuals who acquire money in trade employing it with a spirit that is not to be found once in an age among those who have it put in their pockets by others, without any exertion of their own'.[30] It was Owen Rees who introduced Benjamin Heath Malkin to Pughe: 'I have the pleasure of introducing to your acquaintance my friend Mr. Malkin, who is about publishing a Tour in South Wales. If you can, from your extensive acquaintance with everything that is Welsh render him any service, you will greatly oblige . . .'[31]

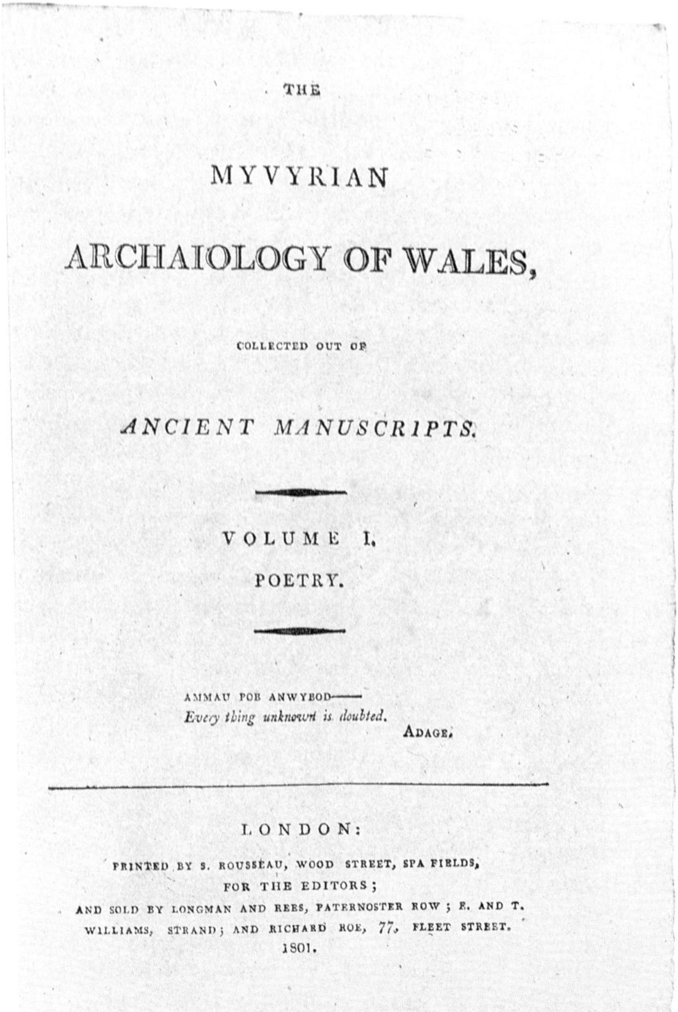

THE

MYVYRIAN

ARCHAIOLOGY OF WALES,

COLLECTED OUT OF

ANCIENT MANUSCRIPTS.

VOLUME I,

POETRY.

AMMAU POB ANWYBOD——
Every thing unknown is doubted.
ADAGE.

LONDON:

PRINTED BY S. ROUSSEAU, WOOD STREET, SPA FIELDS,
FOR THE EDITORS;
AND SOLD BY LONGMAN AND REES, PATERNOSTER ROW; E. AND T.
WILLIAMS, STRAND; AND RICHARD ROE, 77, FLEET STREET.
1801.

Fig. 2   *The Myvyrian archaiology of Wales*
[Edited by Owen Jones, Edward Williams and William Owen Pughe.] (London:
Printed by S. Rousseau ... for the Editors; and sold by Longman and Rees ... E.
and T. Williams ... and Richard Roe, 1801–7.) Reproduced by kind permission
of the National Library of Wales.

Malkin was but one of the antiquaries and travel-writers who became en-
amoured of Wales in this period. Wales was 'discovered' when Continental wars
put paid to sightseeing in Europe, which had been regarded as a vital part of the
education of a gentleman. Travellers in Wales recorded their experiences in print,
fascinated by the strange language and customs, and enthralled by the dramatic
scenery. Interest in the history and literary tradition of Wales was widespread and
the opportunities provided by firms such as Longmans for contact between antiquaries and literati from all parts of Britain could not be other than beneficial.
Malkin married a Welsh woman, as it happened, and settled in Wales.

Owen Rees's brother, Thomas, was also apprenticed as a bookseller but he
followed in his father's footsteps by becoming a Unitarian minister. He was based
in London for much of his career and retained links with the trade in that he was
commissioned to write volumes such as the one on South Wales for the series *The
Beauties of England and Wales*. It is interesting to note that in his introduction to that
volume, he acknowledges the help of his 'intelligent friend, Richard Phillips, Esq.
the able Editor of the Caermarthen Journal; who, besides collecting for me such
information as was to be found in the circle of his acquaintance, kindly availed
himself of the medium of his Paper to procure contributions from other quar-
ters'.[32] His personal connections with the London book trade qualified him to
compile a book which was published posthumously, *Reminiscences of Literary London from 1779 to 1853 ... By Dr. Thomas Rees, with ... additions by John Britton ... Edited
by a Book Lover* (London: 1896). Amongst the reminiscences is an account of a
Welsh bookseller in Paternoster Row, Thomas Evans, who 'in early life ... acted
as the publisher of the "Morning Chronicle", which first appeared in 1770, and in
that capacity had the misfortune to offend Oliver Goldsmith, who went to the
office, and unceremoniously assailed Evans with a stick. The sturdy Welshman,
however, soon recovered from his surprise, and with one blow laid the poet
prostrate on the floor.'[33]

No evidence has come to hand of Evans dealing with the Welsh book trade,
whereas two brothers, Evan and Thomas Williams, specialised in Welsh books.
They left their native Cardiganshire in 1787 and set up business in London.
Thomas returned in 1801 to pursue a career in banking in Aberystwyth but Evan
stayed until his death in 1835, making No. 11 Strand a focal point for the London-
Welsh book trade. He published some of the most important Welsh antiquarian
books of the period, including the short-lived but invaluable periodical *The Cambrian Register*. His stock included books in Welsh and of Welsh interest published
back in Wales and in Shrewsbury and also second-hand books. He confesses to
having 'bought deeply'[34] at the sale of the library of the harpist and antiquary,
Edward Jones, who described himself as 'Bardd y Brenin' (the King's Bard).
Williams, incidentally, often used the term 'Bookseller to the Duke and Duchess
of York' in his imprints. He claimed to have '*grown Gray* in the service of Cambrian
literature'[35] but his services were not always appreciated and he was not welcomed

into the Cymmrodorion Society. He was, however, a member of the Gwyneddi-gion Society.

The Cymmrodorion Society lost impetus after the death of Richard Morris and, in 1770, the Gwyneddigion Society was formed, based in London. The social aspects of the Society are immortalised in David Samwell's poem *Padouca Hunt*:[36]

> In Walbrook stands a famous inn
>   Near ancient Watling street,
> Well stored with brandy, beer, and gin,
>   Where Cambrians nightly meet.

The printer of the poem, Vaughan Griffiths, was in business in London around 1797 to 1812. He printed about half a dozen Welsh books in our period and he receives favourable comments in the correspondence of the Welsh literati, though his involvement with them was not as great as that of the Rees or Williams brothers.

The Gwyneddigion played a more active role in publishing than the Cymm-rodorion, being fortunate in that one of its members was an affluent skinner, Owen Jones, whose son and namesake gained fame as a designer in the worlds of art and book-production. Owen Jones, senior, spent a fortune on Welsh publishing. He sponsored the compilation as well as the printing of the anthology of early Welsh texts known as *The Myvyrian Archaiology*,[37] the title being chosen in his honour since his bardic name was Owain Myfyr. The venture is thought to have cost him between £4000–5000, of which printing would have absorbed £1000.[38] Fortuna-tely, letters sent to Owen Jones have been preserved in the Cymmrodorion library, which was deposited in the British Museum in 1855. Letters of other Welsh literati have survived in various collections and it is interesting to note that Evan Wil-liams's premises were used as a convenient pick-up point for mail and messages.

Williams was a businessman as well as patriot, and this is why he earned unflat-tering epithets such as 'Mr Skinflint'[39] and why he was not always kindly disposed to those who did not use his services as publisher. Samuel Rush Meyrick published his book on *The History and antiquities of the County of Cardigan* by subscription in 1808.[40] He writes to beg William Owen Pughe to send his 3 guineas subscription as the work had cost him £1100, while he had received only £600 in subscriptions. He adds, 'If however you paid Williams the stationer in the Strand, be so good as to send me word immediately, and an order to him to give it up to me as I have had great difficulty in obtaining *even a part* of the subscriptions he has received, from a spiteful hatred he had chosen to shew towards me because he was not the publisher of my book.'[41] The statement is somewhat surprising as Williams had included a five-page advertisement for the work in his *Catalogue of books* in 1808.

When Rhys Thomas failed to complete the mammoth *English-Welsh dictionary* by John Walters at his printing establishments in Llandovery and Cowbridge, it was

Evan Williams who was instrumental in finding a London printer to complete the job. Letters written by Walters to Owen Jones indicate that Jones was arranging the transaction. In August 1793, Walters wrote to say: 'I have sent, by this day's Post, a small box, containing the *Manuscript*, directed for you. . .After removing the shavings, you will find *Hints & Directions to the Compositor, &c*. I leave the conduct of the whole to you'.[42] The printer chosen was an Edward Jones, who does not appear in any of the dictionaries of printers. Edward Jones's bill for the job, addressed to Owen Jones, is to be found amongst the latter's papers:[43]

For printing 32 sheets of the Revd. Mr Walters English and Welch Dictionary at 36/-	£37 12s 0d
For one Sheet of Errata not worked	£1 12s 6d
For 32 Reams of Paper at 15s 6d	£24 16s 0d
Wrappers for the Books	12s 0d
For stitching &c 500 Books	£1 11s 6d
Postage & Letters, Package, Porterage, Booking &c	12s 6d
	£86 16s 6d
By Cash at difft. times	£80
	£6 16s 6d

The 'Correction of the Press' was done by William Owen Pughe.[44] Pughe was a key figure in Welsh publishing; he rendered service as a man well versed in the antiquities of his country, as translator and editor, as a litterateur in his own right and as an amiable confidante. He was also a lexicographer and in this context his contribution to Welsh publishing almost proved disastrous. For an intelligent man, he was extraordinarily gullible. He fell prey to bizarre theories, including those of Rowland Jones, who believed that Celtic was the primeval language from which Greek, Latin, English and Welsh were descended, and Edward Williams ('Iolo Morganwg'), who claimed he had found the bardic alphabet used by Celtic bards. The grammars and dictionaries compiled by Pughe were marred by his misguided views but what was potentially more devastating to printing history was his attempt to devise typographical conventions suited to his theories. They first appear in 1793 and are easily identifiable by the use of z for dd.[45] In 1808, a special fount was cast for a London edition of *Cadwedigaeth yr iaith Gymraeg*, the Bala edition of the same year being in conventional type. No correspondence concerning the casting of the fount has been found, but it may be significant that the book was printed by Samuel Rousseau, who specialised in printing oriental languages. A bardic fount was provided by Pughe for Caleb Stower's *Printer's grammar* (London, 1808) and we know that he persuaded Hugh Hughes, the type-founder, to cut him a fount of bardic type in 1825.[46]

Pughe had volunteered to correct any Welsh tracts published by the Religious Tract Society. He was recommended for the task by Thomas Charles of Bala, a member of the Society and a founder-member of the British and Foreign Bible Society. Pughe convinced him of the merit of his orthography and Charles actually proposed using it for an edition of the Welsh Bible. Fortunately, the sanity of fellow-clerics prevailed.

Thomas Charles had a press at Bala in Merioneth, with Robert Saunderson as printer. Supplies had to be brought from London and Pughe was a useful agent in a crisis: Charles wrote in September 1806, asking Pughe to call on Beale Blackwell the inkmaker '& ask whether they have sent the Ink which has been *twice* ordered before? if not, do they mean to send it? If they do, I wish to have it immediately, or my press must stop'.[47] Pughe had performed similar favours for the Trevecka press, Breconshire. Two letters were despatched to him in 1793.[48] In the first letter, he was asked to call at Caslon's premises in Finsbury Square to see if a fount of new letters, 'small pica body, long primer Rom No1', had been despatched. The second letter, written two days later, hints at panic after news of Caslon's bankruptcy: 'We should esteem it as a peculiar favour if you could procure us a fount immediately from any of the letter founders large enough to compose 16 pages 8vo.' It was to Pughe that Thomas Williams, the drover turned printer, looked when he wanted a supply of Gwyneddigion publications to sell at Dolgellau.[49]

Although printing had arrived in Wales, book-illustration was in a primitive state. Theophilus Jones was able to have his *History of the County of Brecknock* (1805–9) printed by George North of Brecon, but the plates were done in London, under the supervision of Sir Richard Colt Hoare, and they remained in the possession of John Booth, the London bookseller mentioned in the imprint, until he sold them at 5 shillings apiece.[50] Likewise, the superb illustrations, some of which were hand-coloured, used for the editions of the French Chronicles printed at Thomas Johnes's private press at Hafod, in the wilds of Cardiganshire, had to be done in London.

The Hafod Press was in operation between 1803 and 1810, with James Henderson as its professional printer. The folio and quarto editions of Johnes's translations of the chronicles of Joinville, Froissart and Monstrelet are a striking monument to the Press, and they are by no means its only publications. By 1809, however, help with the actual printing was sought; the names of the London printers, Thomas Bensley and Henry Bryer, may be seen in the colophons of certain Hafod books of 1809 and 1810.[51]

Paul Panton, junior, squire in Anglesey, also had a private press, probably a parlour press.[52] He acquired it for his own pleasure but, sadly, none of his handi-work as a printer survives. His supplier and mentor was Luke Hansard, and were it not for the survival of two letters written by Hansard to Panton in December 1794 and 1795, we would know nothing about the venture. That would have been a pity because there is something endearing about the thought that one of the busiest printers in London found time to instruct an Anglesey gentleman in the fine art of printing. Commercial considerations could not have been foremost in the minds of the pupil or the mentor.

By 1820, the close of the period under review, the Welsh book trade had reached maturity. Amateurism was discarded and trade within Wales and with London was conducted on professional lines. There were many changes in Wales during the 18th Century; the country was discovered by industrialists as well as by tourists. Literacy had spread but so had religious dissension, the flames of which were fanned by the Methodist Revival. The French Revolution inspired Welsh radical thought and an abortive French invasion of the Pembrokeshire coast in 1797 awakened patriotic zeal for the defence of the realm. Wales was not an isolated cultural backwater. Literacy had spread and a love of reading was much in evidence. Printers in Wales responded to the increasing demand for publications, and of course for jobbing printing, but they would have been only too ready to admit that without their London links they could not have satisfied their customers. To whatever degree they expanded their business, they would have to turn to London for printing equipment and supplies, and they would rely on London agents for supplying newspapers, journals, novels and books outside their range of publication. For the London book trade, the links were an opportunity for further trade outlets. If they could be strengthened by personal contacts, so much the more pleasant, and potentially efficient, for all parties concerned.

References

1. W.W. Greg, *A Companion to Arber* (Oxford, 1967), p.8.

2. W. Salesbury, *A Dictionary in Englyshe and Welsh* (London: John Waley, 1547).
    W. Salesbury, *A Playne and a familiar introduction, teaching how to pronounce the letters in the Brytishe tongue* (Imprinted at London by Henry Denham, for Humfrey Toy, 1567).

3. R. Prichard, *Gwaith* (London, 1672), sig.a4.

4. *Psalmae gwedi i cynghanedhu. . .Gan Gapten Wiliam Middelton* (Llunden: Simon Stafford a Thomas Salisbury, 1603).
    Rhann o Psalmae Dafydd (Llunden: Simon Stafford dros T.S., 1603).

5. *Llyfr Gweddi Gyffredin* (A Brintiwyd yn Llundain, gan S. Dover, tros Edward Ffowks a Phetr Bodvel, 1664).

6. *Llyfr y Psalmau, ynghyd a Thestament Newydd* (Printiedig yn Llundain gan E. Tyler a R. Holt, ac a werthir gan Samuel Gellibrand. . .a chan Peter Bodvel yng-Haerlleon, a John Hughes o Wrecsam, 1672).

7. W.W. Greg, *A Companion to Arber* (Oxford, 1967), pp.257–8.

8. W.W. Greg and E. Boswell, *Records of the Court of the Stationers' Company, 1576 to 1602, from Register B* (London, 1930), pp.lxxiii–lxxiv.

9. E. Rees, 'A Bibliographical note on early editions of *Canwyll y Cymry*' in *Journal of the Welsh Bibliographical Society*, 10, 2 (1968), pp.36–41.

10. T. Jones, *The British language in its lustre* (Printed 1688, and sold by Mr Lawrence Baskervile. . .and Mr. John Marsh).

11. Reproduced in Thomas Jones's Almanack for 1703. His almanacks were produced under various names; unfortunately, many of them are incomplete and we cannot be sure what form of name he would have used in a particular year.

12. T. Jones, *An Astrological speculation* (London, 1681), p.10.

13. T. Jones, *The British language in its lustre* (London, 1688), sig.X3v.

14. National Library of Wales, (hereinafter NLW), St Davids Probate Records.

15. M. Bromfield, *A Brief discovery of the chief causes, signs, and effects, of scurvy* (London, 1679).

16. Thomas Jones's Almanack for 1708.

17. T. Shankland, 'Diwygwyr Cymry' in *Seren Gomer* (1904), p.16.

18. R.T. Jenkins and H.M. Ramage, *A History of the Honourable Society of Cymmrodorion and of the Gwyneddigion and Cymreigyddion Societies (1751–1951)* (London, 1951), p.11.

19. Ibid. p.13.

20. *Gosodedigaethau Anrhydeddus Gymdeithas y Cymmrodorjon yn Llundain* (Llundain: Printiedig i Wasanaeth y Gymdeithas, gan John Oliver, 1755).

21. R.T. Jenkins and H.M. Ramage, *A History of the Honourable Society of Cymmrodorion* (London, 1951), p.32.

22. NLW Add. Mss. 2545B.

23. *Cofrestr o Gymdeithas y Cymrodorion* (Llundain, 1759).
      Cofrestr o Gymdeithas y Cymrodorion (Llundain, 1762).

24. J.H. Davies, ed. *The Letters of Lewis, Richard, William and John Morris...1728–1765* (Aberystwyth, 1907), pp.389–90.

25. A Welsh advertisement in H. Evans, *Ymddiddan rhwng hen wr dall a'r Angeu* (Caerfyrddin: J. Ross, 1764), sig.Alv.

26. *A General system of nature.* The printing of the seven volumes between 1800 and 1806 was a complicated business and anyone wishing to have details of the volumes should consult No.3322–3331 in E. Rees, *Libri Walliae* (Aberystwyth, 1987).

27. J.B. Nichols, *Illustrations of the literary history of the eighteenth century...Vol.VIII* (London, 1858), p.492.

28. No distinction will be made in this paper between the various names of the firm: Longman & Co.; Longman & Rees; Messrs. Longman, Hurst, Rees & Orme, etc.

29. T. Rees, *Reminiscences of literary London from 1799 to 1853...with additions by John Britton...Edited by a Book Lover* (London, 1896), p.44.

30. NLW, Iolo Morganwg Letters 356.

31. NLW Add. Mss. 13224B, p.431.

32. T. Rees, *The Beauties of England and Wales...South Wales* (London, 1815), p.viii.

33. pp.63–4.

34. Evan Williams to William Owen Pughe. NLW Add. Mss. 13263C, p.513.

35. Ibid. pp.513–4.

36. D. Samwell, *& Padouca Hunt* (London: V. Griffiths, 1800?), p.3.

37. *The Myvyrian archaiology of Wales* [Edited by Owen Jones, Edward Williams and William Owen Pughe] (London: Printed by S. Rousseau...for the Editors; and sold

by Longman and Rees...E. and T. Williams...and Richard Roe, 1801–7).

38. G. Carr, *William Owen Pughe* (Caerdydd, 1983), p.112.

39. Thomas Edwards to William Owen Pughe. NLW Add. Mss. 13263C, p.672.

40. London: Printed by T. Bensley...for Longman, Hurst, Rees and Orme, 1808. Reissued in 1810.

41. NLW   Add. MSS.13263C, p.34

42. British Library Add. MS. 15030, p.169.

43. Ibid. p.172.

44. Ibid. p.167.

45. *Ffurv gweddi* (Llundain: Charles Eyre ac Andrew Strahan, 1793). R. Powell, *Awdyl ar dymhorau y vlwyzyn* (Lundain, 1793).

46. NLW Add. Mss. 13263C, p.560.

47. NLW Add. Mss. 13222C, p.4.

48. Ibid.pp.381 and 375.

49. Ibid.p.331.

50. E. Davies, *Theophilus Jones* (Brecon, 1905), p.27.

51. J.A. Dearden, 'Thomas Johnes and the Hafod Press, 1803–10' in *The Book Collector* (Autumn, 1973), p.335.

52. E. Rees and G. Walters, 'Thomas Pennant and Paul Panton Jr: their printing contacts with George Allen and Luke Hansard' in *Journal of the Printing Historical Society*, 7 (1971), pp.54–63.

Scottish books for America in the mid 18th Century

WARREN MCDOUGALL

Introduction

IN EXPLORING THE availability of Scottish books in America in the mid 18th Century, I consider these aspects: the extensiveness of book exports to America from Scottish ports; the nature of the books sent by merchants to American country stores; the trade in Bibles from Adrian Watkins and Alexander Kincaid of Edinburgh to David Hall of Philadelphia; the American connections and activities of booksellers of the Scottish Enlightenment – Kincaid and Bell, and Hamilton and Balfour; the evidence of Scottish books in American catalogues of the 1750s and 1760s.

The book scene in Scotland at the time may be summarised this way. In the fourth decade of the century, the Scottish booksellers were defending a copyright action brought against them by the booksellers of London. The idea of reprinting a great variety of books for the home market, and of exporting them – America was a beacon – inspired the Scots, and even before the successful outcome in the Court of Session, they began a new Scottish reprint trade. From 1743 in Glasgow and 1748 in Edinburgh, certain English titles began to be reprinted openly, with Scottish imprints, at prices below London rates. From 1750, the Glasgow and Edinburgh printers and booksellers were competing to put out a wide range of reprints in literature, philosophy, history, economics, science and theology. This growth spurred the publication in Scotland of original work by Scots authors, particularly by the booksellers Hamilton and Balfour, and by Kincaid and his successive partners Donaldson and Bell. Another feature of the Scottish book scene was the publication of French authors, in the original and in translation.[1] Fine editions of the classics were printed, famously, by Foulis at Glasgow, but also by Hamilton, Balfour and Neill and by Ruddiman at Edinburgh. The printing of cheap editions of Bibles and New Testaments was continued by the King's Printer in Scotland, at the period of this study by Adrian Watkins 1748 to 1758, and thereafter by Alexander Kincaid. New Testaments, catechisms, prayer books and psalm books were printed by a variety of other printers. Cheap Scottish editions of popular religious writing, and children's books, were also being produced.[2] An ocean distribution network for Scottish goods was well established. Prominent among shippers were the Glasgow tobacco merchants, who had a trade running between the main Clyde ports to America, the West Indies, Ireland and Europe. Many of their ships unloaded tobacco, rum and sugar in Scotland, took on a cargo of manufacturd goods, and headed back across the Atlantic. Some of these goods were destined for their system of stores set up in Virginia and Maryland, where they were offered in exchange for tobacco.[3] The ships belonging to tobacco and other merchants were wide ranging and enterprising. Space was used for their own cargoes or contracted out to agents or syndicates. Scottish captains were given a considerable say in arranging cargoes, and even destinations. In 1759, the tobacco firm Buchanan and Simpson of Glasgow had one of their ships at London for a refit. They wrote to Captain James Colhoun that he and the London agent should try for a freight from there to Dublin, or failing that to Virginia; if not those, then to Halifax or some part of continental America; failing that to some port up the Florida Straits. In the event, they were displeased when Colhoun turned down freight to Philadelphia and Quebec and chose to go to New York, because by this time they had a cargo for Maryland.[4] Such a firm also had schemes for insurance – whether the vessel were going by convoy or running it alone 'north about' around the top of Scotland or Ireland – and what to pay in ransom if a ship were captured by privateers or the French.[5] And the Scots reading public in general was very well informed, through newspapers, of the American trade: arrivals, departures, wrecks, captures, and even where Scotland-bound ships broke off from the convoy.[6]

Book exports from Scottish ports

The amount and the value of Scottish books sent to America in the period can be calculated from the records of shipping, which are extant from 1742–3 in the form of Custom Collectors' Quarterly Account Books; summaries for Scotland as a whole are recorded from 1755.[7] For the purposes of this paper, I have examined the Quarterly Accounts of Leith, Greenock and Port Glasgow from 1742 to around 1760, and the other Scottish ports to 1755.

The Port of Leith, a mile north of Edinburgh, mainly sent books to South Carolina and the West Indies in the 1740s and 1750s.[8] The amounts are not large compared with the Clyde exports, but the periodic shipments are indicative of an organised trade. The ship *Industry* of Leith, loading at Leith for Charleston, South Carolina, picked up 14 *Monthly Magazines* in 1748, six hundredweight of books in 1749, and two hundredweight of books in 1753, 134 Bibles in 1754. In Charleston in 1752 was Robert Wells, a Scotsman, who learned the bookselling trade in Edinburgh, so he might have been one of the recipients.[9] At Leith, the ship's captain James Strachan, on his way from London to South Carolina in June 1754, on the ship *Mercury*, took on 56 pounds of books under his own name, presumably to sell on his own account. Jamaica received seven hundredweight of books

Newspapers kept booksellers and other merchants informed about the movement of ships. At right, Hamilton, Balfour and Neill's *Edinburgh Chronicle* for 1759 carries an account of how three Scottish ships left an American convoy, from St Kitts, to head for Port Glasgow. At left is Moll's *Mappe Monde*, 1748. The Hamilton, Balfour and Neill edition of *Bishop Burnet's History of his own time,* 1753, has one of their typical clean and spacious title-pages. The plate of Gilbert Burnet, not part of the edition, is a link with the enterprising Alexander Kincaid. As Hamilton and Balfour advertised the first Scottish printing of *Burnet's History*, to their chagrin Kincaid and Donaldson brought to Edinburgh the pirated Dutch version printed by Thomas Johnson. The owner of the Hamilton, Balfour and Neill copy had several of the Dutch plates inserted. At the bottom right is the Hamilton, Balfour and Neill *Anacreon*, 1754, in a contemporary binding.

through Leith in 1750 and 1754, Virginia a hundredweight around this time. The *Bettsey* took five hundredweight of books to Antigua in 1760. The first reference I have seen of distribution of books directly to Canada from Leith is 1 April 1761 when the *Wolfe* of Leith, a 100-ton ship sailed by six men and Captain Alex Alexander, took on four hundredweight of books for Quebec.

From the Port of Montrose, the *Delight* of Dundee took a hundredweight of unbound books to Virginia in 1751; the lack of binding is unusual – most books were sent from Scotland bound.[10] At Perth, half a hundredweight of bound books was shipped to Jamaica and the Leeward Islands in 1752,[11] while at Aberdeen, merchants were sending various quantities of books ('two cases', 'two boxes' 'fifty pounds weight' etc.) to Virginia from 1748.[12] While the Port of Kirkwall in Orkney did not ship British books in this period, ships stopping there *en route* from Amsterdam to New York and Boston paid customs duty on books acquired in The Netherlands.[13]

In the West of Scotland, books were shipped to Virginia from Ayr.[14] One ship's captain going through Ayr was Alexander Hutcheson, whose name also turns up a number of times on different ships taking books from the Clyde ports to America in the 1740s and 1750s, and who sometimes exported books on his own account.[15] At Ayr in January 1744, Hutcheson was in command of the *Concord* which took 164 pounds of books to Virginia; in December 1746, he was captain of the *America*, which had gone to France to unload tobacco, and had called back at Ayr, where it took on two hundredweight of books plus a large general cargo, and sailed to Virginia. Port Irvine (which incidentally was involved in the trade in books between Scotland and Ireland) shipped books to Charleston, South Carolina.[16] There was a large shipment of books (2,180 pounds) from Irvine to Philadelphia on 27 May 1754. This was on the snow – or three-masted ship – *Grizie* of Irvine, Captain James Cameron loading the books on behalf of James Campbell and Company.[17]

The principal Scottish ports for book exports to America were Greenock and Port Glasgow.[18] Between 1743 and 1760, Greenock and Port Glasgow shipped around 86.5 tons of books valued at £19,000 to America and the West Indies.[19] Nearly half of the total (40.3 tons) was for Boston, while 23.3 tons went to Virginia, 18.7 tons to Philadelphia. Other consignments in this period were for Maryland, New York, South Carolina, Antigua, Jamaica, St Christopher and St Martin. The books could go on from these ports to other destinations: David Hall of Philadelphia sometimes was sent Scottish books via Boston, while the 2.5 tons of books exported from Port Glasgow to New York in 1759 were for Hall – Bibles from Adrian Watkins of Edinburgh and assorted titles from Hamilton and Balfour.[20]

Some of these consignments were in small quantities, others very large. At Greenock in March 1744, on two ships loading for Boston, the *Marrion* took on two shipments of books weighting 74 hundredweight, while the *Prince George* of

Glasgow took on 18 hundredweight. There were bigger book cargoes than this going to America.[21] Some years saw feverish activity. The Customs Collectors' Quarterly Accounts for Greenock in 1747 show that fourteen ships took books to America that year – eight to Virginia, four to Boston, one to Philadelphia, and one to Maryland. One ship, the *Endeavour* of Greenock, loaded for Philadelphia in late February, and was back at the beginning of November loading for Virginia. Various combinations of merchants put 31 different loads of books on the fourteen ships, in quantities ranging from 5 tons (on the *Annabella* for Virginia, Captain Thomas Knox, on 19 February) to just a few pounds.[22] One of the vessels, the *Page* of Irvine for Boston, had taken on six different book shipments at Port Glasgow prior to moving on to Greenock. Three other ships set out with books from Port Glasgow in 1747, to Boston, Virginia and New York.[23] As in other years at the two ports, many of the merchants sending manufactured goods and books in 1747 were tobacco merchants.[24]

Printed material going from Scotland was not all in the form of books. On 31 August 1756, Joseph Scott and James Warden and Company shipped 233 reams of 'printed papers' to Boston on board the *Nancy*, Captain William Hastie. There is no indication in the Quarterly Accounts of what these were.[25]

Distribution of books by tobacco merchants

The partnership of Semple, Jamieson and Lawson set up a store in Portobacco, Charles County, Maryland, in 1750, bringing in at the start a range of books, in small quantities, bought from the Glasgow bookseller John Gilmour; these are listed by title and price in a store ledger.[26] Gilmour, where he could, would have sent the cheaper Scottish editions that were now becoming available, including his own. Glasgow editions, printed by either Foulis or Urie, included the *Spectator*, *Guardian*, Cervantes's *Instructive Novels*, *Hudibras*, *Paradise Lost*, Ray's *Wisdom of God*, Parnell's *Poems*, *A Select Collection of Modern Poems* (printed by Urie for Gilmour, 1744), Wollaston's *Nature Delineated*, Locke's *Essay Concerning Human Understanding*, and the Edinburgh and Glasgow edition of Tillotson's *Works* of 1748.[27] Possibly Scots editions were Young's *Night Thoughts*, Rollin's *Belles Lettres*, and Ramsay's 'Songs' – *The Tea-Table Miscellany*. London books at the store included *Clarissa*, *Pamela*, *Roderick Random*, *Peregrine Pickle*, *Tom Jones*, Eliza Haywood's *The Fortunate Foundlings*, *Cato's Letters*, Thomson's *Works*, Shakespeare's *Plays*, Pope's *Homer's Iliad*, Ovid's *Art of Love*, and Bailey's *Dictionary*. The store ledgers show that the literature was added to over the next few years. Some books were also sent to a second company store, at 'Saint Marys'.[28]

The names of the clergymen, doctors, farmers, storekeepers, military men, gentry and others, and the books they bought, are recorded in the Charles County store's ledger and day books.[29] Customers paid for their books with crop tobacco, the usual rate in 1752–53 for books being 100 pounds weight for every 7s. sterling due. (The barter for general merchandise was one pound of tobacco for every penny due.) Thus Eleanor Smoot in 1753 paid 1s. for a milk pot and 50 pounds of tobacco for Ramsay's 'Songs', which were valued at 3s. 6d.; Rev. Theophilus Swift paid 1257.5 pounds of tobacco for Rollin's *Roman History* in 1752, 50 pounds for *Paradise Lost* in 1753. Thomas Hynson Marshall in 1752 bought the *Spectator*, worth 17s. 6d., *Tatler*, 12s., *Guardian*, 6s., *Clarissa*, £1. 8s., and Rollin's *Ancient History*, £1. 10s.; he was charged a higher rate of 100 pounds of tobacco per 7s. 6d. sterling, and, what with 1s. 6d. for a bottle of snuff, he owed 1247 pounds.[30]

From 1757 until 1763, when the partnership consisted of John Semple in Maryland and James Lawson in Glasgow, there were seven shipments of books and stationery from Glasgow to the Maryland outlet, amounting to £93. This included unspecified books, presumably literary works, ordered by Thomas Marshall and by Isaac Campbell, who had also bought literature at the store previously.[31] But the other titles were now narrowed considerably, to children's books and religious works. The firm sent (with the price paid, per dozen, to Glasgow bookseller Gilmour in brackets): 10 dozen ordinary Bibles (19s. 6d. to 20s. 6d.); 11.5 dozen New Testaments (6s. to 7s. 6d.); 12.5 dozen spelling books, usually Dyche's edition specified (9s.); 10 dozen prayer books (15s.); 2.5 dozen prayer books on fine paper (20s.); 12.5 dozen battledores (1s. 2d. to 1s.6d.); 12.5 dozen primers and 8 dozen royal primers (2s. 6d.); 9.5 dozen psalters (5s. 6d. to 6s.); a folio Bible at £1. 12s. and a folio Bible with Apocrypha at £1.16s.[32] In addition, the firm's London agent bought from Andrew Millar, and shipped from London to Maryland, £25 worth of theological and medical books, along with one *Universal Magazine* for 1762 and a copy of *The sermons of Mr. Yorick*.[33]

The tobacco merchants Buchanan and Simpson of Glasgow sent similar book consignments to four American outlets. Andew Buchanan, merchant in Newport, Charles County, North Potomac, Maryland, was shipped on 21 January 1760 (with the Buchanan and Simpson charge per dozen): 1 dozen common Bibles (19s.); 1 dozen New Testaments (8s.); 1 dozen prayer books (15s.); 1 dozen psalters (5s. 6d.); 1 dozen horn books (1s.); 1 dozen primers (2s. 6d.); a large church Bible with prayer book and Apocrypha at 15s. Similar book consignments were sent to the same store on 21 March and 29 July 1760.[34] On 31 March 1760, Martin Brimmer, Merchant in Boston, was sent 3 dozen Bibles with Scots Psalms and clasps (20s. 6d.) and 6 dozen New Testaments (7s. 6d.).[35] On 29 January 1761, Thomas Williamson, merchant in Southampton County, James River, Virginia, was sent, at similar prices, 6 dozen Bibles; 4 dozen New Testaments; 4 dozen spelling books; 6 dozen primers; 4 dozen prayer books, small, bound in turkey and gilt (30s, a dozen); 4 dozen prayer books in calf, gilt (24s.); 6 dozen prayer books in sheep, plain (18s.). In addition, there was a set of Smollett's *History*, London, 11 volumes, and in another shipment, the *Universal Magazine* and *Gentle-*

man's Magazine for 1759 and 1760.[36] Buchanan and Simpson supplied another store in Maryland with books. Andrew Buchanan at Newport was aked to forward to 'John Somervell & Co.', merchants, Potomac. a chest containing 6 Bibles, half with Psalms, 1 Dozen New Testaments, 1 dozen prayer books (£1. 1s.), 3 Bailey's *Dictionary* (6s. each), 2 dozen 'histories' (6s. each) 6 Tate and Brady's *Psalms* (10d. each).[37]

A comparison with the book stock of an established store in Charleston, South Carolina, suggests these Scottish exports were typical of a certain trade. John Laurens, a saddler who also sold a range of general goods, had a similar assortment of books. An inventory made in 1747 showed 25 dozen primers, £12.10s.; 3 gilt prayer books, £2.5s.; 23 'sets' of psalm books, £2; 7 dozen and 9 Assembly catechisms, £3; 7 dozen and 7 Dyche's spelling book, £24; 5 dozen psalters, £12; 5 'Testament Plasters' and 4 horn books, £2.[38]

Bibles for Hall of Philadelphia from Watkins and from Kincaid of Edinburgh

The Scotsman David Hall took over Benjamin Franklin's bookshop in 1747, and became Franklin's printing partner the following year, printing the *Pennsylvania Gazette*; he had a successful career that lasted until his death in 1772. The Papers of David Hall have produced a number of significant studies of his bookselling in Philadelphia and his relationship with British suppliers. The focus has been on the London trade, particularly on his main agent, William Strahan, although Watkins, Kincaid, and Hamilton and Balfour have been touched upon.[39] In this essay I explore further Hall's dealings with the Edinburgh men and the distribution of Scottish books.

For his Bibles, Testaments and Psalms Hall turned to the holder of the Patent in Scotland, at first to Adrian Watkins. Watkins supplied Hall with upwards of 4000 Bibles and 6000 New Testaments between 1750 and 1760, for which Hall paid £980. There were five shipments to Hall, the first apparently from Greenock, the others from Port Glasgow, directed to Hall through Boston, Philadelphia and New York.[40] Hall advertised his first collection of Bibles from Watkins on 27 June 1751 in the *Pennsylvania Gazette* as: 'Just imported from Scotland, by the Way of Boston, and to be sold by David Hall, at the Post-Office in Philadelphia, by the Dozen, or single, Quarto, Octavo, Twelves, and Eighteens Bibles, fine and coarse; Likewise Prayer Books and Psalm Books.'[41]

Typical of Hall's orders to Watkins was one sent from Philadelphia on 8 December 1753. Hall's letter, and the relevent Scottish customs record, give a clear picture of the process. Hall ordered: 1000 common Bibles (i.e. ordinary duodecimo), all with clasps, 750 with Psalms; 1500 Testaments (500 with clasps and Psalms, 1000 without); 25 pocket Bibles with gilt bindings.[42] Watkins had them carried to Port Glasgow, where on 2 September 1754 they were put aboard the *Cassandra*, of the Philadelphia/Jamaica run, Captain Alexander Hutcheson. The Customs Collectors recorded the 2500 Bibles and Testaments as 1700 pounds of bound books, British.[43] Three and a half months later Hall wrote to Watkins to say they had arrived; the whole transaction had taken a year. Hall had, as usual, a complaint about the shipment. Previously, he had been dissatisfied with inadequate insurance and poor packing; now he said Watkins had not used him well, sending Testaments printed in a bad brevier rather than a good long primer.[44]

Hall was irritated on this and on other occasions by Watkins's short credit. The King's Printer in Scotland was not inclined to trust this overseas customer. Strahan, therefore, as well as ordering books, had to stand as surety on the first order and always pay on Hall's behalf. Sending word of a Bible shipment in 1757, Strahan said to Hall, 'I told you that Watkins refused to give more than two months Credit for the Scots Bibles, but he afterwards thought better of it, and agreed to accept a bill from me payable in six months, so the Cargo was shipt the 17th of Oct[obe]r'.[45] In 1758, Strahan said Watkins was 'a strange Fellow to deal with'. The Bible patent was now in Kincaid's hands, he said, but it would be some years before Kincaid had sufficient Bibles to ship in quantity.[46]

The final straw for Hall was the state of a large shipment he received from Watkins in March 1760: the *Jean* had taken four months to sail to New York from Scotland; Hall said that when the books reached him, they were in 'a very shattered Condition, owing to the bad Package of them; and the Testaments fall short of the Number in his Invoice, and a great Part of the Clasps rubbed off'. Again Hall mentioned the short time to pay – six months credit from the time the books left Scotland represented stiff terms – and he asked Strahan to approach Kincaid.[47] Books from Hamilton and Balfour had arrived on the same ship much bashed-about, but they were giving him a year's credit with a 5% discount if he paid within twelve months, and he liked the arrangement.[48]

Strahan spoke to Kincaid in London and promised Hall that Kincaid 'will serve you better, and give a longer Credit. He is now here, and returns to Scotland tomorrow, and I intend to see him as far as Cambridge in his Way. We are very Intimate, and he is indeed much of a Gentleman. He comes here generally once a year to buy Paper'.[49] Hall received his first Kincaid Bibles in 1761 with his usual mild grumbles: 'I have received a Chest of Books from Scotland, via New-York, from Mr. Kincaid, I am told, but have no Letter with them. It is very odd, that People should send Goods by one Vessel, and Invoices by another.'[50]

Curiously, Hall forgot that he received the books and had to be reminded by Strahan to pay for them, in 1764.[51] This was after Hall had written to Kincaid, introducing himself: 'You, no Doubt, will be a little surprised at receiving a letter from me, as I never had the Pleasure of any Acquaintance with you, tho' many many years ago, now, I knew you in Edinburgh.' Hall said he sold a great quantity of common duodecimo Bibles, Testaments, and prayer books. He asked Kincaid to send 2000 common duodecimo Bibles, half with Scots Psalms, all with clasps; 100 fine-paper quarto Bibles, with Apocrypha and Scots Psalms; 100 coarse-paper quarto Bibles with Psalms; 2000 Testaments, half with Psalms and all with clasps; 100 small gilt pocket Bibles, with Scots Psalms and a trial batch of various kinds of prayer books. Hall preferred a ship from Leith to Philadelphia, but one from Leith or Glasgow to Boston or New York would also do.[52] Kincaid was an efficient merchant and had the books, shipped on the *Wallace*, Captain Moodie, in Hall's hands within eight months. Hall said the books had come out in very good order and he had no fault to find with them, except that the Testaments should have two clasps, not one.[53]

In all, between 1764 and 1771, Kincaid sent 7500 duodecimo Bibles, upwards of 1200 pocket Bibles and 11,000 Testaments, along with quarto Bibles and prayer books.[54] When Strahan in 1770, having obtained the Bible patent in London, approached Hall asking him to distribute his Bibles in America, the Philadelphian explained how the Scots had cornered the market as far as he was concerned:

As to your first Query, what Sorts of Bibles and Prayer Books are most saleable here? I answer, the Common Twelve Bibles for Schools, is the only one that sells in any Quantity here, and all over North America. And as to Prayer Books, the smaller the Size, the greater the Sale, owing to the Cheapness of them. Testaments, which you do not mention, the lowest priced, from Seven to Eight Shillings a Dozen, likewise sell in considerable Quantities. The coarse Scots Quarto Bibles, about 6*s*. a Piece, sell a little, as do the Pocket Bibles, Eighteens and Twenty-fours, neatly bound. And Kincaid prints a Quarto Bible, on fine paper, and binds it handsomely in Calfskin, of which I have sold some. These are the Sorts chiefly imported here from Scotland; but the common Twelves Bibles, and Testaments, are the only Articles worth mentioning...

And as to my taking large Quantities, and retailing them to my Brethren on the Continent, I can say nothing about it, till I know the Quality of your Goods, and the Prices. But I am really afraid, that as the Scots common Bibles, and Testaments, come so low, you will find that it will not be in your Power to sell yours any Thing like as so cheap; and it is the Cheapness of these Articles altogether, that makes them go off in such Numbers.[55]

During the space of 20 years, Hall received a considerable quantity of Scots Bibles, New Testaments and prayer books, in various editions bearing the imprints, 'Edinburgh, Printed by Adrian Watkins, His Majesty's Printer' and 'Edinburgh, Printed by Alexander Kincaid, His Majesty's Printer'. They were cheap, if not especially well printed.[56] Hall's book trade served Philadelphia and district, and more distant points.[57] Strahan viewed him as a continental distributor. Hall, offering in his 1763 book catalogue to sell books to public libraries and to give good rates to 'those that buy to sell again', said he would sell 'as cheap as any other Bookseller or Stationer on the continent'.[58] He might well have distributed his shipments from Watkins and Kincaid in a wide geographical area.

Alexander Kincaid and his partner John Bell

Kincaid published, among other works, the philosophical writings of the Scottish Enlightenment, on his own in the 1740s, and in the partnerships of Kincaid and Donaldson 1751–58 and Kincaid and Bell 1758–71. Usually the firm published their new authors in conjunction with Andrew Millar of London, and later also with Thomas Cadell, in books printed at Edinburgh or London. The Edinburgh–London promotion of new Scots writing was a growing trend in the 1750s, which took into account the aspirations of the leading Edinburgh booksellers and the belief by Scottish men of letters that they needed a London outlet for money and fame.[59] Kincaid was involved in publishing: David Hume, *Essays, Moral and Political* (1741–2), *Political Discourses* (1751–52), *Essays and Treatises on Several Subjects* (1753); Lord Kames, *Essays Upon Several Subjects Concerning British Antiquities* (1747), *Essays on the Principles of Morality and Natural Religion* (1751), *Elements of Criticism* (1762), *Introduction to the Art of Thinking* (1761); Adam Smith, *The Theory of Moral Sentiments* (1759); Alexander Gerard, *An Essay on Taste* (1759), *Dissertations on Subjects Relating to the Genius and the Evidences of Christianity* (1766); Thomas Reid, *An Inquiry into the Human Mind, on the Principles of Common Sense* (1763); Adam Ferguson, *An Essay on the History of Civil Society* (1767). All of these works were sent to America as published as part of the Kincaid practice, as is shown below, to ship his own books and anything else of merit printed in Scotland.

The letter books kept by Kincaid's partner John Bell between 1764 and 1771 contain details of Kincaid and Bell's American trade, including books sent to individuals. Dr William Shippen of Philadelphia had an account with Kincaid and Bell.[60] Dr John Witherspoon, at Princeton University, relied on the firm a number of times, and appears to have been supplied with copies of one text on a sale-or-return basis, a grammar. On 27 August 1771, the factor appointed to oversee the dissolution of the Kincaid and Bell partnership, sent (via David Dale of Glasgow) a box of books valued at £25. 18s. 7d. to Dr Witherspoon, President of the College of New Jersey. The factor wrote to Witherspoon saying he was also shipping £5. 7s. 10d. worth of books Witherspoon had bought at the Kincaid and Bell auction of November 1769, and sought to clear up other matters on the firm's day-books: 'There are none of the Martin's Philosophy to be had either at London or here. If the Grammars are not all disposed of, you'l please return them by the first Vessel either for Glasgow or this side of the Country.'[61]

Kincaid and Bell's business outlets in America included – besides Hall of Philadelphia – William Millar, John Mein, Jeremy Condy and William Hyslop and Company at Boston, and James Rivington at New York. In 1770, young James Taylor, bookseller in Charleston, South Carolina, was approached as a possible distributor and was asked also to sound out his former master, Robert Wells of Charleston.

Hall and Kincaid were corresponding directly with each other over Kincaid's Bible Business. John Bell, handling the correspondence in the Kincaid and Bell publishing partnership, thought well of Hall and twice sent him unsolicited shipments of the latest Scottish books. Hall acknowledged the first lot, for £62. 9s. 3d., with the resigned pessimism about trade he often displayed: 'Bookselling, at present, is quite overdone here, and Money prodigiously scarce; However, as they are come, shall do what I can to dispose of them, and remit you as soon as possible; But send no more without hearing from me to that Purpose.'[62] The books included more than 50 copies of Bailey's *Universal Etymological English Dictionary*, 20th edition, 1764, which Kincaid and Bell published (anonymously) along with John Balfour and Patrick Neill; Hall mentioned the Bailey especially to Balfour since Balfour had also sent him copies.[63] One can presume that Kincaid and Bell's current editions, such as Kames's *Elements of Criticism* and Gerard's *Essay on Taste*, were also in the shipment. In 1767, when Kincaid and Bell sent Captain Alexander Rammage of the *Concord* to Boston to collect debts, the firm took the opportunity to put on board £36. 10s. 6d. of books for Hall. They told him these were either new books or new editions of books of reputation in Scotland; they believed he would have no difficulty in selling them, and they wanted no payment until he had done so.[64]

Hall had a ready market for popular religious works. Along with a Bible order in 1769, he asked Kincaid for Scottish editions of:

6 Henry's Works, 6 Vols, Folio; 1 Bunyan's Ditto; 6 Flavell's Ditto; 50 Pilgrim's Progress, small, three Parts; 12 Bunyan on the Covenants; 50 Come and Welcome to Christ; 50 Grace Abounding to Sinners; 36 Solomon's Temple Spiritialised; 36 Barren Fig-Tree; 36 Sighs from Hell; 24 Holy War; 6 Luther on the Galatians; 36 Gospel Sonnets, with Notes; 36 Dixon's Psalms, with Notes; 36 Travels of True Godliness, 36 Ditto of Ungodliness; 36 Allen's Alarm; 36 Fox on Time; 24 Dyer's Believers Golden Chain; 12 Flavell on the Heart, 12 Ditto's Husbandry Spiritualised; 36 Confessions of Faith, large, 60 Ditto small; 36 Vincent's Catechism, 36 Ditto on Judgement; 12 Guthries Saving Interest in Christ; 12 Flavell's Token for Mourners; 6 Derham on the Commands; 12 Willison's Sacramental Catechism, 36 Ditto's Example of plain Catechising; 12 Henry on Prayer, 36 Watts on Ditto; 36 Frances Spira; 36 Afflicted Man's Companion; 24 Boston's Fourfold State; 24 Baxter's Call to the Unconverted; 24 Life of Christ, Small; 24 Life of God in the Soul of Man; 12 Wellwood's Glimpse of Glory, 12 Drelincourt on Death, Small; 50 Russell's Seven Sermons; 50 Mason's Penitential Cries; 3 Calvin's Institutes; 6 Harvey's Dialogues, Scots Edition, 6 Ditto Letters, 24 Ditto Meditations.[65]

Hall had ordered a similar list of books from John Balfour in 1765 and James Magee of Belfast in 1766.[66]

John Bell wrote to James Rivington in New York in 1767 asking for a remittance for previous transactions, and offering books. Kincaid and Bell were printing a new, better-quality edition of Bailey's *Dictionary*, on paper costing 2s. a ream higher than their edition of 1764; if Rivington could take 500, they would sell him copies at 3s. 4d. each bound. They also offered Stackhouse's *History of the Bible*, 6 volumes, 20s. bound; their new publication, Adam Ferguson's *History of Civil Society*, quarto; new editions of Kames's *Principles of Equity*, folio enlarged, and *Elements of Criticism*, 4th edition, Adam Smith's *Theory of Moral Sentiments*, 3rd edition, with its additional 'Dissertation', Walker's *Sermons*, *Spectator* 12s. bound, and *Guardian*, along with the other books commonly printed in Scotland on 'the most reasonable terms.'[67]

Two of the Kincaid and Bell customers in Boston were Scotsmen, William Miller and John Mein, who followed a long line of Scottish booksellers and printers to that town.[68] Miller, a bookseller from Scotland, became associated with James Rivington in London and set up in Boston from 1762 to 1765 as a Rivington partner.[69] He ordered books from Kincaid and Bell and on 27 March 1765 they wrote saying they had sent £131. 10s. worth, packed in three trunks and a box, aboard the *Douglas*, Captain Manderson. A number of the books were sent on a sale-or-return basis, but the firm hoped Miller could dispose of them. A second order from Miller had arrived and was promised for the next vessel; meanwhile, Kincaid and Bell had put some of these books in a box of books for John Mein, and they asked Miller to send to Mein for them.[70]

John Mein came from Edinburgh in 1764, started off with a street stall and became a considerable bookseller, selling Scottish and English editions, and setting up the first circulating library in Boston.[71] His library catalogue of 1765 (see below) contains many Scottish books, evidently purchased from Kincaid and Bell. By 1767 his account with Kincaid and Bell stood at £234. 4s. 9d. and the firm said if he could not pay the whole at once, they expected him to remit £150 immediately, since they had had to pay 'ready money' for other publishers' books, and they had paid for the binding long before. However, they continued to offer him books. As with Rivington, they said he could have Bailey's *Dictionary* at 3s. 4d. a bound copy if he took 500, although they said he would have to pay at once. In addition to Ferguson's *History of Civil Society*, Kame's *Principles of Equity*, and Smith's *Theory of Moral Sentiments*, they also offered David Hume's *Essays and Treatises*, Adam Dickson's *Treatise of Agriculture*, volume 1, and Thomas Reid's *An Enquiry into the Human Mind*, along with the other books printed in Scotland.[72]

William Hyslop and Company of Boston owed Kincaid and Bell £261 in 1765.[73] In 1767, a further £54. 19s. 4d. worth of books was shipped at Hyslop's request, aboard the *Mary*, Captain William Welshman. But Bell was concerned to hear that Hyslop had been unable to dispose of many of the books previously sent on 'return'. He thought that popular works such as Thomas Mair's *Book-Keeping Methodiz'd* and Kames's *Elements of Criticism* must certainly have sold in Boston. He asked Hyslop and Co. to make a further effort to sell the returnable books to their usual outlets, even if at a cheaper rate than the invoiced price, but if that failed, to pack them securely in trunks and put on board the first vessel for Leith, since many of the books 'are as good here as money'. Bell was disappointed that £50 worth of Bibles, sent at a cheap rate, had not been paid for. He hoped Hyslop and Co. would remit £150 along with returned books.[74]

Kincaid and Bell's dealings with Jeremy Condy of Boston illustrate their custom of exporting current Scottish books on speculation and their willingness to take unwanted books back if necessary. The Condy Account book refers to some of the editions received from the Edinburgh firm. In 1760 or 1761 (Condy gives both dates), Mrs Condy accepted in her husband's absence at London a number of Edinburgh publications, including those of Hamilton, Balfour and Neill. And in October, 1764, Condy received a consignment of £54. 1s. 10d. worth of books, on the *George and James*, Captain Montgomerie, noting in the accounts they were 'returnable if not sold, being sent without order'. Condy, accordingly, returned on the *Jenny*, Captain Hector Orr, on 6 October 1767, the Kincaid and Bell edition of William Wilkie's *Epigoniad*, (1759), 3 copies at 2s. 1½d. each; Hamilton and Balfour and Neill's *Plutarch's Lives*, 6 volumes (1758), 6 sets at 17s. 6d. each; returned, too, was the London edition of Duncan Forbes's *Works*, 2 volumes (1753) which Hamilton and Balfour had published in conjunction with Wilson and Durham, 4s. From Kincaid and Bell's 1764 consignment Condy returned a Scottish edition of James Hervey's Theron and Aspasio *Dialogues*, 43 bound in sheepskin at 3s. 6d. each and 116 bound in calf at 3s. 8d. Since he was returning books, Condy went through the Kincaid and Bell shipment which Captain Orr had brought on his voyage to Boston in August 1767, and sent back Gerard's *Dissertations on Subjects Relating to the Genius and Evidences of Christianity* (1766) on the October return to Scotland.[75]

The books retained from the 1760/61 shipment and sold by Condy were the Edinburgh *Shakespear*, 8 volumes (1753), which had been printed for Kincaid and Donaldson, Hamilton and Balfour, and other Edinburgh booksellers; 6 copies of Rollin's *Ancient History*, 10 volumes (1758), printed for Hamilton and Balfour, Kincaid and Donaldson, and W. Gray; 6 copies of Rollin's *Belles Lettres*, 4 volumes (1759), Kincaid and Bell, Gordon, Donaldson and Fleming; Saxe's *Reveries* (1759), Alexander Donaldson; Alexander Gerard's *Essay on Taste* (1759), Millar, Kincaid and Bell; 4 copies of an Edinburgh edition of *Cocker's Arithmetick*; and the *Medical Essays and Observations, Published by a Society in Edinburgh*, 5 volumes in 6 parts, (1753), Hamilton, Balfour and Neill. Other titles received over the years are not recorded in the Account Book. One Kincaid and Bell publication which Condy certainly received was Reid's *An Inquiry into the Human Mind*: the inventory of Condy's estate in 1768 included 11 copies of the book.[76]

The books Condy received on the *Jenny* in August 1767 had mostly been ordered by him, and were despatched from Edinburgh to Glasgow, 'in two trunks marked I.C. No. 12 Boston' on 24 April. Bell said that the firm had been obliged to add two or three books to the order so as to fill up the trunks – if the Gerard was one of those extras, it would explain why Condy promptly sent it back. Bell said if Condy found it impossible to dispose of the large amount of Hervey's *Dialogues* by keeping them another year, they should be returned, although he hoped Condy would send them to Hall at Philadelphia, Rivington at New York or Mein at Boston. The current shipment evidently included Bibles, since Bell was moved to describe how profit was lost if there was extended credit: 'perhaps You will scarcely believe what I now shall tell you – that if you Don't Remit in Nine Months for Bibles we are Absolutely Losers, unless other Books are mixt with them: I am Determined to Send no more to America or any where unless other Books are likewise ordered'. However, Bell said, he would be well pleased if Condy paid for the present books in 12 months, 'but when a credit is taken for years, it hurts much'.[77]

The money and returnable books owed by Condy, Mein and Hyslop began to worry Kincaid and Bell and in September 1767 Bell instructed Captain Alexander Rammage of the *Concord*, at Leith, to visit these gentlemen to get either books or money, money preferably. (They were unaware that Condy's returnable books were on a ship to Scotland.) Captain Rammage was to present a £50 draught to Condy, and £150 draughts to both Mein and Hyslop. If Mr Hyslop's partners created any difficulty, the Captain should wait to see Hyslop himself: he came to Boston only once a week or once a fortnight.[78] The Captain proved to be an excellent debt collector, and Bell was pleased. Condy paid Rammage £50. Mein gave the Captain £111, and awaited instructions as to what unsold books should be returned. To reward Mein, Bell set down a list of the latest publications including Witherspoon's *Essays*, 3 volumes, and *Sermons* – and promised to give low prices on any order, on the understanding payment was made regularly.[80] Hyslop either had showed up at Boston, or his partners were not as difficult as feared, and Rammage was given around £97 and Kincaid and Bell £100 in other payments. In return, the grateful Bell offered Hyslop & Co. the 'most choice' books printed in Scotland, which they could pay in their own time, and as an inducement, said he would add Bibles in any amount they wished.[81]

Kincaid and Bell used another ship's master, Captain Urquhart of the *Avon*, to sell books in South Carolina in 1770. They sent three trunks of books valued at £64 to his ship and said he should use his own judgment and discretion in selling them: he could always return them. Bell suggested that James Taylor of Charleston, lately apprenticed to Robert Wells, might help. If Captain Urquhart could persuade Wells himself to take the books, a credit of 12 months could be given, but no one else was to be offered this.[82] Bell also wrote to Taylor explaining that two of the trunks contained 200 copies of Bailey's *Dictionary*. He added that if Taylor or Wells wanted to place an order sometime, they could have all the Scottish books and many English ones 'upon the most reasonable terms'.[83]

The success Kincaid and Bell had in distributing books in America arose from their eminence as Edinburgh booksellers and publishers, a willingness to send books speculatively and give attractive terms that included returns and extended credit, and a knowledge of and access to America that enabled them to take direct action, through ships' captains, to sell books or collect debts.

Hamilton and Balfour

Gavin Hamilton and his cousin and brother-in-law John Balfour were members of a talented and influential family grouping: the Hamiltons and Balfours and their relations were involved in university life, the church, law and medicine and had mercantile interests. Gavin was an Edinburgh Bailie of stature and a life-long improver. He began bookselling in 1730 and formed the partnership with Balfour in 1739. Hamilton and Balfour took on Patrick Neill as printing partner in 1750 to take advantage of the new printing opportunities opening up in Scotland. Their aim was to export more books than they imported, to give the printed quality of Edinburgh books a name in the world, to promote Scottish authors and disseminate culture. The firm became Edinburgh University Printer and printer to the city of Edinburgh in 1754. Their newspaper, *The Edinburgh Chronicle*, an ambitious eight-page production that was published thrice weekly at its height, appeared from 1759 to 1761. After a brilliant run of 12 years, the Hamilton, Balfour and Neill partnership was dissolved in 1762 and all three went their separate ways.[84]

Hamilton and Balfour, along with Neill, reprinted English authors and titles, such as Swift, Pope, Bishop Burnet's *History of his own time*, Algernon Sidney's *Discourses concerning government*, Sir William Temple's *Works*, *The Spectator*, and Restoration and early 18th-century English dramatists, and they participated in the first Scottish edition of Shakespeare's *Works*. They also printed the *Psalms of David*, in metre, regardless of not holding the patent. Original Scottish work, however, was a feature of their publishing.

They published new work, in medicine and science, by Alston, Francis Home, Whytt, Monro, Porterfield, the Edinburgh Philosophical Society, the Royal Infirmary and the Royal College of Physicians. New work in the arts included that of the blind poet Thomas Blacklock, Balfour of Pilrig, a number of pieces by Sir David Dalrymple, the plays of John Home, most notably *The Tragedy of Douglas* (1757), *Fragments of Ancient Poetry* (1760) – the first Ossian book by James MacPherson – David Hume's *History of Great Britain* volume 1 (1754), Alexander Carlyle, Adam Ferguson, Robert Wallace, William Robertson, Forbes of Culloden, William Wilkie, the *Edinburgh Reviewers* of 1755–6 (including Adam Smith and Hugh Blair). They also published French works in the original and in translation – Montesquieu, Voltaire, Duguet, Rollin – and school and university texts in English and Latin (Gregory's *Geometry*, Masson's *English Spelling Book for Schools*, Clarke's *Introduction to the Making of Latin*; Sallust, Livy [printed by Ruddiman], Phaedrus, Anacreon, Virgil, Plutarch's *Lives*). They were noted as fine printers of the classics: their editions of Volusene, *De Animi Tranquillitate Dialogus* (1751) is an example of their high quality. And as Printers to Edinburgh University they printed medical theses in sufficient quantities, it would appear, to be distributed commercially.

Hamilton and Balfour had a number of American associations. Gavin had two brothers in Maryland, both physicians, Dr John Hamilton and the man of letters Dr Alexander Hamilton, and the family corresponded; Gavin also gave travellers letters of introduction to friends and army officers in America.[85] American students attending Edinburgh University Medical School came to the Hamilton, Balfour and Neill printing office to have their theses printed.[86] Benjamin Franklin met them when he was in Edinburgh in 1759, and at his suggestion they sent £57. 16s. worth of books to one of his partners, James Parker of New York. Parker had business difficulties and was unable to sell the books or pay for all of them; when Balfour later asked Franklin to arrange legal action, Parker sent an anguished letter to Edinburgh saying he had never asked for the books in the first place, and had accepted only because Franklin had recommended them.[87] In the 1750s, on the recommendation of William Strahan, Hamilton and Balfour sent books to Franklin's nephew, Benjamin Mecom, who set up business in Antigua and then in Boston; Mecom went bankrupt and Franklin had to arrange to clear the debt.[88]

Hamilton and Balfour became interested in David Hall as an American outlet in 1750. They at first suggested that Strahan in London take their books at a discount and sell them to Hall along with his own, but Strahan told them to send Scottish books directly to Hall, who always paid promptly and deserved all the profits. Strahan remarked later he could not match the low price of books 'printed or pirated in Scotland' – copy money was not paid on reprints, and printing and binding were cheaper there; he had asked that Balfour charge Hall the lowest rate possible, and he presumed Balfour always did this.[89] Balfour, who carried out the correspondence with Hall, sent £34. 7s. worth of books on speculation, and said the Philadelphian could either sell the books on behalf of Hamilton and Balfour or buy them himself at the trade price. Hall bought them, paying £37. 11s. 9d., which included 10% insurance, in a bill payable in London in six months.[90] When Hall pointed out, through Strahan, that he needed more time to make a profit himself, the Edinburgh firm gave more generous terms for future transactions. If Hall paid within a year, he could claim an extra 5% discount.[91]

Altogether, the Hamilton and Balfour partnership sent Hall nearly 3 tons of books in six shipments: on (the dates of departure) the *Triton*, Captain Shirley, from London, 1750; the *Royal Widow*, Captain Cunningham, Port Glasgow to Philadelphia, October 1757, reaching its destination by 12 December, when some of the titles were advertised in the *Pennsylvania Gazette*; the *Cleveland*, Captain Andrews, Port Glasgow to Philadelphia, September 1758, acknowledged 24 February 1759; the *Jean*, Captain Corbett, Port Glasgow to New York, October 1759, the books arriving in Philadelphia in late March 1760; the *Barrington*, Captain Daniel McKirdy, Greenock to New York, August 1761; the *New Bumper* to New York, Captain Brown, August 1762.[92] The firm also sent Hall a large quantity of Irish Bibles which they had bought for him from their connections in Belfast, the printers David and John Hay, but Hall did not like the risk and expense of dodging

Customs with books from this source.[93] Balfour continued to send books to Hall from Edinburgh after the partnership with Hamilton broke up in August 1762.

Hamilton and Balfour sent their own books and the books of others. The 1750 shipment, which arrived by February 1751, included Bibles and two significant Scottish publications of the time, 6 sets of their own consortium's *Works* of John Tillotson, 1748, 10 volumes, and 9 sets of the 8-volume Glasgow *Spectator* of 1745.[94] From 1751 these and other books associated with Hamilton and Balfour can be traced in the long, cramped advertisements Hall placed in the *Pennsylvania Gazette*. The Tillotson and the *Spectator* are listed 30 May 1751. *The Edinburgh Entertainer: Containing Historical and Poetical Collections*, a school book that Hamilton and Balfour and other Edinburgh booksellers had published by September 1750, is noted 10 December 1751.

Hamilton, Balfour and Neill editions were also sent to Hall by his main supplier, Strahan. Robert Whytt's *An Essay on the Vital and Other Involuntary Motions of Animals*, published in Edinburgh 24 Octobner 1751, appears in the *Pennsylvania Gazette* 16 April 1752. Buchanan's *History of Scotland* 2 volumes (1751–2), and Robert Wallace, *A Dissertation on the Numbers of Mankind*, published in Edinburgh 6 February 1753, are listed in Hall's advertising broadside in 1754.[95]

The second shipment to Hall, in 1757, contained a variety of books valued at £51. 16s. 10d. Hall asked Hamilton and Balfour to continue to send as great an assortment as possible – but not, however, works of divinity.[96] The advertisement in the *Pennsylvania Gazette*, 15 December 1757, shows what some of the Edinburgh books were: David Hume's *History of Great Britain*, volume 1, Hamilton, Balfour and Neill, 1754; William Maitland, *The History of Edinburgh*, Hamilton, Balfour and Neill, 1753; The Edinburgh Philosophical Society's *Medical Essays*, 5 parts in 6 volumes, Hamilton, Balfour and Neill, 1752; Algernon Sidney, *Discourses Concerning Government*, 2 volumes, Hamilton and Balfour, and Daniel Baxter, Glasgow, 1750; Sir William Temple's *Works*, 4 volumes, Hamilton and Balfour and other booksellers, 1754. A further advertisement, 2 March 1758, added *A Select Collection of English Plays*, 24 plays bound up in 6 volumes, Hamilton and Balfour, 1755; John Smith's *Select Discourses*, edited by Sir David Dalrymple, Hamilton, Balfour and Neill, 1756; Bishop Burnet's *History of His Own Time*, 6 volumes, Hamilton, Balfour and Neill, 1753; Thomas Simson, *An Inquiry How Far the Vital land Animal Actions . . . can be Accounted for Independent of the Brain*, Hamilton, Balfour and Neill, 1752. The *Shakesepear's plays* referred to may have been the Edinburgh 8-volume *Works* of 1753.

In his acknowledgement of the £102. 12s. 4d. worth of books in the third shipment, 1758, Hall told Hamilton and Balfour never to send books in sheets, since the binding costs were very high in America. He spelt out the three or four kinds of books he wanted. For the time being he had enough copies of 15 Hamilton and Balfour, or Hamilton, Balfour and Neill editions – *The Edinburgh Entertainer*, *Medical Essays*, Temple's *Works*, Whytt and Simson on *Vital Motion*; Abraham Stanyan,

An Account of Switzerland (1756), Matthew Decker's *Foreign Trade* (1756; Hamilton and Balfour's, although there is no name on the imprint); *Plutarch's Lives* (1758); William Leechman's sermon, *The Wisdom of God in the Gospel Revelation* (1758); Robert Whytt's *An Essay on the Virtues of Lime-Water in the Cure of the Stone* (1752, second edition 1755) and *Physiological Essays* (1755); Charles Alston, *A Dissertation on Quick-Lime and Lime-Water* (1752, second edition 1754); Francis Home, *Principia Medicinae* (1758); James Grainger, *Historia Febris Anomalae Batavae* (1753); the Royal College of Physicians's *Pharmacopoeia Collegii Regii Medicorum Edinburgensis* – as well as 21 other Scottish publications, including editions by Urie and Foulis.[97]

'As to the other Books in your Invoices,' Hall continued in this letter, 'you may send me an Assortment of them as soon as you please; and any other good Copies, you may have by you, but send nothing that is bulky; and remember to let them be lettered, and neatly bound. Unbound Books, I told you before, will not do.' He asked for the other books shown on their invoices, and 'any other good Copies you may have by you'. This is an invitaion to the firm to continue to send their range of good editions. Hall said he also wanted Hamilton and Balfour to send *Confessions of Faith*, prayer books printed in Scotland, and sermons along the lines of Andrew Gray's and Robert Russell's. He added: 'An Assortment of Chapman Books, all in the comical or wonderful strain, will also do.' When he next asked for a Hamilton and Balfour shipment, Hall repeated, 'let the Assortment be of the best Authors, and all new books among them'. He wanted recent editions from Scotland, not old stock.[98]

Hamilton and Balfour and their partner Neill produced or were associated with more than 340 publications in the period 1750–62. It seems reasonable to conclude that much of what they printed was sent to Hall in Philadelphia, along with other contemporary Scottish work, and that the range of their output was either sold directly by Hall or distributed by him in America.

Scottish books in American catalogues

Contemporary catalogues of American booksellers contain many Scottish editions. Hamilton and Balfour books had a number of distributors. At Philadelphia, William Bradford's 1755 catalogue includes the *Works* of Duncan Forbes, jointly published by Hamilton and Balfour, and Wilson and Durham of London in 1753; a Bradford catalogue of 1760 has William Wilkie's *Epigoniad* (either the Hamilton and Balfour 1757, or Kincaid and Bell 1759 edition), Sir William Temple's *Works*, 4 volumes (1754) and the 10 volume Rollin's *Ancient History*, (1758).[99] In Philadelphia also, William Dunlap's 1760 catalogue has the Edinburgh Philosophical Society *Medical Essays* (1752).[100] At New York, Garret Noel's catalogues contain a number of the firm's books: that of 1755, Alexander Monro, *The Anatomy of the Human Bones and Nerves* (1750), Forbes's *Works*, and David Erskine, *Lord Dun's*

Familiar and Friendly Advice (1754); the 1759 catalogue, Thomas Blackwell's *Memoirs of the Court of Augustus*, 2 volumes (1753–6); the 1762 catalogue, Francis Home's *Principiae Medicinae* (1758), and William Porterfield, *A Treatise on the Eye*, 2 volumes (1759).[101] The College of New Jersey Library in 1760 has Colin MacLaurin's *An account of Sir Isaac Newton's Philosophical Discoveries* (1748), published by Millar and Nourse of London, and which Hamilton and Balfour and Kincaid had taken an interest in selling.[102] Kincaid and Bell's David Hume, *Essays and Treatises*, and Smith's *Theory of Moral Sentiments*, are in that Bradford 1760 catalogue. Mair's *Book-keeping* is in the 1755 catalogue of Garret Noel of New York, Smith's *Theory of Moral Sentiments* and *Gerard on Taste* are in the 1762 catalogue.

Kincaid and Bell supplied John Mein of Boston with a wide variety of books. The *Catalogue of Mein's Circulating Library; consisting of above twelve hundred volumes, in most branches of polite literature, arts and sciences* (Boston, 1765), contains around 200 Scottish editions, printed mainly at Edinburgh and Glasgow, although several are from Aberdeen.[103] Mein hoped to lend the books at £1.8s. a year, 18s. a half year, or 10s. 8d. a quarter and was inspired to identify the editions by giving place and date of publication. There are a few Hamilton and Balfour editions in the library: Sidney on Government (1750), Pascal's *Thoughts* (1750), Rollin's *Ancient History* (1758), *A Supplement to Dr. Swift's Works* (1753), and Sir William Temple's *Works* (1754). A considerable number of the Edinburgh books were published by Alexander Donaldson, including original work and the cheap reprints that he and printing partner John Reid were also producing to compete in the Edinburgh and London markets: they include the Donaldson edition of Goguet's *The Origin of Laws, Arts and Sciences* (1761), *Plutarch's Lives* (1763), *Swift's Works* (1761), *The Works of Alexander Pope* (1764), and Donaldson and Reid editions such as *Bossuet's History of France* (1762), *Buchanan's History of Scotland* (1762), *The Adventures of Gil Blas* (1764), *Le Diable Boiteux* (1760), *Adventures of Gaudentio di Lucca* (1761), *The Tea-Table Miscellany* (1760), *A Select Collection of the Best Modern Poems, by Milton, Addison, Dryden, Pope, &c* (1763), *Free Mason's Pocket Companion* (1763), *Cocker's Arithmetic* (1763), and *Doddridge's Sermons to Young People* (1762).[104] There are many Foulis, Urie, and Glasgow and Edinburgh editions of popular divinity and reprints of English and French literature. In an appendix, Mein gives the prices of the Bibles and prayer books he was receiving from Scotland. A subsequent publication by Mein, *A catalogue of curious and valuable books, to be sold at the London Book-Store* (Boston, 1766?) includes among the editions received from Kincaid and Bell, Kames's *Elements of Criticism* and *Essays on the Principles of Morality and Natural Religion*, Reid's *An Inquiry into the Human Mind*, Smith's *Theory of Moral Sentiments* and Gerard's *An Essay on Taste*.[105]

Summary and Conclusion

The activity at the Scottish ports shows that considerable quantities of books were being sent to America, especially to Boston, Virginia and Philadelphia, in the middle of the 18th Century. This essay has focused on several of the participants: the tobacco merchants Semple and Lawson and Buchanan and Simpson, the King's Printers Adrian Watkins and Alexander Kincaid, and the leading Edinburgh partnerships of Kincaid and Bell and Hamilton and Balfour, who demonstrate in their shipments the kinds of books that were readily available. Kincaid and Bell were selling directly to Boston, Philadelphia, New York and South Carolina; Hamilton and Balfour successfully to Philadelphia, to booksellers who in turn would be distributing to others. The appearance of Scottish books in the booksellers' catalogues referred to is evidence of their spread, but the geographical extent of the distribution has still to be explored. This might be done by taking the editions of particular booksellers and printers and comparing them with local newspaper advertisements and catalogues. The productions of the enterprising Hamilton and Balfour and Kincaid and Bell could be a starting point for this part of the century.

References

1. See my paper, 'Copyright Litigation in the Court of Session, 1738–1749, and the Rise of the Scottish Book Trade', *Edinburgh Bibliographical Society Transactions*, vol.V part 5 (1988), pp.2–31.

2. For the Bible patent in Scotland see John Lee, *Memorial for the Bible Societies of Scotland* (Edinburgh, 1824); his *Additional Memorial on Printing and Importing Bibles* (Edinburgh, 1826). pp.108, 121 and appendices, refers to other printers of New Testaments and church books. For Scottish books generally see the Eighteenth Century Short-Title Catalogue and the National Union Catalog pre-1956 Imprints. Particular studies are cited below.

3. T.M. Devine, *The Tobacco Lords: A Study of the Tobacco Merchants of Glasgow and their Trading Activities c.1740–90* (Edinburgh, 1975), and *A Scottish Firm in Virginia 1767–1777: W. Cuninghame and Co.* (Edinburgh, 1984), pp.ix–xv. Barbara Crispin, 'Clyde Shipping and the American War', *Scottish Historical Review*, xli (1962), pp.124–134. J.H. Saltow, 'Scottish Traders in Virginia, 1750–1775', *Economic History Review*, 2nd ser. xii (1959), pp.83–98.

4. Scottish Record Office (West Register House), CS96/507, Buchanan and Simpson Letter Book 1759–1761, ff.24, 42, letters of 28 December 1959 and 22 February 1760. The various MSS of the company are described in *Scottish Record Office, Court of Session Productions c.1760–1840* (Public Record Office, 1987).

5. SRO (West), CS96/507. f.11 verso, 25 November 1759 seeking abatement on insurance of a convoy ship, and asking for an insurance rate for a ship going to the

West Indies from Cork or Dublin north about: 'she is defenceless, and we intend her to run it.' f.42, 21 February 1760, giving Captains Buchanan and Andrews authority to ransom their tobacco to up to two-thirds of the value. See Richard Pares, *War and Trade in the West Indies, 1739–1763* (London, 1963).

6. *The Edinburgh Chronicle*, 4–9 August 1759, p.327, says the *Jean and Betty*, Captain Alexander, the *Mally*, Captain Langmuir, and the *Crawfurd*, Captain Lees, had arrived in Port Glasgow after five weeks' sail from St Christopher, having parted with the Convoy in latitude 42 degrees, and longitude about 42 degrees West from London.

7. SRO, E504 Series, Scottish Collectors' Quarterly Accounts; RH2/4 and RH20, copies of the Public Record Office Customs 14, Ledgers of Imports and Exports, Scotland. I give a table of exports from Greenock, Port Glasgow and Leith, 1743–55, and Scotland as a whole 1755–62, in 'Copyright Litigation . . . and the Rise of the Scottish Book Trade', pp.14–17.

8. SRO, E504/22/1–9, Leith, 1742–61. Ships' size and numbers of crew are given in the 'victualling bills' in the Accounts.

9. Wells dealt mainly in imported books at 'the Great Stationery and Book-store on the Bay', one of the largest book stores in North America. Isaiah Thomas, *The History of Printing in America* (New York and London, 1971), II, p.240. *The Papers of Henry Laurens*, ed. George C. Rogers, Jr. (Columbia, South Carolina, 1976), V, p.274n.

10. SRO, E504/24/2. Montrose, 1748–52.

11. SRO, E504/27/2, Perth, 1748–53.

12. SRO, E504/1/3–4, Aberdeen, 1748–53.

13. SRO, E504/26/1–2, Orkney, 1743–55: 11 Sept. 1748, *Thistle*, Captain Henry Aitken, for Boston; 17 Sept. 1748, *Charming Polly*, Captain John Kelletas, for New York; 30 August 1749, *Maria*, Captain Thomas Randall, for New York.

14. SRO, E504/4/1–2, Ayr, 1742–56.

15. e.g. at Port Glasgow 6 Sept. 1755, Alexander Hutcheson and William Kay shipped 450 pounds of books aboard Hutcheson's vessel, the *Royal Widow*, bound for Jamaica/Philadelphia. SRO, E504/28/7.

16. SRO, E504/18/1–2, Port Irvine, 1742–52: 10 August 1751, *Jenny*, of Irvine, Captain Hugh Paterson, for Charleston.

17. SRO, E504/18/3, Port Irvine, 1752–56.

18. SRO, E504/15/1–9, Greenock, 1742–60; E504/28/1–9, Port Glasgow, 1742–60.

19. I calculate the value at £11 a hundredweight, the median figure used by the Customs in 1755 for bound British books being exported to America: SRO, RH2/4/10–11, Ledgers of Imports and Exports, Scotland (Copy of PRO Customs 14), 1755–62. For further details of book valuation see 'Copyright Litigation. . .and the Rise of the Scottish Book Trade', pp.15–17.

20. SRO, E504/38/9, Port Glasgow. In the *Jean*, Captain James Corbett, for New York. On 19 October 1759, the merchants James Dunlop, Thomas Hutcheson and

George McFarlane shipped linen, woollens and other goods, including 400 pounds of bound books that Hamilton and Balfour had sent by carrier from Edinburgh. On 27 October, the agents Charles Hutcheson (a Greenock bookseller) and Robert Gregory put on board 15 boxes of bound books, weighing 2,950 pounds, on behalf of Watkins. The voyage took an exceptionally long time – David Hall said the passage was 'above four months' – and the books did not reach him in Philadelphia until late March 1760. American Philosophical Society, Hall Letter Book, Hall to William Strahan, 5 March and 31 March 1760, Hall to Hamilton and Balfour 2 July 1760.

21.   On 18 Aug 1754 on the *Cassandra* for Philadelphia, Captain Alexander Hutcheson, James Wardrop and James Main shipped 31,150 pounds of books (along with woollens, thread, thread stockings, haberdashery, tanned leather and gloves). Wardrop was a tobacco merchant (*The Tobacco Lords*, p.184).

22.   SRO, E504/15/3, Greenock, 1747.

23.   SRO, E504/28/3, Port Glasgow, 1747.

24.   They include Andrew and John Cochran, James Donald, Robert and Thomas Dunlop, Richard and Alexander Oswald, Andrew Blackburn, Andrew, Robert and James Buchanan, Robert Findlay, Allan Dreghorn, Alexander Stirling, Archibald Ingram, John Murdoch, James Deniston, William Gordon, Andrew Syms and Robert Bogle. (See *The Tobacco Lords*, pp.177–184, for a catalogue of these Glasgow merchants.) The merchant Robert Gilmour is often associated with book shipments in this period, including 1747. He was later a member of the tobacco partnership of Dunmore, Blackburn and Co. (*The Tobacco Lords*, p.188).

25.   SRO, E504/15/7, Greenock, 1756.

26.   SRO (West), CS96/1179/1, Ledgers (Charles County, Maryland), Semple, Jamieson, Lawson mss: the first ledger [A] starts with two lists of books bought from Gilmour. See *Scottish Record Office, Court of Session Productions c.1760–1840* for the various Maryland and Glasgow mss relating to the company.

27.   For Glasgow books see: Philip Gaskell, *A Bibliography of the Foulis Press*, second edition (Winchester, 1986); Hugh McLean, 'Robert Urie, Printer in Glasgow', *Records of the Glasgow Bibliographical Society*, 3 (1913–14), pp.89–108; R.A. Gillespie, 'A List of Books printed in Glasgow 1701–1775' (unpublished FLA Thesis, 1967).

28.   SRO (West), CS96/1179/1, Ledger F: 15 April 1755, Saint Marys store, accounts for 4 sets *Spectator*, 2 sets Tillotson's *Sermons*, 1 set Rollin's *Belles Lettres*, 1 set Thomson's *Works*, 1 set *Revolution of Genoa*, 4 *Whole Duty of Man*, 2 *Night Thoughts*, 1 *Paradise Lost*, 1 Ramsay's *Songs*, 1 *Hudibras*, 1 Shakesepeare's *Works* (three volumes wanting), and 1 set *Gil Blas*.

29.   SRO (West), CS96/1177–8 (Day Books 1750–68), and CS96/1179/1–3, CS96/1180, CS96/1181/1, CS96/1182/2 (Ledgers and indices 1750–68).

30.   SRO (West), CS96/1179/1, Ledger B.

31.   SRO (West), CS96/189, Ledger (Glasgow), p.19, cargo of April 1762; a list of books bought by Campbell 5 November 1751 is in CS96/1177 (Day Book, Charles County).

32. SRO (West), CS96/1185, pp.9, 80 on the *Charming Sally*, Captain James Mont-
    gomerie, April 1757; p.131, on the *Bettsey* February 1759; p.267, on the *Jamieson*,
    Captain Montgomerie, January 1760. CS96/1186, pp.52, 73, on the *Nancy*, Captain
    Montgomerie, March 1761; p.187, on the *Lawson*, Captain Stephen Rowan, Sep-
    tember 1761. CS96/187, pp.18–19, on the *Lawson*, Captain Rowan. April 1762;
    p.75, on the *Potomac*, Captain Thomas, April 1763.

33. SRO (West), CS96/1186, pp.145–46, on the *Polly*, Captain John Johnston, April
    1761; CS96/1187, p.65, on the *Nelly*, Captain Johnston, April 1763.

34. SRO (West), CS96/503, p.79, on the *Fair Lilly*, Captain Henry White; p.105, on the
    Menie, Captain Colin Buchanan; p.185, on the *Fair Lilly*, Captain Robert Morison.

35. SRO (West), CS96/503, p.128, on the *Robert*, Captain Thomas Watson.

36. SRO (West), CS96/503, p.314, on the *Binning*, Captain James Colhoun; p.335, on
    the *Planter*, Captain Alexander McTaggart.

37. SRO (West), CS96/502, p.104, on the *Fair Lilly*, Captain Morison, April 1762.

38. *The Papers of Henry Laurens*, ed. Philip M. Hamer, (1968), I, p.376. I presume
    'Testament Plasters' were plaster ornaments.

39. American Philosophical Society, Hall Papers. Robert D. Harlan, 'A Colonial
    Printer as Bookseller in Eighteenth-Century Philadelphia: The Case of David
    Hall', *Studies in Eighteenth-Century Culture*, 5 (1976), pp.335–369, 'William Strahan's
    American Book Trade, 1744–6', *Library Quarterly*, 31 (1961), pp.235–44, and
    'David Hall's Bookshop and its British Surces of Supply', in *Books* in *America's
    Past: Essays Honoring Rudolph H. Gjelsness*, ed. David Kaser (Charlottesville, Va.,
    1966), pp.2–23. The American context is described in Stephen Botein, 'The Anglo-
    American Book Trade Before 1776: Personnel and Strategies', in *Printing and Society
    in Early America*, ed. William L. Joyce and others (Worcester, Mass., 1983), pp.48–
    82. See also Edwin Wolf II, *The Book Culture of a Colonial American City: Philadelphia
    Books, Bookmen and Booksellers* (Oxford, 1988).

40. APS, Out-Letter Books, Hall to Watkins, 29 June 1751, 23 November 1751, 19
    November 1752, 8 December 1753, 18 December 1754; Hall to Strahan, 27 Sep-
    tember, 20 November 1750, 28 March, 28 June, 7 September 1751, 21 March, 1
    November 1752, 18 December 1754, 7 October 1755, 20 February 1758, 5 March,
    31 March 1760. Hall Account Book, 1748–67, Watkins and Strahan accounts.
    Franklin Papers (54.61), letters of Strahan to Hall, refer frequently, 1753–60, to
    Watkins and his shipments.

41. *The Pennsylvania Gazette 1728–1789*, *a Reprint Edition* (Philadelphia, 1968).

42. APS, Hall to Watkins.

43. SRO, EH504/28/6, Port Glasgow.

44. APS, Hall to Watkins, 18 December 1754.

45. APS, Franklin Papers, Strahan to Hall, 12 December 1757.

46. APS, Franklin Papers, Strahan to Hall, 10 June 1758.

47. APS, Hall to Strahan, 31 March 1760. See also n.20 above.

48. APS, Hall to Hamilton and Balfour, 2 July, 15 November 1760.

49.   APS, Franklin Papers, Strahan to Hall, 21 June 1760.

50.   APS, Hall to Strahan, 28 June 1761.

51.   APS, Franklin Papers, Strahan to Hall, 4 June 1764.

52.   APS, Hall to Kincaid, 17 March 1764.

53.   APS, Hall to Kincaid, 20 November 1764.

54.   APS, Hall's further orders to Kincaid for Bibles are in letters of 17 December 1765, 13 November 1766, 12 June 1767, 11 June 1768, 2 December 1769; he also acknowledges a further shipment 29 April 1771.

55.   APS, Hall to Strahan, 6 February 1770.

56.   John Lee said Adrian Watkins produced a great number of Bibles, some of them very indifferently, as the duodecimo of 1748, others not contemptibly, as the octavo of 1754, while Kincaid 'never produced any thing that ranked above mediocrity'. He lamented that Scots Bibles had not been printed by such 'contemporary artists' as Thomas Ruddiman, and Hamilton, Balfour and Neill of Edinburgh, and Foulis and Urie of Glasgow. *Memorial for the Bible Societies in Scotland*, pp.184–5.

57.   'A Colonial Printer as Bookseller in Eighteenth-Century Philadelphia', p.355. Botein, p.56, notes that the chief importers in other port towns such as Boston and New York also acted as wholesalers to smaller tradesmen in the same vicinity and in the countryside.

58.   *Imported in the last vessels from Europe and sold by David Hall, at the New Printing-Office, in Market Street, Philadelphia, the following Books, &c.* [1763?], no.41386 in *Early American Imprints, 1639–1800 Series*, and *Supplement*, ed. Clifford K. Shipton (New York, and Worcester, Mass., Readex Microprint, 1963–). Cited hereafter as *EAI*. No.48 in Robert B. Winans, *A Descriptive Checklist of Book Catalogues Separately Printed in America 1693–1800* (Worcester, Mass., 1981).

59.   'Copyright Litigation . . . and the Rise of the Scottish Book Trade', pp.22–9.

60.   Bodleian Library, Mss Eng. Letters C.20–21, Kincaid and Bell Letter Books, 2 volumes: I, f.64, to Hall 17 September 1767. See also APS, Hall to Kincaid, 20 September 1766. I thank John Feather and Nancy Drucker for alerting me to the American connections in the Kincaid and Bell Letter Books.

61.   Bodleian, Kincaid and Bell, I, f.83v, James Taylor to David Dale, Glasgow, 27 August 1771; f.84, to John Witherspoon, New Jersey, same date.

62.   APS, Hall to Kincaid and Bell, 20 November 1764.

63.   APS, Hall to Balfour 20 December 1764.

64.   Bodleian, Kincaid and Bell, I, f.64, to Hall, 17 September 1767.

65.   APS, Hall to Kincaid 2 December 1769.

66.   'Copyright Litigation . . . and the Rise of the Scottish Book Trade', p.19 for the Balfour books. APS, Hall to James Magee 4 February 1766.

67.   Bodleian, Kincaid and Bell, I, f.37, to Rivington 22 April 1767.

68.   Thomas, II, pp.226–230, for Scots in Boston.

69.   Thomas, II, p.229.

70. Bodleian, Kincaid and Bell, I, to Miller 27 March 1765.

71. John Eliot Alden, 'John Mein, Publisher: An Essay in Bibliographic Detection', *The Papers of the Bibliographical Society of America*, 36 (1942), pp.199–214.

72. Bodleian, Kincaid and Bell, I, f.35. The current account was for books shipped to Mein 8 March and 24 October 1765 and 13 June 1766 (I, f.62).

73. Bodleian, Kincaid and Bell, I, f.24 note of 12 April 1766.

74. Bodleian, Kincaid and Bell, I, f.36, to William Hyslop and Co. 22 April 1767.

75. American Antiquarian Society, Condy Account Book, Kincaid and Bell accounts, pp.157–8.

76. Elizabeth C. Reilly, 'The Wages of Piety: the Boston Book Trade of Jeremy Condy', *Printing and Society in Early America*, pp.83–131, p.126

77. Bodleian, Kincaid and Bell, I, f.38, to Condy 24 April 1767.

78. Bodleian, Kincaid and Bell, I, f.65, to Captain Rammage.

79. AAS, Condy Account Book, p.158.

80. Bodleian, Kincaid and Bell, I, ff.102–103, to Mein, 5 August 1768.

81. Bodleian, Kincaid and Bell, I, f.104, to Hyslop and Co., 6 August 1768.

82. Bodleian, Kincaid and Bell, II, f.46, to Captain Urquhart, 24 August 1770.

83. Bodleian, Kincaid and Bell, II, f.47, to James Taylor, 25 August 1770.

84. See my papers 'Gavin Hamilton, Bookseller in Edinburgh', *The British Journal for Eighteenth-Century Studies*, I, (1978), pp.1–19, and 'Copyright Litigation . . . and the Rise of the Scottish Book Trade'. My 'Gavin Hamilton, John Balfour and Patrick Neill: a Study of Publishing in Edinburgh in the 18th Century' (unpublished Ph.D. thesis, University of Edinburgh, 1974), contains further biographical and bibliographical material. See Appendix below (pp.187–232) for 'A Catalogue of Hamilton, Balfour and Neill Publications, 1750–1762'.

85. Maryland Historical Society, Dulany Papers, Alexander Hamilton, letters to family and friends 1739–43, and subsequent correspondence from members of Hamilton family in Scotland. National Library of Scotland, MS.6506, 1–22, John and Alexander Hamilton to Gavin Hamilton includes a 1755 journal on the battle of Duquesne and a letter from John, Maryland, 7 May 1755, referring to Gavin's friend Sir Peter Halkett, Scots bearing letters, and to books sent by Gavin.

86. Clemens Crooks of St Christopher (1753), James Jay of New York (1753), Valentine Peyton of Virginia (1754), Thomas Bulfinch of New England (1757), Thomas Clayton of Virginia (1758), William Shippen of Pennsylvania (1761), and William Smibert of Massachusetts (1762). Their imprint appears also on the thesis of Theodore Bland of Virginia (1763).

87. J. Bennet Nolan, *Benjamin Franklin in Scotland and Ireland 1759 and 1771* (Philadelphia, 1938), pp.47–9. *The Papers of Benjamin Franklin*, ed. L. W. Labaree and others (New Haven and London, 1759–), XII (1968), pp.251–2, John Balfour to Franklin, 2 September 1965. APS, letter from James Parker to Hamilton and Balfour, 3 January 1766, which confirms that Franklin arranged the 1759 shipment.

88. *The Papers of Benjamin Franklin*, XII, pp.251–2, XI (1967), pp.240–1.

89.   J.A. Cochrane, *Dr Johnson's Printer: the Life of William Strahan* (London, 1964), pp.78–9. APS, Franklin Papers, Strahan to Hall 13 October 1764.

90.   APS, Hall to Hamilton and Balfour 7 September 1751; Hall to Strahan 2 February 1751, 7 September 1751.

91.   APS, Hall to Hamilton and Balfour 24 February 1759.

92.   APS, Hall Account Book, 1748–1767. SRO E504/28/8–9, Port Glasgow, 1756–60, E504/15/10, Greenock, 1760–62.

93.   APS, Hall to Hamilton and Balfour, 3 March 1763, saying he had to pay £1. 14*s*. 6*d*. after Customs seized a shipment at Carlingford in Ireland. Hall to Balfour, 20 November 1764, on another shipment: 'books from Ireland are seizable here, so that they were obliged to be landed, and Stored at New-Castle, 35 Miles from Town, and sent up slyly, which occasioned a Risk, and an extraordinary Expense, which they will not bear: Therefore shall be obliged to you, not to order any more Books from that Quarter for me, as there are now always two of the King's Ships at least in our River'.

94.   APS, Hall to Strahan 2 February 1751.

95.   *Imported in the last ships from London, and to be sold by David Hall* [1754], *EAI* 46086, Winans 21.

96.   APS, Hall to Hamilton and Balfour, 24 April 1758.

97.   APS, Hall to Hamilton and Balfour, 27 March 1759. Urie publications included the histories of Scotland by Robert Lindsay of Pitscottie and William Drummond (1749), and Bayle's *Gustavus Adolphus* (1757). Foulis Press editions included *Cicero*, 20 volumes (1748–9).

98.   APS, Hall to Hamilton and Balfour, 22 December 1760.

99.   William Bradford, *Books just imported from London* (1755), *EAI* 7368, Winans 25; *A catalogue of books. Just imported from London* [1760?], *EAI* 8555, Winans 34.

100.   *Books and stationary* [sic], *just imported from London, and to be sold by W. Dunlap* [1760], *EAI* 8587, Winans 37.

101.   Garret Noel, *A catalogue of books* (1755), *EAI* 7519, Winans 26; *A catalogue of books* (1759), *EAI* 8447, Winans 33; *A catalogue of books, &c.* (1762), *EAI* 9222, Winans 44.

102.   *A catalogue of books in the Library of the College of New-Jersey* (1760), *EAI* 8683, Winans 36. 'Copyright Litigation ... and the Rise of the Scottish Book Trade'. p.23.

103.   *EAI* 10069, Winans 54.

104.   Donaldson and Reid printed upwards of 88 titles 1760–5. These are described in a paper of the Court of Session cases relating to the partnership, *February 28, 1769. Unto the Right Honourable the Lords of Council and Session, the Petition of Alexander Donaldson Bookseller in Edinburgh*, Appendix, pp.37–4, collected with three other papers in NLS R.234.b.2. See also 'Copyright Litigation ... and the Rise of the Scottish Book Trade', pp.13–14.

105.   *EAI* 41642, Winans 59.

Printers and Booksellers
in Dublin 1800–1850[1]

CHARLES BENSON

ON 13 OCTOBER 1821 William Wakeman, the wholesale agent in Dublin for the London publishing firm of Baldwin, Cradock and Joy, and also a bookseller on his own account, gave evidence about the book trade to the Commissioners of inquiry into the collection and management of the revenue arising in Ireland. He was asked:

> Do you know anything of the printing of books here? – It is comparatively nothing in Ireland, except a description of Catholic books of a very cheap sort, which are sold at so low a rate, that they could not be printed in England for the same money, and also a few school-books used exclusively in Ireland.
>
> Is it diminished or increased? – since the Act of Union it is almost annihilated; it was on the same footing as America previous to that time, and every new book was reprinted here; but since the Copyright Act has been extended, that cannot now be done openly.[2]

Wakeman and Charles Palmer Archer, another bookseller, who gave evidence on 26 October 1821 both regarded the trade in imported books, despite its considerable increase since 1800, as being severely restricted by the prevailing system of importation duties, drawback of these duties and their attendant administrative expenses. So great were the latter that neither regarded it as worthwhile to claim the drawback of duty (which was at the rate of three pence per pound weight) on small parcels. These often contained periodicals which Archer said 'we are obliged to import by mail, for the sake of expedition, the expenses on which are considerable, and which, in fact, leaves very little, and in some instances *no profit* to the importer'.[3]

Twenty-one years later, in 1842, the novelist William Carleton wrote in the preface to a new Dublin edition of his *Traits and Stories of the Irish peasantry*:

> In truth until within the last ten or twelve years an Irish author never thought of publishing in his own country, and the consequence was that our literary men followed the example of our great landlords; they became absentees, and drained the country of its intellectual wealth precisely as the others exhausted it of its rents. Thus did Ireland stand in the singular anomaly of adding some of the most distinguished names to the literature of Great Britain, whilst she herself remained incapable of presenting anything to the world beyond a school-book or pamphlet.

It had not always been so. There was indeed a radical difference in trading conditions for the book trade after 1801. The coming into force of the Act of Union on 1 January 1801 amalgamated the previously separate kingdoms of Great Britain and Ireland into one United Kingdom. This brought in its wake a Copyright Act which for the first time put Irish printers and publishers under the same legal constraints as their British counterparts.[4] Prior to 1800 there was no copyright law in Ireland, and the Dublin trade flourished, largely as a reprint trade, supplying in great measure the intellectual needs of the country, and, particularly towards the end of the century, building up a large export business to North America. Though there was a custom of recognition of copyright in Dublin, the local book trade was, understandably, unable to build up a pool of authors in the absence of a legal framework. Authors with manuscripts to sell headed to London.[5]

The Dublin trade came under increasing economic and political pressure in the 1790s. The squeeze on profit margins came in considerable measure from increased taxation on paper imposed by the Irish Parliament. In 1795 the duty was raised steeply, coming with various incidental charges to between 4 and 5 shillings per ream depending on size. This moved both master printers and journeymen to petition early in 1796 against its renewal. The journeymen averred

that in consequence of said duty the price of printing paper has been so enhanced that the printing of elegant editions of several useful and valuable works has declined, and an increased importation of books substituted, to the manifest injury of petitioners and their families; that a considerable number of the printers of Dublin were heretofore employed on editions of works to be exported to America, which was found to be greater in amount than the home consumption, but since the new duty on foreign paper, and the extravagant rise in the price of Irish paper added to the inadequacy of its supply, their employment in that line has in great measure ceased.[6]

Political pressure was exerted particularly on the periodical press, the editors and proprietors of which became liable to draconian penalties if they stepped out of line. So effective was the legislation that all opposition papers ceased publication in 1798. Of the five still publishing, three were subsidised by the government, two very quietly pursued a neutral line.[7] The prominent Catholic bookseller Patrick Byrne wrote to Mathew Carey in Philadelphia on 16 October 1798 in worldweary strain, 'After spending the better part of my life in trade in the Capital of this Kingdom, I am now determined to spend the remainder of it as an American Farmer – I write to you for advice and assistance in fixing myself in that situation'.[8]

At the start of the new century Ireland stood united with Great Britain in law, but the majority of the people differed vastly from the English in religion, and a significant proportion differed in language as well. In Ireland access to political power, even at so low a level as the Corporation of Dublin, was denied to the

Roman Catholic majority. Catholic relief acts in 1778 and 1792 had eased the burden of the penal laws and enabled Catholics to play a more prominent part in economic life. Though the use of English continued to increase a large number of people were solely Irish speaking.

With the mainstay of their trade, the reprint business, gone, the printers faced an uncertain future. The booksellers had the extra financial burden of importing a higher proportion of their stock. Outsiders saw opportunities: John Cooke, brother-in-law of Joseph Butterworth, came over from London and settled on Ormond Quay, close to the Four Courts, as a law bookseller.[9]

Advertisements in the newspapers, and records in the one printer's ledger known from the early 19th century suggest that the printers survived largely on jobbing work, though contracts to print for any official organisation or society were great lifelines.[10] An advertisement from J. and J. Carrick on the occasion of their removal from Bedford Row to 29 Bachelor's Walk in 1804 shows the range of a middle-ranking printer. They claimed to have spared no expense

to render their press a general, complete and expeditious medium of mercantile and public intelligence. They have imported likewise a quantity of new and beautiful type from the first foundry in England, and laid in a stock of fine papers for such publications as may require elegance of typography and ornament . . . Advertisements, cards, auction and handbills, large posting bills, etc. worked off in a few hours without disappointment. Circular letters, mercantile receipts, shopbills, catalogues, &c, leases, rent rolls, ejectments, and legal, military and naval forms of every description executed with expedition and correctness on the same moderate terms as have rendered their office so remarkable.[11]

Work commissioned by the bookseller Matthew Neary Mahon from the printers Graisberry and Campbell in January 1805 included:[12]

1000 copies of the sixth edition of *Intercepted letter* [by J.W.Crocker]
250 bills for the Wickam cruizer 8°
250 bills for the Buckingham cruizer 8°
200 Letters ruled for the Lawyers' Corps 4°
100 Letters ruled for the Attorneys' Corps 4°
100 Bills for the sale of whiskey
250 *Observations on the Habeas Corpus Act*
1000 *Familiar epistles to Frederick E Jones* 12° [by J.W.Croker]
1000 *Cutchacutchoo* 12° [by J.W.Croker]

It is not easy to get accurate accounts of the sizes of printing establishments. Though presses were required to be licensed from 1798, and this requirement continued until 1839, the licences have not survived in the State Paper Office.[13] The information for the first thirty years comes from auction and sale advertisements. One in *Saunders's Newsletter* on 24 September 1821 offered the following:

'To be sold two good presses, fit for newspaper work, an imposing stone several large troughs thickly leaded, five frames, about twelve pair of cases, a few brass galleys, and a variety of other articles useful in a printing office.' When the equipment of *The Star*, edited and partly owned by Joseph Timothy Haydn, was sold on 4 August 1826, in consequence of money owing at the Stamp Office, the materials on offer included 'one large iron printing press, one common press, a large imposing stone, several pairs of cases and stands, a quantity of printing type, chiefly long primer'. A report after the sale suggested that 'the whole may have produced £200'.[14] When M. Woodmason was sold up in April 1826 he had three large printing presses.[15]

More extensive information is available from the mid-1830s about one of the larger establishments. Philip Dixon Hardy devoted the entire issue on 10 May 1834 of the *Dublin Penny Journal* to 'a familiar description of printing in all its branches'. This was largely to celebrate his new steam-press which after several months' trial was now working smoothly. In addition to the difficulty of finding mechanics who could work it, the machine had been 'originally placed in an upper story of our office, the tremor produced by its working, so shook the entire house, as to render it necessary to remove it to the ground floor'. Output with two boys attending the machine was put at 1500 impressions an hour. However, he notes that make-ready time was so lengthy that 'it would not be worthwhile printing any number under two thousand on it'. Included in the article is a view of Hardy's press room showing five iron presses and he claimed to have a Stanhope, a Clymer, a Columbian, and a very neat press made by Joseph Aldritt of Dublin. In his evidence to the Select Committee on Combinations of Workmen given on 18 June 1838 Hardy was asked how many men he had been employing in 1835. His reply was 'I had, I think, at times, 15 men, who were employed regularly by the week, and I have had 15 or 20 others at case and press, less or more, as business required.' He had that year also seven to nine apprentices.[16] In 1841 J.S. Folds gave evidence to the Court of Queen's Bench that in June 1840 he had 24 journeymen and 5 apprentices working for him. His intention to increase the number of apprentices provoked a strike which lasted for over six months.[17]

The number of apprentices had been a long-running grievance with the journeymen printers. On 2 April 1825 they placed a lengthy advertisement in *Saunders's Newsletter* because they

feel called on, in duty to themselves and the public, to lay open and expose an iniquitous system of fraud and imposition, practised by petty master printers in this city, and the provincial towns throughout Ireland, on a credulous and unsuspecting community. These men, alive only to what affects themselves and reckless of the evil consequences that must result to others from a prosecution of their interested schemes, contrive to impose on the public, by representation of the prosperous state of the printing business – of the respectability and intelligence of the members of that art – of the golden prospects that await a young man on completing his apprenticeship, &c. – and hold out a variety of other hopes and expectations, equally vague and illusory until they fill their establishment with apprentices, from the parents of each of whom they have extorted a large fee, under the pretence of teaching the lads the art of printing–a stipulation for the performance of which they have neither a competent knowledge nor sufficient means.

In fact, the journeymen complained

the art of printing in this country, at no time prosperous, has been for many years rapidly decaying under the withering influence of English monopoly. In proportion as the trade has declined (strange to say) in the same, if not in a greater proportion, have hands multiplied, and the causes have already produced a reduction in the price of literature. Indeed to such a degree has that reduction taken place, and so naturally have our interests suffered, that no trade or profession requiring an equal proportion of intelligence is so badly paid as printing. In most of the establishments in Dublin, an intense and unremitting application during sixteen hours in the day and six days in the week, is requited by a pittance so trifling, as to be insufficient for the comforts of the applicant himself, independent of his wife and family . . . For themselves they are determined to protect, by all legal means, that business, which has become, by a toilsome and irksome servitude their hard earned and only property.

In the general business slump the following year the letterpress printers established a Committee for the relief of the unemployed printers. Apart from subscriptions within the trade, they felt 'urged, by the force of necessity alone, to seek a participation, on behalf of their numerous unemployed brethren, in the benevolent sympathy which the pressure of distress has created'.[18] The Committee's progress report in early October indicates that it had relieved 140 cases from the weekly subscriptions within the trade of £30. 7s. 6d. and in the weeks ending 23 September and 30 September it had aided 27 and 32 people respectively. Rates of payment from the fund ranged from 7s. 6d. down to 2s. 6d. in the week, with the majority getting 5s.[19] Distress was such that some printers even ended up working on government outdoor relief schemes, breaking stones.[20]

The journeymen finally took action to curb abuse of the apprenticeship scheme when a delegate meeting of the Irish Typographical Union agreed on a rule book on 15 September 1836 which, *inter alia*, stipulated that 'after the 15th day of September 1836, no office shall employ a greater number of apprentices than the proportion of one to two men permanently employed, two to four, three to six; and where more that [*sic*] are employed, the number of apprentices may be increased to four; but on no account shall that number be exceeded. Where more are now under indenture, the introduction of others shall be resisted by all legal means, until the number shall be reduced to the prescribed limits'. [21] P.D. Hardy admitted to the Committee on Combinations of Workmen in 1838 that apprenticeship was abused,

'I believe, from knowing Ireland tolerably well, that in many towns in Ireland, there are offices conducted altogether without a journeyman, where lads are trained as printers; they have come to Dublin, when out of their time, perhaps only half knowing their business, or perhaps not half knowing it; but still they have served seven years, and are printers; and also in Dublin, there are printers who do not employ men at all, but train lads; and if any means could be devised to protect the men in any way, I should say it would be but fair that men having got a good education, and having served seven years, should not be obliged to hunt the world for employment'.[22]

But he objected to the principle of the union's rule. Michael Staunton, proprietor of two Dublin papers stated to the same committee, 'I know that latterly the apprentices have greatly multiplied; I think there has been a growing abuse in that regard. Small printers, speculating on casual works, have taken in apprentices almost without limitations'.[23] Thomas Daly, secretary of the union, was of opinion that no more than 140 of the 260 journeymen printers in Dublin had anything like permanent work in 1838, and the union had assisted 120 members to emigrate in the preceding four years.[24]

Notwithstanding this tale of very real misery there was an extensive amount of printing going on. In the first two decades, besides the usual local sermons, trials and chapbooks, a considerable number of books were published by subscription. Though these included the expected quota of feeble poetry, other works were more solid. In 1804 one author recognised the poor state of the Irish market *vis-à-vis* the English one. James Gordon wrote *A new history of Ireland* which was published in quarto in London. But the author wished 'to accommodate his country men with a cheap edition' and advertised proposals for a Dublin edition to be printed in 8°, and undertook to stay in Dublin to correct the sheets.[25]. Some copies were to be printed on a very fine paper at £1. 2s. 9d, others on paper of a lesser quality at 17s. 4d . A total of 281 subscribers wanted 560 copies of this edition. In 1808 642 subscribers accounted for 767 copies of Leonard MacNally's two-volume *The justice of the peace for Ireland*. The publisher H. Fitzpatrick put himself down for 100 sets. In 1815 a total of 473 people subscribed for 1004 copies of Nicolas Caussin, *The holy court*, while 1230 subscribers took 1246 copies of A. Atkinson's *The Irish Tourist* in the same year. A feature of the subscription lists of the first two decades is the number of distinctly Roman Catholic books published in this way, many of which are quite slight devotional works. Of a total of 95 lists traced so far between 1801 and 1820 as many as 16 fall into this category. I have no doubt that this level of subscription publishing represents in some measure a political statement. Not all the publishers of these slight books were entirely engaged in the book trade: one edition of Henry VIII, *Defence of the seven sacraments* was printed and sold by James Griffen, at his Manufactory for Sewing Silk, School and Prayer Book, Lege Twist, Account Book, Thread, Tape, Quilting Worsted, Hardware and Ironmongery Ware-house, 33, New

Row, in about 1817. By 1822 he had added gunpowder to his wares!

In common with Great Britain the number of books published by subscription tails off towards 1850 and many of the later lists have evidence of extremely hard work by the author in persuading his neighbours to support him. The 659 subscribers for Patrick Donnelly's poem *Love of Britain* published in 1824 come almost entirely from a twelve-mile radius of his home village of Athboy in Co. Meath. Of the 528 names in Matthew Archdeacon's novel *Everard* in 1835, no fewer than 449 come from west of the Shannon, mainly from Co. Sligo.

About 1817 the business of school-book publishing really took off with the publishing activities of the Society for the Education of the Poor (otherwise known as the Kildare Place Society), who provided cheap educational literature in an endeavour to supplant pernicious works.[26] The Society's literary assistant Charles Bardin was examined by the Commissioners on Education in Ireland on 2 December 1824.[27] He gave their objective as being 'to publish moral works, and to blend as much instruction with them as possible', while avoiding offence to individual religious opinions. Their success was marked by the sales figures that he quoted to the Commissioners. Since 1817 they had sold 65,000 copies of Cottin's *Elizabeth*, and 60,000 of Aesop's *Fables*. They had had 30,000 copies of Captain Cook's *Voyages* printed since April 1820, while of their purely educational books an edition of 10,000 copies of the *Dublin Reading Book* was exhausted in 1822, and a further edition of 50,000 copies was ordered. Their *Dublin Spelling Book* was an even greater success; 50,000 copies were printed at the end of 1819, and a second edition of the same size was in the press when Bardin gave his evidence. By 1824 the normal edition size ordered by the Society was 10,000 copies. In 1831 the Commissioners of National Education began to publish their own school-books, which again had to be very carefully written to avoid offending religious interests. These, besides their captive domestic market, succeeded well in the export trade. In 1850 Longman and Co. and John Murray complained to Lord John Russell in a protest about the state interference in the trade that 'they find that the books printed for the Irish Commissioners of Education, supplied to schools in England patronised by the English Commissioners, amount to about a fourth part of the whole; and this quantity is exclusive of those sold by the agents of the Irish Commissioners in London and elsewhere'.[28] The extensive popularity of the Irish works is shown by the imprint of the Commissioners' *An introduction to the art of reading*, third edition, Dublin, 1850 which lists booksellers in London, Liverpool, Edinburgh, Montreal, and Halifax, Nova Scotia.

It is not yet possible to produce statistics on the subject range of Dublin printed books of the period but observations in libraries and newspaper advertisements show that school-books, directories, sermons (principally preached to members of the established Church of Ireland), and pamphlets on local controversies such as primary education, Catholic emancipation, and tithes predominate; these are all the stuff of provincial printing. A couple of features which distinguish the Dublin trade from other provincial centres, however, are the extensive medical and legal publishing.

During the 18th Century there had been some reprinting of medical texts, but Irish medicine came of age in the mid-19th Century and there was a substantial body of original publication. The Dublin works of Colles, Graves, Cheyne, Corrigan and Stokes secured international recognition for Irish clinical medicine. From about 1820 there was also a marked rise in the number of law books for the Irish market. Despite the existence of a native legislature, there was curiously little Irish writing on law in the 18th Century. The market after the Union clearly became identified as a profitable one; text-books, law reports and manuals for amateur magistrates abound. Hodges and Smith found it worthwhile to take a 2½-column advertisement in *The Nation* newspaper on 23 November 1844 entirely devoted to a list of over 60 law books which they published. In 1838 P.D. Hardy had no doubts about the good prospects for the printing trade had it not been for the activities of the trade union: 'In my own case, I should have gone to a very great extent, for I had opened a concern not only here, but in America; I sent a young man to the United States and to Canada. I have an agent in the States and in Canada, and one even at Van Diemen's Land; so that I would have carried on a very considerable trade in printing works in Dublin, as they do in London, and sending them abroad'.[29]

The Dublin bookbinders are turning out to be a much more numerous body than I had suspected. I am finding considerably more than C. Ramsden lists.[30] Their work, or course, covers the entire range from the heights attained by George Mullen, James Adams, Gerald Bellew, and Thomas Mullen down to the humble operator slapping linen covers on chapbooks.[31] The explanation for their number lies in part in one of William Wakeman's answers to the Commissioners of Inquiry into the Collection and Management of the Revenue arising in Ireland in 1821; 'many of the booksellers here are now in the habit of getting their books in sheets; there is a difference of a penny to twopence a volume in binding a school-book and three-pence to four-pence on a larger book between Dublin and London; leather is much cheaper in Dublin, and labour also'.[32] According to Charles Bardin in 1824 school-book binding 'is done by people of an inferior class, who take it home to their own rooms, and therefore the competition cannot be expected to be very extensive among them, executing as they do only 500 or a 1,000 at a time'.[33]

Some advertisements by Thomas Mullen when setting up in 1827 will give an idea of the competition. He

asserts and asserts truly that he is the cheapest and best bookbinder in Dublin. The following facts will go far to prove the truth of this. He served his apprenticeship to his father's brother, the late Geo. Mullen of Nassau Street, and most book men know that in this case his name alone is a tower of strength. T. Mullen has also the advantage of having been finisher to the best establishments in London. Being a workman, and executing the principal part of his trade with his own hands, is it not likely that books will be bound cheaper and better at his establishment than at others, where finishers are employed at heavy salaries. Octavos neatly bound at 1s. each and 12mos as low as 9d.[34]

Mullen immediately got into a price war with Alexander Panormo, proprietor of a Cheap Bookbinding Establishment in 11 Pitt Street who was 'under the determination of not being excelled by any other house in Dublin. His prices are very low, and his specimens not inferior to any other binder in this city. Octavos strongly bound at 9d. and 12mos only 6d.'[35] In October Mullen announced that he had reduced his prices by 25% which he claimed left them 'at least, 50 per cent lower than the prices of any other respectable bookbinder in Dublin'. He was ready to give references from distinguished noblemen and gentlemen who had honoured him with their patronage. His range of prices ran from the basic octavos at 9d. up to twelve guineas.[36] Panormo failed to last the pace and was sold up as an insolvent debtor in 1828. Competition remained fierce: Mullen reduced his prices by 10% in 1829 though a defensive note in the advertisement hints at pressure from the trade 'Now be ye not angry at this announcement, my Brother chips, ye know there is no agreement among us, therefore I break none'.[37] The number of bookbinders listed in the street directories gradually falls during the 1840s though this may reflect more binding work being done in printing offices as against outwork rather than an absolute fall in output.

Turning to bookselling we reach an area littered with unquantifiable factors. As in the 18th Century, many booksellers carried other lines to supplement their incomes. A few lucky ones were agents for charitable societies. Just how profitable this could be is apparent from the evidence of William Watson to the Commissioners on Education in Ireland. In the year 1821 his mother was the bookseller of the Association for discountenancing Vice and made a trading profit before overheads of over £1900 on publications sold for the Society.[38] The majority of the books sold were imported from Great Britain, and these imports had increased rapidly immediately after the Act of Union.[39] Some Dublin wholesalers had extensive relationships with London publishing houses, especially John Cumming who was in business as a wholesale and retail bookseller and publisher from 1811 to 1848. Copies of his account with Colburn and Bentley in the early 1830s show him owing £1136. 9s. 4d. at the end of November 1831. Having paid this bill, his account at the end of August 1832 shows him owing £1559. 11s. 10d.[40] These accounts show him to be acting as a commission agent with a 10% margin on sales, with Colburn and Bentley paying advertising charges and accepting returns. In early 1837 successive advertisements announce that he had been appointed sole Irish agent for Edward Moxon, Charles Tilt, and Effingham Wilson.[41]

A number of booksellers published stock catalogues which give an indication of the size of businesses. Harriot Colbert's *Catalogue of ancient and modern books, c.* 1802, lists 2844 items, while Matthew Neary Mahon's *Catalogue of books in various languages and classes* in 1813 had 6199 books. The largest stock of all is listed in catalogues I have not yet found. It was for the auction sale of Bennet Dugdale's stock in trade after his death in 1828. It was claimed the stock contained 60,000 volumes and catalogues were to be published weekly.[42] My disbelief in the size faded with the knowledge that the auctions went on for eleven months.

An altogether more modest affair was Richard Harman's *A catalogue of modern books now selling at unusually low prices* in 1830 listing 1135 items with two extra pages full of instructive and amusing publications for young people. Harman's short career as an independent trader began with an announcement in *Saunders's Newsletter* on 15 December 1828 that he intended to set up at 73 Dame Street as a bookseller, publisher, and stationer. His puff announced that he 'served his time in one of the *first houses* in this city, and afterwards held a *confidential* situation in the office of *His Majesty's Printers* for nearly 10 years'. So he was probably in his early thirties. He goes on to say 'Binding, Letter Press, Lithographic and Copperplate printing, executed in the best manner and on the shortest notice'. By 27 December 1828 he had his shop open, concentrating on juvenile literature, and having a seasonable variety of ladies and gentlemen's almanacs and pocket memorandum books. In May 1820 he made a bid for the lawyers' patronage as he proposed to open reading rooms which he intended to supply not only with the reviews and newspapers but also with the various statutes which he could obtain quickly through his connection with G. Grierson, the King's Printer.[43] In late October he announced plans for a weekly periodical to be called *The Friend*.[44] Domestic disaster struck when his son died of inflammation of the lungs aged only five months. By 2 April 1830 he was determined to quit business immediately, published the catalogue of stock, and put the house up for sale.[45] His last appearance in the papers is as an insolvent writing clerk in 1832.

The large and enterprising firm of Grant and Bolton published a series of catalogues from the late 1820s. A bargain in their 1833 *General catalogue of cheap second hand books* of 4415 books was the anonymous *Sense and sensibility*, London, 1813, 3v, 12°, very neatly half bound at eight shillings, with a note indicating that it would sell at £1. 3*s*. in London. Their *Catalogue of second hand books, in every branch and department of literature* in 1836 included in the 8987 items a copy of Shakespeare's *Comedies, histories and tragedies* London, 1664 at six guineas with the remark that it was 'the scarcest of the early editions of our immortal bard, nearly the whole of the impression having been destroyed by the great fire in London; this edition is marked at £18-18-0. in the London catalogues'. Two years later their *Catalogue of a very extensive collection of second hand books* of 7928 items was issued as a classified list in seven broad divisions as follows: '1. Holy Scripture 2. Divinity, Theology. 3. English history, biography and miscellanies. 4. Irish ditto. 5. Novels, tales and romances. 6. Greek and Latin classics with books in most of the ancient and modern languages. 7. Books printed at the Aldine presses.' What is most interesting in this list is item 1341: 'Luther (Mart.) Opera, Germanicé, 14 vols, small 4°. *neatly half bound*, 4*s*. 6*d*. per vol. Wittem., 1519. The above volumes contain some very curious tracts of Martin Luther, in the German language and character, to be disposed of in separate volumes'. William Ullathorne, missionary in Australia, and late Bishop of Birmingham, later recorded being in Dublin at the time: 'At leisure times I was fond of searching into old bookshops, picking up what I thought might be useful in Australia, where books in those days were very scarce. In Dame Street Dublin, I thus picked up a great rarity, no less than the collection of the original tracts, pamphlets, and sermons of Martin Luther, without any of those expurgations of his abusive language and obscenities which were effected in the collected editions of his works. They were bound up in a dozen quarto volumes'.[46]

The 1840s were darkened in Ireland by the Great Famine of 1845–47. The population declined from 8,175,124 in 1841 to 6,552,385 in 1851. Besides the appalling destruction of life there was widespread economic disruption. This was reflected in the book trade. A survey of the reports of insolvencies and bankruptcies in the official journal, *The Dublin Gazette*, shows a total of 284 instances between 1801 and 1850. Of these 73, or just over 25%, occurred in the five years 1844–48. Some of the biggest firms crashed. Andrew Milliken, whose firm originated in the 1770s, went bankrupt in 1844; his assets were bought for £7,500 from the assignees. J.S. Folds, one of the largest printers, went bankrupt in 1845; Richard Coyne, the Catholic bookseller and publisher, and William Curry the publisher went in 1847. The most conspicious survivor into the 1850s was James Duffy, with a business firmly based on the triple pillars of Catholic piety, schoolbooks and nationalist literature.

The half-century closes with the trade sadly disturbed by the economic consequences of the Famine, but showing signs of vigour in the quality of work, with the publication in 1851 of the greatest monument of the Dublin University Press, the 6 volume bilingual edition of the *Annals of the Four Masters*, and in quantity, with the massive exports of the school-books of the Commissioners of National Education. Though the lot of the small men in any branch of the trade was hard, so far as I have discovered only two committed crimes for which they were hanged; the one was an engraver who for want of business started printing bank notes without authorisation,[47] the other a barrow bookseller who engaged upon a highway robbery which failed.[48]

References

1.   These are preliminary reflections on studies which are primarily intended to produce a directory of the Dublin book trade in the period.

2.   *Third Report of the Commissioners of Inquiry into the Collection and Management of the Revenue arising in Ireland,* House of Commons, 1825, appendix 2, p.15.

3.   *Ibid.,* appendix 3, p.16.

4.   41 Geo.III c.107.

5.   For the authoritative study of the 18th Century trade see Pollard, M., *Dublin's trade in books 1550–1800,* (Oxford, 1989).

6.   *Journals of the House of Commons of Ireland,* (Dublin 1796–1802), XVI, p.193.

7.   Inglis, B. *The freedom of the press in Ireland 1784–1841,* (London, 1954), pp.108–12.

8.   P. Byrne to M. Carey 16 October 1798. Historical Society of Pennsylvania, Lea and Febiger Collection, MS 7746.

9.   *Dublin Journal (Faulkner's)* 13 April 1802.

10. Graisberry and Campbell's business for the Dublin Society was worth £242. 12s. 1d. in 1802, and £300. 2s. 1d. in 1802, and had the merit of punctual payment. Graisberry and Campbell, *Ledger* 1797–1806. Trinity College Dublin MS 10315, openings 58, 72, 73.

11. *Hibernian Journal* 14 November 1804.

12. Graisberry and Campbell, *Ledger* 1797–1806 Trinity College Dublin MS 10315, opening 123.

13. 38 Geo.III, c. 18, Ireland.

14. *Saunders's Newsletter* 4 August 1825, 5 August 1825.

15. *Saunders's Newsletter* 18 April 1826.

16. *Second Report from the Select Committee on Combinations of Workmen,* House of Commons, 1838, p.43.

17. *Saunders's Newsletter* 16 April 1841.

18. *Saunders's Newsletter* 19 September 1826.

19. *Saunders's Newsletter* 3 October 1826.

20. State Paper Office OP/588T/727/90.

21. *Second Report from the Select Committee on Combinations of Workmen,* House of Commons, 1838, p.101.

22. *Ibid.,* p.26.

23. *Ibid.,* p.52.

24. *Ibid.,* pp.97, 101–2.

25. *Hibernian journal* 18 June 1804.

26. Moore, H.K., *An unwritten chapter in the history of eduction,* (London, 1904), pp.214–15, 245–8.

27. *First Report of the Commissioners on Education in Ireland,* House of Commons, 1825 Appendix 206, pp.464–5.

28. Goldstrom, J.M., 'The correspondence between Lord John Russell and the publishing trade', *Publishing History* XX (1986), p.11.

29. *Second Report from the Select Committee on Combinations of Workmen*, House of Commons, 1838, p.28.

30. Ramsden, C., *Bookbinders of the United Kingdom (outside London) 1780–1840* (London, 1954).

31. Work by George Mullen is illustrated in Craig, M., *Irish Bookbindings*, (Dublin, 1976) pp.21–2; work by Thomas Mullen is in Foot, M.M., 'A binding by Thomas Mullen of Dublin c. 1827–30', *The Book Collector* 35 no.4 (1986) pp.494–5.

32. *Third Report of the Commissioners of Inquiry into the Collection and Management of the Revenue arising in Ireland*, House of Commons, 1822, appendix 2. p.15.

33. *First Report of the Commissioners on Education in Ireland*, House of Commons, 1825, appendix no.206, p.465.

34. *Saunders's Newsletter* 18 January 1827.

35. *Saunders's Newsletter* 23 January 1827.

36. *Saunders's Newsletter* 16 October 1827.

37. *Saunders's Newsletter* 28 November 1829.

38. *First Report of the Commissioners on Education in Ireland*, House of Commons, 1825, appendix 180, p.385.

39. Pollard, M., *Dublin's trade in books 1550–1800* (Oxford, 1989), pp.154–5.

40. Bentley papers BL Add. MS 46640, ff.68ᵛ, 85ʳ.

41. *Saunders's Newsletter* 14 February, 24 April, 2 May 1837.

42. *Saunders's Newsletter* 11 March 1828.

43. *Saunders's Newsletter* 1 May 1829.

44. The British Library holds nos.1–10.

45. *Saunders's Newsletter* 2 April 1830.

46. Ullathorne, W., *The autobiography* (London, 1891–1892) v.1, p.136.

47. *Saunders's Newsletter* 14 August; 3, 11, 19 November 1818.

48. *Saunders's Newsletter* 3, 8 January 1828.

Publisher, pedlar, pot-poet:
The changing character of
the broadside trade, 1550–1640[1]

TESSA WATT

ONE FINE DAY, some time between 1557 and 1565, somewhere between Tamworth, Staffordshire and London, a minstrel named Richard Sheale was robbed of 60 pounds of gold, which he was taking to the city to clear his debts. Not one to miss an opportunity, Sheale had soon turned the sad story of his misfortune into a song, and used it to elicit help from sympathetic listeners. One of these listeners copied the ballad into a commonplace book along with four of Sheale's other songs, leaving us a glimpse into the lifestyle and repertoire of a minstrel in the early years of Elizabeth's reign.[2]

Richard Sheale still belonged to the medieval system of musical patronage, travelling with his harp under the protection of the Earl of Derby. His position was superior to that of a common broadside ballad-seller, who was usually a masterless man with no such immunity from the vagabondage laws.[3] Nevertheless, Sheale lived not far from that nether world of vagrants: his wife was a pedlar woman, his friends were alehouse-keepers (who helped him brew a pot of ale when he was out of pocket), and his debts forced him to go begging abroad with his song. And although some of his pieces were apparently improvised, others show signs of contact with the broadside ballad trade. 'Remember man thy frail estate' is typical of Protestant moralising broadsides of this period, and 'Chevy Chase' was almost certainly circulating in print.[4] Sheale's epitaph for the Countess of Derby is recorded with a long-winded title in typical broadside form, which suggests it was composed for the press:

the epith off the dethe off the ryghte honorable lady Margrete countes of Darbe, which departyde this world the xix[th] day off January, and was buryede the xxiii[ti] off Phebruary, in anno Domini 1558, on whosse soll God have mercye, Amen, quothe Rycharde Sheale.[5]

Comments of other minstrels like Sheale suggest that songs learnt from print or manuscript copies were incorporated into their repertoire.[6] The minstrels' high degree of mobility ensured that ballads could travel the length and breadth of the land in this way. Sheale himself was based in Tamworth, Staffordshire, but his working route cut a great diagonal swathe across the country. His travels took

him over 100 miles south-east to London, and also some 80 miles in the opposite
direction, north-west to Ormskirk in Lancashire, where he attended the Countess
of Derby's funeral.[7] Ballads could travel along these minstrels' routes, cut loose
from their printed form, and adapted or 'recreated' by the individual performer.

Some half a century later, in 1616, William Brown described the typical ballad-
seller in the marketplace. Gone is the harp, and any pretence of musical skill: the
performance is not an end in itself, but only a pretext for selling the printed
artefact, the broadside.

> . . . Ballad-mongers on a Market-day
> Taking their stand, one (with as harsh a noyce
> As every Cart-wheele made) squeakes the sad choice
> Of Tom the Miller with a golden thumbe,
> Who crost in love, ran mad, and deafe, and dumbe,
> Halfe part he chants, and will not sing it out,
> But thus bespeakes to his attentive rout:
> Thus much for love I warbled from my brest,
> And gentle friends, for mony take the rest . . .[8]

The seller squeaks or chants out the ballad to draw in the customers and get them
hooked by the plot. However, this anonymous ballad-seller is not primarily a
musician at all, but a pedlar – either working indpendently, in the style of Autolycus, or in the hire of the ballad publishers.[9] A passage from Henry Chettle's *Kind
harts dreame* [1592?] describes the latter type of arrangement:

> . . . no stationer, who after a little bringing them uppe to singing brokerie, takes into his
> shop some fresh men, and trusts his olde searvantes of a two months standing with a
> dossen groates worth of ballads. In which, if they proove thrifty, hee makes them prety
> chapmen, able to spred more pamphlets by the state forbidden then all the bookesellers
> in London . . .[10]

The spread of petty chapmen selling ballads in this period is a measure of how
far print was infiltrating the oral culture. Printed wares were becoming increasingly familiar objects in the daily lives of those on the fringes of literacy. As
Nicholas Bownde commented in 1595:

> You must not onely look into the houses of great personages. . . but also in the shops of
> artificers, and cottages of poor husbandmen, where you shall sooner see one of these
> newe Ballades. . . than any of the Psalmes, and may perceive them to be cunninger in
> singing the one, than the other.[11]

Bownde even claims to have witnessed the interesting situation of illiterate cotta-
gers pasting up ballads on their walls in order to 'learne' them later:

and though they cannot reade themselves, nor any of theirs, yet will have many Ballades set up in their houses, that so might learne them, as they shall have occasion.[12]

This audience, at the end of the century, appears to have broadened considerably from that of the early Elizabethan years. Many of the early broadside ballads were written for a small coterie: epitaphs of gentry and merchants, or contrived literary invective between members of a London-centred elite.[13] When Richard Sheale wrote his epitaph for the Countess of Derby in 1559, it is likely to have been run off in a small number of copies and distributed to his patron's 'lovyng frenddes', perhaps by Sheale himself.[14] Early Elizabethan ballads were sometimes billed as 'A warning to London' or addressed to 'London dames'; by the second quarter of the 17th Century they were much more commonly given titles like 'The cooper of Norfolke' or 'A pleasant new northerne song, called the two York-shire lovers'.[15] This is not to say that 16th-Century ballads did not reach across much of the country: we hear that polemical ballads were passed around in the village alehouses of Cambridgeshire and Norfolk in the 1550s, 'cast in the streetes of Northampton' in 1570, and so on.[16] However, by 1624, the ballad sheet had apparently become a common artefact even in 'northern' villages, where they were stuck up on walls as a cheap form of decoration. In that year Abraham Holland satirised the popularity of the broadside:

As in North-Villages, where every line
Of Plumpton Parke is held a work divine.
If o're the Chymney they some Ballad have
Of Chevy-Chase, or of some branded slave
Hang'd at Tyborne, they their Mattins make it
And Vespers too, and for the Bible take it.[17]

The spread of the ballad was possible because of growing literacy. As Margaret Spufford has convincingly argued, statistics based on signatures are probably gross underestimates of *reading* ability.[18] Reading was taught before writing, and it is likely that many more rural people could get through the text of a broadside ballad than could sign their names to a Protestation Oath. David Cressy's figures for early-modern England may only represent the proportion of each group which remained in school from age seven to eight when writing was taught.[19] Amongst husbandmen and labourers especially, there may have been a large number who attended school up to the age of six, and learnt the primary skill of reading, but who were whisked away to join the labour force 'as soon as they were strong enough to contribute meaningfully to the family economy'.[20]

Nevertheless, improvement in the separate skills of reading and writing would have depended generally on the presence of schoolmasters and the foundation of village schools. On the graph of literacy, readers would probably form a dotted line running parallel above writers, so that the two skills followed the same 'dynamics'. David Cressy has described the first half of Elizabeth's reign as a period of 'educational revolution', with advances in ability to sign in all social groups for those schooled between 1560 and 1580. In East Anglia, husbandmen of this generation improved from 10% to 30% fully 'literate', yeomen from 45% to 75%, and tradesmen in Norwich from 40% to 60%. From 1580 to 1610 was a period of 'educational recession', followed by a recovery during James's reign and 'pronounced improvement' in the 1630s.[21] The growing specialisation of the ballad publishers coincided with this second phase of 'educational revolution', and may reflect an increasing awareness of lower social groups as a potentially lucrative market for print.

The broadside ballad, as both song and printed text, was at the cutting edge of this 'revolution'. We should not think of print as simply replacing oral culture, but of a complex interaction of the printed word with existing cultural practices. R.S. Thomson has shown that the successful ballads which made up the publishers' core 'stock', reprinted generation after generation, are the same ones which have survived as familiar 'folksongs'.[22] The areas from which collectors like Cecil Sharp drew their material can be matched fairly closely with the routes covered by pedlars carrying broadsides in the 18th and 19th Centuries. Thomson argues that the ballads collected from the oral tradition by folk enthusiasts in the last two centuries in fact owe their survival to the reinforcement of the printed word.[23]

The period under study in this paper, the late 16th and early 17th Centuries, is the crucial one in which the specialist trade in ballads and other cheap or 'popular' print came into being. By 1624, the leading ballad publishers had collected together the copyrights to a stock of ballads, formed themselves into a syndicate called the 'ballad partners', and organised themselves for more efficient storage and distribution of the printed sheets. Unfortunately no inventory survives for a ballad publisher of this period, and references to ballad-sellers in local records are thin on the ground. It has so far proved impossible to chart the route of any pedlars of print with certainty for this period, let alone to draw up a comprehensive map of the distribution network. The question of the spread of printed wares must be approached obliquely, looking at changes in the publishers' strategy and output; at the character of the broadsides themselves; at the literary evidence setting broadsides in a cultural context; as well as the 'hard' evidence referring sporadically to ballads and ballad-sellers.

In the rest of the paper I will look more closely at the main links in this growing chain of paper – the publishers, the pedlars and the poets – first in the early Elizabethan years, and then half a century later. Together these groups developed into an increasingly specialised industry, distributing cheap printed wares to a widening readership across the country.

Publishers

The closest thing the Elizabethans had to a broadside tycoon was the printer–publisher Richard Jones. He produced the largest number of ballads (164 titles entered in the Stationers' Register) and spanned a period from 1564 to 1602. Jones was only one of some 40 publishers who registered at least one broadside with the Stationers' Company during its first decade.[24] However by 1586 the records begin to show the accumulation of large numbers of ballads in a few hands. In that year a Star Chamber decree ordered stationers to bring in their old copies which had not been properly authorised.[25] Jones registered 123 ballads, listed on a separate sheet of paper which has unfortunately not survived.[26] (His nearest competitor was Edward White, with 36 titles.)

However, ballads were not Richard Jones's only trade: he also published 106 distinct books and pamphlets, not counting multiple editions.[27] Jones was by Elizabethan standards a 'popular' printer, producing only two works in Latin, and none of the staple text-books for the schools and universities: he catered for 'lay' rather than 'learned' culture. Yet his clientele consisted, it appears, of gentry and wealthy London merchants. Almost half his corpus was made up of full-length books, many addressed to 'young gentlemen' 'young courtiers' 'To the Gentlemen Readers' or to specific members of the Court and City elite.[28] Jones's list included books about foreign lands, addressed especially to merchants;[29] news pamphlets about political events in England and the Continent;[30] play texts (usually at least nine sheets quarto); and verse collections, usually retellings of classical myths, tangled in Renaissance allegories and conceits.[31] Some of Jones's authors claimed to write for 'everie man from the highest to the lowest: from the Richest to the poorest', but did so in works of over 300 pages, which would have cost a minimum of ten pence unbound.[32]

Jones did publish a handful of cheap and portable pamphlets which could be considered as the precursors of the 17th-Century chapbook. Philip Stubbes's *A christal glasse for Christian women* was his account of the life of his wife Katherine, who died in childbirth at the age of twenty. Commonly known as 'Katherine Stubs' the slim quarto pamphlet was first published in 1591 and a century later was still sold as a 'double-book' by the chapbook publisher William Thackeray.[33] In 1635 William Cartwright mentioned the title as part of the standard selection of religious tracts and sermons sold outside playhouse doors from a wooden box:

I shall live to see thee
Stand in a Play-house doore with thy long box,
Thy half-crown Library, and cry small Books.
Buy a good godly Sermon Gentlemen –
A judgement shewn upon a Knot of Drunkards –
A pill to purge out Popery – The life
And death of *Katherin Stubs*.[34]

Pedlars of 'small books' were stock figures of the London streets in the early 17th Century; a print of 36 'criers of London' shows a man with a wooden box of 'Alminaks' hanging from his neck.[35] This sales method was probably well established even by Jones's time for distribution within the capital; but how far his wares travelled out into the countryside is a question on which the records are mute.

In 1602, the same year that Richard Jones printed his last book, John Wright gained the freedom of the Stationer's Company. He was a founding member of the 'ballad partners', a group of six of the less wealthy booksellers who gradually, during James's reign, accumulated the copyrights to the most successful ballad titles. The six included John Wright's two brothers Cuthbert and Edward together with Thomas Pavier, Henry Gosson, and John Grismond. The partners' first entry in 1624 is a registration of 127 ballads, of which as many as two-thirds had already been published by the year 1586. By the 1630s the partners had a near monopoly on the publication and distribution of the most popular ballad titles. They formed a close-knit little dynasty bound by ties of apprenticeship, patrimony and marriage; a dynasty which was to dominate the trade for the rest of the 17th Century.[36] John Wright's own apprenticeship line leads directly through William Gilbertson, Charles Tias and Thomas Passinger, to John Back, Josiah Blare and Thomas Passinger (2); all familiar names from the chapbook imprints in Margaret Spufford's *Small books and pleasant histories*.

John Wright, like the rest of the 'ballad partners' was a bookseller, not a printer.[37] The primary function of the partnership does not appear to have been collaboration in the actual production of the ballads, but rather, their distribution.[38] The individual ballad sheets bore the imprint of one partner or another, but the broadsides were all stored in a communal ballad warehouse, and sold to hawkers at a standard rate set by the partners. According to a court case of 1630, their rate was 13s. 4d. per ream, or a third of a penny each.[39] There are various indications that distribution was a particular skill of these booksellers. John Wright sold a number of titles (at least seventeen) published by other stationers; an indication of his access to markets which they could not reach from their own shops.[40] His shop was located in Giltspur Street just ouside Newgate, well placed for carriers going west or north-west from the city. It was near the market at West Smithfield, where chapmen gathered to purchase wares of all kinds. By 1624, Francis Coules, Francis Grove and John Trundle (other leading ballad publishers) were all located in the Newgate/Smithfield area.[41] Smithfield was still the main neighbourhood for ballad and chapbook publishers in the late 17th Century. Routes to the south were covered by another cluster of shops on London Bridge, where Henry Gosson was now set up.[42]

The partners' improved distribution, and consolidation of copyrights to the ballad titles, was accompanied by a new emphasis on what we would now call 'marketing strategy'. The most striking change was the institution of woodcut pictures as a standard feature. In the 16th-Century collecitons, no more than roughly a quarter of the ballads have some kind of woodcut decoration. For the period 1600-1640, more than five-sixths of extant ballads are illustrated.[43] This visual packaging would have increased the appeal for an audience on the fringes of literacy. Many a non-reader must have first encountered these printed texts through their function as decoration, in neighbours' homes or in the public alehouses. As Wye Saltonstall commented in 1631:

A Country Alehouse.
Is the center of the Towns good fellowship, or some humble roof't cottage licens'd to sell Ale. The inward hangings is a painted cloath, with a row of Balletts pasted on it.[44]

This standard décor is confirmed by Izaak Walton, who in 1653 described a visit to

an honest Alehouse, where we shall find a cleanly room, Lavender in the windowes, and twenty Ballads stuck about the walls.[45]

The broadside stuck on the wall must have played an important part in the process of 'typographic acculturation' in England.[46]

   Although the ballad partners' stock was not limited to ballads, their overall output had begun to shift. There was a greater concentration on ephemeral or 'popular' material such as sensational news pamphlets and plays, suggesting increasing specialisation in printed wares for a wider market. Henry Gosson's special line, apart from his 80 ballad titles, was in the pamphlets of John Taylor, the 'Water Poet', of which he produced thirty. John Wright was in fact the most substantial of the 17th-Century ballad publishers I have looked at, putting out fewer ballads and more full-length books. Yet less than half his non-ballad works ran to four sheets or more, as opposed to almost two-thirds for Richard Jones.[47] His output included plays and news pamphlets; not the sober political reports published by Jones, but more sensational stories of murders, earthquakes and monstrous births, complete with title-page woodcuts.[48]

   Wright's most important contribution to the book trade was as a pioneer of a new genre, the penny chapbook – a small pamphlet which gradually became standardised in a format of 24 pages (or sometimes less), in octavo or duodecimo. These chapbooks were the little books which Samuel Pepys was later to bind together as 'penny merriments' and 'penny godlinesses', although they appear to have cost twopence by the time he was collecting.[49] John Wright, together with a preacher called John Andrewes, was effectively the inventor of the penny godliness, of which he had published a dozen titles by 1640. 'Penny chapbooks' in general account for 20 titles, or one-quarter of his total surviving non-ballad output. The growth of the chapbook trade is a subject ouside the scope of this paper, although I will touch on it again later.[50] However, the development of these little books is an indication of how the ballad publishers were reaching out to new markets by producing books which were cheap, portable and suitable for the rudimentary reader.

The 1620s was the decade in which the 'ballad partners' organised themselves into a specialised syndicate for the distribution of their wares. The evidence also points to this as the period when the same publishers began consciously to acquire the copyrights to small books, which could be carried over long distances in a pedlar's pack. By sending these chapbooks along the distribution networks they used for their ballads, they could reach potential readers who had until then been unlikely to purchase the printed word except in broadside form.

Pedlars

If we now move from the publishers to their agents, the pedlars, we again see evidence of how the printed word was making inroads into rural culture. Our mid-16th-Century minstrel, Richard Sheale, is a transitional figure between the predominantly (though certainly not exclusively) oral tradition of the professional minstrel, and the print-based performance of the ballad seller. [51] The distribution networks for printed wares may have been extensions of the routes along which songs were disseminated by minstrels, waits and travelling interlude players. Rather than treating the distribution of print as a completely new and isolated phenomenon I will look at it in the context of these older lines of travel and communication.

The story of Richard Sheale suggests how a minstrel could act as a cultural conduit spanning great geographical and social distances. His association with the Earl of Derby apparently guaranteed him an audience amongst the Earl's acquaintances:

And my lord Strang also on me dyde tak compassion.
For whos sakys I thank Gode I have ban well regardyde,
And among ther lovyng frenddes I have ben well rewardyde.[52]

However, their payments were not enough to keep body and soul together, and it seems that Sheale was also involved in the chapman's trade:

But I hade frenddes in London whos namys I can declare,
That at all tymys wolde lende me xx^{lds} worth off ware . . .[53]

He may have been buying silks and linen for his wife, who was a specialised chapwomen, working the fairs and markets of Staffordshire:

. . . at fearis and merkyttes she solde sale-war that she made,
As sherttes, smockys, partlyttes, hede clotthes, and othar thingges,
As sylk threde, and eggynges, shurte banddes, and stringes . . .[54]

The couple may well have travelled to markets as a pair, he singing and she selling. The contacts of Sheale and his wife between them covered the entire social scale, from the noble Lancashire household, to the shops of London tradesmen, to the Staffordshire markets, to the world of the local alehouse-keepers in Tamworth (who helped him to make an extra five pounds from brewing ale, a common last resort for the poor).[55]

This wide range of social contacts suggests the folly of any attempt to draw a line between 'elite' and 'popular' culture in this period. Most of the minstrels who played in noble households were themselves from humble social backgrounds. For example, the Register of the Freemen of the City of York records the sons of a grocer, a wright, a tailor, a porter, a labourer and two tapissers becoming musicians in Elizabeth's reign.[56] The songs of the minstrels must have permeated the lives of their families, neighbours and friends in these other trades, and we should think of distribution in social as well as geographical terms.

Songs travelled to the nether regions of society through familial and social contacts. They also travelled to the distant regions of Lancashire, Yorkshire and Norfolk via a network of itinerant performers. The high degree of mobility amongst waits and other minstrels meant that the songs they performed were disseminated to all corners of England, including the far north. In Newcastle, between February and August 1562, the Chamberlains' Account Books record payment to groups of waits who had travelled from towns in County Durham, Cumberland, and Yorkshire; and to minstrels from Ireland and Scotland.[57] Over the Christmas season in 1614-15, Carlisle was visited by the waits of Lancaster, Lincoln and even Bristol.[58] Between these relatively official visits, there were many wanderers. The accounts of Carlisle and of neighbouring Naworth Castle show a number of payments each year to musical nomads such as 'a piper that came out of Lankyshire', 'two fiddlers at the gate', 'a knightes musicions yat came oute of Yorkshyer' and 'j scotes gentlewomanminstrell'.[59]

Not only did the Bristol waits make the long voyage north to Cumberland, but northern waits came south. In 1633, Coventry was a stop-over for the waits of Preston, Halifax, Ripon and Kendal; as well as, more predictably, from cities within a radius of 50-odd miles, like Shrewsbury, Derby, Nottingham and Newark.[60] Nor was the music of the waits heard only in the major towns and cities. In 1511, 28 townships of western Cambridgeshire contributed sums towards a pageant of St George, held at the village of Bassingbourn. Minstrels and waits were hired, for a lump sum of 5s.11d., to come out into the countryside from Cambridge for three days.[61]

Court cases over songs which were libellous or politically contentious indicate that it was common for waits and minstrels to carry printed or written copies of the texts they performed.[62] However, since the songs were learnt by heart, the audience received them in oral form. The direct dissemination of printed ballads fell to a different class of traveller, the petty chapman, whose unskilled performance (as we have already noted) was primarily a sales pitch for the printed text. The high level of vagrancy in this period provided the ballad partners and other publishers with a large army of potential distributors. General statistics for the vagrant population indicate that two-thirds were single, primarily male, and that (between 1570 and 1622) an astonishing two-thirds were under the age of 21.[63] Writing around 1592, Henry Chettle gives the impression of ballad-singing youths flooding the countryside, coming into conflict with the older minstrel tradition:

... As vile it is that boyes, of able strength and agreeable capacity, should bee suffered to wrest from the miserable aged the last refuge in their life (beggery excepted) the poore helpe of ballad-singing.[64]

Since ballad sellers were most often guildless, 'masterless' men, our records of them come almost solely from their prosecutions as vagrants. The most frequent references to 'ballad singers', as such, outside London can be found in Norwich, the second city of the realm. A half-dozen ballad singers appear in the Norwich Court Books from 1600 to 1640, with orders forbidding them to practise their trade and sometimes exiling them from the city. In the Norwich records the singing and selling of ballads are invariably mentioned together. William Nynges was part of a husband-and-wife team, both ordered in 1605 not to 'singe nor sell any Ballettes within this Cytty after this day upon payne of whippynge'. In 1614, James Dickon was 'Inioyned not to singe Ballades nor to sell eyther Ballades or Alminackes in the market after this day'. Alexander Lawes was 'forbidden to use sellynge or singinge of Balletes' in 1629, but was apprehended again 13 years later, when the authorities seized 'thirty Libellous & scandalous ballettes which he was singinge of in this Citty & puttinge to sale which were burned in the open market'.[65] These real-life balladeers may have had no more musical talent than the squeaking ballad-monger with his performance of 'Tom the Miller', described above. But the fact that they did sing confirms again that the ballad was considered to be a performance, and not just a printed text to be sold and read, detached from its tune.

Ballad-sellers also reached the Wiltshire record books, which include the rare survival of a 'register of passports' for vagrants apprehended in Salisbury.[66] In 1616 'Apprice Williams, a ballad-singer and vagrant' was sent home from Salisbury to Goldhanger in Essex. In 1630 'Edward Kerbye, a ballad-seller, wandering' claimed he came from Holborne, London.[67] Another London man, Walter Plummer of Southwark, was stopped at Trowbridge fair in 1620, 'carrying with him a store of ballads to sing in his travels'. And in the 1650s, when ballads were banned, singers were arrested in Devizes and Bristol.[68]

Ballads were even to be found lying about on the roads of Wiltshire, according to a petty chapman at Stalbridge fair accused of stealing money: 'he sayeth that he found itt folded up in a Ballad in the highway neare Warminster'.[69] Even if this is a fabrication, the fact that such a story sprang immediately to mind shows how commonplace ballads were in this region. Ballad-sellers apprehended in this area were quite likely to be on their way from London heading further south and west. Of those vagrants described as 'chapman', 'chapwoman' or 'petty chapman' caught in Salisbury between 1598 and 1640, most were either from London (four of them) or from the southern and western counties of Hampshire, Somerset, Dorset and Devon (eight).[70] These chapmen probably plied their wares at least as far as the towns they described as home; and some of them may have been carrying ballads among the other trinkets in their packs.

Unfortunately nothing like the Salisbury register appears to survive for the midlands or the north, and other sources for the history of vagrancy are sparse in these areas.[71] My search through a number of the quarter sessions records available in print yielded nothing on 'ballad-singers' or 'ballad-sellers'.[72] This may be partly a problem of terminology: very few of the vagrants appear to have called themselves 'ballad-sellers' as such. In A.L. Beier's statistics on the occupations of vagrants, they may be among the 7–10% of vagrants described as 'petty chapmen'.[73] Others may be hidden among the 'apprentices and servants' who made up almost a quarter of Beier's masterless men c.1620–c.1640.[74] Still others, trained in any number of trades, may have sold ballads on the side, or for brief periods between other jobs. The fluidity of 'occupations' is epitomised by the Wiltshire man who was 'sometimes a weaver, sometimes a surgeon, sometimes a minstrel, sometimes a dyer, and now a bullard'.[75]

The paucity of 'ballad-singers' or 'ballad-sellers' in the records is not just a semantic problem, then, but may tell us something about the degree of specialisation in the trade. Pedlars carrying just ballads were probably much less common in this period than those carrying ballads as a sideline with other wares, like Shakespeare's pedlar Autolycus.[76] Cases in the Court of Requests from the 1590s on show that chapman from the midlands and south-west, as well as the home counties, were following regular trade routes to and from London.[77]

Ballads and pamphlets may also have travelled with the carriers. In *The carriers cosmographie* (1637), John Taylor listed the inns around London where carriers could be found on specific days of the week, bound for over 200 towns across Britain, and able to deliver goods and letters to the remotest regions of Scotland, Wales and Cornwall. Regular destinations in the north included Halifax, Wakefield, Doncaster, Preston, and many other towns in between.[78] The carriers of York (to give one example) arrived at the sign of the Bell without Ludgate every Friday, and left again on Saturday or Monday. Goods sent to York could then be sent on 'any waies north, broad and wide as farre or further than Barwicke', while from Lancaster they could be 'conveyd to Kendall, or Cockermouth'.[79] The existence of regular carrier services, together with the evidence that chapmen's routes to the extreme north and south-west were already well established by the end of the 16th Century, suggests that we should think of a national market for cheap print, and not merely a metropolitan area. In 1641, the author of *The downefall of temporizing poets* claimed there were 277 ballad-sellers in London. If he was right in his count, it is likely that by then these London-based pedlars alone covered much of the country in their wanderings.[80]

Pot-poets

The spread of the printed ballad was possible only by the disengagement of the song from any intimate attachment to a particular singer. Even if the minstrel did not invent a song from scratch, he made it his own property by 'recreating' it in an oral performance. Richard Sheale's songs were recorded in a commonplace book with his name inscribed as the author, though he was certainly not the original creator of the ballad of Chevy Chase, which bears his name. But for the pedlar the ballad was no longer personal property in this way; it was a commodity to be sold, like other commercial wares.

Not only was the printed song increasingly detached from its singer, but also from its author. In the 16th Century, most ballads named the author on the broadside, either by full name or initials. The ballad-writers were not generally a separate breed of journalists, but came from a cross-section of respectable professions. We have ballads written by a merchant-tailor of London (William Fulwood), a silk-weaver (Thomas Deloney), as well as dramatists and stationers (Thomas Preston, John Awdeley).[81] Even clergymen put their names to godly versions of the most popular secular ballads. William Kethe, Protestant divine and Marian exile, was the author of several anti-papist ballads.[82] John Cornet was another ballad-writing minister, and Thomas Brice spent his energies writing moralisations of the great contemporary collections of courtly love poetry.[83]

The social and educational status of these reforming versifiers is in stark contrast to that of the ballad-writers half a century later. In the early Elizabethan period the closest thing to a ballad hack was William Elderton, famed for his drinker's red nose. Yet this prolific writer was also a respectable professional: he was an attorney at the Sheriff's Court in London, in 1562. A decade later he was Master of the Boy Actors of Eton College, and then the Children of Westminster School, posts of some importance.[84] Elderton's counterpart in Charles's reign was Martin Parker, the most famous and popular ballad-writer of the 17th Century. Parker seems to have been an alehouse keeper, a steep drop from an attorney on the social scale.[85] By this time the association of ballad-writers with low-life and vice was complete. The typical pot-poet described by John Earle in 1628 is a mercenary hypocrite: 'sitting in a bawdy house he writes God's judgements'.[86]

Not only were the ballad hacks sliding further down the social scale; they were also becoming increasingly anonymous. Although the Elizabethan 'ballad' had sometimes been a traditional 'folksong' adapted from an unidentified source, it

was more often the wit or polemic of an individual author.[87] However, by the early
17th Century, authors were seldom named on the broadsides – with two sorts of
exception. The first was for the very rare ballad hacks whose names seem to have
carried with them a popular following, such as Martin Parker and Laurence Price.
The second kind of named author was the narrator and main character of the
ballad (sometimes a fabricated *persona*): criminals' last repentance ballads are the
most common examples of this suppositious narrator–author.

With these exceptions, the standard ballad of the early 17th Century went into
the world authorless. The original names attached to the popular 'stock' ballads
were simply dropped off the broadsides as the copyright changed hands.[88] What
had once been an author's medium – a vehicle for propaganda and personal
opinion, or for building a popular reputation as a story-teller was now largely a
publisher's medium, governed by time-tested commercial dictates. The ballad was
not so much an individual creation as a piece of public property, known to an
increasingly broad audience.[89] The skill of the anonymous ballad hack was largely
one of gathering songs and stories from oral sources, converting them into
suitable printed form, and sending them off across the countryside to a new and
wider public.

Of course the process of re-packaging 'traditional' culture was as old as the
publishing industry itself, and the ballad writers were part of this heritage. In 1568
the printer Robert Copland described how his customers pestered him with
requests for copies of their favourite stories, such as the jest of the 'seven sorrows'
of woman. Copland suggested he might print the tale if a copy were brought to
him, and was told:

I have no boke, but yet I can you shewe
The matter by herte, and that by wordes fewe
Take your penne and wryte as I do say
But yet of one thyng, hertely I you praye
Amend the englysh somewhat if ye can . . .[90]

Oral culture passed into print this way, and printed stories seeped into the oral
culture. Inns and alehouses were centres for the exchange of news, jokes and
merry tales: the Coventry mason Captain Cox was described as being able 'to talk
as much without book as ony Inholder betwixt Brainford and Bagshot'.[91] In 1626
John Taylor published his collection of *Wit and mirth: chargeably collected out of
taverns, ordinaries, innes, bowling-greenes and allyes, alehouses, tobacco-shops, highwayes, and
water-passages*.[92] Even if some of the anecdotes were chestnuts from old jest
books,[93] given Taylor's popularity the stories were likely to end up in the 'allyes'
and 'alehouses' once the printed collection appeared.

The 17th-Century ballad-writer Martin Parker was a product of this storytelling
culture. Apparently he made a living as an alehousekeeper, and would have been
well placed to pick up stories and songs, to try out his own on the clientele, and to

judge what would be popular in cheap printed form.[94] Not only was he a prolific ballad-writer, and also an early participant in the development of a new publishing format, the penny chapbook. Parker's chapbook titles were sold and distributed by the ballad publishers, and seem to have been aimed at his faithful ballad-buying public. The broadside industry found a new way of 'spreading the word' by sending these cheap and portable little books along the same distribution network as the ballads.

For his first of these little pamphlets, registered in 1630, Parker updated the Elizabethan morality tale, *Robin conscience*, in a sixteen-page octavo format. The original is a classic Protestant manifesto, in which the young Robin urges his idolatrous family to 'have a respect unto Christ's Testament'.[95] Martin Parker's version leaves out the Protestant message, and links morality to social responsibility, as the 'Conscience' figure visits tradesmen, gentlemen and yeoman and is turned away. In the end it is only 'mongst honest folks that have no lands. But get their living with their hands' that 'Conscience' is finally welcomed.[96] *The king and a poore northern man* (1633) also deals with topical social ills (in this case wicked lawyers), and seems to be appealing to readers at the bottom levels of rural society. It tells the story of a poore Northumberland man who, being cheated by a lawyer, went to the king himself to have things set right. The most striking thing about these early 'penny merriments' is the proliferation of woodcuts, in a period when most cheap pamphlets were illustrated only on their title-page. *The king and poore northerne man* contains seven pictures in only 24 pages octavo: a visual novelty which was no doubt an attraction to those with limited literacy skills.

The sale of these little books is described by Parker himself in *Harry White his humour*, a chapbook miscellany of puns and aphorisms written in 1637. Apparently they were hawked by pedlars in the same manner as ballads, and their price was twopence:

Harry White is glad at the heart to see the young men laughing, the maides smiling, some drawing their purses, others groping in their pockets, some pretty lasses feeling in their bosomes for odde parcells of mony wrapt in clouts: for these are evident presages of his good fortune: ah what dulcid musick it is to his eares, when he heares his audience cry, joyntly, give me one, give me two: change my mony says one, here is a single twopence says another.[97]

In Parker's preface (addressed to his character Harry) he even suggests the number of copies to be sold: 'thus wishing that thy humour may be satisfied with tenne thousand two peny customers, I commit thee to thy humour'.[98]

The figure of 10,000 may be an arbitrary artistic invention, rather than a factual statement about print runs. Nevertheless, the ballad publishers of the 1620s and 1630s had clearly hit upon a publishing formula with enormous potential. As we know from Margaret Spufford's work on the late 17th Century, by the Restoration chapbooks had become numerically more important than broadsides in the output of the so-called ballad publishers. In 1664 just one publisher, Charles Tias, had around 90,000 octavo and quarto chapbooks stored in his shop, house and warehouse. This is a substantial stock when one considers that the entire annual production of almanacs was 300,000 to 400,000 in this period, and that this number provided one almanac for every three families.[99]

The early chapbooks evolved directly out of the broadside trade, sharing the same black-letter type, the same crude woodcuts, the same writers and publishers. They were often in verse, and told of stories and heroes already familiar, such as the anonymous *Tom Thumb, his life and death* (1628), or Martin Parker's *A true tale of Robin Hood* (1632), both in 24-page octavo format. Indeed, the chapbook was sometimes merely a balled text printed over a number of pages. *The pleasant and sweet history of patient Grissell* was first registered as a broadside in 1565–6, and was still on sale in a ballad catalogue of 1754.[100] It told the story of Grissel, a poor girl married to a noble marquess, who tested her by taking away her babies and sending her back to her father's cottage for sixteen winters. As in all the versions of the story, which dates back to before Boccaccio's *Decameron*, Grissel bears all this 'most milde and patiently' and is eventually reunited with her 'gracious lord'.

Around 1640, the 'partner' John Wright took the ballad text, spread it out over 24 pages octavo, and adorned it with seven woodcuts, mostly generic pictures of gentlemen with plumed hats and ladies with fans. For the chapbook, a prose introduction and conclusion were added, persuading women to learn patience, humility and obedience from Grissel's example. The verse text was divided into little chapters and headings: 'How patient Grissell was sent for the wedding, and of her great humility and patience' (and so on). The editorial policy of chopping longer works into small units with headings was also followed by the publishers of the French *bibliothèque bleue*, apparently on the understanding that readers with only basic literacy skills 'would rely on short, easily deciphered self-contained segments, and would require explicit signposts'.[101] Patient Grissel demonstrates concretely the movement of the ballad from oral into print culture. The song which had been frozen into broadside form for commercial distribution had now moved a step further into book form, to be read rather than sung.

The spread of cheap printed wares came about through a chain of demand and supply, running from the provincial reader to the London press and back again. The newly-literate buyer in the marketplace wanted familiar heroes, lots of woodcuts, and a simple text to a popular tune. The alehouse poet acted as a cultural conduit, absorbing news, stories and songs, and regurgitating them in ballad metre. The ballad publishers – lesser stationers without lucrative copyrights to the bestselling primers and religious guides – were forced to carve out new markets for their broadsides and pamphlets. To this end they organised themselves into a partnership, sharing a warehouse and an improved distribution network.

The final link in the chain was the pedlar who carried the printed product back out to the buyer in the provinces. He is difficult for the historian to trace in this period, appearing in the records only when he is caught picking pockets at a fair, or arrested for vagrancy. Many of the pedlars were rootless, masterless men and women, driven to hawking ballads and chapbooks as a last resort. By the end of the 17th Century they were at least 2,500 strong, counting only those who were registered in the first year of the 1696–7 Licensing Act. One contemporary estimate put the real number at 10,000.[102] Oddly it was the large population of vagrants – that underclass so complained of by moralists – whose growling bellies were responsible for the spread of the printed word to the far corners of the land.

References

The place of publication is London unless otherwise stated.

1. For a fuller account of the broadside and chapbook trade in this period, see Tessa Watt, *Cheap print and popular piety 1550–1640* (Cambridge, forthcoming [1991]).
2. Bodleian MS Ashmole 48. Reprinted in Thomas Wright, ed., *Songs and ballads, with other short poems, chiefly of the reign of Philip and Mary* (1860), especially pp.157–60. Hyder E. Rollins, 'Concerning Bodleian MS Ashmole 48', *Modern Language Notes*, 34 (1919), pp.340–51.
3. Elizabeth's statute of 1572 applied the vagrancy laws to all 'common players in interludes and minstrels' who were not under aristocratic or royal patronage. The provisions of this statute were reiterated in a vagrancy Act of 1597. (A.L. Beier, *Masterless men: the vagrancy problem in England 1560–1640* (1985), p.96.)
4. Wright, *Songs and ballads*, pp.24, 54. On Chevy Chase, see R.S. Thomson, 'The development of the broadside ballad trade and its influence upon the transmission of English folksongs' (Cambridge PhD, 1974), ch.2; Claude M. Simpson, *The British broadside ballad and its music* (New Brunswick, New Jersey, 1966), p.99. The first entry of Chevy Chase to the 'ballad partners' in 1624 (Arber, IV, 131) almost certainly records a transfer of a ballad already in print.
5. Wright, *Songs and ballads*, p.179.
6. In 1554, a Norfolk minstrel whose apprentices were accused of singing a song against the mass was asked 'if they had eny bookes of songes', which indeed they did. (*Records of Early English Drama. Norwich 1540–1642*, p.34. Henceforth 'REED.') In 1611, a York wait said he was given a copy of a libellous song along with 'diverse other songs' by the waits of Louth in Lincolnshire. (REED York, p.535).
7. Wright, *Songs and ballads*, p.181.
8. William Brown, *Britannia's pastorals. The second booke* (1616), p.11.
9. For Autolycus, the most famous of literary ballad sellers, see William Shakespeare, *The winter's tale* [written 1610–11], especially IV, iii–iv.
10. Henry Chettle, *Kind-harts dreame. Conteining five apparitions, with their invectives against*

abuses raigning [1593?], sig.C2v.

11. Nicholas Bownde, *The doctrine of the sabbath* (1595), p.242.

12. *Ibid.* p.241.

13. For a list of epitaphs see Hyder E. Rollins, *An analytical index to the ballad-entries in the Stationers' Registers: 1557-1709* (1924), 2nd. edn. with intro by Leslie Shepard (Hatboro, 1967), pp.67-71. For an example of literary 'flyting' see the Churchyard-Camel controversy of 1552 which was probably indecipherable to those outside a small clique. There are thirteen of these broadsides surviving in the Society of Antiquaries (Broadsides 20-32).

14. Wright, *Songs and ballads*, p.160.

15. 'A warning to London by the fall of Antwerp' [1577?] in H.L. Collmann, ed., *Ballads and broadsides chiefly of the Elizabethan period . . . now in the library at Britwell Court* (1912) #69. (Henceforth 'Collmann'.) 'A proper new balade expressying the fames, Concerning a warning to al London dames' [1571], Collmann #71. 'The cooper of Norfolk [*c.* 1627], Pepys Ballads (Magdalene College, Cambridge), I, 400. 'A pleasant new northerne song' *c.* 1630], Pepys, I. 240.

16. REED Norwich pp.34-5. Margaret Spufford, *Contrasting communities. English villagers in the sixteenth and seventeenth centuries* (Cambridge, 1974), p.245. 'An answer to a papisticall byll, cast in the streetes of Northampton . . .' (Collmann, p.171).

17. A[braham] H[olland], 'A continued inquisition against paper-persecutors' in John Davies, *A scourge for paper-persecutors, or papers complaint, compil'd in ruthfull rimes, against the paper-spoylers of these times* (1624), sig.A2v of the section by Holland.

18. Margaret Spufford, 'First steps in literacy: the reading and writing experiences of the humblest seventeenth-century autobiographers', *Social History*, 4 (1979), pp. 407-435. See also Keith Thomas, 'The meaning of literacy in early modern England' in Gerd Baumann, ed., *The written word. Literacy in transition* (Oxford, 1986), p.103.

19. David Cressy, *Literacy and the social order. Reading and writing in Tudor and Stuart England* (Cambridge, 1980).

20. Spufford, 'First steps in literacy', p.129.

21. Cressy, *Literacy and the social order*, pp.168-71.

22. The term 'folksong' in this paper is used to describe any song which was sung for several generations, whether or not its survival was reinforced by printed versions. It is not intended to imply any theory of 'popular' or 'communal' origins.

23. Thomson, 'Development of the broadside ballad trade', especially map.

24. Hyder E. Rollins, 'The black-letter broadside ballad', *Publications of the Modern Language Association*, 34 (1919), p.260. He found 30 more names on unregistered extant copies before 1580.

25. Edward Arber, ed. *A transcript of the registers of the Company of Stationers of London 1554-1640* (5 vols. 1875-94), II, pp.807-12. Henceforth 'Arber'.

26. Arber, II, 452.

27. For a full catalogue see Tessa Watt, 'Cheap print and religion, *c.* 1550 to 1640',

(Cambridge PhD, 1988), pp.507–13.

28. *A short-title catalogue of books printed in England, Scotland & Ireland and of English books printed abroad 1475–1640*. 2nd edn. Begun by W.A. Jackson & F.S. Ferguson. Completed by Katherine F. Pantzer. 2 vols. (1976–86) 3631, 21593, 20402, 16674, 3633, 19880. (Henceforth 'STC').

29. *The voyage and travaile of M. Caesar Frederick, merchant of Venice, into the East India*, trans. Thomas Hickock, 1588.

30. e.g. STC 333, 11694, 13092.5.

31. Thomas Procter, *A gorgious gallery of gallant inventions* (1577); Nicholas Breton, *A floorish upon fancie* (1577) and Anthony Copley, *Wits fittes and fancies* (1595).

32. John Norden, *A sinful mans solace* (1585), 336 pages, 8°.

33. STC 23381. *A cristal glasse for christian women. Contayning an excellent discourse of the life and death of Katherine Stubbes.* 1591. Margaret Spufford, *Small books and pleasant histories. Popular fiction and its readership in seventeenth-century England* (1981), p.266.

34. William Cartwright, *The ordinary, a comedy* (written *c.*1635), III, v, in *The plays and poems of William Cartwright*, ed. G. Blakemore Evans (Madison, 1951), p.317. John Mico, *A pill to purge out popery*, was first published in 1623. (*Ibid.*, p.644).

35. Arthur M. Hind, *Engraving in England in the sixteenth and seventeenth centuries*, 3 vols. Vol.3 compiled by M. Corbett and M. Norton (Cambridge, 1952–64), III, 367 and pl.212. British Museum, Dept. of Prints and Drawings (Authorities for Artists, Vol.II, period V). The plate appears to date from the reign of Charles I. It was recut after the Restoration, and sold by I. Overton at the White Horse. The rat-catcher who occupied the large central panel in the pre-1640 plate was replaced with a man holding books, and a scroll labelled 'Buy a new Booke'. (The almanack seller still remained as one of the 36 smaller figures.) This alteration appears to reflect the burgeoning of the 'small book' trade after the Restoration, as described in Spufford, *Small Books.*

36. See Watt, 'Cheap print', pp.89–102 and fig.85. A detailed account of the events leading up to the formation of the partnership has already been given in Thomson, 'Development of the broadside ballad', Part I, chs.1–2.

37. The only exception was John Grismond.

38. Cyprian Blagden, 'Notes on the ballad market in the second half of the seventeenth century', *Papers of the Bibliographical Society of the University of Virginia*, 6 (1953–4), p.167. Gerald D. Johnson, 'John Trundle and the book-trade 1603–1626', *Studies in Bibliography*, 39 (1986), p.189.

39. Testimony of John Hamond in Chancery Interrogatories over the Symcocke patent. Cited in William A. Jackson, ed., *Records of the Court of the Stationers' Company 1602 to 1640* (1957), p.xxi.

40. Johnson, 'John Trundle', p.189.

41. John Trundle, who had kept shop at his famous sign of the 'Nobody' in Barbican, moved down the road to Smithfield in 1624.

42. Spufford, *Small books*, map #1 on p.114.

43. See Watt, 'Cheap print and religion', pp.105–7.
44. Wye Saltonstall, *Picturae loquentes. Or pictures drawne forth in characters. With a poeme of a maid*, sig.E10v.
45. Izaak Walton, *The complete angler; or, the contemplative man's recreation* (1653), facs. edn (1876), p.49.
46. Term used by Roger Chartier in a discussion of the *images volantes, placards,* and other ephemeral print which was circulated and posted up in French cities. (Roger Chartier, *The cultural uses of print in early modern France,* trans. Lydia C. Cochrane (Princeton, 1987), p.159.)
47. See Watt, 'Cheap print', Appendix H.
48. For example, STC 4768, 6553, 12630, 18786, 25840.
49. The word 'penny chapbook' throughout this paper should be understood as a description of a specific format, rather than of price.
50. For an account of the development of the chapbook trade see Watt, *Cheap print and popular piety,* chs.7–8.
51. There was never such a thing as a 'pure' oral tradition in medieval Europe: songs like those of the troubadours were available in manuscript copies, which fed back into the tradition. See for example Lee C. Ramsey, *Chivalric romances: popular literature in medieval England* (Bloomington, Indiana, 1983), pp.233–4.
52. Wright, *Songs and ballads,* p.160.
53. Wright, *Songs and ballads,* p.157.
54. *Ibid.,* p.158
55. *Ibid.,* p.160
56. Walter Lincoln Woodfill, *Musicians in English society from Elizabeth to Charles I* (Princeton, 1953), p.244.
57. REED Newcastle, pp.30–2. In these examples, I am choosing peak periods of the year, but not exceptional years.
58. REED Cumberland. Westmorland. Gloucestershire, pp.80–1.
59. Woodfill, *Musicians in English society,* p.261. REED Cumberland. Westmorland. Gloucestershire, pp.66, 90.
60. REED Coventry, p.434.
61. Spufford, *Contrasting communities,* p.248; *Small books,* p.229.
62. REED York, p.535. REED Norwich, pp.34–5.
63. This fell from 67% to 47% for the years 1623–1639. Beier, *Masterless men,* pp.51–5, Tables III & IV.
64. Chettle, *Kind harts-dreame* [1592?], sig.C3v.
65. REED Norwich, pp.126, 141, 200–1, 237.
66. 'Register of passports for vagrants 1598–1669' in Paul Slack, *Poverty in early-Stuart Salisbury,* Wiltshire Record Society, vol.31 (Devizes, 1975).
67. *Ibid.,* pp.49, 58.
68. Beier, *Masterless men,* p.98.
69. British Library, Harleian MS 6715, fol. 98v.

70. Slack, *Poverty in early-Stuart Salisbury*. From London and environs: Register #82, 152, 288, 476. From the south and west: #144, 156, 192, 293, 344, 366, 387, 551.

71. Beier, *Masterless men*, p.35. Excepting Cheshire and Somerset, Beier's statistics on vagrants' occupations do not stretch more than 100 miles from London. (Table XI is drawn from London, Wiltshire, Essex, Leicester, Norfolk, Somerset and Chester.)

72. For records covered see Watt, 'Cheap print and religion', pp.34–5 n.81. After a wide sampling of printed records, the negligible returns for the volume of material covered did not seem to justify visits to the various county record offices on speculation. I have therefore been forced to rely on the long-term and wide-ranging work on poverty and vagrancy by scholars such as Paul Slack and A.L. Beier.

73. Beier, *Masterless men*, Table XI. 7.7% of vagrants were listed as petty chapmen in *c.*1520–1600; 7.1% in *c.*1600–*c.*1620; 9.8% in *c.*1620–*c.*1640.

74. *Ibid.* 16.3% in *c.*1520–*c.*1600; 21.9% in *c.*1600–*c.*1620; 23.2% in *c.*1620–*c.*1640.

75. Woodfill, *Musicians in English society*, p.128.

76. Shakespeare, *The winter's tale*, especially IV, iii-iv. In *The great reclothing of rural England: petty chapmen and their wares in the seventeenth century* (1984), pp.88–9, Margaret Spufford examines the items in Autolycus's pack, which included linen, cambrics and lawns, haberdashery and small courtship gifts, as well as ballads.

77. See Watt, 'Cheap print and religion', pp.36–7.

78. John Taylor, *The carriers cosmographie; or a briefe relation of the innes in and neere London* (1637), sig. B2, B3, C, C3.

79. *Ibid.*, sig.C3, A2v.

80. Cited in Thomson, 'Development of the broadside ballad trade', p.178.

81. See Watt, 'Cheap print and religion', pp.71–2, 109.

82. DNB. 'A ballet declaring the fal of the whore of Babylone' (a 32-page pamphlet, described in DNB) and 'Of misrule's contending with God's worde by name' [1553?], Society of Antiquaries, Broadsides, #16.

83. John Cornet, 'An admonition to Doctor Story', Collmann #33. Brice's 'Courte of Venus moralized' was registered in 1566–7. *The Court of Venus* (*c.*1538), which contained five poems by Wyatt, had been through its third edition in *c.*1563. *Songs and sonnets* ('Tottel's miscellany', 1557), by Wyatt, Surrey and others, must have been the inspiration for Brice's 'Songs and Sonnettes' which appeared in 1567–8. Neither of Brice's collections survive.

84. Hyder E. Rollins, 'William Elderton: Elizabethan actor and ballad writer', *Studies in Philology*, 17 (1920), pp.205–6, 216.

85. Susan Aileen Newman, 'The broadside ballads of Martin Parker: a bibliographical and critical study', Birmingham PhD (1975), I, 2.

86. John Earle, 'Micro-cosmographie' (1628). Quoted in Natascha Wurzbach, *Die englishe straßenballade 1550–1650* (Munich, 1981), pp.403–4.

87. There are only twenty extant broadsides of 'traditional folksongs' prior to 1640, according to Thomson, 'Development of the broadside ballad trade' p.57. However, Thomson does not discuss the possibility that other ballads may have been

'folksong' in the 16th and 17th Centuries, even if they have not survived into the 20th Century.

88. Because the 16th-Century copies do not survive, we do not, in most cases, know the authors. An exception is Thomas Deloney who included ballads like 'The Duchess of Suffolk' in his own printed collections (*Strange histories, of kings, princes, dukes* (1602); *The garland of good will* (1631), repr. in *The works of Thomas Deloney*, ed. F.O. Mann (Oxford, 1912).)

89. The shift to timeless, authorless ballads was not total or permanent. During the Civil War and Interregnum the ballad was seized as a polemical weapon; outlawed in 1649, with flogging as punishment for sellers and singers. But in 1655–6, when Cromwell reimposed effective licensing, the ballad publishers re-registered their copyrights to the favourite 'stock' ballads.

90. Robert Copland, ed., *The seven sorowes that women have when theyr husbandes be deade* (1568), prologue.

91. Spufford, *Small books*, pp.65–7.

92. Printed for H. Gosson, sold by E. Wright. It ran through five further editions.

93. Such as *A, C, mery talys* (1526?).

94. Newman, 'The broadside ballads of Martin Parker', I, 2.

95. *The book in meeter of Robin conscience* [c.1565?]. Another edition printed by Edward Allde [1590?]. Reprinted in W. Carew Hazlitt, ed. *Remains of the early popular poetry of England* (4 vols. 1864–6), III, pp.225–47.

96. Martin Parker, *Robin conscience, or, conscionable Robin* (for F. Coules, 1635), p.15. Entered to M. Sparke 20 April 1630; assigned to F. Coules 13 June 1631.

97. Parker, *Harry White*, sig. B2v.

98. *Ibid.*, sig. A4.

99. Spufford, *Small books*, pp.100–101.

100. Arber, I, 296. William and Cluer Dicey, *A catalogue of maps, histories, prints, old ballads, copy-books, broad-sheets and other patters, drawing-books, garlands, &c.* 1754. STC 12384: 'A most pleasant ballad of patient Grissell' [c.1600].

101. Chartier, *Cultural uses of print*, p.249.

102. Spufford, *Small books*, pp.115–16.

A few shillings for small books:
the experiences of a flying stationer
in the 18th Century

MICHAEL HARRIS

ON THE AFTERNOON of Tuesday 12 June 1827 the rambling career of David Love reached its conclusion and he was laid to rest in the churchyard of St Mary's Nottingham. He was in his 77th year and to the end he pursued his avocation as hawker and ballad-writer with dogged good humour and determination. At the age of 75 he had taken the road to Hull to sell his halfpenny sheets, was arrested for vagrancy and sentenced to two weeks on the treadmill. His last work contained an account of this experience and he cried it through the streets of Nottingham in his familiar, broad Scotch accent.[1] This paper is primarily about David Love and about the way in which he fitted into a sector of the book trade which has a remarkably low visibility.

The itinerant trade in print is almost a blank for the whole of the 18th Century although the period is bracketed by some striking material. On the one hand, there is the marvellously rich view of the 'paper workers' of mid-19th Century London by Henry Mayhew.[2] Using his established combination of interviews and statistical analysis he presents a picture of the contemporary street trade which reaches to the lowest levels of commercial activity. On the other, there is the recent work on the ballad and chapbook trade of the late 17th and early 18th Century by Margaret Spufford.[3] Her starting point was the Pepys Collection of chapbooks at Cambridge but, unlike other modern investigators, she pursued the material into the difficult areas of production and distribution. Making use of wills, inventories and the records of the Court of Orphans in London she brought into view the flood of ballads and chapbooks which were being pumped out by the printer/publishers centred on London Bridge and Smithfield. Of course, as with any pioneering work of this sort, there are some rough edges. She does not, for example, follow through her selective comments on the 1730s. Twenty years later, just before the removal of the houses from London Bridge in 1761, there is evidence for the continuation of large-scale output from this location. The presence of at least one printer, William Edwards, whose office was made up of two houses run together, as well as several stationers, suggests that the street-literature business on the Bridge continued to flourish.[4] Equally, Spufford has nothing to say about the obscure network of individuals printing ballads and chapbooks, often of a highly

83

contentious sort, from obscure corners of the town. Francis Clifton and his cronies, who were forcibly dragged into public view during the second and third decades of the 18th Century, represent a further layer of output perhaps mainly intended for local consumption. When, in 1720, Clifton had his type kicked in by the authorities he also lost about 2,000 printed ballads ready for distribution.[5]

Spufford's account of the distribution network of hawkers and pedlars, which extended into her book on the *Great Reclothing of Rural England*,[6] is again pioneering work. She was the first to demonstrate the value of the licensing records generated by the Act of 1697 and to show how wills and inventories can be used at this modest level. Even so, as she freely admits, such material can only reach a little way through the system. Over 2,500 people took out licences but the legislation excluded and continued to exclude large categories of itinerant traders. Anyone selling a range of printed material, Acts of Parliament and licensed almanacks amongst other variably promising items, as well as those selling wares of their own making, were exempt. David Love never held a licence during his long career and was not acted against on that account.[7] In the same way wills and inventories are inevitably a by-product of success, and swathes of the poorer hawkers and pedlars fail to appear in such a respectable setting. Ellen Vickers and her illiterate daughter, Sarah Ogilby, and the one-legged man and his companion who sang ballads at the corner of the Old Bailey are among the twenty or so London hawkers who dealt with Clifton and his associates.[8] Such people can only be located in that dismal repository compiled by political hatchet men, the State Papers Domestic.

Although, as Mayhew discovered, it is particularly hard to categorise the activities of the men and women working as itinerant traders in print, as a further preliminary it seems worth attempting to establish two broad distinctions. First, the division between the street sellers using London or some other urban centre as a regular base and those long-distance travellers also working the towns but constantly on the road. Clearly there was considerable overlap as personal circumstances or economic fluctuations propelled people from one line of activity to another. At the same time, the town-based traders often moved around surburban circuits, covering as much as 60 miles in a day. However, even if the distinction blurs in the context of an individual's working life it can be used to establish an underlying difference. The 'straw hat' women[9] and the semi-destitute hawkers working the London streets in the early decades of the 18th Century were, like the majority of the subjects of Mayhew's investigation, locked into the economy of the capital. David Love, on the other hand, though he spent several years in London and finally settled in Nottingham, was irretrievably peripatetic and must be classified as a long-distance traveller.

The second broad distinction is between the hawkers working in a more or less tied relation to printers and the highly miscellaneous freelancers. This variable working relationship provided the frame for Patricia Hollis's useful classification

Fig. 1   'David Love, The Nottingham Poet, 1824', attributed to George Scharf
and reproduced in Alfred Docker, 'Old English Characters', *The Connoisseur* 83
(January–June 1929), p. 156. Copy from the Local Studies Library, Nottingham.

of the hawkers of the unstamped London newspapers of the 1820s and 1830s and it is within the setting of newspaper production that the links between printer and hawker were at their closest.[10] Hollis's 'core venders' were sometimes 'regularly employed as street shopmen' and there are clear indications of this sort of relationship throughout the 18th Century. During Queen Anne's reign the *British Apollo* was delivered across the London area by men and boys regularly employed to cover fixed walks and with responsibility for collecting subscriptions and contributions. How far and on what terms hawkers continued to be employed by the printers of London newspapers is far from clear. Subsequent evidence for this sort of arrangement is confined entirely to the local press. During the 1720s the *Northampton Mercury* and the *Gloucester Journal* provided readers with information on the routes followed by their chapmen and the *Journal* named each of the thirteen men employed in its distribution.[12] Almost 60 years later the accounts of the *Hampshire Chronicle* included payments for training and equipping the newsmen[13] and it seems likely that the printers of most successful local weeklies had a number of hawkers on the strength. The relationship was not always secure, as the notices offering rewards for the arrest of absconding newsmen makes plain:

John Chambers, a Tall, Thin, Black Man about 6 foot high or better, who used to Travel with the Northampton Mercury to Leicester and Thomas Moss, a short well sett Fellow, very much Freckled in the Face, and who Limps with his Right Leg, who also travell'd the Road with the aforesaid Mercury from Northampton to Whitney, are run away from their Master's Service with a considerable Quantity of Goods.[14]

Three years earlier in 1718 Henry Crossgrove had reason to insert in his paper the *Norwich Gazette*:

Note, That the Fellow with the Crutches, sells my News no longer, I have turn'd him out for several Abuses; therefore pray take Care of being deceived.[15]

In the ebb and flow of casual work at the lowest economic level the distinctions between the regular employee and the self-employed freelance can never be clearcut. Even so, the distinction can work, as the experiences of David Love will show.

The obscurity of the hawkers of print and the confused and ambivalent character of their position gives the personal record of David Love, hawker or flying stationer, a considerable value. His autobiography, which has never been used in this or any other context, appeared in two versions – first, in what seems to have been intended as a series of eight-page chapbooks in verse.[16] The copy in the British Library which contains the account of the earliest part of his life was printed by John Marshall in Newcastle, probably at the beginning of the 19th Century. Although stated on the title to be 'Part 1' and ending with the words 'To be continued' I have not been able to trace any more of it. Secondly, Love published a completely overhauled version, mainly in prose but with large chunks of narrative verse inserted, which was published in Nottingham in 1823 by the radical printers Sutton and Son.[17] Getting it into print was a complicated process. Love issued the first eight-page number as a specimen of the paper and type, publication 'to go on regular, when he has got a sufficient number of Subscribers to defray the Printing charges'. In the event it appeared fortnightly in 22 numbers at one penny each and ran through at least five made-up editions.[18] The writing is vigorous. A patronising obituary in the *Nottingham Journal* pointed out that his verses did not possess 'the ease of Pope, the correctness of Johnson, or the grandeur of Milton; they were frequently prosaic and sometimes (like himself) hobbling in their gait'.[19] Of course, such comments entirely miss the point. Street literature, as Mayhew well knew, had to be mediated in a peculiarly direct way between writer, singer or speaker and purchaser, and Love and his colleagues had no interest in attempting a high-gloss product.[20] Some self-censorship occurred between the two publications. Love is less inclined to dwell on his youthful indiscretions by the 1820s, partly perhaps as a concession to changing times and taste. In the early chapbook version there was a good deal of romping in Scottish barns with the female servants.

Then oer each other we did tumble,
Tho' we were hurt we did not grumble,
For rakes, & boards, we made them rumble,
                And laugh'd aloud
Then one another we did jumble
                All in a crowd.[21]

The tone of the later publication was more discreet. Neither version contains overt political comment and there is much less of the religious frenzy that characterises the nearest equivalent work, *Some Account of the Travels of John Magee Pedlar and Flying Stationer in North and South Britain in the years 1806 and 1808*. Magee, an Irishman with a radical past, published his material in Paisley in 1826.[22] It consists largely of spiritual exhortation and the wildness of his material at least serves to emphasise the restraint and clarity of David Love's text. I do not intend to retell here the story which Love writes in his own highly entertaining words. If his chronology is not always secure the sequence of experiences is clear enough. What I want to suggest is the way in which the *Life* reflects some of the characteristics of the itinerant trade in print and also locates its author within a general system of bookselling.

David Love shared the low – even the negative – status of the great majority of the hawkers of ballads and chapbooks. Although an interest in the trade could be passed on through families,[23] most seem to have come to it as a last resort, either in response to personal disaster or as a bottoming-out in a process of downward mobility. Patricia Hollis's list of the hawkers of unstamped newspapers included a bewildering range of depressed tradesmen.[24] The point has been usefully made

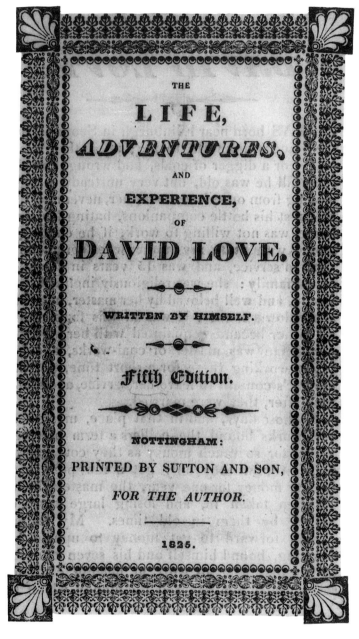

THE

LIFE,

ADVENTURES,

AND

EXPERIENCE,

OF

DAVID LOVE.

WRITTEN BY HIMSELF.

Fifth Edition.

NOTTINGHAM:

PRINTED BY SUTTON AND SON,

FOR THE AUTHOR.

1825.

Fig. 2   Title-page of fifth edition of Love's autobiography, 1825.

that the street selling of cheap commodities, of which print was one of the cheapest, represented the purest form of capitalist welfare.[25] People on the brink of toppling over the boundary of subsistence could turn to hawking and the link between this form of activity and begging was very close indeed. Among the chapbooks in the British Library are a few low-key items deliberately produced as an appeal to charity rather than as a commercial proposition. A disabled soldier, a bookbinder subject to fits and a blind china mender were among those whose survival depended on hawking religious material specially repackaged in chapbook form.[26] In fact, begging was regularly integrated with the highly erratic street economy. Thomas Holcroft as a child in the 1750s was sent to beg from house to house while his parents sold the miscellaneous objects of their street trade[27] and in the case of David Love, begging and hawking formed part of a single line of acitivity. Initially, desperate circumstances, desertion of the family by his shiftless father and his mother's blindness, forced him into selling small books. Later when his arm was crushed in a mining accident he was thrown back, still as a young man, on to the final resource of cheap print. The publication statements on some of his own work drew attention to his lameness[28] and throughout his life local circumstances, robbery, illness or bad harvests, obliged him to return to begging. This sometimes involved the sale of a printed petition[29] but was as often a simple appeal for charity. In Bristol, the Isle of Wight and London, Love was obliged to beg the money he needed for another round of publishing or stock purchase. This sort of primary money-raising launched or sustained many freelance hawkers without access to credit or other resources. The mechanism began to operate at a very low level. In 1725 George Parker, petitioning against the application of the Stamp Tax to cheap London newspapers pointed out that

Poor and miserable *Blind Hawkers*, whose deplorable Circumstances greatly deserve Compassion will, by supressing these Half-penny News Papers, . . . be absolutely deprived of getting their Bread; for divers of them, who are Industrious, and have but a Penny or Three-Half-Pence, for a Stock to begin with in the Morning, will before Night advance it to *Eighteen Pence* or *Two Shillings*, which greatly tends to the comfortable support of such miserable Poor and Blind Creatures who sell them about the Streets.[30]

Ironically, when David Love again met up with his father in the 1780s, he found that a mining injury and advanced age (he was then nearly 90) had forced him to take up selling godly books which were brought from him out of charity.[31]

The abject status of most hawkers, their method of work and the overlap with begging all contributed to the lasting notion that the itinerant traders were part of a criminal sub-culture. Many definitions of the term hawker in the legal reference books of the 18th Century rehearse the old conjunction of street selling with sharp practice and link the practitioners with the idle poor.[32] This view, reinforced by reports and comments in the local press and elsewhere,[33] had practical effects. Love was often harassed by magistrates for breach of the peace or vagrancy, and, like John Magee, was taken up in the sweeps of common lodging houses that followed outbreaks of local crime.[34] On one of his circuits Love was arrested consecutively in Newcastle, Durham and Hull. He was not seriously disturbed. Of his experience at Hull he wrote, 'as I was singing the Child's Dream, a religious song, the mayor passing by, in less than a quarter of an hour a constable put me in the house of correction'. He was soon released and was back on the streets singing his ballads 'but not so loud'. [35]

As Margaret Spufford clearly indicated, not all the socio-economic movement of hawkers and pedlars was in a downward direction. The trade was potentially profitable, if not respectable, and individuals could accumulate a substantial property. This was often manifested in a shift to shopkeeping, although, as David Love's experience indicated, such a move was not necessarilly the result of a life-time's struggle. His first wife was a farmer's daughter who had some difficulty in coming to terms with his low status.[36] Love acknowledged that she could have aspired to marry a shoemaker and he needed all his skill as a patterer to win her over. It was possibly as a result of her social aspirations that in his twenties he turned shopkeeper and opened a general store near Falkirk. His capital at the time amounted to £1.18s. and his shop was stocked entirely on credit from a grocer, a baker, a draper and a hatter in the nearby town.[37] The effort to sustain his new position was a desperate one. He was obliged to revert to hawking small books and ballads to finance his business, although he did so 'a long distance from our home, being ashamed that any should know I was again turned a flying stationer'.[38] His wife, who was described in hostile terms as given to 'abusive talk', constantly harangued him about the shame and disgrace of returning to ballad singing and he agreed instead to hawk the unsold shop goods. The results were dire. On one occasion, while carrying a large quantity of bargain-rate looking-glasses under his arm and in his pack, he fell over a style and smashed the lot. He managed to sell some of the fragments but it was symptomatic of the difficulties that accompanied this attempt at upward mobility. Before long the business broke and although he ended up poorer than he started, Love was probably relieved to be back on the road where 'a few shillings would set me up with small books and I was sure of selling them'.[39]

Love's attempt at general retailing did not in itself represent a change of direction. Just as the local booksellers and printers dealt in an extended range of consumer durables, so the pedlars and hawkers with whom they worked carried a wide range of low-cost commodities. Print was David Love's primary commercial interest but he also handled the conventional 'nick nacketories'[40] which could give him access to a wider market. After a spell in the Nottingham workhouse, for example, he toured the area selling cotton balls, needles, thimbles, 'the best and stoutest laces' and buttons.[41] This sort of combination had characterised the content of the pedlar's tray since the 16th Century. At the same time, David Love moved through a series of professions which provided a counterpoint to his life as a flying stationer and emphasised the erratic character of experience at this level of the trade. Following his disastrous spell as a collier and in spite of having had less than a year of formal education, he became a village schoolmaster. He managed to accumulate forty pupils but as he 'got no more than a penny each week for readers and three half pence for writers'[42] he was unable to live on the income and after five months was back on the road. During the American War Love joined the Duke of Buccleugh's South Fencibles, a regiment which contained more than its fair share of physically disabled soldiers and was guaranteed not to leave Scotland.[43] This turned out to be a short-term success ('These were the golden days of David Love') but a medium-term failure. He was arrested for writing a personal lampoon on a sergeant's wife and held pending court-martial. In his usual pragmatic way Love spent his time in the military prison learning to play the violin. On his wrongful acquittal he returned to print, cashing in on the poems he had written during his three years in the service.[44]

Love's association with print could itself carry him in unexpected directions. Many of the itinerant traders offered their customers a selection of medicines some of which were home-made. Among the disapproving newspaper reports of the 1730s was an account of a widow from Trowbridge in Wiltshire who travelled in abortifaisant pills containing gunpowder who blew herself up during their preparation.[45] More conventionally the newsmen and hawkers employed by printers such as Robert Walker and the Diceys offered an assortment of cure-alls alongside the products of the press.[46] In this way Daffy's Elixir and Dr Bateman's Pectoral Drops became household names across the nation during the 18th Century. David Love does not appear to have peddled medicines. However, his access to medical information in printed form gave him the opportunity to set up briefly as a practitioner, combining social benefit with commercial advantage. His casual practice was based on 'a famous book of foreign recipes' (unidentified) and 'the London and Edinburgh Dispensatory'.[47] Although he claimed he had never intended to turn quack doctor, he was always ready to treat 'any poor creature for a small trifle'.[48] This line of alternative medicine ended when he lent his three books to a Bristol shopkeeper who sold up and disappeared.

The variety of Love's work experience can be seen in some ways as a side-effect of his irresistible impulse to ramble. Itinerant trading was often the by-product of low circumstances and personal desperation but, as Mayhew disapprovingly indicated, it could also result from an unwillingness or inability to settle.[49] This seems partly to have been Love's case. He was always ready to get moving and his erratic circuits criss-cross each other through his autobiography. John Magee also covered long distances. A substantial section of his *Travels* is supposed to be about his journey from Paisley in Scotland to Woolwich in Kent.[50] On the way back he travelled from London to Newcastle by ship, a form of transport which also figures in Love's writings. Magee is inclined to dwell on the difficulties he experienced – uncontrolled dogs, hostile clergymen and dreadful weather among other things. Love was both more buoyant and more mobile. Much of his career in England was spent travelling the roads of the Midlands and the North. He coincidentally buried two of his three wives at Rugby[51] and frequently turned up at Nottingham, York, Newcastle, Hull and other towns across the region. He returned to Scotland more than once, experiencing some hair-raising (and brilliantly described) storms at sea.[52] Love's narrative is itself a rambling affair and does not always allow for a precise reconstruction of his routes. However, he can be located in urban centres across the south of England. He spent variable periods in Bristol, Salisbury, Newbury in Berkshire and Gosport in Hampshire. All the time from the 1780s he circled around London feeling the irresistible pull of the metropolis with its real and imagined commercial opportunities. He made three visits, the last some time around 1810 when he travelled from Nottingham to Paddington by canal.[53] By one of those strange interconnections which suggest continuity at the lowest level of the trade, Love on this occasion rented an unfurnished room up two pairs of stairs at number 42 Fleet Lane. This was a convenient location for getting around the City and suburbs as well as being close to the Fleet Market. He was probably unaware that it was in Fleet Lane that Thomas Gent, Francis Clifton and Robert Walker had all established their low-key printing offices during the early decades of the previous century.[54] Still under the shadow of the debtors' prison, the area did not prove fortunate for Love and after being forced back on to private charity he returned with his family to Nottingham for a spell in the workhouse.

Competition on the London streets could be ferocious, particularly in winter. However, for most of his career Love was working an active market. The huge volume of street literature revealed by Margaret Spufford is itself an indicator of the depth and extent of popular demand. A single London Bridge wholesaler, Charles Tias, at his death in 1664 had a stock of about 90,000 printed chapbooks, enough for one in every fifteen families in the country. He also held more than 37,000 ballad sheets and when this is extended by the output of his fellow publishers, and when the annual torrent of almanacks is added, enough for one in every three families by the mid-17th century, it is possible to suggest the existence of a flood of print seeping into the most obscure rural areas.[55] There is no reason to suppose that demand flagged though it was diversified and partially rerouted through the local trade and David Love's personal experiences seem to suggest a brisk response to his material. As he worked the fairs and markets and knocked on innumerable doors he often underestimated demand. Writing of an early excursion to the three-day Whitsunbank Fair in Scotland to sell his ballads, he described how there were 'a dozen hands holding out for them at once'.[56] He sold out on the first day and wished he had brought 2,000 more songs. Whether or not this was a realistic assessment he claimed to have experienced a similar sell-out on the Isle of Wight and twice referred to print runs of 3,000 copies of his own work.[57]

The identification of focal points of demand was part of the long-distance traveller's business and both Magee and Love homed in on garrison towns. Magee ended
his walk from Scotland at Woolwich while David Love spent some time at Gosport, described in 1791 as 'a large town and of great trade especially in time of
war'.[58] Gosport had two substantial dockyards and was a short ferry ride from
Portsmouth. Here 'the sailors gave sixpence or a shilling as freely for a book, as a
half penny is given elsewhere when times are hard'. Love described how they
eagerly purchased 'printed silk ribbands and paper slips in great numbers, with
various mottoes, which I sold speedily, getting what I asked for them'.[59] Of
course, demand was not always predictable, as the pessimistic Magee pointed out:

As I carry with me in my travels a few pious books and sermons for sale, when I enter any
house, and shew these articles, the common salutation I get is, We want no good books;
for we have more good books than we have time to read. Others cry, We cannot read, we
would rather have something to eat and to drink; Others would run and shut the door,
when they saw me coming. Some would call for ballads, play books, or political pamphlets; so very different is the taste of men. Their conduct justifies the common proverb,
>   Many men, many minds,
>   Many women many kinds.[60]

Such difficulties were aggravated by a general downturn in the economy of the
poor. Both Magee and Love found that by the 1820s problems of unemployment
and declining living standards had put a brake on the capacity of working people to
lay out small sums on print.[61] Unfortunately, neither provide much detail about
their customers. All through the 18th Century women figure as prominently as
men as purchasers of cheap print. In the 1720s the Jacobite ballads were snapped
up, as a London newspaper put it, by 'abundance of scoundrels of both sexes'[62] and
Love certainly targeted young women at fairs as well as on the doorstep. It is hard
to get much further than this in relation to the sub-groups within the working
population who kept the two men on the move.

In catering for this high, though not always stable, demand, Love sold both his
own work which he had printed locally and a cross-section of the materials which
were sold by booksellers and printers located along his routes.

I have composed many rhymes,
On various subjects and the times,
And call'd the trials of pris'ner's crimes,
>   The cash to bring
When old I grew, composed hymns
>   And them did sing.[65]

From a preliminary search it appears that almost all Love's occasional material, at
least in its original state, has disappeared. However, it is clear from the *Life* that his
main line of output was the ballad constructed from recycled personal experience.

This approach was sometimes refined to accommodate more generalised themes. In London he offered his customers an elegy on a cat, a piece on St Bartholomew's Fair and another on the cries of London.[64] Even so, much of Love's verse, like that of Mayhew's running patterers, had the buzz of current interest about it. A good example of the process by which local events were transmuted through print by way of his composition, appeared in his account of a stop-over in Berwick-on-Tweed. Here Love witnessed an attempt by some constables to arrest a coachman on the suit of a widow made pregnant and jilted. The arrest drew a 'great crowd', a promising portent, and Love, after collecting the details of the case, set to work:

I went in haste to my lodging, and soon composed a song, which I entitled, 'The Wanton Widow of West-Gate, or the Coachman clapped in Limbo'. I got it printed, and had them bawling in the streets the same evening; there was none to oppose me, and I sold them very quick.[65]

So quick, in fact, that he had to be supplied by a boy who 'brought them to me, by three or four quires as I sold them'. The appeal of current information, particularly if based on sex or violence or both, was great in itself but the method of marketing could be crucial. As one of Mayhew's informants stated, 'a good stout pair of lungs and plenty of impudence' was enough to carry a running patterer through the market.[66] Love certainly satisfied both criteria but his particular skill in drumming up business appeared in his account of the disposal of a single sheet as Gosport:

The printer had a good many papers, concerning an essay to assassinate the King. I bought twenty quires of them, but being stale, I could not sell them. Then I ran through the streets, as if half a score had been calling papers behind me, crying, it is all found out and the rogues will be hung no doubt. This was my call wherever I went; but some people said we have found out you; this we knew some weeks ago; others asked me what is found out? I said, buy it, and you will see. Then I went off to another place, and so on till I sold them all.[67]

The ballads composed by David Love, like his small books, were continuously recycled and reprinted, and sorting out the bibliographical structure from the surviving materials is almost impossibly complicated. Perhaps his most successful verse publication in book form was his collection of *Original Poems* apparently published at several locations.[68] At Gosport Love claimed to have sold 1,000 copies of the 24-page book at four pence on common and sixpence on fine paper.[69] It was said to be mainly composed of Love's early verse. Nothing was ever wasted. The final version of his autobiography was itself a compendium of his life's work. As well as a full text of his separately published *Journey to London*, it contained his religious poems[70] and, most strikingly, a long collection of pious acrostics on the names of some of his customers. The writing of short verses to order formed a profitable line of work for Love and was advertised in his imprints and title pages.[71]

Although he also dealt in other people's material Love seems to have had little or no interest in the stereotype items which had been in circulation for a century or more and which formed the principal stock-in-trade of the Diceys and the major local dealers. He is sparing with detail but he cetainly handled trials and dying speeches as well as quantities of small religious books with which, particularly after his conversion in 1796, he was temperamentally in tune. Wherever he went he checked out the local printer's and bookseller's stock for likely items, mainly on current events. In Dumfries, where 'a bookseller took me to his shop to let me see all his assortment of songs and small books', Love bought a few quires of a paper entitled 'A full and true account of the absurdities of Mrs Buchan, who had invented a new religion' and sold them very successfully.[72]

Having identified some of the elements in David Love's autobiography which link him to a general system of itinerant trading in print, I want in the rest of this paper to suggest how he fitted into the structure of the shop-based book trade. One of the primary characteristics of the trade at large was the intricacy of its organisation. Through the multiple processes of production and distribution a very large number of individuals meshed together, working at tasks which at times overlapped and merged and at other times became separate specialisations. The interdependence of the various sectors of the trade was nowhere clearer than in the relationship between the printers of popular literature and the miscellaneous community of freelance hawkers. Each relied on the other, and the printers, as well as engaging in the conventional strategies of loan and debt, did all they could to support the activities of their primary distributors. The Old Bailey publishers of Jacobite ballads explained the meaning of such enigmatic items as *No Fence for Rogues, turn in, turn out, turn up, turn down, turn which way you will, you cant save your Bacon*, suggested how they could be called and, unreliably, indicated which were safe.[73] During the 1740s the printers of unstamped newspapers were said to have established a bank to bail out the hawkers with 'true Hearts and sound Bottoms' who carried their material.[74] In this case the extent of the street trade on which the mutual engagement was based was striking. When Anne Mahoney, alias Irish Nan, was arrested on the outskirts of London in 1743 she was carrying over 400 unstamped papers.[75] The dependence of the local printers on such flying stationers as David Love was suggested at the time of his arrest at Hull. 'My wife', he wrote, 'informed the printer, who printed my song, that I was in confinement by the mayors's order; he instantly went to the mayor, and said, if you stop my paper-sellers, I shall be obliged to shut up my printing office'.[76] He was released almost at once. Love's apparently haphazard movement across large tracts of England and Scotland was prescribed by the presence or absence of book-trade representatives in the towns he visited. He was propelled along his circuits by his ability to raise money through the services of the local trade. The way in which this worked in practice was graphically described in the

Life during his account of a journey back from Scotland in about 1814:

> We rested three times on our return, first at Berwick-upon-Tweed, where I reprinted one of my books, and called the town; I got as many books before-hand, as carried me to Newcastle-upon-Tyne; there again I reprinted. called the town, and got books to bring us to Leeds in Yorkshire. I did the same at Leeds, which enabled us, by the Lord's blessing, to come to Nottingham.[77]

Love as a freelancer worked within an established framework, negotiating terms with the printers and booksellers along his routes. All the way through the 18th Century the use of such imprint statements as 'printed for the company of running stationers' itself suggests a sense of corporate interest.

Love's relationship to the static members of the trade varied widely in intensity. In most cases he simply passed through the area, composing and printing, buying and selling, on his way to the next urban centre. However, he occasionally established a higher degree of commitment to a local printer/bookseller and his *Life* is particularly useful in indicating how this was organised. As a Scot, Love was representative of a large number of itinerants who moved south across the border under various kinds of economic pressure. On one occasion in Scotland he found himself sharing a barn with 39 other travellers, 'some blind, others lame, some packmen, others ballad singers, fiddlers, pedlars, gypsies of every description'.[78] Competition alone must have driven many such individuals southward where they formed part of a highly mobile work force. Margaret Spufford identified a substantial community of Scotch chapmen at Tetbury in Gloucestershire in the 1690s[79] and, with the Irish, they formed a large and usually unpopular group among the itinerant traders. They also formed part of the pool of labour which sustained the local book trade. When the printer Thomas Gent, himself with Irish connections, listed the six journeymen he employed at York in the 1720s he revealed the extent of his reliance on migrant labour.[80] Four came from Scotland, including a former 'stroller' and 'a sort of interloper', and one from Ireland. He had a generally low opinion of their character, describing one of the Scots as a false loon and the Irishman as 'little better, when mellow than a lunatic, and quite drunk a perfect madman'. Collectively he referred to them as 'ungrateful vermin'. Nonetheless, as they passed through his printing office, they kept his business ticking over and the Scots and Irish were probably more important in supporting the local trade than is usually acknowledged. It seems that David Love's experiences conformed to a familiar pattern of casual employment and may have been shaped by an established Scotch connection.

His periods of semi-formal engagement as workman and hawker were never more than temporary. It may be that Love had a number of spells within the print trade and that he engaged himself to the Mr Evans who printed his poems during his second visit to London.[81] The *Life* only contains two such episodes, the first and most durable with a printer/bookseller in Gosport. This was probably John

Stead who by the early 1780s was acting as agent for the *Hampshire Chronicle* although he was not listed in Pendred's directory of the local trade.[82] Love refers to his employer as William Steed, but this may be a combined Scotification and memory lapse. In any case a good idea of the retailing side of his business is provided by the shop advertisement written by David Love and included, with a similar item for a Leicester grocer, in the *Life*. He sold a comprehensive selection of books including Bibles, large histories, novels, school books and music primers together with stationery, playing cards, coffin furniture, pomatum and Scotch snuff. The list is a long one:

Best Blacking Balls for Boots and Shoes,
Receipts, how you the same may use;
Harvey's Gunpowder I have got
Single and double; Patent Shot;
And Paper Hangings, Fancy Borders
You'll have according to your orders;
Great choice of Prints of every kind,
In my Book Shop for you I'll find;
New Almanacks both stitch'd and sheet,
Of every sort you'll have complete.
Ladies and Gentlemen, and such as choose,
May send their Advertisements for the News;
Your Orders shall be done with speed most fervent,
By WILLIAM STEED, who is your humble servant.[83]

Love settled in a furnished room in Gosport and began to work for Stead in a way which offered a combination of security and independence:

Mr. Steed, a book printer, employed me in his printing office, to assist his servants at the press, and folding books, pasting up bills, and carrying parcels to Portsmouth or wherever he pleased to send me.[84]

The flexible nature of their terms was such that when it rained Love worked in the printing office but when it cleared up he went out on the road selling his own and Stead's materials. Love seems to have become a useful adjunct to the business. Sometimes Stead gave him books to sell locally or across the water in the Isle of Wight. Sometimes Love speculated on his own account:

All the bound books, both old and new, in Stead's shop that were not saleable, and odd volumes incomplete, I bought very cheap; I got a large stall full and sold them pretty well.[85]

This was the sort of activity that some local booksellers, including Nevill Simmons of Sheffield and Michael Johnson of Lichfield, undertook on their own account.[86] Clearly each benefited from the other and Love claimed that Stead offered to set him up in a large furnished house in Gosport to sell books for him on a permanent basis. The pull of London proved too great for Love but after a short and disastrous excursion to the capital he returned to Gosport. Stead at once offered to re-employ him on commission, offering to put him in the way of earning £1 in a single day.

> There is a great Fair at Newport in the Isle of Wight which is kept but once a year; you will get there in time, and there will be none to oppose you for no bookseller will cross the water. I will credit you with as many books as will draw five pounds; what you do not sell you can bring back, and they can be sold afterwards. I was astonished at his civility, being a few shillings in his debt.[87]

Subsequently, Love's wife was drawn into the arrangements. It was agreed that while he worked in the printing office, she would take four-pounds worth of books, half of which had been paid for by Love, on a six-day circuit through the Island. As was so often the case things ended badly. His wife got fuddled with drink, was robbed of her takings ('gold, silver, and copper all in one bag') and had to be rescued.

In all, Love seems to have worked in Gosport for about a year.[88] Whether he was one of a series of casual employees hired by Stead is not clear from the *Life*. Nonetheless, his experiences reflect the ebb and flow of labour through the trade and on at least one other occasion he was drawn into printing-office work. Luke Pennington, a printer, possibly with Scotch connections, had taken over Thomas Gent's office in Minster Coffee-Yard, York and in 1789 had embarked on the production of Matthew Henry's *Bible* in weekly parts.[89] This ambitious and labour-intensive project, which was underway when Love arrived in the area, involved the regular employment of six journeymen and a good deal of confusion.

> One day [Love wrote] a great misfortune happened, one of the journeymen lifting a large form to set on a press for correcting, instead of carrying it perpendicular, carried it slope ways, which all fell into *pie*. None but printers and type-setters know the time, pain and difficulty, to distribute all these letters into different boxes.[90]

Being experienced in working in print Love took a furnished room in Pennington's house and was hired 'to gather up types, clean out the office' and carry parcels.

Although he is sparing with personal details in the *Life*, on this occasion he provides a clear indication of how local circumstances could initiate a new phase of rambling. The problem arose from the fact that Pennington, 'a stout good looking man' of about thirty, had married his former employer, a widow by that time over fifty. Mrs Pennington seems to have regretted the move. She often invited the Loves into her parlour and moaned about her second husband. 'But now, said she, I have married a rogue, and made him a gentleman; he has no love

Fig. 3   David Love in old age. Anonymous portrait. Copy from the Local
Studies Library, Nottingham.

or regard for me, for his drinking and gambling will be our ruin, he is often out all night long with his whores'. As Love remarked, 'Wither (sic) all this was true I cannot tell; but this I know to my sorrow, she was full of jealousy'. In the event Love's second wife Mary, herself about fifty, and Mrs Pennington for whom she worked fell out when both were 'mellow with liquor, as was too often the case'. Mrs Pennington in a fit of sexual jealousy, 'went up stairs, took a hammer and nails, and blocked up a door that opened out of the paper warehouse, into my room, thinking (no doubt) that her husband made too free with my wife.'[91] There followed a confused episode involving anonymous letters and at the end of three months the Loves abruptly decamped. Apart from the human interest of the incident, it does bring into view some of the character of life in the confined spaces of a local printing office.

One of the reasons for indulging in this anecdote is to suggest the hazy outline of a business which is usually presented in clear and self-contained terms. Imprints and account books, though of immense value, have failed to get at David Love and his transient equivalents who were as much a part of the trade as the carefully labelled printers and booksellers. As a trained printer and member of the Stationers' Company, Thomas Gent would have rejected any comparison with Love, the unskilled son of an itinerant collier and domestic servant. However, their experiences do coincide in ways which are not just a matter of geography and chronology. Both were outsiders. Gent had served his apprenticeship in a London ballad house and his long-term association with popular literature pushed him to the margins of the respectable trade. Like Love, Gent wrote ballads and chapbooks throughout his career and their shared experience of this form of authorship was reflected in the structure and content of both their autobiographies. As Gent's personal circumstances deteriorated his career moved closer to Love's. By the 1760s he was dealing largely in chapbooks and almanacks and was forced to take up itinerant selling around York. He was painfully aware of his shifting status:

A *London* Stationer train'd, my Bread to get;
Now RUNNING One. A moving Epithet.[92]

Love was not a member of the book trade in any formal sense but his experiences fit into a system which embraced the London high-flyers as well as the usually destitute and often disabled street traders.

David Love was born at Torriburn near Edinburgh in 1750 and for over 70 years was on the road engaged in spreading the word. The specifically religious overtones of this phrase are appropriate to Love as the frame of much of his life and writing was supplied by his religious conviction. During his declining years in Nottingham he suffered the fate of becoming a local character and was known derisively, and much to his annoyance, as 'Old Glory'.[93] A long section of his

Life rehearsed the circumstances of his 'conversion' and the verse which it contained is full of spiritual exhortation. Even so, it was not overwhelmed by the sort of apocalyptic fervour that characterised the writing of John Magee. Love's material, as I hope I have indicated, provides a clear-headed view of the world. Magee also revealed an interest in political radicalism. Although he tried to rationalise this in terms of madness induced by the spectacle of human suffering,[94] he was still driven by his sense of the unregeneracy of society. Such views were alien to Love. He had some harsh words for the rich; 'though they have great superfluities, yet they would rather let a poor creature starve, ere they would keep him or her alive out of their unnecessary expences or store'.[95] However, his general line was humanitarian rather than revolutionary. He comes over as an unambitious, good-hearted person, a member of a sector of the book trade which has sunk below the horizon. Reading modern studies of the 18th Century it is hard to imagine the existence of such people living and working outside the orbit of middling society. Love was part of what Thomas Gent described as 'the under class of my fellow creatures'[96] and any attempt to reconstruct the period, particularly in terms of book-trade history, has to accommodate his still shadowy presence. His experiences open up an area of popular culture, supported by print, which itself has been pushed to the margins of research. It is time that Love, with his few small books, was given the attention he deserves. His own modest verses concluding the *Life* can also end this paper:

Now thanks to my subscribers all,
Who were so kind and free;
When I did at their houses call,
The Numbers bought from me.

I can't express my gratitude,
For favors manifold.
You all to me have prov'd so good,
Perhaps, because I'm old.

I hope your favors still to gain,
To please my friends I'll strive;
I trust my labor's not in vain,
If thereby I may thrive.

When round I to each house did go,
Many did me befriend;
I hope you will continue so,
Until my days shall end.

Postscript: illusion and reality

I am grateful to Sheila Lambert for raising, with shrewd irony, the issue of the 'reality' of Love's material. How far does his account represent a 'true' statement of a lifetime's experience? Was Love in some sense a construct of his own or even somebody else's imagination? Such questions are particularly difficult to answer in relation to a man whose personal record appeared only in print. His experiences lie mainly outside the conventional apparatus of external verification. Love was arrested often enough. However, the chance of picking up a reference to a casual prosecution for vagrancy is slight. Love's footsteps, like those of a traveller struggling through a snow storm, were clear but ephemeral. After a short time the passer-by finds only a smooth surface. Following publication of the autobiography Love's status as a local character gave him an independent existence in the writings of middling observers. More telling, the imprint statements on his surviving publications link him to different parts of the country at times which coincide with the chronology of the *Life*. If his existence is hardly in doubt, the details of his experiences remain untested. It can only be said that they are entirely consistent with what is known both about the contemporary trade and the general structure of itinerant selling. Across a substantial stretch of time an army of individuals appear and disappear through records of one sort or another engaged in activities of exactly the kind that Love described. Of course, the use of the word 'adventures' in the title of the *Life* contains an echo of a fictional representation of events. On the other hand, its inclusion may simply indicate Love's sense of what was needed to sell his serial on the streets. I prefer to give him the benefit of any doubt. His integrity, underpinned by a sincere religious conviction, seems clear. As with any such account, his memory may be at fault on occasion and the temptation to embellish may not always have been resisted. Even so, the *Life* carries conviction and in the course of time I expect that additional information will emerge to ratify some of the detail in his invaluable account.

References

1.   These details are compiled from William Hone, *Every-Day Book* (London: 2 vols., 1827) vol. 2, cols.225–230 (with a portrait), 1575; *The Table Book* (London: 2 vols., 1827) vol. 2, cols. 177–181; the *Nottingham Journal* 4406, Saturday 16 June 1827, containing an obituary of Love. Unfortunately the equivalent issue of Sutton's *Nottingham Review* is missing from all known holdings of the paper. To these references can be added the useful and unexpected entry for David Love in the *Dictionary of National Biography*. I am grateful to Giles Mandelbrote for bringing this item to my notice.

2. Henry Mayhew, *London Labour and the London Poor* (London: 3 vols., 1851) particularly vol. 1, pp.213–308.

3. Margaret Spufford, *Small Books and Pleasant Histories; Popular Fiction and its Readership in Seventeenth-Century England* (Cambridge: Cambridge University Press, reissue 1985). Her other work on education and literacy also has a high value in this area of popular culture.

4. Information on the occupants of the houses on the Bridge prior to reconstruction can be found in the Corporation of London Record Office, Comptroller's Bridge House Papers *c.* 1603–1850, Box 3. The material includes a detailed survey of the properties in 1753–4 by the architect George Dance. Some detail on the stationers on the bridge appears in Ambrose Heal, 'Old London Bridge Tradesmen's Cards' in Gordon Home, *Old London Bridge* (London: The Bodley Head, 1931), pp.308–324. Also in the rather erratic list in Victor E. Neuberg, *Popular Education in Eighteenth Century England* (London: Woburn Press, 1971), pp.156–66.

5. Francis Clifton to Charles Delafaye, (1720), Public Record Office, London (hereafter PRO), State Papers Domestic (hereafter SP) 35. 21/75.

6. Margaret Spufford, *The Great Reclothing of Rural England: Petty Chapmen and their Wares in the Seventeenth Century* (London: Hambledon Press, 1984).

7. The legislation in force from the middle of the 18th Century is rehearsed in successive editions of Richard Burn's *Justice of the Peace*, first published in two volumes in 1755. By dealing in the stock of various English printers and booksellers David Love made himself liable to prosecution for not having a licence. However, because much of the material he sold was his own work he was able to establish a *de facto* immunity.

8. Examination of Ellen Vickers and Sarah Ogilby, 25 January 1718, PRO, SP 35. II/14(i). Also further examinations of the same date, SP 11/14(2) and 14(3). Vickers had worked as a hawker since Dr Sacheverell's trial in 1710. The one-legged man and his companion were described by Richard Shaw, an informer, in a letter to Delafaye of 6 March 1720, SP 35. 25/94. Subsequently Shaw occasionally identified them in manuscript on the printed ballads he sent in to the Secretary of State's office. For example, *The Church-man's new Health* (MS 18 November 1721), SP 35. 29/23,

9. Reference to 'a straw hat lady' sent 'to the House of Correction to hard labour' in a letter from Dan Combes to Delafaye 22 January 1722, PRO, SP 35. 31/154.

10. Patricia Hollis, *The Pauper Press* (Oxford: Oxford University Press, 1970) particularly pp.171–91.

11. William F. Belcher, 'The Sale and Distribution of the *British Apollo*' in Richmond P. Bond, ed., *Studies in the Early English Periodical* (Chapel Hill: University of North Carolina Press, 1957), pp.73–101. The level of work discipline was suggested in the attempt to enforce the use of 'respectful language', *ibid*, p.95.

12. *Gloucester Journal*, Monday 9 April 1722. Such distributors may have worked exclusively for a newspaper printer/publisher. However, the indications are that their income, like that of the miscellaneous agents, was generated by sales rather than

assured by regular payments from the employer. See, for example, the claim that the hawkers had deserted 'Mr. Hasbart's News' as 'it was not worth their going about with them', *Norwich Gazette* 607, Saturday 24 May 1718. I am grateful to David Stoker for this reference.

13. Christine Ferdinand kindly provided me with the reference to the *Hampshire Chronicle* from the account book for 1781–1783 which she describes elsewhere in this volume, PRO, Exchequer 140. 91.

14. *Northampton Mercury* Monday 30 January 1721. Cited in Robert S. Thomson, 'The Development of the Broadside Ballad Trade and its influence upon the Transmission of English Folksongs' (Cambridge University, unpublished Ph.D. thesis, 1974), p.97.

15. *Norwich Gazette* 598, Saturday 22 March 1718. Nearly three months later the *Gazette* carried a notice signed by 'Thomas Howlett, the Lame Fellow with Crutches' admitting that he had vented scandalous reports against its printer, Henry Crossgrove, at the instigation of his ex-partner Hasbart, *Norwich Gazette* 610, Saturday 14 June 1718. My thanks are again due to David Stoker for this reference.

16. *The Life of David Love. Part 1 Containing his Birth, Parentage and Education with Several Curious Transactions During his Youth* (Newcastle: 'For the Author by J. Marshall, Old Flesh Market, Newcastle', n.d.), 8pp. There is no illustration on the title.

17. There is a certain amount of repetition in the work itself as Love sometimes covered tha same period in both verse and prose. For the later version he added a glossary of Scottish terms as footnotes to the text. The elder Sutton who founded the printing business and set up the *Nottingham Review* was said himself to have started out as a 'walking stationer', *Notes and Queries* (hereafter *N&Q.*) 7th Ser., vol. 8(July–December 1889), p.333.

18. The publication notice was dropped by the 5th edition (1825) but there are no indications of any changes to the text. The British Library holds a copy of the 3rd edition (1823) with the portrait and there are other copies of various 'editions' at the County Library, Nottingham (3rd (1823), 4th (1824), 5th (1825)) and at the National Library of Scotland (5th). There are a number of copies in private hands including my own from the Nottingham Mechanic's Institute (5th) and one in the possession of Giles Mandelbrote (4th). Tipped into the Mandelbrote copy is a half-sheet broadside entitled *Some Account of the Last Hours of David Love, Who Died on Tuesday, June 12th 1827*, printed in Nottingham for Elizabeth the wife of David Love. This item also describes 'A wonderful miracle, being a hint of the life and sufferings of David Love.'

19. *Nottingham Journal* 4383, Saturday 6 January 1827.

20. Mayhew, *London Labour*, vol.1, p.220.

21. Love, *Life* (Marshall), p.6.

22. I am grateful to the Local Studies Librarian at the Central Library, Paisley for providing me with a photocopy of this text. There are no indications of any previous edition.

23. See, for example, the evidence given by a 'private Hawker' whose father had followed the same line of work in the *Old Bailey Proceedings* 12, 13, 14 July 1716, p.2.

24. Hollis, *Pauper Press*, p.174.

25. David Alexander, *Retailing in England during the Industrial Revolution* (London: Athlone Press, 1970) p.62.

26. Publications in a volume of chapbooks in the British Library, 1076. h.2 (1–47). An early 19th-Century broadside in the British Library, *Margaretta* (London: n.d.), contains a large illustration of a young woman selling slip ballads over some short verses which end 'Relieve my woes &c.', *Factotum*, 30 (December, 1989), p.24.

27. *Memoirs of the Late Thomas Holcroft, Written by Himself* (London: 3 vols., 1816), vol.1, pp.23–5.

28. David Love, *A Few Remarks on the Present Times* (no place or date), 8pp. 'Printed for, and Sold by the Author, a Lame Man; Who Makes erses [*sic*] on any Subjects, if mployed [*sic*].'

29. Love, *Life* (Sutton), pp.78–9.

30. Notice in *Parker's London News* 988, Wednesday 17 March 1725.

31. Love, *Life* (Sutton), p.82.

32. For example, entries under 'Hawkers' in John Cowel, *A Law Dictionary* (London: new edition, 1727); Giles Jacob, *New Law Dictionary* (London: new edition, 1722).

33. For references to a variety of hostile comments on pedlars and hawkers published in London and local newspapers see Jeremy Black, *The English Press in the Eighteenth Century* (London: Croom Helm, 1987), p.263, n.40. Love himself gave an account of some of the frauds he had met with amongst his fellow travellers, *Life* (Sutton), pp.19–23.

34. *Ibid.*, p.103; Magee, *Account*, pp.20, 34–5.

35. Love, *Life* (Sutton), p.104.

36. Love, *Life* (Sutton), p.104. Love's third and last wife, Elizabeth Laming (*d.* 1853), also had social aspirations which caused him some difficulty, *N&Q*, 7th Ser., vol.8, pp.234, 411–12.

37. Love, *Life* (Sutton), pp.29–30.

38. *Ibid.*, p.31.

39. *Ibid.*, pp.37–8.

40. Use of this term appeared in the *Universal Spectator* 180, Saturday 16 February 1734.

41. Love, *Life* (Sutton), p.144.

42. *Ibid.*, p.14.

43. *Ibid.*, p.41.

44. Most of the itinerant individuals whose careers were the subject of a printed record were at some time or other engaged with the military. John Magee joined the army during the American war and spent several years serving in Irish regiments, while James Allan, the Northumberland piper, made a regular profit from enlistment and desertion. In spite of his deformities the pedlar-poet Dougal Graham was at least a camp follower of the Pretender's army in 1745. Magee, *Account*, pp.41–2; James

Thompson, *A New, Impartial, and Authentic Life of James Allan* (Newcastle: 1828); George Macgregor, ed., *The Collected Writings of Dougal Graham* (Glasgow: 2 vols., 250 copies, 1883), vol. 1, p.12.

45. *General Evening Post* 226, Thursday 13 March 1735.

46. For Walker see Michael Harris, 'Paper pirates; the alternative book trade in mid-18th Century London', in Robin Myers and Michael Harris ed., *Fakes and Frauds* (Winchester: St. Paul's Bibliographies, 1989), pp.47–69. The Diceys, who became the most substantial London-based distributors of ballads and chapbooks, were said to have set up in business as itinerant sellers of medicines; Thomson, 'Ballad Trade', p.91

47. The works whose titles are closest to this ambiguous statement are Nicholas Culpeper, *Pharmacopoeia Londoniensis: or the London Dispensatory* first published in London in 1659 and the *Dispensatory of the Royal College of Physicians in Edinburgh* first published in Edinburgh in 1727. However, the most frequently reprinted works containing prescriptions and bearing a close relation to these titles are *Culpeper's English Physician* first published in London in 1652 and still in print and the *Pharmacopoeia Collegii Regia Medicorum Edinburgensis* first published in Edinburgh in 1722 and reaching a tenth edition in 1817.

48. Love, *Life* (Sutton), p.77.

49. Mayhew, *London Labour*, vol.1, p.218.

50. Magee included in his *Account* the distances marked on mile stones from Paisley to Woolwich and back which he had recorded in a notebook, pp.3–5.

51. Love, *Life*, (Sutton), p.83.

52. *Ibid.*, pp.120–22.

53. *David Love's Journey to London* (Nottingham: Shorrock and Son, n.d.).

54. *The Life of Mr. Thomas Gent, Printer, of York, Written by Himself* (London: 1832), p.143; *The Butler and Steward's Key* (London: 'Printed by F.C. in Fleet Lane', (1718), PRO, SP 35. 66/66; Harris, 'Paper pirates', p.64.

55. Spufford, *Small Books*, pp.98–9. Cyprian Blagden, 'The Distribution of Almanacks in the Second Half of the Seventeenth Century', *Studies in Bibliography*, vol.11 (1958), pp.107–116.

56. Love, *Life* (Sutton), pp.32–3. The titles of the ballads given in the *Life* were *The Pride and Vanity of Young Women, with Advice to Young Men that they may take care who they marry* and *The Pride and Vanity of Young Men, with advice to the Maids, to beware of becoming ensnared by their flatteries, and enticing words.*

57. On 'a rainy harvest' and *Redeeming the time . . .*, Love, *Life* (Sutton), pp.80, 86.

58. *The Universal British Directory* (London: 5 vols., (1791)), vol.3, p.182.

59. Love, *Life*, (Sutton), p.67.

60. Magee, *Account*, p.18.

61. For example, Love, *Life*, (Sutton), pp.80–81; Magee, *Account*. pp.7, 18.

62. *Weekly Journal or British Gazetteer* 1317, Saturday 25 April 1719.

63. Love, *Life* (Sutton), p.15.

64. *Ibid.*, p.151.
65. *Ibid.*, p.38.
66. Mayhew, *London Labour*, vol.1, p.235.
67. Love, *Life* (Sutton), p.66.
68. The British Library copy of Love's *Original Poems* has a London imprint and a date which has been firmly interpreted as 1791. However, the last figure is not legible under the laminate although it may once have been. If the entry is correct then the preliminary statement that it had 'been printed six times' already, means that the Gosport 'edition' of about 1794 was yet another reprint of a successful work. I have been unable to trace another copy.
69. Love, *Life* (Sutton), pp.65–6.
70. David Love, *A New and Correct Set of Godly Poems, for the Benefit of all Christians of every Denomination.* In nine parts ((Culross?): printed for and sold by the author, (1782)), 16 pp. 12°. This is how the British Library copy, missing since October 1987, is described in the ESTC. P.A. Hopkins has kindly informed me that there is a copy dated 1783 in the National Library of Scotland.
71. One of his title statements reads –
    'Who can on names Acrostics make,
    In a poetic strain;
    To please you, he great pains will take,
    All for a little gain.'
    Love, *Life* (Sutton), p.77.
72. *Ibid.*, p.38.
73. Examination of Ellen Vickers, 25 January 1718, PRO, SP 35. 11/14(3); *A New Song Commemorating the Birth Day of her Late Majesty Queen Anne* (London: 1718) with manuscript note 'Eliza Robinson. The New Ballad You may sing it but fear not', PRO. SP 35. 11/20(1).
74. Michael Harris, *London Newspapers in the Age of Walpole* (London and Toronto: Associated University Presses, 1987), p.29. Clifton on at least one occasion offered to bail any hawker arrested for carrying his material, statement by John Lightbody 20 July 1720, PRO, SP 35. 21/75.
75. She was said to have been arrested on seven separate occasions; Harris, *London Newspapers*, pp.30, 40.
76. Love, *Life* (Sutton), p.104.
77. *Ibid.*, p.125.
78. *Ibid.*, p.17.
79. Spufford, *Reclothing*, p.27.
80. Gent, *Life*, pp.173–4.
81. Possibly a member of the Evans family connected, through Richard Marshall, with the Diceys, Leslie Shepard, *John Pitts: Ballad Printer of Seven Dials* (London: Private Libraries Association, 1969), p.37.
82. John Stead, printer, was listed in *The Universal British Directory* under Gosport

(*c*.1791) and a John Stead was among those polled in the 1790 election for the County of Southampton. I am grateful to Christine Ferdinand for identifying John Stead at Gosport as an agent of the *Hampshire Chronicle*, December 1781–83, PRO, Exchequer 140. 91, f.76.

83. Love, *Life* (Sutton), pp.68–70.

84. *Ibid.*, p.65.

85. *Ibid.*, p.67.

86. Spufford, *Small Books*, pp.124–5.

87. Love, *Life*, (Sutton), p.73.

88. Love seems to have been in Gosport in 1794 as he vividly described the English and French ships limping into harbour after Lord Howe's victory of 1 June, *Ibid*, pp.66–7.

89. Robert Davies, *A Memoir of the York Press* (Westminster, 1868), pp.339–40. Davies cites imprints from Gent's Coffee-Yard address while Love described Pennington as 'Printer in Minster-Yard'. Otherwise the accounts coincide, Love, *Life* (Sutton), p.104.

90. *Ibid.*, p.105.

91. *Ibid.*, p.106.

92. Thomas Gent, *The Contingencies or Changes of this Transitory Life* (York: (1761)), p.15. See also Davies, *York Press*, pp.228–30.

93. The representation of Love and his fellow hawkers as local characters had some early precedents in London. For example, 'Old Bennet' figured in John Dunton, *Life and Errors* (London: 2 vols., 1818), vol.1, p.236. and in the broadside *The Mercury Hawkers in Mourning* (1706), Society of Antiquaries of London.

94. Magee. *Account*, pp.30–1.

95. Love, *Life* (Sutton), p.4.

96. Gent, *Life*, p.129.

Single sheets from a country town:
the example of Exeter

IAN MAXTED

WHILE PRINTED BOOKS from earlier centuries survive widely and show from their sturdy format that they were intended for posterity, there was a vast body of printed material which was produced with no thoughts of long-term survival. In its time such material was more immediately available to wide sections of the community than books but anyone who studies this body of literature today is in the position of a palaeontologist who has to reconstruct antediluvian landscapes from the evidence of scattered fossils. Seldom does one come across rich limestone deposits like the archives of Cheney of Banbury[1] or Sprang of Tunbridge Wells,[2] and one cannot be certain that these are typical. This paper does not quarry a rich vein but picks over the scattered survivals of single sheet items produced by the presses in Exeter in the 18th Century. I shall, however, be obliged to cast my net to include other Devon towns and to reach forward to the 19th Century to fill gaps in the record.

During the course of collecting materials for a checklist of Devon imprints[3] I have located 288 single sheet items printed in Devon, 246 of them printed in Exeter. Of the remaining 42, thirteen were printed in Plymouth. As far as the date of publication is concerned 92 were printed before 1780, 98 in the 1780s and 93 in the 1790s.

These figures do not include printed forms, the first items that I propose to deal with, which were among the earliest categories of printed material to be produced in Exeter where the printing press found a permanent home in 1698 when Samuel Darker set up business. Six books or pamphlets are recorded for this first year but this number of imprints on books is surpassed by five different imprints on apprenticeship indentures as well as two on sacrament certificates in that same year.

Dickinson has studied apprenticeship indentures for Exeter[4] and examined the archives of several parishes. Work on the quarter sessions records has extended the range of material available and shows that, up to 1730, seven printers in Exeter supplied at least 42 different indentures to 15 different booksellers in Exeter as well as one each in Plymouth and Totnes. At times forms were printed for different booksellers from the same setting of type, only the imprint being changed. As well as apprenticeship indentures other types of form included removal orders, orders in bastardy, publicans' recognizances and, from 1754, the

APPRENTICESHIP INDENTURES PRINTED IN EXETER TO 1730

Printer→ / Bookseller↓	Anon	S. Darker	S. Farley	Farley & Bliss	J. Bliss	P. Bishop	G. Bishop	A. Brice	E. Farley
[Unspecified]									
Thomas Butter	1698–14		1702–11	1706?		1716?			1729?
Walter Dight	1698				1709				
Charles Yeo	1698		1703–5?	1706					
John Pearce	1698								
Edward Score	1720?		1703					1720	
Philip Bishop			1706?						
Philip & Margery Yeo			1708?		1708?				
John March			1709?–23				1720?		
B. Smithurst (Plymouth)			1710						
Philip Yeo	1713?		1710?				1722	1720	
Nathaniel Thorne							1720?		
Jane Butter	1720								
R. Legassicke (Totnes)								1724?	
Jane Pring	1727								
Margery Yeo	1728?								1728?
Aaron Tozer									1729?
Thomas Butter II									1729?

largest of all, the marriage register books. There were more than 450 parishes in Devon guaranteeing a steady demand for forms but such work would be intermittent, a couple of days' work a year probably sufficing for the county's requirements of apprenticeship indentures. The surviving numbers of titles of books or pamphlets in Exeter seldom reached double figures each year before the 1780s, so that printers required other sources of work to keep their presses from being idle for long periods.

Many found an answer in the publication of a newspaper. Of the seven printers supplying apprenticeship indentures in Exeter to 1730 six published newspapers. Samuel Darker, Exeter's first permanent printer, died early in 1700 but his partner Samuel Farley had probably established the *Exeter post-man* by 1704. His son Edward Farley took over a later title published by Samuel in the 1720s. In 1709 Joseph Bliss established the *Exeter post boy*, in 1714 Philip Bishop founded the *Exeter mercury*, and after his death in the King's Bench prison in 1716, he was succeeded by his son George. Andrew Brice established the *Postmaster* in 1717 after absconding from his master Joseph Bliss.

It is difficult to assess the circulation of these early provincial newspapers. From 1712 to 1725 most newspapers consisted of $1\frac{1}{2}$ sheets in order to qualify them as pamphlets. As such, they were liable to pay only three shillings stamp duty for an entire impression instead of one penny for every single sheet in an edition or a half-penny for every half-sheet. When this loophole was blocked in 1725 Andrew Brice announced in the 23 April issue of *The postmaster* that he would have to pay an additional £100 or more in duty annually. This indicates a circulation of at least 24,000 sheets per year or 300 $1\frac{1}{2}$-sheet newspapers per week. Prior to the change in the law on stamp duty the newspaper cost $1\frac{1}{2}d$ per issue; afterwards the price of the single sheet newspaper which the disgruntled Andrew Brice revived on 30 April, under the new title of *Brice's weekly journal*, rose to $2d$.[5] The progressive rises in newspaper stamp duty to a minimum of $1d$. in 1757, $1\frac{1}{2}d$. in 1776, $2d$. in 1789, $2\frac{1}{2}d$. in 1794 and $3\frac{1}{2}d$. 1797, together with the rising price of paper, resulted in a charge of $6d$. for a newspaper by the end of the century. The wages of an Exeter labourer rose from about $6s.$ $9d.$ in 1700 to $8s.$ a week during the second half of the century while a craftsman's wages rose from $10s.$ a week in 1710 to $12s.$ in 1790.[6] It can be calculated that the cost of a four-page weekly newspaper in the 1790s might be the equivalent of perhaps £5.00 in today's prices. By 1793 the printer of the *Exeter gazette* boasted a circulation of about 1,000 copies, not dramatically more than Brice could have achieved 70 years previously. Even in 1837 its successor, then called the *Exeter and Plymouth gazette*, had a circulation of little more than 2,000 according to the evidence of returns of newspaper stamps, and this was considerably more than any other Devon newspaper; the *Devonshire chronicle* managed to survive on a circulation of a mere 250 copies.[7]

Where they could get them people had a preference for London papers whose news was that much fresher. However, the print run of London newspapers was not large enough to satisfy the provincial demand so that the printers in provincial towns acted as relay posts, multiplying the numbers of copies for local distribution and adding local advertisements. Such work could occupy a press for one day a week and would still leave time for other work. Significantly, the gathering of advertisements and other matter for inclusion in the newspaper set up communications networks which helped the production and distribution of much of the remaining output.

Besides the newspaper advertisements, which helped them to survive even with limited circulations, the printer was called on to produce separate advertisements and posters. I have traced about 15 in 18th-Century Exeter. Advertisers include booksellers, carpenters, coach services, linendrapers, and an umbrella maker with the fitting name of B. Dryer.

One special form of advertisement was the playbill (*see* Fig. 1). The theatre in Exeter was only open during the season, so work was not guaranteed for the whole year, but Exeter playbills survive from as early as the 1750s. Although complete sets have not survived, it would appear that printers frequently produced a separate playbill for each day's performance. For example, the playbill for the performance of *The Castle of Andalusia* on 12 August 1783 described it as 'never acted here' while a separate playbill for the following day describes it as 'acted here but once'. In addition the printer had other alterations to make because a different farce was acted at the second performance.

The printing press could provide a wider audience for the individual who had something to say. Sermons are the prime example of such early vanity publishing, but on a smaller scale Exeter provides several examples of printers being approached to publish specific statements. Perhaps the most unusual of these is entitled *Balloon-concerns*. It was a quarter sheet written in 1786 by an east Devon farmer John Wipple who complained that a hot-air balloon had damaged his crops.

Official notices were another source of work for local printers. Indeed the Council of Exeter appointed a series of local printers for this purpose, although official work could not have been a great source of income for a printer judging by the long series of vouchers in the Devon Record Office containing accounts presented by tradesmen to the Corporation of Exeter in the 18th Century. In the year 1793/4 R. Trewman and Son held both the stationery and the printing and advertising contracts and presented an account for £35. 10s. 3d. Of this however only £11. 9s. 6d. – less than one third – was for printing and advertising and only £8. 14s. for the actual printing work. This can be broken down as follows:

Sept 19 1794	Printing 300 invitation cards	10s. 6d.
Oct. 1 1794	Printing 500 invitation cards	17s. 6d.
Oct 21 1794	Printing 5000 foolscap 8° audit receipts	£1. 16s. od.
Mar 31 1795	Printing 2000 sheets pot folio	

Fig. 1   A playbill of 1784. Westcountry Studies Library (Devon Library Services).

	to regulate the market	£4. 10s. 0d.
May 15 1795	Printing 200 large invitation cards	7s. 0d.
June 30 1795	Printing 300 quarto bills	
	materials of the wool market for sale	6s. 0d.
Sept 18 1795.	printing 200 large invitation cards	7s. 0d.

Besides printing four batches of invitation cards, one batch of forms and two posters in the course of that year, Trewman received payments totalling 5s. for dispersing two of these publications and £2. 10s. 6d. for insertions of four official advertisements into his paper, usually for two weeks each.

The payments for dispersal were high in the case of the 300 quarto bills for the sale of materials for the wool market, being one-sixth of the cost of printing, and this could imply that bill-posting was included as well as simply delivering. The extent of bill-posting in 18th-Century Exeter is not clear; nevertheless it was the most immediate method of 'spreading the word', so deserves some consideration.

Within a year of Darker's setting up his press in 1698 he printed Sir Bartholomew Shower's speech at the Guildhall on declaring the results of the poll in the parliamentary election.[8] In it Shower referred to two critical publications entitled *Queries* and *Little reflections* which had been posted at the Guildhall, but it is not clear whether these were in print or manuscript. Early illustrations of Exeter do not make it clear to what degree announcements and other material were posted around the city. Artists and engravers tended to omit the ephemeral or disfiguring. Nevertheless an engraving of the Theatre in Exeter dated 1804 does show a large board hanging from the side wall and there is evidence of posters pasted on a wall of a neighbouring property.[9] An engraving of the Guildhall dated 1829 shows that notices were posted on the pillars of the arcade[10] and an engraving of St John's Hospital in the High Street made in 1831 shows a considerable accretion of posters on one of the walls.[11] At about that date there was a considerable number of 'gentlemen of the paste and brush' as the *Exeter and Plymouth Gazette* designated them on 26 April 1833. It described them as 'a jealous class of fellows, and not upon the best terms with each other. The placards of Mr George R--- excited a considerable degree of envy ... and they determined to show him up in a new light; accordingly, in the bills for sale of the Bishop's Court estate, they permitted the first line to remain, where the celebrated auctioneer's name appeared in conspicuous characters, and underneath they posted the exhibition of a large sea monster, now showing here at 6d. per head; and the placard consequently read ..."Mr. George R---, the Great Greenland Whale"'. By 1848 there was certainly a sufficient quantity of paper being pasted on walls in Exeter to occupy individuals full-time, for in that year John Knight of Smythen Street is listed as a bill-poster in the local trade directory.

The fact that so many single sheets are printed on one side only indicates that there must have been a tradition of posting these up, even indoors. Paper was expensive and printers could have economised by printing on two sides using the technique of work and turn if there was any prospect of this type of material being widely accepted in that form. Where broadsheets are printed on two sides they are often using the back of waste paper. For example *The speech of Oliver Cromell*, [*sic*] *upon dissolving the Parliament* was printed by Elizabeth Brice to her usual atrocious standard on the verso of *An account of a most daring highway-robbery, committed on Saturday night last, near Kingsbridge*, a title which would soon lose its currency as it was clearly dated 28 April 1784.

Political broadsheets were prime candidates for posting on walls but no such material has been traced for Exeter until the election of 1761. Andrew Brice, who deals with a wide range of activities at the hustings in *The Mobiad*, a verbose poetical account of Exeter elections during the 1730s, makes no mention of election posters, but he notes that this was a depressed period in Exeter's economic fortunes, a depression which is certainly reflected in the drop in printing activity, and it may be that there was neither the money nor the printing presses available to produce election literature. However from the 1760s this lack was more than compensated for, and for 1790 a particularly fine set of some 30 election squibs survives in the Devon and Exeter Institution. It includes a large number of songs and poems whose titles give some indication of the level at which much of the election was conducted:

A new copy of verses called the niggardly barber's blaggardly action.
A new copy of verses called smoke his old bacon.
Bampfylde for ever, no sneaking contractor.
Old Turkey-Legs has got the gripes.

James Baring was particularly lambasted, being designated 'Old Turkey-Legs', 'Old Griping Jack' or 'Poking Old Jack O'.

However it is impossible to be clear about the full extent of Exeter election literature until 1812. In that year the printer Robert Cullum gathered together all the squibs, addresses and other papers in a volume entitled *The spirit of election wit*. For the uncontested City of Exeter election of that year he lists 17 items and for the election for the county of Devon he records 38 items. While reproducing the text of the addresses he omits the imprints. Fortunately, this gap is filled by a collection of many of the original items in the Westcountry Studies Library which show that five printers in Exeter, one in Plymouth Dock, one in Bath and one in London were used. For 1818 he repeated the exercise[12] and managed to round up 68 items leading up to the city election and 87 leading up to the county election, some of them published a couple of years before the actual poll as prospective candidates were staking their claims.

Even outside the period of the hustings local political issues could give rise to a flurry of pamphlets and leaflets. A collection survives in the British Library generated by a dispute over the Exeter Corporation of the Poor in 1784. The background to several such exchanges in Tiverton is provided by a series of letters written by the Tory town clerk of Tiverton, Beavis Wood, to his MP, Sir Dudley Ryder.[13] He was always critical of radicals or 'crabs' as he termed them, among whom he placed the historian of Tiverton, Martin Dunsford. On 5 February 1793 he wrote that Dunsford and his disaffected associates had provoked disloyal expressions. Complaint had been made to the mayor who summoned the radicals and warned them to be more careful what they said in the future. Wood wrote that a paper was 'dropt and handed around the town, which altho' insignificant caused some laughing on all sides. And I put it up in my office window that all might read it as they passed.'

One week later, on 12 February, he wrote that, in order to please some of his friends, 'who did not like to be too much laughed at and in order to promote a more general amusement', he wrote and put up another paper, 'which made the Mayor help to the laugh of the patriots'. The authorities were not having much success that month as an attempt at a holiday to burn the works of Tom Paine 'went off heavily' with very few attending; and Ryder felt that this caused Tiverton to have 'a very disaffected and disloyal character throughout the country'.

In order to support the character of the Corporation the Mayor of Tiverton held a Common Council on 15 February when the resolutions were published but not put in the newspapers. On 19 and 25 February Beavis Wood put out two advertisements under the name of Pam 'in order to keep on the laughs by the desire of my loyal assistants. This I fancy made the patriots resolve to attack the last resolution of the corporation and they now appeared to expect something very particular to be laughed at.' Within a couple of days the expected leaflet appeared. Wood wrote on 28 February 'In order to ridicule the last Corporation resolutions now approved a few of the printed papers signed *Bunyan senior*, by way of burlesque, but it produced more groaning than laughing and yet went off very well as a joke. The loyalists again desired me to think how a parody might be put out to Bunyan'. This clearly occupied Wood for some little time as he did not write again until 11 March: 'I published the paper of Snap as a parody to Bunyan, which turned the laugh all round again and kept the little Dr. Abell in his water for some days'. Abell was the local apothecary, a man of wit but a prodigious drinker whose addiction led him at times to outrageous behaviour. Wood expressed the hope that this would be the end of 'all this idle amusement and no harm or any degree of ill will had been produced by it as could be discovered'. However, Wood was wrong. On 16 March he wrote that someone had become a little serious with him and he had received a letter through the post. 'I wrote the note under it and put it up in my window for all (who chose) to read them. By which means I have had as many attendants before my door as at any country private shop.'

These extracts show the atmosphere in which such squibs were generated, and also demonstrate how they circulated through a mixture of word of mouth, written and printed messages. There is no surviving evidence for a printing press in Tiverton before 1797 and such items would probably have had to be printed in Exeter, some twelve miles distant.

It is difficult to assess the amount of printed material produced by Exeter presses during this period. We do not know the number of presses owned by each printing house, or the extent to which they were kept active. Certainly printers did not rely solely on printing work, as can be seen by their extensive involvement with patent medicines and a wide range of stationery and other products. Nor is it known what staff a typical Exeter printer had at his disposal. Andrew Brice gives the impression that for long periods he was undertaking all the functions of the printing office single-handed,[14] but many printers had apprentices – if the regular newspaper announcements that they had absconded are anything to go by. Bibliographers have assumed that a typical press was able to turn out one average edition sheet printed on both sides each day. But this assumes a normal edition size in the London trade of 1,000 to 1,500 copies and a printing shop where the numbers of compositors and pressmen were balanced and the presses kept continuously active. Many of the editions in Exeter must have been much smaller, but they could vary considerably in size. It has been seen that Trewman's official orders ranged from 200 to 5000 copies. In 1788 Davidson claims that 20,000 copies of *A genuine account of the trial of William Smith and John Richards* were sold around the gallows by Stoke Church near Plymouth.[15] Besides, ephemeral items were printed on one side of the paper only and several titles could be produced on one sheet. In 1782 *Rodney victorious, or the Spaniards defeated* shared the same half sheet as *Capt. Ephraim, or the Yankee entertainment*. This is surpassed by an example dating from 1782 where *The maid's lamentation on the loss of her shepherd* is found on the same quarter sheet as *Rodney triumphant and France humbled*, both of them slip songs headed by crude woodcuts printed by Thomas Brice. The whole sheet could have contained eight such pieces, all printed off in a few hours (*see* reproduction on page vi, above).

Taking Trewman as a sample printer and 1791 as a sample year a few calculations can be made. I have traced four books printed by Trewman in this year, although some smaller items may have disappeared without record. Three are books of poems, by Downman, Hallaran and Kendall, made up of fourteen, thirteen and three sheets respectively. The most substantial work was *An elementary treatise, by way of an essay, on the quantity of estates* by Richard Preston, an octavo of 684 pages or 43 sheets. This produced a total of 73 sheets, theoretically 73 days' work. A further 52 days would be taken up by his newspaper. Two broadsheets are recorded and other official work might take another week or so of his time. So far only 22 weeks of work for a single press has been accounted for, leaving the theoretical capacity for a single press to produce a couple of hundred sheets of popular literature. Proof that Trewman had at one stage employed his press in the production of such material is given by the imprint of *The prodigal daughter; or the disobedient lady reclaim'd*, an eight-page chapbook printed in the 1770s; the imprint reads 'Exeter: Printed by R. Trewman, behind the Guildhall, where country shopkeepers, travellers, and others, may be supplied with a variety of old and new ballads, patters, penny histories, &c. &c. &c.'

The printer had to be certain of his distribution system before producing large quantities of such material. The newspaper networks are described elsewhere in this volume and the newsmen doubtless aided in the dispersal of this material along their regularly traversed routes. Far more irregular but equally important was the army of flying stationers, chapmen, hawkers, patterers and travellers. They were a motley collection of individuals who at times became well-known characters. One early 19th-Century Exeter itinerant, Tommy Osborne, even had his portrait lithographed. It shows him as a shabby person in a patched suit and battered hat hopefully offering an old bound volume while other books and papers are tucked under his arm and in a bag hung over his shoulder. He achieved the dubious distinction of being adopted as a candidate at the Ide burlesque election of 1812. The squibs which circulated on the occasion indicate that he was a shambling character, and his fondness for the bottle let him down. On his way home he confessed, 'I full into the Kennel . . . and most unluckily gamboged my best breeches and very much deranged the cuticle of my posteriors'. This may have cost him the election and the next we hear of him is his setting off for Alphington goose fair. He died in 1823, aged 41; life on the road seems to have taken its toll as he looks older and quite broken down in his portrait.[16]

Others survived the rigours of this way of life somewhat longer. Mrs J. Drew died in Exeter in 1801, aged 99. During the winter months she had been a courier or retailer of almanacks for the printer of the *Exeter and Plymouth gazette*. As Woolmer had only established that newspaper in 1792 she must have been braving the muddy lanes of Devon well into her nineties.[17] Such a vagrant existence must have attracted many of the misfits in society. Thomas Liscombe, widely known as a hawker who supplied Devon and Cornwall with ballads and similar materials, was arrested for the murder of Sarah Ford, the wife of a farmer in Kingsbridge, South Devon, at the end of 1812. He also confessed to the murder of a girl named Margaret Huxtable, in nearby Dodbrook.[18]

Such extremes of behaviour must have been exceptional, but the hawkers were anxious to turn a penny as best they might. Brice[19] gives us a picture in the 1750s of the people in the country eagerly receiving execution broadsheets. In reply to questions about their authenticity 'the honest vociferator would have fifty oaths ready to vomit forth, that "tis the right, tho' the devil himself had been author and printer too". The hawker would take his parcel of broadsheets from the press that had it ready first, even if it was a day before the execution 'the better to secure the run, as the term is; that is to get the start of others. As a paper is a paper to the country-folk, contain what it will; so money is money to the patterer and the grub, come how it may . . .'.

The origins of such ephemeral material are very hard to identify. Some of it was probably written by the hawkers themselves either working on a freelance basis or under commission from the printers who were well aware of the local demand for gallows literaure. Elizabeth Brice, for example, may have sponsored the account of Catherine Giddy (*see* Fig. 2) which clearly had an excellent sales potential. Some 25 examples of execution broadsheets published in Exeter during the 18th Century have so far been traced[20] and the printers occasionally revealed how far they were prepared to go to obtain the authentic accounts from which their publications were compiled.

In April 1752 Andrew Brice explained[21] why he had been unable to satisfy the public in providing them with details of the execution of William Jennings. He had received a message directed to his printing office in Northgate Street from the condemned man with the words 'I beg to see you this afternoon, as soon after dinner as you can'. He accordingly went to the prison where he found the prisoner, together with the chaplain and the warder. Jennings informed him that he had been recommended to him as the proper printer of what he had drawn up, to be published after he had been dispatched. The chaplain urged the prisoner not to be hasty and to avoid maliciousness. Jennings was agitated that the whole truth might not be told but said that he would send for Brice on the following day. The next day Brice was handed the confession but as soon as he had put it in his pocket the warder burst out violently 'Mr. Brice, I'd have you take care what you do. I'd not be in your coat for 500l. And I'll acquaint Mr. (mentioning a name) this minute . . .'. Brice replied 'Why, I pray? What concern has he in this case? Besides, do you take me for a fool or madman, that I know what I have to do in my own affairs?'. As the prisoner looked apprehensive, Brice gave in to a request from the warder 'Pray, Mr. Brice, let me have the paper, and you shall have it again tomorrow morning.'

On his way home Brice met with one of the chief officers who offered him the opportunity to ride in the coach with the prisoner to the place of execution. He arrived at the gaol and was present while the chaplain ministered to the prisoner, assuming that the confession would be handed over at the foot of the gallows. The crush of the crowd prevented his boarding the coach but he managed to reach the gallows in time. Just as the wretched prisoner was about to ascend the ladder Brice forced his way through the crowd and asked for the paper 'Ah! Sir', said the condemned man 'I am very sorry I have given you so much trouble but Mr. . . . has got it, and you must apply to him for having it'.

Brice was displeased, the more so when he discovered that the gentleman referred to had never received the paper, and his subsequent tirade in his newspaper casts interesting light on the role of the printer in producing this form of literature. When ministers visited condemned prisoners and urged them to make a full confession this was regarded as part of their penance. But for Brice it was not enough that it be made 'clandestinely or in hugger-mugger, but in order to

ACCOUNT OF THE

MURDER,

Committed by Catherine Giddy on her Male Baſtard Child.

CAtherine Giddy, a widow, aged 28, had three children by her late husband, two of whom are ſtill alive. She lived at Plymouth Dock, and earned a livelihood as a boatwoman. A ſhort time ſince, the perſons of the houſe ſhe lodged in taxed her with being with child ; but ſhe denied it with an oath.

In the beginning of this preſent June, a woman of the ſame houſe going to the neceſſary, found Giddy in the corner in great pain, and asking her diſorder, Giddy ſaid ſhe had a violent cholic fit. The woman left her, and ſoon after returned, when by what ſhe ſaw believing Giddy had been delivered, ſhe looked into the vault, and ſaw the child's feet juſt above the filth. She immediately called aſſiſtance, and the infant was taken out with ſome ſmall remains of life but ſoon expired.

The mother was taken into cuſtody ; and as it appeared, that ſhe conſtantly denied her pregnancy, and even in the laſt extremity when aſſiſtance is moſt required ; that ſhe had not the leaſt preparation for her delivery, which (having had three children) ſhe muſt know to be at hand ; and as it was clear, that ſhe had taken the babe from the floor, and wilfully caſt it alive into the vault, the Coroner's Jury gave a verdict of Murder, and ſhe was yeſterday committed to High Goal.

June 22, 1782.

EXON: Printed by E. BRICE, near Eaſt-Gate.

Fig. 2 A broadsheet printed by 'E. Brice', 1782. Westcountry Studies Library (Devon Library Services).

its being dispers'd abroad in print'. Although the chaplain put the condemned into a proper frame of mind to make his confession, it was normally left to the printer or one of his agents to take it down in writing, or if the prisoner chose to write it himself, the minister would give it to the printer. At times Brice was able to persuade the prisoner when the chaplain could not, and one of the main arguments he used was 'that it being to be published [*sic*], it was probably the best amends or restitution, he could in his circumstances make to an injured and offended world in general, and it might be so drawn up as to tend to the correction and edification, as well as information, of numbers, even at a distance.' The public, thought Brice, had a right to expect a confession, something more important to him than his 'righteous gain'.

Whether sincerely or not, Brice saw the production of these broadsheets as a public duty and was quick to attack those whom he saw as capitalising on the execution. As a footnote to *The confessions or declarations of John Price* executed in 1737 he wrote: 'As people are impatient at waiting long for such papers as this present, and others are usually published by other hands under the false pretence of being dying speeches, I am persuaded to publish this half sheet as 'tis; which shall be follow'd with the speeches, &c. at the execution with all speed possible.' Indeed for a time Brice gave up the unequal struggle of competing with these unscrupulous rivals. He claimed: 'We should be asham'd of appearing as t'were in common, and in that respect as on a level with the sorry grubs who now scandalously swarm here; such wretched ones are they for authors, however either of them may be qualified as a worthy printer's journeyman!' Brice avers that the most illiterate criminal would be ashamed to have 'such nonsense and false English charged upon him even when he is going to the gallows'. 'The bulk of populace, incapable of making due distinction, buy them as the real last dying words of malefactors, at their very execution-place, even before they are turn'd off the ladder.' He abhors such practices and after a stirring crescendo announces to the reader of his paper: 'The world is therefore requested, in justice, to take notice, that of the three several grubaean papers, which will probably issue from as many presses tomorrow here, and the same day be cry'd perhaps fifty miles remote, Andrew Brice has nothing of his writings in either one', unless, he added derisively, 'a modest young sparck, according to his wonted knack of plagiarism, slaps in some embellishing sentences or so, borrow'd from *my* former publications'.

This statement reveals incidentally how much of this ephemeral material must be lost. Brice indicates that there were at that time three presses in Exeter beside his own but no other active printer is recorded from the evidence of surviving imprints in the early 1750s. Possible candidates are Joseph Drew and one of the Farleys, perhaps Mark, known to have been active in the late 1740s, and Thomas Brice, Andrew's 'pushing nephew', who was printing later in the 1750s.

Brice's vituperation did not kill all of these dubious practices. Even as late as 1866, when one might have expected better communications to have made people more aware of current events, a broadsheet embellished with a crude woodcut appeared entitled *Execution of Mrs. Winsor at Exeter, for the barbarous murder of Mary Jane Harris's child*. A rough and ready job had been done on the woodcut which seems to have depicted a gallows for a mass execution. The central section had been excised and an amorphous blob on the end of a line did duty for the Torquay baby farmer who was to be hanged. Some hastily concocted verses described *inter alia* that:

Those children belong to some poor girl
    That had been lead astray
Mrs. Winsor would take them to nurse
    As long as they would pay.
She would murder them – yes, strangle them
    For this paltry gain,
But putting them between beds
    Or pressing the jugular vein.

And it goes on to relate that 'when culprit and hangman stood side by side a fearful yell rose from the assembled crowd, and the excitement only ceased when the culprit, who struggled but little, ceased to exist'. The printer should have been less hasty. According to Cossins[22] she was respited twice and eventually sentenced to penal servitude for life. The grave was dug, the gallows were erected and Calcraft the hangman came down to Exeter twice but Winsor was never hanged.

An even stranger case is presented by a broadsheet bearing the imprint 'J. Catnach, printer, 2 & 3, Monmouth-court, 7 Dials' which relates *The life, trial and execution of Mary White*. Mary White, aged 19, was executed at Exeter for the murder of her master and mistress, although protesting her innocence. Smith, one of her admirers, who was a spectator, stung with guilt and horror, rushed through the crowd, exclaiming 'I am the murderer!' and delivered himself into the hands of justice. The details in the broadsheet are circumstantial. The execution is helpfully dated 'Saturday last', the murdered couple kept the 'large inn at Exeter', White is an appropriate name for injured innocence and Smith is sufficiently anonymous. Unfortunately for Catnach, Cossins gives a full list of executions in Exeter from 1795 to 1877 and there is none named White. In fact it is a prime example of Catnach's catchpenny items.

Such bogus material (or 'cocks', as the running patterers of Mayhew's day termed them) was not confined to execution broadsheets. The case of the cannibals of Clovelly can serve as an example. *The history of John Gregg, and his family of robbers and murderers* is preserved in an eight-page chapbook in the Pearse Chope collection at Bideford. It is anonymous and without imprint but can probably be assigned to the later 18th Century. It reports how the Gregg family took up their abode in a cave near Clovelly on the north coast of Devon where they lived 25 years without visiting any town or city. During this time they robbed above 1000 persons, and ate the corpses of all those whom they robbed. They were eventually discovered and the king himself came with 400 men to hunt them out. Their cave was discovered containing 'such a multitude of arms, legs, thighs, hands and feet, of men, women and children hung up in rows, like dry'd beef and a great many lying in pickle'. John's charming family, consisting of his wife, eight sons, six daughters, eighteen grand-sons and fourteen grand-daughters begotton by incest were taken to Exeter and next day conducted under a strong guard to Plymouth where they were executed without trial.[23]

The printer could make minor amendments to an existing chapbook to fit his copy as he composed it, but the authorship of most ephemeral material is uncertain. Exeter had its Grub Street as well as London but much of the material must have been written by the printer himself or, as Brice suggests, by his journeyman. The Brice family seem to have had a particular flair for this and actually signed some of their poetic endeavours.

A typical example is Brice's *Address of thanks from the English virgins of sixteen to the Hon. Charles-James Fox, for his zeal to obtain an amendment of the Marriage-Act, to enable females to marry at sixteen and males at eighteen. Put into rhyme by their typographic amanuensis, Thomas Brice.* (*See* Fig. 3.) It dates from 1781 when the reform of the marriage laws was under consideration and its consists of eight stanzas of rumty-tumty stuff decoratively laid out in two columns within a frame of printer's flowers. It begins:

Thou dear dearest Charles Fox,
Whose firm courage no shocks
Of grey-bearded prejudice awe;
Warmest thanks now receive
From all girls whose breasts heave
For marriage according to law

The marriage acts continued to exercise the wits of Exeter for some time as indicated by an advertisement under the heading 'matrimony' in the *Exeter flying post* in July 1784:

Several boarding school misses, who are Wards of Chancery, who never hope to be married according to the strict laws of the Court of Celibacy, and who are in the wishing age of husbandising, offer themselves for better for worse to any sprightly young fellows of genteel address and good family, who have no fortunes, and who are willing to take a trip to Scotland, to Ireland, to America, or, in short, to any part of the world. If no better offers, they are resolved to go off with the dancing-master, the writing-master, the music-master, the drawing-master, or even with a footman, in cases of necessity. Apply at No. 2, in Non-Preservative Grove, Anti-Virgin Terrace, in most parts of England. N.B. Bring the marriage act in your pocket, a wedding-ring, and a close cap or two.

This indicates a London origin since houses were not numbered in Exeter at that

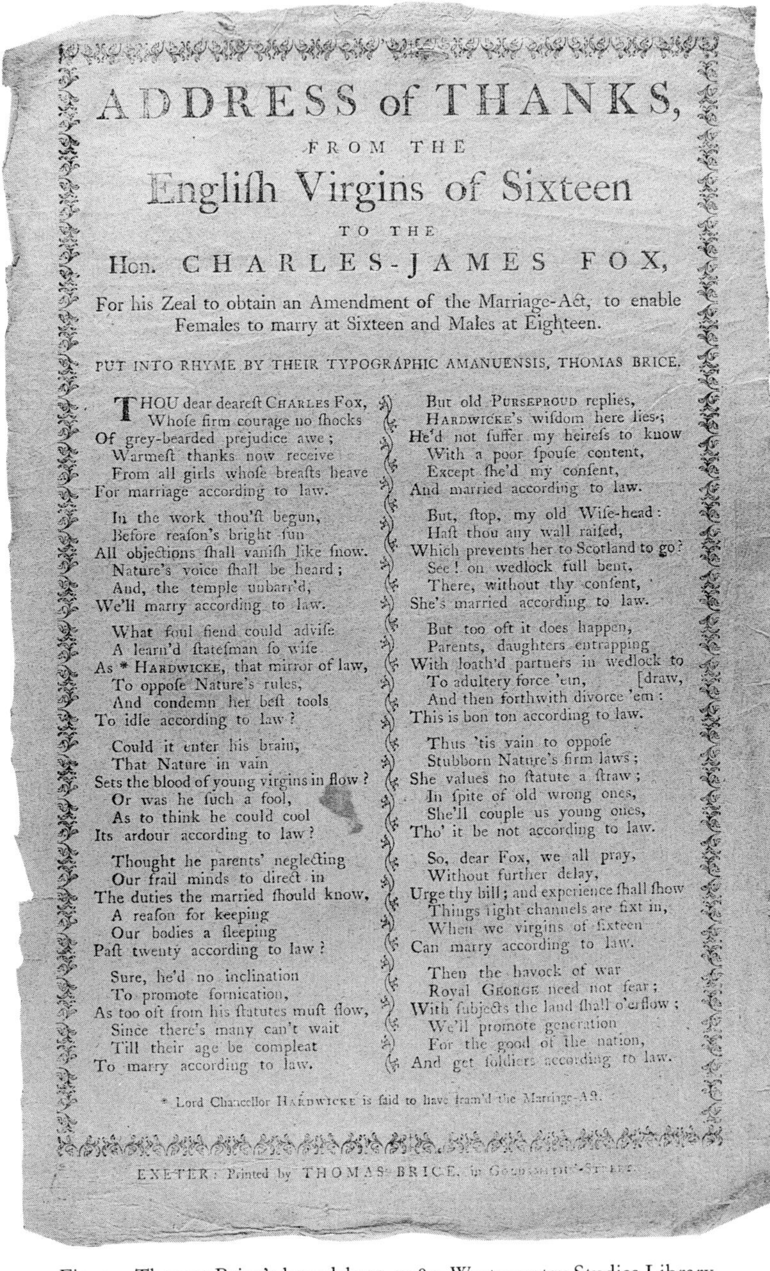

ADDRESS of THANKS,

FROM THE

Englifh Virgins of Sixteen

TO THE

Hon. CHARLES-JAMES FOX,

For his Zeal to obtain an Amendment of the Marriage-Act, to enable
Females to marry at Sixteen and Males at Eighteen.

PUT INTO RHYME BY THEIR TYPOGRAPHIC AMANUENSIS, THOMAS BRICE.

THOU dear dearest CHARLES FOX,
  Whofe firm courage no fhocks
Of grey-bearded prejudice awe;
Warmeft thanks now receive
From all girls whofe breafts heave
For marriage according to law.

In the work thou'ft begun,
Before reafon's bright fun
All objections fhall vanifh like fnow.
Nature's voice fhall be heard;
And, the temple unbarr'd,
We'll marry according to law.

What foul fiend could advife
A learn'd ftatefman fo wife
As * HARDWICKE, that mirror of law,
To oppofe Nature's rules,
And condemn her beft tools
To idle according to law?

Could it enter his brain,
That Nature in vain
Sets the blood of young virgins in flow?
Or was he fuch a fool,
As to think he could cool
Its ardour according to law?

Thought he parents' neglecting
Our frail minds to direct in
The duties the married fhould know,
A reafon for keeping
Our bodies a fleeping
Paft twenty according to law?

Sure, he'd no inclination
To promote fornication,
As too oft from his ftatutes muft flow,
Since there's many can't wait
Till their age be compleat
To marry according to law.

But old PURSEPROUD replies,
HARDWICKE's wifdom here lies;
He'd not fuffer my heirefs to know
With a poor fpoufe content,
Except fhe'd my confent,
And married according to law.

But, ftop, my old Wife-head:
Haft thou any wall raifed,
Which prevents her to Scotland to go?
See! on wedlock full bent,
There, without thy confent,
She's married according to law.

But too oft it does happen,
Parents, daughters entrapping
With loath'd partners in wedlock to
To adultery force 'em,   [draw,
And then forthwith divorce 'em:
This is bon ton according to law.

Thus 'tis vain to oppofe
Stubborn Nature's firm laws;
She values no ftatute a ftraw;
In fpite of old wrong ones,
She'll couple us young ones,
Tho' it be not according to law.

So, dear Fox, we all pray,
Without further delay,
Urge thy bill; and experience fhall fhow
Things right channels are fixt in,
When we virgins of fixteen
Can marry according to law.

Then the havock of war
Royal GEORGE need not fear;
With fubjects the land fhall o'erflow;
We'll promote generation
For the good of the nation,
And get foldiers according to law.

* Lord Chancellor HARDWICKE is faid to have fram'd the Marriage-Act.

EXETER: Printed by THOMAS BRICE, in Goldfmiths-Street.

Fig. 3   Thomas Brice's broadsheet, 1781. Westcountry Studies Library
(Devon Library Services).

date, and it may have been copied from a spoof advertisement which had found its way to the printer's shop.

Brice had previously tried his hand at putting into verse an extract from the *London Gazette* of 2 December 1780 in his *Remonstrance of the American officers* and doubtless a number of the anonymous pieces were his, particularly those with political content, such as *The Dutch answer to the British manifesto*, a quarter sheet of verse which probably appeared in 1781 and seems quite sympathetic to the Dutch. Whoever the authors, political comment was seldom far away in such poetical effusions and the authors must have assumed that their readers would have a fair degree of interest in, if not knowledge of, events in the world outside Devon.

More than one-fifth of 18th-Century single sheet items produced in Devon are totally in verse, perhaps an indication that the broadsheets would be declaimed to an audience by the running patterer or chaunter, or read aloud by the subsequent purchaser. This verse includes much political literature, some of it highly controversial. In 1754, for example, Mark Farley was sentenced to one year's imprisonment for printing a seditious song on the anniversary of the Pretender's birthday.[24] At times the verses form only part of the broadsheet and are followed by an explanation of the events which had inspired them. Several sheets on Rodney's naval campaigns in the early 1780s are examples of this. *Rodney's complete victory over the French fleet*, a half sheet printed by Thomas Brice in 1782, has sixteen four-line stanzas in two columns in the top half of the sheet in which Jove announces to the gods that he will assist Britannia to remain queen of the seas. The political jibes sit awkwardly with the Olympian imagery. In one stanza Jove declaims:

Take stout Hercules with you and charge him to scour
From wrong'd Britain its Augean filth;
Thro' Shelburne and Rockingham then I'll restore
To my island its glory and wealth.

The lower half of the sheet proceeds to explain the allusions in the verses to Rodney's defeat of the French off Dominica on 12 April 1782 with details of the ships in the French and English fleets, often with the numbers of their guns given.

Other poetry appears to be more purely sentimental in tone. There are half a dozen slip songs recorded for the 1780s, each with a crude woodcut heading the verses on the strip of paper. They include such plaintive offerings as *The Maid's lamentation on the loss of her shepherd* which appeared in 1782 with a woodcut of a shepherdess, and, dating from about 1785, a fragment of a slip song probably entitled *The lamenting shepherd*. In 1790 the same theme of lost love was being elaborated in *The Young Maid's complaint for the loss of her shepherd*.

Yet even these songs often had the background of current events. *The sorrowful lamentation of Miss Sarah West* which appeared in 1782 has Rodney's naval campaigns as its background. She 'lost her life with her sweetheart on board the formidable man of war commanded by the brave Rodney'. A few years later the new penal settlement in Australia forms the background to *Botany Bay, a new song*, and has as its first line 'My dear girl, I'm safe landed at Botany Bay'. Other songs in the same format, such as *Rodney triumphant and France humbled* which appeared in 1782 with a woodcut of a sailing ship, are more purely patriotic.

Popular sentimental literature could appear in prose too, as for example *Beauty's admirer; or, the lover in Cupid's snare*. The printer, probably Elizabeth Brice in about 1783 to judge by the apology for typographical style, explains: 'The following is a copy of a letter sent by Mr. W. . . to Miss S. . . upon seeing her at the Theatre'.

Besides liking to be shocked by execution broadsheets, informed by political tracts and touched by slip songs, the public wanted to be amused, and the printers were able to supply them with a wide range of humorous material. To modern eyes the most amusing aspect appears to be the names of the characters. In an eight-page half-sheet *The new mystery and art of gossiping* printed in about 1783 by Thomas Brice, 'in Goldsmiths'-Street; where travellers and shopkeepers may be supplied' we meet Mrs Chitchat, Ruth Keepcounsel, Madam Prateapace, Peg Babtongue and Johnny Smellsmock. In June 1782 Brice produced a half-sheet of mock-dramatic text printed in two columns on one side of the sheet entitled *The duellists, a farce, performed at the Theatre real, in Heavitree, last Monday* in which the *dramatis personae* are 'Nicholas Notchcheek a barber, and James Jockeywell a groom, boxing, attended by Matthew Muffin and Barnaby Burncake, two bakers, and a crowd of devout worshippers of Saint Monday'. Both items are peepshows into the daily life of the common sort in the gin-shop or in the street.

The occasional use of dialect would appeal to the country folk while having an appearance of quaintness for the better sort, as in the case of the *Exmoor scolding, in the propriety and decency of Exmoor language* which ran into many editions, or the broadsheet *A dialogue about the hairy man, which passed last Saturday between Goody Goosecap, Gaffer Coldpoll, and Farmer Slyfox, at Ide near Exeter* published about 1785. The printers were clearly cultivating a market among the labouring classes in the towns and countryside.

The burlesque elections which took over the inoffensive village of Ide, just outside Exeter after the parliamentary elections catered for a wider public. [25] At least nineteen broadsheets were printed for the Ide burlesque election in 1812 by Cullum, Trewman, Hedgeland and Besley, all of whom had printed for the parliamentary election. They presupposed an awareness of politics for there are allusions to personalities in the real election of 1812 when the Whig Samuel Colleton Graves stood for Devon against John Pollexfen Bastard and Sir Thomas Dyke Acland on a platform of peace and reform – a brave stand at the height of the Napoleonic wars. He polled only eight votes against the 823 of Bastard and 840 of Acland. One of the Ide broadsheets was signed by 'a Graves-Digger' which would be a cause of knowing laughter among those of the readers who had been following the elections.

In the years after the Napoleonic wars the foundations laid by the printers in the later 18th Century were built on; after a period underground, radical literature began to be circulated more openly. On 7 July 1819 the *Black Dwarf* printed a letter from an unnamed pamphlet-seller in Exeter who had fallen foul of the authorities:

On Monday I opened a shop in South Street, for the sale of political pamphlets on the side of reform, and exhibited the contents of the Dwarf, on the outrage of the magistrate. In a short time it met the eyes of the parties concerned; and I had sold but few of them, when an officer of the excise, and a constable, entered the shop, with a warrant, and arrested me, not for selling the pamphlets, but for a fine of ten guineas for having sold cider, without a licence, some months ago! They made a seizure on the goods, and took me before the mayor, (a terrible fellow this mayor!) at the guildhall. He said it would have been better had I never been born; that I had done more injury to the morals of this city than I could do good while I lived. I was forthwith committed to the new prison, which had been opened for the first time that morning. Some friends immediately came forward, and opened a subscription to pay the fine, which was done on the Wednesday. At about five I went to the Mayor to demand my goods, but he told me it was an unseasonable hour, and I must wait until the following morning. When I saw him in the morning, he stated the inaccuracy of some points mentioned in the Black Dwarf, and I promised they should be corrected. He then endeavoured to persuade me to decline selling the publications; in reply to which I told his worship that I was determined to persevere in the sale, as I had fortunately some enlightened and able friends to support me. I was desired to name them; but I did not feel it necessary to satisfy his worship. My goods were delivered to me again, and I recommence business to-morrow.

This incident is part of a continuing attempt to suppress radical literature in Exeter. The writer later refers to a shoemaker's premises which had been raided, but none of this appears to have ben mentioned in the local newspaper, the *Exeter flying post*.

In the 1880s the polymath vicar of Lew Trenchard, Sabine Baring-Gould, was scouring Devon for folksongs.[26] He soon found that the farmers and yeomen were not a suitable source for this type of material. All the songs they knew were such as had been published early in the 19th Century in song books or broadsheets. It was necessary to drop to a lower level (as he terms it) and seek out men that could neither read nor write. Many of the words Baring-Gould was hearing were corruptions of broadside ballads, the texts of which had been received by printers from itinerant singers who had received them orally, and he was often able to verify this from his large collection of printed ballads. He found the older folksongs, unadulterated by recent printed versions, among such informants as stonebreakers, road-menders, hedgers and thatchers in the remote fastnesses of Dartmoor or north Devon.

Popular culture at the start of the 19th Century, the formative years of Baring-Gould's informants, was an interesting mixture of printed and oral tradition. The village bard and travelling hawker were a prominent part of rural life, written and printed sheets were being posted around the towns and villages and pinned on tavern walls. The hustings were a time for speeches and printed squibs; during the assizes country yokels were snapping up execution broadsheets; each week newspapers were being read to interested groups and passed around the villages, as a disapproving Beavis Wood reports from Tiverton.[27] It was a period of active participation in the communication process, quite unlike today's passive acceptance of what the mass media pump at us. By the later 18th Century the mental baggage of common people in Devon was no longer exclusively made up of orally transmitted folklore, it was also weighted down with printed material. Since Elizabethan times hawkers must have penetrated the rural areas of Devon with its scattered hamlets but it was during the last decades of the 18th Century that the printing press began to reach the smaller towns in Devon, facilitating a much greater diffusion of a wide range of printed material among the folk in the villages and countryside. This literature began to broaden their horizons and prepare an eager market for the deluge of print which became available in the following century. It is not to the newspapers of the 19th Century that we must look for the birth of an informed public in Devon but to these earlier single sheets from the country towns.

References

1. *John Cheney and his descendents* (Banbury, 1936); Feather, John. *The provincial book trade in eighteenth century England* (Cambridge: Cambridge University Press, 1985), pp.105–6, ff.

2. Alston, R.C. 'A provincial printer at work, 1793–1800'. *Factotum*, 10 (Dec. 1980), pp.6–7.

3. Maxted, Ian. *Books with Devon imprints: a handlist to 1800* (Exeter: J. Maxted, 1989). Many references to individual titles in this paper can be explained by reference to this work. The published list contains a few more titles than are represented by the figures given in this paper, which was prepared some months before its publication.

4. Dickinson, M.G. 'Early Exeter printers and booksellers 1669–1741', *Devon and Cornwall Notes and Queries*, 29 (1962), pp.128–38.

5. Brushfield, T.N. 'Andrew Brice and the early Exeter newspaper press', *Transactions of the Devonshire Association*, 20 (1888), pp.178–9.

6. Hoskins, W.G. *Industry, trade and people in Exeter 1688–1800*, 2nd edition, (Exeter: University of Exeter, 1968), pp.129–31.

7. *Returns of newspaper stamps 1837–50*, House of Commons papers 1851 (42), vol. 17 pp.516–29.

8. Shower, Sir Bartholomew. *The substance of what Sir Bartholomew Shower spake at the Guild-Hall, Exon, August 19th, 1698* (Exeter: Printed by Sam. Darker and Sam Farley, 1698).

9. 'Exeter' (London: T. Woodfall, 1804). Aquatint (J.V. Somers Cocks. *Devon topographical prints 1660–1870: a catalogue and guide* no. 1000).

10. Deeble, W. 'The Guildhall, Exeter' (London: R. Jennings, 1829). Steel line engraving (Somers Cocks no. 984).

11. Sprake, C.J.G. 'Saint John's Hospital, Exeter' (Exeter: C.J.G. Sprake, 1831). Steel line engraving (Somers Cocks no. 892).

12. *The addresses, speeches, squibs, songs, &c. which were circulated during the recent general election ..., compiled by R. Cullum*, (Exeter: R. Cullum, 1818).

13. Wood, Beavis. *Georgian Tiverton: the political memoranda of Beavis Wood 1768–98, edited with an introduction by John Bourne* (Exeter: Devon and Cornwall Record Society, 1986), pp.134–6.

14. Brice, Andrew *The mobiad: or, the battle of the voice* (Exon: Brice and Thorn, 1770).

15. Davidson, James *Bibliotheca Devoniensis* (Exeter: Roberts, 1852), p.96.

16. Maxted, Ian. 'The little crawling pamphleteer', *Antiquarian book monthly review* vol. 13 no. 11, November 1985, pp.426–9.

17. *Monthly magazine* Aug. 1801, p.84.

18. *Monthly magazine* Jan. 1813, p.568.

19. *Brice's weekly journal* 17 Apr. 1752.

20. Maxted, Ian. '... a most laborious, dreadful and shocking murder ...' *Factotum occasional paper 3* (1983) pp.2–6.

21. *Brice's weekly journal* 17 Apr. 1752.

22. Cossins, James. *Reminiscences of Exeter fifty years since*, 2nd edition, (Exeter: William Pollard for the author, 1878), pp.40–1.

23. Coxe, Antony D. Hippisley. *The cannibals of Clovelly: fact or fiction?* (Bideford: Bideford Community College, 1981). This work includes a facsimile of a chapbook which rehearses a story probably originating in Galloway in Scotland.

24. Jenkins, Alexander. *The history and description of the city of Exeter ...*, (Exeter: P. Hedgeland, 1806), p.207.

25. *The spirit of election wit* (Exeter: Cullum, 1812).

26. Baring-Gould, Sabine. *Further reminiscences 1864–1894*, (London: John Lane, 1925) pp.184–215: 'Folk songs, 1887–88'.

27. Chalk, E.S. 'The circulation of XVIII-century newspapers' *Notes and queries*, vol 169 (1935) p.336.

Local Distribution Networks
in 18th-Century England

C.Y. FERDINAND

THE BODY OF THIS PAPER derives from two sets of material – first the manuscript archives of the Winchester-based *Hampshire Chronicle* for 1778 to 1783; and second the evidence of a run of the *Salisbury Journal* from its beginning in 1736 until 1785, when Benjamin Collins, the *Journal*'s main proprietor, died. Since the *Hampshire Chronicle* documents are so new and so important to the study of the 18th-Century provincial newspaper trade, it might be useful to start with a history of their discovery and the general implications of the find.

In their search for printed material in the Public Record Office in mid-1988, 18th-Century Short-Title Catalogue team members came across a box in the Exchequer records that contained a run of the *Hampshire Chronicle*.[1] Further investigation discovered that the *Chronicle* was only one exhibit in the case of Wilkes versus Collins. Accompanying the newspaper were a couple of its account books. More searching found another box with more account books and, in another section of the Exchequer archives, the plaintiff's Bills (or Interrogatories) with the defendant's Answers – both describing in slightly different versions how the newspaper was run. These, so far as is known, are the only 18th-Century provincial newspaper account books to have survived.[2] This is the only precise record there is of any country newspaper's methods of distribution, agent's fees, print runs, circulation figures, advertisement charges, returns, and so on; these documents are therefore of special significance to the study of the provincial newspaper trade in the 18th Century. Taken as a whole they provide a more complete, more accurate picture of the making and running of a moderately successful provincial newspaper than has hitherto been possible.

In August 1772 a schoolmaster-turned-bookseller, James Linden, established his *Hampshire Chronicle* in Southampton with the backing of other proprietors who, he claimed, were 'dispersed in many parts of the County, as well as other parts of the Kingdom'.[3] Now Benjamin Collins had considered Southampton and that whole port area to be *Salisbury Journal* territory since at least the 1750s – in fact Linden had found it useful to advertise in the *Journal* from 1759 and was himself one of Collins's newsagents by 1770. However, Linden's *Hampshire Chronicle* was a direct threat to the circulation of the *Salisbury Journal* and although Linden had timed his bid to coincide with temporary administrative difficulties in his competitor's office and boasted in 1773 that there had been a '*very great Increase of the Sale of the* Hampshire Chronicle',[4] he was no match for the experienced (perhaps it is not unfair to say unscrupulous) commercial-man Collins, and he was compelled to sell out in 1778.[5] On 18 May 1778 a partnership was formed by Thomas Baker (of Southampton), Benjamin Collins, his son Benjamin Charles Collins, and John Johnson (all of Salisbury), John Wilkes (of Winchester), and John Breadhower (of Portsmouth) to purchase the copyright of the *Hampshire Chronicle* from its bankrupt founder. Soon after the new partnership was formed under the slightly misleading name of T. Baker and Co. (for Baker soon dropped out of the venture and Benjamin Collins in fact held the controlling interest), the *Chronicle* moved to Winchester, partly because the more central location promoted more efficient distribution. This new proprietorship was dissolved 24 March 1783, and later in 1783 John Wilkes, the Winchester proprietor, brought a suit in the Court of Exchequer against his former partners. The partners' newspaper account books are preserved in the PRO as exhibits to this Exchequer case.

The Exchequer documents include:

(1) A weekly account of *Hampshire Chronicle* advertisements from 18 May 1778 to 19 May 1783 in four folio volumes;[6]

(2) A cash book covering 18 May 1778 to 24 March 1783;[7]

(3) An account book (Ledger B) for 1781 to 1783;[8]

(4) The marked-up office copy of the *Hampshire Chronicle*, 11 May 1778 to 31 December 1781;[9]

(5) Minutes of one meeting of the partners 23 November 1778;[10] and

(6) John Wilkes's Bills with Benjamin Collins's Answers.[11]

To describe them now in more detail: the advertisement books give a weekly account of all the paid advertisements in the *Hampshire Chronicle*, with details of who placed the order, the number of times the notice was to appear, the price paid, the account to which the charge was made, and the total weekly revenue from advertisements. Considered with the office copy of the newspaper itself, it is possible to deduce accurate rates for advertising and to tell whether reductions were offered to partners, to other members of the book trade, and for multiple advertisements. It is also possible to calculate the newspaper agents' total weekly allowances for soliciting advertising customers.

The cash book is a record of both cash payments made to the partners (usually for advertisements) and cash paid out on behalf of the partners. The entries on the 'paid out' side of the book are particularly illuminating. Expenses for training 'fresh newsmen' are recorded in a relatively discursive and informative style, as well as payment for the daily and weekly newspapers from which the *Hampshire Chronicle* – like other provincial newspapers – derived much of its own news, an express news delivery service (which it shared with the *Salisbury Journal*), editing and printing costs, the particular expenses of moving the newspaper from Southampton to Winchester in 1778, and miscellaneous expenditures for items like blank ledgers, paper, and cord.

Ledger B includes credit accounts for regular customers, the partners, the agents, and the newspaper itself. Only fairly conjectural figures for provincial newspaper circulation have been available until now: the Paper Account in Ledger B records exactly how many copies of the *Hampshire Chronicle* were printed each week from 24 September 1781 through 24 March 1783, and even includes the number of papers returned for credit, so it is possible to say precisely how many copies of a provincial newspaper were printed and sold each week. Corroborating evidence is found in the account of the exact quantity of paper bought and of how much of it was stamped.

The minutes of the 1778 meeting (which were fortuitously left in one of the account books) not only reveal that provincial newspaper proprietors employed local people to supply news, but also suggest that there were standard rates for such a service. (Thomas Baker in this case was to be paid 'the same Allowance . . . for furnishing Intelligence, as is allowed to him at Salisbury'.) Allowances for selling advertisements and for distributing the newspaper are discussed as well. Perhaps most important is the information that newspaper agents sometimes expected a salary in addition to a discount for their role in the distribution of a paper, giving a new dimension to the lists of agents compiled from the colophons of 18th-Century provincial newspapers.[12]

Because no provincial newspaper account books were known to exist, historians of the provincial newspaper usually have had to rely for evidence on the newspapers themselves (when the newspapers in fact survived). Another of the exhibits in the case of Wilkes versus Collins is a bound volume of the *Hampshire Chronicle* containing an unbroken run of more than three and a half years of the paper, corresponding to the dates of the account books. A complete run does exist in the present *Hampshire Chronicle* office in Winchester and is also available on microform,[13] but the advertisements in these 190 numbers in the PRO are marked in manuscript with details of how long the advertisement was to run and how much was paid for it: this evidently formed the working copy for the weekly advertisement account books. Copies in the *Hampshire Chronicle* office are clean. In addition, notices in the *Chronicle* for May 1778 give details of the transfer of ownership from James Linden to the new proprietors.

Finally the Bills and Answers clarify the roles the plaintiff and defendants (all of them partners from 1778 to 1783) had in purchasing the *Chronicle*, removing the paper from its home in Southampton to Winchester, printing it, and managing it.

These documents provide a uniquely detailed record of the commercial structure and administration of a country newspaper in the 1770s and 1780s. In spite of this uniqueness, they can be taken – with some reservations – as representative of other country newspapers of the time. The *Chronicle*, for example, was run by a group of proprietors who made critical decisions at a series of half-yearly meetings: group ownership and management by committee have been well documented for several London newspapers and is understood to have been the general practice in the capital.[14] (This has partly to do with the risks involved in setting up a periodical, partly to do with the model of the London congers, the groups of booksellers who joined together to purchase the copyrights in the more expensive, more profitable, riskier books; both the risks and the model of joint proprietorship would have held true in the provinces.) While group ownership of provincial newspapers has not been documented in the same way, their imprints imply that such arrangements existed.[15] Circulation figures documented for the *Chronicle* fit in with estimates for other 18th-Century country newspapers. The same is true for advertising rates, discounts for agents and other distributors, accounting practice, and so on – the account books and bills confirm much that is already known or speculated about 18th-Century provincial newspapers. But they supply the detail and the consistency that have been missing from other narrations.[16] The Exchequer documents provide a useful account of how one newspaper, the *Hampshire Chronicle*, worked, but even more important, in this case something is also known of its specific inter-relationship with another provincial newspaper, the *Salisbury Journal*, the copyright of which was also owned and managed by Benjamin Collins. All of this has a bearing on the mechanics of country newspapers and their distribution networks.

What can be said now about the distribution and circulation of country newspapers and other goods? First of all, that such matters were the life of the newspaper and had very much to do with its administrative structure. Without effective distribution the paper would lack credibility as an advertising medium, it would find few subscribers, and it would generate little income. The overall management of the *Hampshire Chronicle* was left to a series of proprietors' meetings that were scheduled at six-monthly intervals in different locations. It was at these meetings that decisions were made about just how the paper was to be distributed: who was to be employed to carry the bundles of newspapers to outlying agents and at what rates, what restrictions were to be placed on news-carriers, where agencies should be encouraged, who should train the newsmen who actually delivered the paper to subscribers, and so on. These same decisions had to be made for the *Salisbury Journal* of course, although the evidence points to a unilateral process – Benjamin Collins evidently took over sole proprietorship from his brother William in 1740 and continued in that style until 1770 when he sold shares in the copyright. (He bought them back about 1775.) In the case of the *Chronicle*, with its owners living about twenty miles from each other, it was necessary that one proprietor, the printer-bookseller John Wilkes in Winchester, take charge of daily maintenance, including printing and accounting. This was the top level of management for a country newspaper – either a single owner, or a group of booksellers and/or printers (usually) who joined together to run their investment.

The next level was composed of the paper's newsagents. These were other business people (frequently, but not always, booksellers, sometimes even proprietors of other newspapers) who agreed to organise local distribution. The proprietors of the *Hampshire Chronicle* were themselves expected to act in this capacity – in fact John Breadhower was invited to join the other proprietors, 'conceiving that many of such Papers might be distributed and sold at Portsmouth ... in Case they had a Partner residing there and interested in the Success of the said Undertaking'.[17] It had been generally understood that these were independent agents, whose income derived in part from commissions on the advertising they brought in and from discounts on the newspapers and other goods (particularly books and medicines) they sold through newspaper channels. The minutes of the first meeting of the *Chronicle*'s proprietors in November 1778 demonstrate that at least some of these agents expected a salary: for example, Thomas Baker of Southampton had charged the proprietors 'Five Shillings per Week for Agency' – unreasonably, they decided, although Baker was still allowed sixpence per dozen (the usual halfpenny each) to see that the *Chronicle* reached the customers.[18] The same document shows that some newspaper agents also furnished 'Intelligence' on a regular basis and were paid to do so. The Exchequer records list the agents by name, their locations, and numbers of papers distributed each week.

It is about this middle level of management – the newsagents – that there can be greatest discussion, for these men and women are the most readily documented. It was important that consumers know exactly where they could place their advertisements, subscribe to the newspaper, send literary and local news contributions, and pay on their accounts, so newsagents' names and addresses frequently appeared in long lists after the newspaper's imprint. They were mentioned in advertisements for books and medicines and they sometimes placed notices of their own. In contrast, at the level of ownership and then in the lower ranks of newsmen, carriers, and postboys, what might be called a hidden commercial infrastructure was in place. There were reasons to disguise the true ownership of a paper – Benjamin Collins, for example, was publicly anxious that the *Journal* be seen at all times to be a family-run, family-owned paper, and yet, because a Solicitor's Instructions Book has by chance survived in the Wiltshire Record Office, it is known that Collins sold shares in the *Salisbury Journal* to other Salisbury booksellers after 1770,[19] shares that he bought back in 1775.[20] Collins held a controlling interest in the *Hampshire Chronicle* from 1778 to 1783, yet he is never mentioned in the imprint, possibly because he also owned the competing *Salisbury Journal*, possibly because he may have helped to engineer the bankruptcy of the *Chronicle*'s previous proprietor. His involvement is known only through the Exchequer documents. And if there were ever any records of the lowest level of distribution, they would have been kept by the newsagents, but none of these accounts seem to survive. Certainly the existence of people who carried and cried

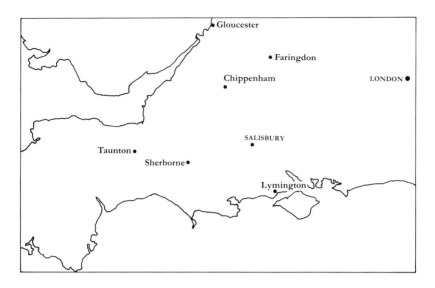

Map 1   *Salisbury Journal* agencies 27 February 1739

the newspaper is recorded and a good idea can be formed of what they did and when, but very few names and even fewer precise routes are known.

The newsagents' most significant role of course was in their efficient organisation and management of local distribution networks – they were the ones responsible for getting the newspapers, books, medicines, and related goods to the customers. By plotting the places from which they worked, the geographical area of distribution for a provincial newspaper can be described fairly accurately. There is some justification for using the lists of agents in this way, for a real correlation can be seen when sources of advertising are compared with locations of agencies; that is to say, provincial newspaper advertising usually originated in and around towns with news agencies, and it is certain that at least a few copies of the newspaper were distributed from these agencies each week.[21] Agents were an essential condition of a healthy income from advertising and subscriptions.

Fifty years of the *Salisbury Journal* provide a good example of how provincial newspaper proprietors, through their newsagents, shaped and reshaped an area of readership and distribution. Map 1, which shows the placement of *Journal* agents in February 1739, defines an expansive catchment area (averaging 57 miles from Salisbury), thinly populated by only seven newsagents outside of Salisbury. Its extent and shape were determined both by the times and by the commercial and personal contacts of William and Benjamin Collins. An agency in London was almost obligatory for a provincial concern with any hopes of success, for London was the main provider of books, medicines, stationery, and other commodities. Successful country booksellers, including those who set up news-papers, acted as entrepôts for such staple items, developing and servicing the local retail market in return for wholesale goods – this was an arrangement that made sound commercial sense for both parties.[22] In the case of the *Salisbury Journal*, the Collins brothers probably had no trouble deciding on Thomas Astley at the Rose in St Paul's Churchyard as their London agent, a bookseller with whom William Collins had been working for some years.[23] Then in Faringdon their agent was someone named Poole.[24] Although it is about 60 miles to the north of Salisbury, Faringdon was where the two Collins brothers were born and they still maintained connections there, notably with the Baldwin family. The Gloucester agency, in the person of Gabriel Harris,[25] might well have been set up in direct competition with Robert Raikes's well-established *Gloucester Journal*. In its first few years the *Salisbury Journal* openly competed with its Gloucester rival. This was particularly evident during the Melksham weavers' riots in 1738–9 when the two papers took opposite positions (Raikes supporting the weavers; and Collins – typically – supporting the clothiers).[26] But, as was often the case, competition gave way to co-operation, if not combination, and by 1755 Raikes had himself become a *Salisbury Journal* agent. There may have been a similar situation in Sherborne where the printer William Bettinson began publishing the *Sherborne Mercury* early in 1737, within months of the *Salisbury Journal*. The two towns are just over 35 miles from each other, so there was likely to be some initial competition, yet when the typography of the *Salisbury Journal* noticeably im-proved in October 1737, it was because Bettinson had taken over its printing. For a time the *Salisbury Journal* was in effect a local edition of the *Sherborne Mercury* and William Bettinson was a newsagent for the *Journal*.[27]

The placement of *Salisbury Journal* agents in 1739 suggests some of the factors involved in the establishment of a local distribution network. The proprietors' family and private business connections no doubt influenced the shape of the newspaper networks. And there were commercial forces at work of course: the relative lack of competition in the late 1730s allowed for an extended catchment area (Wiles lists under 25 country newspapers in operation in 1737).[28] As the provincial reading market was not fully developed, the potential subscribing population was scattered. The physical condition of the roads also had an influ-ence: communications had improved with the new bye- and cross-post services after 1720, but few roads in Wiltshire were turnpiked until the boom after 1750. Established commercial carrier networks also played their part.

After 1739 there was a gradual, almost uninterrupted, contraction and concen-tration in the network. As early as 1741 there was a clear indication of what was to become undisputed *Salisbury Journal* territory, the area to the north-west around Devizes, and there is a suggestion of a network extending to the coastal area south-east of Salisbury. Devizes was a great cloth centre and the roads round there, extensively used by the clothiers to dispatch goods, place orders, and

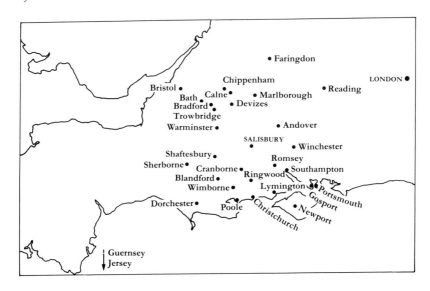

Map 2   *Salisbury Journal* agencies 24 October 1757

receive payment, were the first in Wiltshire to be turnpiked.[29] Devizes and Newport were important additions, for the agents there were to form a small consortium, or network-within-the-network, with Benjamin Collins in the 1740s: the names of Benjamin Collins, Thomas Burrough, who was a member of an important Devizes snuff and tobacco family, and Richard Baldwin junior in Newport, who was Collins's first apprentice and a member of the Faringdon and London book-trade family,[30] frequently appeared together at the head of lists of booksellers in trade advertisements and they evidently provided a higher level of service for each other than they did for other country colleagues.

John Newbery, who was associated in the early 1740s with the *Reading Mercury*, was a potential competitor, and yet he too became an agent for the *Salisbury Journal* in 1742, for his name appears in the list of newsagents after the imprint of 23 March for that year. Evidently the very close business and personal connections between Newbery and Collins led them to forestall unproductive squabbling over territory. These two booksellers collaborated in writing and publishing books for what was becoming a very profitable children's market; they bought and sold shares in copyrights from each other; and when Newbery died in 1767 his will included mourning rings for Benjamin Collins and two others.[31] 1742 also saw early attempts to set up an agency in the western port town of Bristol.

Lists of *Salisbury Journal* newsagents for 1746 and 1755 show similar attempts to establish a geographically broader subscribing market, with agencies in

Exeter, Oxford, Faringdon, Gloucester, and Bristol. Personal agencies in these distant towns apparently proved impractical, and they either disappeared from *Journal* lists, or gave way to coffee-house subscriptions. The inclusion of coffee houses in the network had certain commercial advantages – the number of newspapers provided each week might have been smaller than that sent to a bookseller-agent, but the problem of newspapers returned for credit probably would have been eliminated and potential advertisers would have had access to whole files of the paper at the coffee house. (And remember that advertising brought in most of the profits – a situation that holds true with newspapers even today.)

The map for October 1757 (Map 2) demonstrates the strong recovery of the *Salisbury Journal* after a Stamp Act in July that raised the duty on each copy of the paper by a halfpenny and on each advertisement by a shilling. Of course this was not a dull, news-less time of 'profound Peace', but the beginning of the Seven Years' War and public thirst for news overrode some of the effects of the new tariffs – just as the Government expected. Provincial newspaper editors could also make the most of the greater price-differential between the London papers and the weekly country papers – Collins was quick to point out that his *Journal*, with the best of the news culled from London and continental printed periodicals as well as from written sources, was far less expensive than any single London paper. A comparison between the agencies in 1755 (before the Stamp Act) and the agencies in late 1757 (after the Stamp Act) shows that in response to the greater demand for news, the trend towards concentrated and comprehensive distribution had accelerated.

Some time around 1770 Benjamin Collins sold shares in the *Salisbury Journal* to his former apprentice George Sealy and the local Salisbury printer John Alexander. He claimed to have bought back the shares in 1775. There seem to be signs in the disposition of network agencies between 1770 and 1775 that there were difficulties under the new management: for one thing the number of towns with newsagencies dropped from 30 in 1757 and 1770 to only 22 in 1773, rising to 25 in 1775. The Instructions Book mentioned earlier gives some support to that inference, for the solicitor concerned was acting on behalf of one of the temporary partners, who was trying to claim for debts incurred during those years.

By 1785 the lists of newsagents bear little evidence of the bumpy 1770s. When Benjamin Collins died early in 1785, the *Journal* had been under renewed family control for about ten years and there was a well-defined area of distribution, densely populated with 57 agents who were on average 29 miles from Salisbury. That is more than eight times the number of agencies in 1739, and concentrated in a much smaller area.

Conjectural circulation figures can give some idea of the scale of the *Salisbury Journal*'s market – after all one of the main aims of the newspaper proprietors in developing a distribution network was to encourage and service a local reading

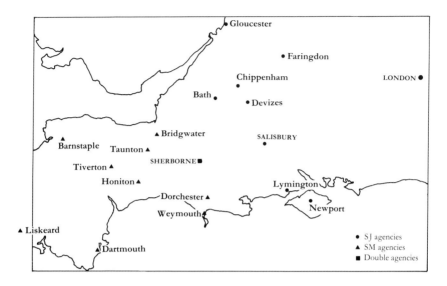

Map 3   *Salisbury Journal* and *Sherborne Mercury* agencies 15 December 1741

population. No exact numbers for *Journal* subscribers exist, but the commercial optimism of one very early Salisbury printer, Samuel Farley, may be noted: he thought that 200 subscribers would keep his *Salisbury Post Man* going in 1715. (It failed.) In the 1740s the *Journal*, which was a very successful provincial newspaper, probably had about 2000 subscribers, and perhaps 3000 in the late 1760s. By 1780 its proprietors claimed 'upwards of 4000'.[32] Obviously many more read the paper than bought it, although how many more will never be known.

That is part of the story of the *Salisbury Journal*'s distribution network in the mid-18th Century, and the same story might be told of other carefully managed provincial newspapers – an expansive, but diluted distribution network in the early part of the century when competition was not so fierce; and then a gradual reshaping as a natural catchment area was defined.

The evidence of Newbery and Bettinson suggests that it was commercially desirable to co-operate or combine with potential competitors in other towns, and the effect of these interactive tactics may be seen in the distribution networks of the *Sherborne Mercury* and the *Reading Mercury* relative to that of the *Salisbury Journal* at the same time. In both cases there was a division of territory into two distinct catchment areas, rather than an expensive struggle over the same market. William Bettinson distributed the *Sherborne Mercury* primarily from Sherborne west as far as Cornwall, leaving the area between Sherborne and Salisbury for Collins. Bettinson kept a *Salisbury Journal* agency and although Collins did not then reciprocate, Collins did concede Taunton to Bettinson, at least temporarily.

(*See* Map 3.) Likewise the *Reading Mercury*, already in business for 20 years and much the stronger of the two papers in 1743, allowed the *Salisbury Journal* to develop the area to the north-west around Devizes. The only overlap was in London and Oxford, as well as in Reading and Salisbury, where there were mutual agencies.

The story was different for the *Hampshire Chronicle* and its distribution network. By the time James Linden left off his *Salisbury Journal* agency to buy into the newspaper trade in 1772, provincial newspapers in general had multiplied and Southampton in particular, where Linden had been in business as schoolmaster and bookseller, had been an important part of the *Journal*'s market for at least fifteen years. (Newspaper owners in Reading could not have been happy to find a competitor in Southampton either, and Linden might well have been the anonymous 'frivolous, contemptible Fellow' against whom the editors of the *Reading Mercury* warned 'their candid Readers in a Certain Quarter of Hampshire' early in 1773.)[33] Linden probably saw an opportunity for himself in the difficulties the Salisbury paper was experiencing, and he seems to have felt that there was a genuine need for a Hampshire newspaper. The editor of the *Salisbury Journal* responded immediately, first by omitting the news of the *London Gazette* in order to pre-empt the new rival, and second by publishing a 'card' in the 17 August 1772 number of the *Journal*. It is worth quoting the card in full for what it has to say about distribution and advertising:

A CARD.

THE SALISBURY JOURNAL presents his most respectful compliments to his Readers in general, throughout the county of Hants, and hopes, as he has been their faithful servant for upwards of thirty years past, and punctually supplied them with the earliest and most authentic intelligence during the whole time, that they will take no part in the very unnecessary opposition forming against him, in one part of their county, but continue to give him their usual kind reception, and he will make it his constant endeavour still more and more to merit their favours.

** The SALISBURY JOURNAL is, without exception, the most extensive Country Paper in the kingdom, being circulated weekly by upwards of twenty distributors, (besides the mails, carriers, and other conveyances) in the most regular manner, throughout the counties of *Wilts*, *Hants*, and *Dorset*, part of *Somersetshire*, *Gloucestershire*, *Berkshire*, and *Oxfordshire*, the isles of *Wight*, *Purbeck*, *Jersey*, and *Guernsey*; and to numbers of Gentlemen residing out of the reach of the distributors, it is constantly sent by the post; also to some of the most public Coffee-houses in London; from whence it may reasonably be concluded there is not the least occasion for any other News-paper in this part of the kingdom, (so amply supplied already) on any pretence whatever, especially at a time of profound Peace, when there is so very little stirring, that even a single column of the SALISBURY JOURNAL would easily contain all the material news of the whole week.

Indeed to the Merchant, the Tradesman, the Manufacturer, and, in short, every Man of Business, the great number and variety of Advertisements in an old established Journal, are not only matter of amusement, but of real use, which a *new paper*, printed in a corner of the county, hemm'd in on one side by the sea, without any resource of country, but what is already supplied, on the other, can never attain to, as the inutility of advertising thererin is too obvious to need the least observation to be made thereon.

THE EDITOR.

Map 4 shows what the editor of the *Salisbury Journal* had against the *Hampshire Chronicle*. James Linden and Company were attempting to establish a readership within the *Salisbury Journal*'s south-eastern and eastern territory, as well as in the lucrative Bath market. There was even a *Hampshire Chronicle* agency in Salisbury just around the corner from the *Journal*'s printing office – not a collaborative arrangement with Collins and Company, but an apparently competitive agency in the person of Edward Easton II. In fact, of the sixteen towns from which the new *Hampshire Chronicle* was available, ten had well-established *Journal* agencies. The *Salisbury Journal* fought back with new agencies in Stockbridge, Whitchurch, and Cowes to reinforce its network by 1775.

Yet the area Linden staked out for his *Hampshire Chronicle* was a manageable one and, in spite of what his Salisbury antagonist had to say, the location in Southampton had certain advantages – he could dispatch the paper early to the Isle of Wight by the packet boats, thus arriving ahead of the *Salisbury Journal* there (later the packet boats were to take the *Chronicle* to Jersey and Guernsey); he had quicker access to port news; he retained connections with London in the book-sellers Bedwell Law and George Robinson, and in several coffee houses; and his distribution network could ensure that his nearby subscribers received news and goods before those of the *Salisbury Journal*. So Linden answered the Salisbury editor with a card of his own, thanking him for 'the very polite and unsolicited manner in which he has advertised the HAMPSHIRE CHRONICLE' and hoping that his own claims of a broad network 'will obviate any idle and frivolous cavils as to the place of Publication'.[34]

For a time Linden appeared to be successful. He was advertising for more distributors within a year;[35] his agency towns increased to 22 by 1775; and, while his agents did include a baker, a tallow chandler, a dealer in rum, and a couple of innkeepers and shopkeepers, at least half of them had book-trade connections, which may be viewed as a healthy sign.[36] But by May 1778 Linden was bankrupt and, far from being reconciled by having ready buyers (that is Collins and Company) for his 'Property, right and title of printing and publishing [the *Hampshire Chronicle*] ... together with the Printing Materials',[37] he remained defiantly in Southampton with plans to begin a rival paper of the same name. The Exchequer documents offer some explanation for Linden's resentment; for

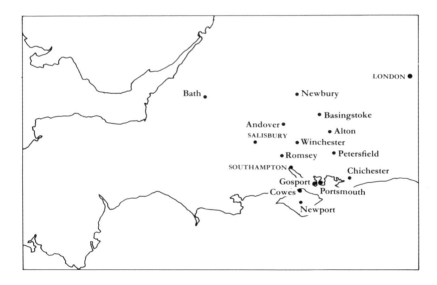

Map 4   *Hampshire Chronicle* agencies 24 August 1772

example the new owners were able to buy the business at a knockdown price because Linden's legal agents had delayed the sale. No doubt Linden was also behind the 'several unfavourable reports . . . industriously propagated relative to the sale of the said Paper'.[38]

What is known of Linden's agents – namely their numbers, names, and addresses – is derived primarily from the first six volumes of the *Hampshire Chronicle*, for the account books for those years have not survived. More about the agents can be discovered under the new management in 1778. In fact the agents are the group best represented in these records. For example the account books record exactly how many papers each agent received each week, and how many were returned for credit each half year. The numbers varied considerably from agent to agent and even within the same agency. J. Blake in Southampton (Thomas Baker's replacement) took about four dozen stamped *Chronicles* each week and at least that many blanks.[39] His allowance was 6*d.* a dozen for the duty-paid papers, twice that for the blanks. He also made a commission on advertisements, 3*d.* each for 118 in the first half of 1782. J. Blanch in Arundel started out in 1781 with a dozen papers weekly, then eight papers, then only six, of which three dozen and eight papers were returned for the half year. One can only hope that his bookselling business brought in more income. William Dawkins of Gosport, who ran the circulating library, stamp office, bookbindery, stationer's and bookseller's shop, and medical supply in the High Street there, distributed from four to six dozen *Chronicle*'s each week in the early 1780s. He was also paid for furnishing news, at a guinea per half year. It is no surprise to find the enterprising Dawkins among the *Salisbury Journal* agents too. Elizabeth Martin in Waltham took the lowest number – eight papers a week in 1781, only four in 1782 – yet she seemed to know her market well; only six papers were returned for credit in a six-months period. The papers distributed through the agents can be measured against production figures for the *Chronicle* as a whole.

In the early 1780s Wilkes generally printed editions of between 1050 and 1100, plus usually 51 or 56 blanks, according to Ledger B. An extra 200 copies, probably for casual sale, were printed of the 11 November 1782 issue, which brought news via a *London Gazette Extraordinary* of the success of the new British-invented red-hot shot used to fire the Spanish ships besieging Gibraltar. All newspapers that were sold were required to be printed on paper bearing a stamp that represented duty paid to the government (after 1757 this amounted to $1\frac{1}{2}d$. per sheet). The stamp-duty accounts in Ledger B give corroborative evidence of edition size. Sales of the *Chronicle* had dropped as low as a decidedly unprofitable 500 in 1779, which may have been a result of competition from James Linden's re-entry into the market with his short-lived rival *Hampshire Chronicle*. But by the 1780s Wilkes and his partners were back to circulation figures of over 1000. This, along with advertisement sales and competent management, should have been sufficient to produce a reasonable income. The production figures do not vary by much in the early 1780s, which indicates some stability, and of the 56,193 newspaper stamps paid for between 18 March 1782 and 17 March 1783, less than 2% were returned by the agents for credit. (56,193 divided by 52 weeks gives a weekly figure for stamped papers of 1080.)

Intermediate between the printing office and the outlying newsagents were the distributors. In a general sense anyone who saw to the dispersal of newspapers, including newsboys, agents, carriers, and postmen, was a distributor, but in this particular sense is meant the men who carried bundles of newspapers from the source to the retail agents by whom direct local distribution was then organised. (The distinction is one that was sometimes, but not always, made in the 18th Century.) Information on distributors is almost as scarce as that for the newsmen, since the whole system could run efficiently without the consumer even knowing that distributors existed. While lists of distributors were never published in the papers, their activities would have been recorded in the proprietors' account books. The *Hampshire Chronicle* documents provide the examples of R. and W. Fry: R. Fry made weekly journeys to Poole (about 42 miles from Winchester), dropping papers at Mr Feltham's in Ringwood, Mr Abbet's in Lymington, and Mr Rule's in Poole; W. Fry, who must have been related, made journeys to Sussex (about 38 miles from Winchester) with deliveries to Mr Stapley in Havant and Mr Jaques in Chichester, as well as to an unidentified, unlocated Mr Colebourne. (There was a Mr Colborne working for the *Salisbury Journal* in 1783, but he was based in Sturminster Newton, which is not in the direction of Sussex.) In the early 1780s R. Fry carried from as few as nine dozen and six papers to as many as fifteen dozen five, averaging around twelve and a half dozen. W. Fry delivered only about three dozen papers a week at the end of 1781, but in 1782 he regularly took ten to twelve dozen, and once, in November 1782, he set out with fourteen dozen and eight. They each received a guinea per trip, but apparently did not benefit from a discount on papers delivered; rather it was the agents who could in effect buy the *Chronicle* wholesale at 2½*d.* to retail at 3*d.* Commercial and private carriers, whose distribution networks had long been established, sometimes acted as newspaper distributors too.

Many provincial proprietors also employed an express service to bring the papers and other news from the capital to the local printing offices. While the express riders had little to do with local distribution, it was they who bolstered the country papers' claims to circulate the 'freshest advices' to their readers, sometimes even in advance of the London papers. (This situation existed because some of the London thrice-weeklies, geared to a provincial market, were sent out by the country post before they were issued in London.) The *Salisbury Journal* had used an express service for some time, something that is known because Collins had published apologies for delays – once when his rider had stayed on for additional important news and another time when the rider had dropped his newsbag in the dark and had to turn back.[40] But such services cost money and Collins made certain that his readers knew about this additional expenditure when a tax-propelled price rise was imminent. When Collins and Company became involved in the *Hampshire Chronicle*, the two papers shared these expenses. Benjamin Collins, the most experienced of all the partners, seems to have organised delivery from London, and the account books record half-yearly payments to him 'for bringing Express' at 13*s.* 6*d.* a week. There are also payments of £6 10*s.* to A. Morley in Basingstoke for 'carrying Express 26 weeks' (that is 5*s.* a week) – he probably met the London-to-Salisbury rider to take the London news on to Winchester.[41]

At the lowest level of newspaper distribution were the newsmen, postmen, and carriers who actually delivered the papers to readers. Newsmen were employed directly by the newsagents to deliver the papers and items advertised in the papers, around a circuit designed to meet the needs of local subscribers. They often worked exclusively for one newspaper: because of the potential conflict of interest between Benjamin Collins's two papers, the *Salisbury Journal* and the *Hampshire Chronicle*, it was stipulated that newsmen carry one paper or the other, but not both, at least not without permission. Similar exclusive arrangements held true for other provincial papers. It seems that, in general, a halfpenny *in all* was allowed by the proprietors for local distribution, not counting the costs of long-distance carriage (like the guinea a week to the Frys, or whatever postage was required to get the paper to those 'gentlemen residing out of reach of the distributors'). This probably means that the agents received allowances on the papers, medicines, and books they handled, out of which they paid their newsmen a small wage for walking or riding a prescribed route each week. Occasionally one finds in provincial newspapers the promise of a halfpenny allowance to the neighbour who arranged to collect the newspaper at an agreed location for those out-of-reach gentlemen. While none of the accounts in the Exchequer documents have been connected with newsmen, the records do provide incidental information about this level of distribution. For example, the proprietors paid 4s. 6d. each for leather newsbags; and in 1783 it cost 4 guineas in horse hire and other expenses for one 'Journie with fresh Newsmen to shew them the Road', which shows that on-the-job training was included. The proprietors, newsagents, and consumers must have preferred the tailored delivery service provided by dedicated newsmen, but no 18th-Century newspaper distribution network was able to find every potential subscriber. Sometimes the post office, with its comprehensive national delivery system, incidentally conveyed newspapers, especially to those subscribers who lived well out of the newspaper networks. And it must have been useful for country proprietors to include postmasters among their agents. But customers were usually expected to foot the bill for postal delivery, at least until newsagents lke William Tayler in London began to offer subscriptions to major newspapers on a postage-free basis. Likewise customers who had their papers sent by commercial or private carrier would expect to pay an additional fee.

The distribution network of a provincial paper – developed by its proprietors, organised at a local level by its newsagents, and activated by numerous distributors, newsmen, carriers, and postmen – was integral to its administrative structure. The system was designed to move goods, particularly newspapers, books, and patent medicines, from the printing office to the consumer. When a distribution network was well-run and effective, the newspaper, it seems, had a good chance of surviving profitably – but perhaps more important, these systems meant that country readers for the first time had regular, *easy*, weekly access to books, pamphlets, and newspapers.

References

1. I am grateful to Geoffrey H. Martin, former Keeper of Public Records, for notifying me of the find.
2. Other related account books do exist: there is the bookseller John Clay of Daventry, whose records for different periods between the 1740s and 1780s are being investigated by Jan Fergus and Ruth Portner (see their 'Provincial Bookselling in 18th-Century England: The Case of John Clay Reconsidered', *Studies in Bibliography*, 40 (1987), pp. 147–63; and late 18th-Century day books and ledgers survive

for John Cheney and Sons of Banbury (*John Cheney and His Descendants: Printers in Banbury since 1767* (Banbury: Privately printed, 1936)). But neither business produced a newspaper. There are substantial records for several 18th-Century London newspapers, for example the *Grub Street Journal*, the *General Evening Post*, and the *St. James's Chronicle*, which Michael Harris, among others, has examined (see Michael Harris, 'The Management of the London Newspaper Press during the Eighteenth-Century', *Publishing History*, 4 (1978), pp.99–100, and his *London Newspapers in the Age of Walpole* (London: Associated University Presses, 1987)). A set of books particularly relevant to the provincial newspaper press that might still be around are those for Christopher Etherington's *York Chronicle* – they were discussed by Robert Davies in his *Memoirs of the York Press* (1868), but seem to have disappeared since then.

3. *Hampshire Chronicle*, 24 August 1772.

4. *Ibid.*, 31 May 1773.

5. For a study of Benjamin Collins see C.Y. Ferdinand, 'Benjamin Collins, the *Salisbury Journal*, and the Provincial Book Trade', *The Library*, 6th ser. 11 (1989), pp.116–38.

6. Public Record Office (PRO), E. 140/90.

7. *Ibid.*

8. PRO, E. 140/91.

9. *Ibid.*

10. Found tucked into Advertisements volume, PRO, E. 140/90.

11. PRO, E. 112/1959/147.

12. The main index entry for this subject is 'Agents, lists of' in Roy Wiles, *Freshest Advices: Early Provincial Newspapers in England* (Columbus: Ohio State University Press, 1965); information on newspaper agents has a similar basis in lists published in newspapers in G.A. Cranfield, *The Development of the Provincial Newspaper 1700–1760* (Oxford: Clarendon Press, 1962), pp.192, 198–200, 202.

13. I am grateful to Steve Robinson, present editor of the *Hampshire Chronicle*, for allowing me to consult early numbers of the newspaper.

14. Harris, *London Newspapers*, pp.65–81.

15. Roy Wiles, for example, lists almost 40 pre-1760 partnerships in the index to *Freshest Advices*.

16. Wiles's *Freshest Advices* and Cranfield's *Development of the Provincial Newspaper*, both classic studies, are anecdotal in part.

17. James Linden in the Bills and Answers, PRO, E. 112/1959/147.

18. Minutes, 23 November 1778, PRO, E. 140/90.

19. Wiltshire Record Office (WRO), 761/1. I am grateful to K.H. Rogers, Wiltshire County Archivist, for locating the Instructions Book.

20. Collins himself claims that he bought the shares back in 1775 in the Bills and Answers, PRO, E. 112/1959/147.

21. For example, a comparison of the places of origin for educational advertisements in the *Salisbury Journal* with locations of newsagencies shows a high correlation between the two. However, it should be remembered that agents were not always

listed in the *Journal* – sometimes years passed with no printed notice for agents.

22. John Feather discusses this relationship in his *The Provincial Book Trade in Eighteenth-Century England* (Cambridge: Cambridge University Press, 1983), pp.1–11.

23. Collins and Astley are associated in the imprint of William Diaper's *Brent: A Poem* [1732?], which was 'Printed for William Collins at the Bible and Crown in Silver Street, and sold by T. Astley and R. Baldwin, London'.

24. N. Poole appeared in the *Salisbury Journal* imprint from 1739 to 1742 and later in the 1750s. Poole is not otherwise identified.

25. Evidently the bookseller Gabriel Harris, Jr., probably son, partner, and successor of Gabriel Harris, Sr., who had worked in Gloucester from at least 1702 to 1738. (See H. R. Plomer, *A Dictionary of the Printers and Booksellers Who Were at Work in England, Scotland and Ireland from 1726 to 1775* (Oxford: Oxford Bibliographical Society, 1932), p.116).

26. Wiltshire weavers rioted against their employers in late 1738, causing a good deal of property damage. Three of the weavers were later hanged. Public opinion was divided on the issues, with the *Salisbury Journal*'s editors taking the side of the clothiers and the *Gloucester Journal*'s editor the weavers' side – this local coverage was picked up by the national press.

27. William Bettinson called himself a printer from London, but evidently did not serve a formal apprenticeship there (he does not appear in McKenzie's *Apprentices*). He was listed after the *Salisbury Journal*'s imprint from 27 February 1739 to 23 March 1742.

28. Wiles, *Freshest Advices*, Appendix B: Chronological Chart.

29. Beginning 1706–7 with the Act of 6 Anne c. 26.

30. For the Baldwin–Collins connections see C.Y. Ferdinand, 'Richard Baldwin Junior, Bookseller', *Studies in Bibliography*, 42 (1989), pp.254–64.

31. The two others were Dr Robert James, the man behind James's Fever Powder, and Thomas Greenough of Greenough's Teeth Tinctures. With Collins, who had invented a Cephalic Snuff, and Newbery, who marketed patent medicines, they must have formed something of a medicinal network.

32. Printed *Salisbury Journal* receipt, Salisbury and Wiltshire Museum, Salisbury.

33. *Reading Mercury*, 22 March 1773, quoted in K.G. Burton, *The Early Newspaper Press in Berkshire (1723–1855)* (Reading: For the Author, 1954), p.81.

34. *Hampshire Chronicle*, 24 August 1772.

35. *Ibid.*, 3, 31 May 1773.

36. The imprint for 3 July 1775 reads in part: 'ADVERTISEMENTS for the Paper are taken in by B. LAW and G. ROBINSON, Booksellers, and at the *Chapter*, London, and *Peele*'s Coffee-Houses, LONDON; likewise at the following Places:

[In four columns] At WINCHESTER, Mr. *Greenville*. PORTSMOUTH, Mr. *Carr*, Printer. GOSPORT, Mr. *Breadhower* and Mr. *Douglas*. CHICHESTER, Mr. *Humphry*, Bookseller. SALISBURY, Mr. *Easton*, Printer.

At DEVIZES, Mr. *Burrough*, Bookseller. PETERSFIELD, Mr. *Richardson*, Baker.

ALTON, Mr. *Roe*, Bookseller. BASINGSTOKE, Mr. *Ring*, Grocer. ANDOVER, Mr. *Painter*, Shopkeeper.

At NEWPORT, (Isle of W.) Mr. *Sturch*, Stationer. WEST COWES, (Do.) Mr. *Maynard*, Innkeeper. ROMSEY, Mr. *Brookman*, Dealer in Rum. LYMINGTON, Mrs. *Beeston*, Stationer. HAVANT, Mr. *Stapley*, Bookseller.

At PORTSMOUTH COMMON, Mr. *Harmood*. READING, Mr. *Knight*, Tallow-Chandler. POOLE, Mr. *Lander*, of the Custom-House. FARNHAM, Mr. *Cooke*, Bookseller. CALNE, Mr. *Savary*, at the *Catherine-Wheel*.

37. Notice of the sale of the *Hampshire Chronicle* to 'Mess. BAKER and Co.' in the *Chronicle*, 18 May 1778.

38. *Hampshire Chronicle*, 18 May 1778.

39. Blanks in this case were probably duty-free newspapers intended for the Channel-Island market (with thanks to John Palmer for the suggestion).

40. *Salisbury Journal*, 27 October 1760, 25 March 1765.

41. The evidence suggests that this 'shared' arrangement meant that the *Chronicle* partners paid for the London-to-Salisbury express, as well as for the Basingstoke–Winchester connection, which would have provided in effect a free service for the *Salisbury Journal*.

Egerton Smith and the
early 19th-Century book trade in Liverpool

MICHAEL PERKIN

ON FRIDAY 5 July 1811, there appeared on the streets of Liverpool the first number of a new weekly newspaper, the *Liverpool Mercury*. Priced at seven pence per copy, it was a paper to be 'conducted upon liberal, yet steady, principles', and in most respects it was a typical product of its time. The first number consisted of eight pages set in three columns and contained: an essay on parliamentary reform; 'an impartial transcript of the opinions of the day' extracted from 'the principal of the London and provincial papers'; literary and political correspondence; ship news, lists of vessels arrived, a meteorological diary and tide tables (prominent in all seaport newspapers); miscellaneous extracts from modern voyages and travels; natural history; local verses; births, marriages and deaths; markets; and notices to correspondents. Occasional small woodcuts (ships, inventions, etc.) broke up the text. Publication in volume form with an index proved to be very successful. (*See* Fig. 1) In 1815, 'the no. of sets is not surpassed by any other provincial newspaper or metropolitan'. The indexes 'being printed on unstamped paper cannot be forwarded under frank post free' and were hence sent by canal or coach. By 1820, the distribution pattern had largely been established in the chief towns of the north of England, with agencies in the Midlands, London, Dublin, Edinburgh, Glasgow and North Wales. And by 1855, according to the Stamp Returns after the *Act to amend the laws relating to the Stamp Duties on newspapers and to provide for the transmission by post of printed and periodical publications*, the circulation of the *Liverpool Mercury* was 912,000 copies, well above its nearest county paper rival, the *Leeds Mercury* at 735,000, and only exceeded by the *Dublin Telegraph* among the Welsh, Scotch, Dublin and Irish county newspapers.[1] The chief proprietor, printer, publisher and editor of the *Liverpool Mercury* from its foundation in 1811 until his death in 1841, was Egerton Smith, the main subject of this paper. But in this account I make no claim that his newspaper and related business activities were essentially any different, except in local circumstances, from those of many other successful editor/ proprietor businesses starting from small beginnings in the late 18th and early 19th Centuries, for example James Simmons of the *Kentish Gazette*, Robert Raikes of the *Gloucester Journal*, William Cowdroy of the *Manchester Gazette*, and many others. Moreover the *Liverpool Mercury* was by no means Liverpool's first newspaper.

In fact it was Liverpool's first printer, Samuel Terry, who printed some ten books from 1712 to 1720, who also produced its first newspaper, *The Leverpoole Courant* in 1712, of which no copies are now extant. Without any doubt the most successful printers in Liverpool – and I think this is probably true for most English provincial towns in the 18th and 19th Centuries – were those who developed their businesses around the printing and publishing of local newspapers, which in their turn became the chief agencies for the distribution of London books in the provinces. But the next newspaper to be published in Liverpool was Robert Williamson's *Liverpool Advertiser*, first issued in 1756. This yawning gap of 44 years, and the fact that there was very little printing of any kind in Liverpool in the period, is perhaps best explained by the steadily increasing burden of the Stamp Acts of 1712 and 1725 on small provincial printers. Adam and John Sadler were the first printers with a business of any size in the town. John, the more active son, printed *The Liverpool Chronicle and Marine Gazeteer* from 1757–9, and some 58 books and pamphlets from 1740 to 1765. Robert Williamson has aleady been mentioned: his *Liverpool Advertiser* has claims to be the first provincial newspaper to concentrate on shipping, trade and commerce. Another printer, John Gore, began his rival paper, the *Liverpool General Advertiser* in 1765 and continued both to print and publish it up to his death in 1803. He was succeeded by his son Johnson Gore who published the first Liverpool street directory in 1766, a sequence which has continued under various names up to the present day. Liverpool's most eminent printer, John M'Creery, set up his press in Tyrer Street in 1792, or possibly 1791, and printed about 98 titles there, including books by and for William Roscoe which contain some of his finest typography. He left for London in 1805. Earlier in 1799 Jonah Nuttall, the founder of one of Liverpool's most successful printing and publishing firms, was established in the town, and by 1818 the firm of Nuttall, Fisher and Dixon at the Caxton Press was one of the largest publishers of part-books in the country before the disastrous fire of 7 February 1821 completely destroyed their presses and stock. But apart from Thomas Kaye's effective *Liverpool Courier*, started in 1808, which will be mentioned later, virtually all the remaining fifteen or so Liverpool papers appearing before the establishment of the *Mercury* in 1811 were very short-lived and most of them were trade sheets, maritime or commercial publications.

But to turn now from this thumbnail sketch of the early history of the Liverpool book trade to the particular.[2] It would be wise to identify the person in my title. Egerton Smith was not the first of this name in his family. Book trade historians, I am sure, are not alone in regretting the unnecessary habit of naming sons after fathers without a thought for the problems it causes for future research workers! Egerton Smith I is first recorded in 1759 as continuing the school kept by his father William Smith, writing master. In 1765 he was living in Redcross Street, and in 1774 an address which became familiar – Navigation Shop, Pool Lane – occurs in the directories for the first time. It is probable that about this year he started his printing business, to which he subsequently added that of stationer

THE

LIVERPOOL MERCURY,

OR

COMMERCIAL, LITERARY, AND POLITICAL

Herald;

A WEEKLY PAPER, intended to be formed into a series of ANNUAL VOLUMES,

With a Copious Index to each.

VOL. I.

COMMENCING JULY, 1811,——TERMINATING JULY, 1812.

"SALUS POPULI LEX SUPREMA"

LIVERPOOL:
PRINTED BY EGERTON SMITH AND Co. 18, POOL-LANE

1812.

Fig. 1   The first volume title page of *The Liverpool Mercury*, 1812, with a woodcut vignette by Henry Hole, who worked on Bewick's *British birds*, and for John M'Creery in Liverpool.

and seller of mathematical instruments, charts and maps. We know that he employed a bookbinder in 1781, and that he lost printing equipment in the same fire that destroyed most of Henry Hodgson's stock in Pool Lane – fires at printing offices seem to have been very much an occupational hazard in the 18th and 19th Centuries. Egerton I died in 1788 and his business was carried on for about a decade by his widow Ann, at first on her own, and then with her sons Egerton II (the subject of this paper) and William. There then follows a bewildering series of partnerships over the next half-century and beyond. The evidence for them is derived from directories and newspaper announcements. We often know when partnerships terminated, less often when they were started. The evidence from surviving imprints sometimes confirms, occasionally contradicts, this information. From about 1803 to 1811 (probably after the death of their mother) Egerton II and his brother William were in partnership with Samuel Dawson, both in the stationery and optician's business. William, who died in 1817, left the partnership early as we find Egerton II and Samuel Dawson in partnership from July 1811 as Egerton Smith & Co., the name that recurs up to 1850 and beyond. But over the next 30 years Egerton Smith was also in partnership with F.B. Wright, Thomas Burgeland Johnson (who will figure prominently later in this paper), Moore Galway, James Melling, Edward Rushton (son of the better known blind poet of

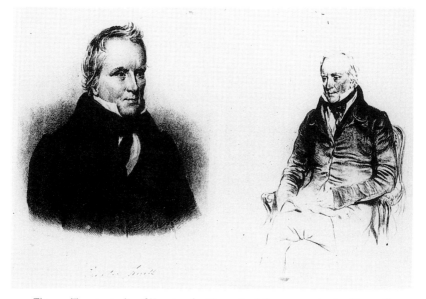

Fig. 2   Two portraits of Egerton Smith: on the left an engraving by Wagstaff after a drawing by Turmeau, undated but probably in the 1820s; and on the right a portrait drawn and lithographed by T. & W. Crane, Chester, probably near the end of his life.

the same name), Edward Melling, John Smith, Thomas Rogerson and William Cockrell Langly. This is but a simplified summary of the complex history of the Smith & Co. partnerships: suffice it to say that Egerton Smith had many varied connections with the Liverpool book trade throughout his business life.

What sort of man emerges from behind this dry record of a business career? The problem with many studies of the personalities in the provincial book trade is how to put flesh onto the bare bones of the facts available. (*See* Fig. 2.) A statue erected to Egerton Smith's memory in 1843 following a public subscription bore the following inscription: 'The indefatigable friend of humanity; the protector of the brute creation; the fearless assailant of oppression in all its forms; the advocate of the universal diffusion of knowledge, of free trade, of civil and religious liberty in every land.'[3] Perhaps some Victorian rhetoric appears here, but as I hope to show, to a considerable extent these claims can be justified by his public acts and publications. Concerning his private life, as I have indicated, the facts are few and far between. He was born, the son of Egerton and Ann Smith, on 19 June 1774 in Pool Lane. One can presume he was educated in Liverpool, but there is no evidence for this. The next hard fact he gives us himself in the *Mercury* of 24 August 1821: 'about the year 1789 I was bound apprentice to a printer, stationer and papermaker of some eminence, in Kendal in Westmoreland'. This master was James Ashburner, and Smith goes on to mention his fellow-apprentice, Michael Branthwaite, 'who now carries on business in the same spot'. If he followed the normal seven-years apprenticeship Egerton would have been back in Liverpool in about 1796, assisting in the family business. In 1820 he married Margaret Wood, who was from a well-known Norfolk family, and they had three daughters, one of whom, Lydia, died in 1828. Egerton's aunt, Mrs Elizabeth Fleetwood, who was possibly related to an earlier Liverpool printer, Robert Fleetwood, died at his house in July 1824 at the advanced age of 93.

Undoubtedly the single most important event in Egerton Smith's life was when he became, at the age of 37, the first proprietor of *The Liverpool Mercury, or Commercial, Literary and Political Herald*. He founded the paper, and here I quote from McMillan, his obituarist, 'not at the expense of his friends and supporters but at his own risk'.[4] And indeed the paper is still with us: it became a bi-weekly in 1847 and a daily in 1863. It was eventually amalgamated with the *Liverpool Daily Post*, which had been founded in 1855, to become, in 1904, the *Liverpool Daily Post and Liverpool Mercury*. The 'Commercial' part of the paper's original title was probably inserted to emulate the city's strong Tory newspaper, *The Liverpool Courier and Commercial Advertiser*, which had been founded by Thomas Kaye in 1808 and was an effective rival throughout the period of Egerton's editorship of the *Mercury*. As one of Liverpool's leading Whigs, part of Egerton Smith's object in founding the *Mercury* was undoubtedly to promote the cause of reform in the Reform Bill struggle.

The *Mercury* also had a central role in Egerton Smith's formation and running of the Concentric Society, a club for Whig intellectuals, and one of seven political clubs started in Liverpool between 1812 and 1830, most of which were aligned to the Tory or Whig factions.[5] It was founded in 1812 after the Liverpool elections and the *Liverpool Mercury* acted as its minute book, faithfully and sympathetically recording all its meetings and speeches. Other supporters in its early days were the Reverend William Shepherd and, until bankruptcy drove him out of politics, William Roscoe. The Society supported the Parliamentary candidature of radicals such as Lord Brougham and was much more active and responsive to domestic, national and other issues than the other Liverpool clubs. It ceased to meet quite suddenly in 1822.

After an unsuccessful attempt to launch another new journal, *The Gleaner*, in April 1817, which failed after two numbers because under the Stamp Act it was classed as a newspaper, Egerton Smith began another new publishing venture. On 28 July 1818 appeared the first number of *The Kaleidoscope, or Literary and Scientific Mirror*, a weekly journal of belles-lettres. The first series ran from 1818 to 1819, and a New Series from 1820 to 1831. Once again Egerton Smith was in sole control as editor, printer and publisher. It was to be 'a familiar miscellany from which religion and political matters are excluded' and it was conducted, Timperley later observed 'with very considerable ability'.[6] After twelve years of reasonable commercial success publication was suspended in September 1831 because of distribution problems. The editor complained that he could always command punctuality of delivery 'before the establishment of railways which have excluded from the various lines of the roads several of the ordinary coaches by which our parcels were, until lately, delivered with punctuality'. Several other factors contributed to the paper's demise: firstly, only one impression was possible because it was printed at the Mercury Office presses and the type had to be distributed soon after the first edition was printed off; secondly, being on unstamped paper it could not be distributed freely though the Post Office; and thirdly, even at local level it could not be sold freely on the streets except by a hawker with a licence.[7]

The *Kaleidoscope*, and to a certain extent the *Mercury*, were also outlets for Eggerton Smith's prolific ideas, inventions and enthusiasms of the moment. To take but a few examples: as early as 1830 he was an enthusiastic advocate of steam engines and railways. He recommended the use of fixed locomotives on canal banks to tow barges, an idea that was not actually tried out until 1890. He invented 'dead-lights' for use at sea; a cork life-saving jacket (he was both a notable swimmer and fencer); a new kind of metronome; and even a bicycle. He promoted baths and wash-houses, and publicised the merits of sea bathing by establishing a floating bath in the Mersey. This was moored off Prince's Pier Head and passage to it was by ferry boat. He also proposed an early form of fish farming with breeding ponds at New Brighton (not something that could be recommended today!) In the *Liverpool Mercury* for 1825 we find him advocating a road tunnel under the Mersey – a project not realised until 1934.

Egerton Smith's newspaper and journal were also the vehicles for his social concerns and philanthropic schemes. He was one of the first leading provincial journalists to denounce the negro slave trade: the West Indian slave-owning interest had tried to ruin his business in the early years. One of his schemes was for a 'Night asylum for the houseless poor' on which he published a pamphlet in 1832. This was first opened in 1816 and has claims to be the first of its kind in England. Warmth and shelter were provided for about 120 lodgers per night. Some years later it became an institution and continued to function until the amended Poor Law was passed making it to some extent redundant. Egerton was also one of the founders of the Strangers Friend Association, for aiding the destitute and visiting the poor in their own homes.

Other publications reflect his interest in education and language teaching. In the *Kaleidoscope* for 1824 there is a 'Report of the origin, progress and present state of the Liverpool Apprentices' and Mechanics' Library, by its originator, Egerton Smith.' This was started as a result of a letter he had received from a Mr Noah, Sheriff of New York, in 1821, recommending the formation of such a library on the plan of those established in New York and other towns in the United States in 1820. After obtaining the approval of a trade protection group, The Guardian Society, he procured a library room and an assistant, and his appeal for books in the *Mercury* was so successful that by 1824 he had about 1200 volumes and numerous pamphlets. In the same year the library was officially supported at a public meeting at which even Thomas Kaye of the *Courier* gave his approval for the scheme. Language teaching was the purpose of a book he published with Dominique Albert in 1831: *Hononymes francaises: or the French hononymous words arranged in sentences*; and in another collaboration with William Dolier he put forward a plan of education for the young backed up with a series of engraved copy-books published in Liverpool in 1828 and several times reprinted up to the 1840s.

In 1833 Egerton Smith printed and published in parts *The Melange, a variety of original pieces in prose and verse*. In the following year the parts were collected into a volume of 634 pages and Messrs Simpkin and Marshall the London booksellers were added to the imprint. The book contains pieces by Egerton largely culled from the *Mercury* or *Kaleidoscope*, but with, in addition, a curious moral fable entitled 'The Elysium of Animals', never before published. The narrator of this fable is a balloonist who is knocked by accident out of the car beneath his balloon and is carried through storm and cloud to a strange land where birds and beasts talk, mainly of their earthly sufferings. The straying balloonist is put on trial before a jury of animals with an elephant as judge. Some of the stories of witnesses – the horse, the bull, the bear, and so on – are described as having recently appeared in a paper. The balloonist is acquitted, but the human race is declared guilty. 'The Elysium of animals' created such a stir when it appeared that it was separately reprinted in London in 1836 at the request of the London Society for Promoting Rational Humanity towards the Animal Creation. McMillan, in his obituary,[8] describes how Egerton Smith had seen an emaciated horse in a heavily laden cart being cruelly beaten by its driver, and how he tried to intervene. In both the original edition and the London reprint of the fable there appears a folded plate of one of George Cruikshank's most powerful etchings, 'The knacker's yard', which must have contributed greatly to the moral indignation aroused by the tale. McMillan quotes a letter from the London Secretary of the Society to Egerton Smith: 'We are quite in despair respecting any success in Liverpool, yourself being the only individual who has expressed any lively interest in our success.' Egerton went on to become one of the founders of the Liverpool Society for the Prevention of Cruelty to Animals.

When we turn to survey the published output of a provincial printing dynasty such as Egerton Smith and Company over a period of more than 50 years we are faced with a number of restraints and difficulties. First, there would appear to be no surviving day-books, ledgers or accounts; secondly, the survival rate for minor material, pamphlets, reports, sermons, ephemera, etc., is lower than it is for books – and it is decidedly the minor material we are dealing with here; and thirdly, we do not have, and are not likely to have, a reliable method of recording the titles and details of books printed by provincial printers for publishers outside their area – since printers' imprints are carefully hidden in most 19th-Century books, and of course often do not appear at all. There are records for only eleven books printed by the Smith partnerships for London publishers, but there must have been considerably more than that. The number of books actually both printed and published in Liverpool amounts to only a few more; it is significant that a number of these were by subscription or paid for by their authors. The risk factor was still too high for large ventures. As one would expect, more than 90% of the titles recorded are in the pamphlet class. These can be roughly categorised as follows: concert and music-hall programmes and libretti (a surprisingly large class); local, official and political pamphlets (perhaps the provincial printer's main staple); religion and sermons (a predictably large group); scientific (mainly reflecting Egerton's interest in the navigation and optical instrument side of the business); society reports and meetings (again a large class); trials; education; medical tracts (especially towards the end of the period); and ephemera of all kinds. The business was largely, then, jobbing-work and printing to order. There is evidence of considerable competition among the Liverpool printers of this period over some regular jobbing contracts, such as the programmes for the Liverpool Musical Festivals, sacred music texts, play-bills, local elections, trials, and the Liverpool Tract Society and other Society publications. To take but one example: the printing of 'The accounts of the Corporation of Liverpool with their Treasurer.' This was for many years the preserve of John Gore and Son, the publishers of *Gore's Liverpool Advertiser*. In 1815 they produced a cumulative edition of the accounts for 1799 to 1815; in the same year a rival set was printed by Egerton Smith and Co. Gore and other firms jostle each other for the contract from 1816 to 1837; Smith and Co. finally get another chance – but only for one year, 1838, and other firms again competed until finally in 1845 Thomas Baines gained the contract.

Let us now turn to the technical side of the business where information is even more scanty. In the absence of records we have to rely on the occasional news item or advertisement. For example, we know that in July 1813 new printing types were acquired for the *Mercury*, and that a year later the engraving and copperplate printing side of the business ceased. In 1829 the Office contained two Imperial presses, a foolscap folio and a foolscap broadside obtained from Messrs Cope and Sherwin in Shoreditch. Another advertisement reveals that in 1832 Napier's Grand Patent Printing Machine, a steam press which could also be operated manually, was operated by hand to print off Mersey views and small hand-bills. By 1835 the business had obviously expanded, with the jobbing printing clearly separated off from the newspaper printing. An advertisement for this year announces considerable additions to the firm's great variety of types to enable book work, catalogues, circulars, cards, posting-bills and account books to be printed; and bookbinding, stationery and patent medicines were still part of the business. In 1838 the circulation of the *Mercury* averaged 6,488 copies per week, and this necessitated the purchase of a more efficient printing machine. The proprietors decided to have a machine constructed for them by Cowper's of Manchester, powered by a steam engine from Monteith, Gibb and Simpson of Liverpool.

Finally, to return to the firm's history, there is the extraordinary story of one of Egerton Smith's many partners, Thomas Burgeland Johnson. (*See* Fig.3.) Whether or not it is typical of Smith's relations with his partners in the book trade it is difficult to say since there is so little evidence about any of the others. Unlike Egerton Smith, Johnson achieved an entry in the *Dictionary of National Biography*. This was not on his merits as a printer or publisher but because of his, ultimately, successful career in London as a writer and publisher on field sports. The author of the *DNB* account merely records that he was 'a printer in Liverpool who after taking to literary pursuits removed to London in 1834 in the hope of improving his prospects'. Timperley in his *Dictionary* is a little more explicit on the Liverpool period, where, he states: 'he . . . passed the greater part of his life in literary pursuits and where at length his prospects became blighted and he removed to London in 1834.'[9] How, or perhaps we might say, by whom were his prospects blighted? I take as a starting point Egerton Smith's 'Narrative of facts' of the dispute between Johnson and himself which appeared in six successive issues of the *Mercury*, 1821–2. 'Sometime in the year 1812, being engaged in the optical, stationery and printing business, and having also to superintend the editorship of the *Liverpool Mercury*, I judged it expedient to admit a partner into the general, or what is termed jobbing printing; and accordingly entered into a connexion with a Mr Johnson, who did not bring into the concern one shilling, a

Fig. 3   A portrait of Thomas Burgeland Johnson reproduced as a frontispiece to his *The Sportsman's cyclopedia*. London: Sherwood, Gilbert, and Piper, 1831.

circumstance to which I should not have adverted had I not known that he has made assertions to the contrary. Out partnership was dissolved on the 5th October 1815. . .'. Egerton Smith then goes on to refute one by one some eight assertions made by Johnson about events which took place during the partnership and after. The ultimate cause of the rupture was the printing by Johnson on the *Mercury* presses of an indecent volume of love letters by the late Mrs Hunter, once a celebrated actress. The sheets were virtually all run off when Egerton Smith, on one of his rare visits to the Printing Office, discovered certain coarse and indelicate passages and there and then ordered the whole edition to be burnt, except 'two copies for my own justification.' Unfortunately I have not been able to trace either so I am not able to provide the reader with any passages! He vowed then to rid himself of Johnson. The other assertions in Smith's 'Narrative of facts' consisted of various financial matters, including alleged unpaid debts by Johnson to a printer's joiner, the embezzlement of funds, etc. Many of Johnson's claims against Smith were made in an extraordinary book he printed in 1819. This was *The mystery of the abbey; or the widow's fireside*, a novel in two volumes, printed for Sherwood, Neely and Jones in London, and published by R.Sutton, Paradise Street, Liverpool. The only copy of this work I have traced was 'Presented to the Athenaeum Library, Liverpool' by the author. It is anonymous, but was undoubtedly written by Johnson, the printer of both volumes, and it is assigned to him by the author of the *DNB* article. The story begins as a conventional 'gothick' cum picaresque tale, involving the usual ingredients of robbery, murder, a priory, a mysterious baronet, etc., intermixed with episodes and references to Johnson's chief interests – dogs, game shooting and hunting. But as early as chapter three there is a strong element of autobiography, when the narrative breaks off to describe the author's 'admittance into the printing office of Plagiary Puff, who in addition to publishing a newspaper, carried on the business of bookseller and stationer', and it goes on to describe how he became a Printer's Devil. The original story is resumed, but from volume two chapter four to the end all pretence at continuing it is dropped, and we meet 'Mr Weatherspoon Plausible' for the first time, undoubtedly intended as Egerton Smith and recognised as such by him in his replies printed in the *Mercury*. 'This wonderful man', Johnson writes, 'was ready to sink beneath the weight of his charitable labours: he had not time to devote to less feeling purposes.' Various other characters and events are introduced which are obviously intended to portray events in the partnership. Egerton Smith in his 'Narrative' describes the novel as 'destitute of wit, good writing, moral or humour. He has scraped together a melange of scurrility and lies, under the expectation that party feeling or private personal enmity would lend a greedy ear to any tale, however preposterous. He was however overshot the mark'. But it is clear that he did recognise himself. After the novel the exchange of insults continued in the *Mercury* and in one of Johnson's journals, *The Liverpool Theatrical Investigator*, which ran from 1821 to 1822 and in which Johnson violently attacked the productions and management of the Theatre Royal, Williamson Square, with which Egerton Smith was closely connected. (*See* Fig.4.) In reply to Egerton's measured 'Narrative of facts' Johnson later returned to the fray with another extraordinary document, 'Hypocrisy unmasked', which consists of extracts from his pieces in *The Liverpool Theatrical Investigator* cobbled together with a commentary.[10] Johnson was obviously a choleric man and in this piece, as we would now say, he 'goes over the top'. Two extracts will give the flavour of the piece: he quotes Smith as one 'who had contrived in less than ten years to "expel" five partners by dissimulation, falsehood and fraud, to promote designs, as interested and base as ever crept from beneath the cloak of one of the most consummate hypocrites, one of the most unprincipalled knaves, that ever gave a murky animation to light-coloured gooseberry Eyes, or ever skulked along the street "like a thief with a shoulder of mutton under his arm." ' And in another passage: 'this conglomerated constellation of mercurial poison, inflated vanity, puffing and plagiarism sets off at top rate by charging Mr Johnson with having ordered upwards of one hundred reams of paper with the intention of fixing the payment on Mr Smith . . .' and so on. And his final paragraph sums up his bitterness: 'His [i.e. Egerton Smith's] object was to prevent the establishment of Mr Johnson in Liverpool as a printer; he has not succeeded but trembles for the possible consequences. For the accomplishment of his diabolical purpose he resorted to the grossest hypocrisy, the most deliberate, the foulest, and most fiend-like falsehood; to swindling in various forms; to all the crooked ways of a well-practised and highly-finished deceiver; to detraction, to calumny, and slander – he has succeeded beyond all possible doubt – in covering HIMSELF in eternal infamy.'

The result of all this cross-fire was in fact rather inconclusive. Egerton Smith took out an action for damages against Johnson in January 1822 at the Borough Court of Liverpool for eleven distinct gross libels in the *Liverpool Theatrical Investigator*, and laid damages at £5. He gave Johnson the opportunity to bring further evidence for them, but Johnson failed to do so, as he was apparently expecting an indictment rather than an action for damages. Egerton Smith won the verdict merely by proving that Johnson had published the libels. We will probably never know the truth of the affair – other than that there was obviously a deep-seated enmity between the two men. Johnson was in a weak position in the partnership, but one feels in reading his replies – however extravagantly phrased – that the fault was not all on his side and that he was not – appearances to the contrary – entirely the rogue that Egerton Smith made him out to be. For instance, there is some evidence that his bankruptcy in 1816 was in fact engineered by the Smith business; certainly his equipment and types were auctioned off before he could immediately re-establish himself. But he was, in fact, not suppressed and continued to print books and journals in Liverpool for a number of years, certainly up to 1834 when he is recorded as in partnership with a John

Burgeland Johnson, possibly his brother. But he never met with much success: a number of his later serials, such as *The Liverpool Examiner*, and, *The Voice of the Country*, both of which appeared in 1832, survived only for a few issues. He was already a sick man when he moved to London, but his books on field sports which he wrote and published there, such as *The Sportsman's Cyclopedia*, were successful and often reprinted.

I have described the Smith–Johnson affair at some length, partly because of its mild entertainment value, but also because it does to a certain extent call into question Egerton Smith's dealings with his fellow members of the book trade in Liverpool. Ten partnerships in less than 25 years does suggest that he was perhaps a difficult man to get on with in a business relationship. But this in no way deflects from his very considerable achievements which I have tried to describe; his philanthropy, his concern for social reform, his interest in education, his inventions, and above all, his establishment and conduct of a highly influential and distinguished provincial newspaper business.

Fig. 4. One of a series of caricatures, drawn and etched by Alexander Mosses, on the rivalry between managements at the Theatre Royal, Liverpool, in 1822: it shows Johnson on the gallows with some of his books and pamphlets consigned to the flames.

References

The sources for this paper not footnoted below are drawn from the files of *The Liverpool Mercury* and other Liverpool serials, together with primary and secondary materials used in the Liverpool Bibliographical Society's Book Trade in the North West Project, Occasional Publications 1 and 2: *The book trade in Liverpool to 1805: a directory*, 1981 (1982); and *The book trade in Liverpool from 1806 to 1850: a directory*, 1987.

1. Alexander Andrews, *The history of British journalism from the foundation of the newspaper press in England to the repeal of the Stamp Act in 1855*, vol.2, 1859, pp.334–7.

2. For a more detailed account see: A.H. Arkle, 'Early Liverpool printers' *Transactions of the Historic Society of Lancashire and Cheshire*, 80, 1929.

3. R. McMillan, *Egerton Smith: a biographical sketch of the founder of The Liverpool Mercury*, 1891. (Reprinted from *The Liverpool Mercury*, Nov.–Dec. 1890.)

4. McMillan, *Egerton Smith*.

5. Barbara Whittingham Jones, 'Liverpool's political clubs, 1812–1830' *Transactions of the Historic Society of Lancashire and Cheshire*, 111, 1960.

6. C.H. Timperley, *Encyclopaedia of literary and typographical anecdote*, 2nd ed., 1842.

7. See also: E.W. Jones, 'A note on The Kaleidoscope'. *National Library of Wales Journal*, 12, 1961–2.

8. McMillan, *Egerton Smith*.

9. Timperley, *Encyclopaedia*.

10. *Hypocrisy unmasked; or, 'a faithfull portrait from the life' of Weatherspoon Plausible! alias Egerton Smith*. Liverpool: printed and published by T.B. Johnson, [*c.* 1821].

The country trade in books

JOHN FEATHER

THE PAPERS in this book give some idea of the range of book trade studies encompassed by the simple word 'distribution'. In fact, as everyone in the trade knows, successful distribution is the key to successful publishing and bookselling. Books are and always have been a minority taste. They are expensive to produce, because they require mass production processes on a scale which is so small as to be barely economic. The trade in printed books has always been a trade involving a small number of producers dealing with a very large number of retailers, most of whom take only a few copies of any one title. That analysis, and the economic problems which it implies, is not unfamiliar to anyone in the trade today, but we can trace similar patterns and encounter similar problems as far back as the second half of the 17th Century, when something resembling a publishing industry first began to develop in this country.

In a short paper such as this, it is possible to do no more than suggest some of the outlines of the country trade.[1] The first and central point is a very simple one: the country trade was distributive rather than productive, despite the fact that some books were indeed produced. The provincial printers have always attracted a good deal of scholarly and antiquarian attention; this is hardly surprising since their surviving products are the most tangible remains of the trade. There is, however, no longer any real argument about the fact that book printing was never, except in a few very special cases, the economic basis of provincial printing businesses.

Successful provincial firms were based upon one or more of three related activities:

First, there were those printers who owned and produced a newspaper. Until well into the 19th Century these newspapers were weeklies, and were important not so much for their news content as for the medium which they provided for local advertising. They were distributed over comparatively large areas around the towns in which they printed, although the number of copies printed was quite small. They were competing in a limited market, but the competition was with the nationally distributed national newspapers rather than other products of the provincial press. Only the very largest towns could sustain more than one local newspaper. The newspaper owners were, until well into the 19th Century, the dominant figures in the country trade. Benjamin Collins and his family in Salisbury are well-known examples; similarly prosperous and influential newspaper owners were to be found in most of the major country towns.[2]

Secondly, there were printers who primarily specialised in jobbing work. The demand for this greatly increased towards the end of the 18th Century as the pace of economic life quickened. The example of the Cheneys of Banbury is well known, but there are many others.[3] They are difficult to document, since jobbing work was, by its very nature, ephemeral, and surviving examples are but the tip of the iceberg. Where there is documentary evidence, however, as there is for a few printers, it is clear that jobbing work was the economic cornerstone of many provincial printing firms, especially in the industrial towns of the North and the Midlands from the 1780s onwards.

Thirdly, some provincial printers were major producers of chapbooks, ballads and similar popular books. It has been argued that the demand for such material was so great that the London printers could not produce enough to satisfy the market outside the capital.[4] We might add that it seems unlikely that the financial returns would have justified the capital costs of national advertising and distribution of such low-value items, which were, therefore, not attractive to the London printers. The London chapbook and ballad trade was, like the provincial trade, essentially local rather than national. Local production was both more efficient and more cost-effective. I have previously somewhat underestimated the importance of this branch of the trade. Again, the survivors are only a tiny fraction of the total output, for there were probably few provincial printers who did not have a hand in chapbook and ballad printing. The specialists, like White and others in Newcastle, are well-known, but that is partly due to the accidents of bibliophilic fashion which have determined what shall survive.

There were, of course, a few printers who really did produce books, and perhaps even made it into a significant part of their businesses. The example of William Eyres of Warrington has often been evoked to show that there were important book publishing activities in English towns other than London.[5] Certainly Eyres's output was very important, and was remarkable both for the quality of the printing and the significance of the books themselves. We should, however, remember two things about him. First, he had the unique advantage of easy access to the group of distinguished men who formed the staff of the Warrington Academy at the very pinnacle of its fame and success; and secondly, he almost always arranged for his books to be distributed through the most important radical bookseller in London, Joseph Johnson.[6] Eyres was as unusual in being a major printer and publisher in a small provincial town as Collins was in being a significant shareholder in London copyrights.

Printing then, although interesting, and not without significance, is not really the central concern of the historian of the country trade any more than it was for the trade's practitioners. We return, in fact, to the topic of distribution, which is, as has been suggested, the real importance of the country booksellers in the wider history of the book trade in this country.

There were essentially four modes of distribution which we need to consider: First, there were books printed and published in London which were also available in the country bookshops, that is, distribution from London to the provinces or national distribution. Secondly, there were books printed in a provincial town, or in one of the other countries of the British Isles, intended for regional distribution only, or for export to a place other than England and Wales, that is regional distribution or distribution for export. Thirdly, there were books printed in the provincial towns which were sold in London as well as elsewhere in the country, or distribution from the provinces to London, as well as national distribution. Fourthly, there were books imported into England and Wales which were sold either in London or in the provinces, or both, that is national or regional distribution of foreign books.

Let us briefly consider these in a little more detail. The first category – books printed and published in London but also available in the country bookshops – includes the vast majority of books printed in England since Caxton set up shop in Westminster. If we confine ourselves to the 18th Century, the typical English book of that period is a 'London' book, in which the only town mentioned in the imprint is London, and no provincial bookseller is, apparently, involved. In fact, advertisements in the provincial newspapers show that many of these books were, as we might expect, widely distributed throughout the country, and that they were readily available in the country bookshops. In fact, they formed the bulk of the retail trade in books in the provinces, just as 'London' books constitute by far the largest part of the total output of the London trade. Let me emphasise this point. The typical 18th-Century English imprint is a London imprint only, but this does not mean that the book was not available outside London.[7]

There are, however, atypical books which do indeed have provincial names in their imprints, and these books reveal a little more about themselves. A few examples help to illustrate this. In Fig. 1, we have the imprint of a pamphlet printed for one of the major London booksellers of the time. It is not, however, typical. William Pine of Bristol, although memorialised by Plomer primarily as a printer, was also an important publisher and distributor of Methodist tracts. This book, in which I think we can assume he had a financial stake, was available from him at wholesale prices, presumably for charitable distribution. The book in Fig. 2 is much more normal. William Mason, the author, was a Canon of York when this poem was published, and that alone is enough to explain why a York bookseller was one of the distributors: it was a convenient means of exploiting the local interest in the book, by providing a distributor in a city where there was likely to be a comparatively high demand.[8] In return, Tessyman got extra business and, probably, rather better trade terms than other booksellers.

The importance of the regional distributors has been increasingly recognised by scholars in recent years, but we must remember that it was the exception not the rule to name them in the imprint. Here we are using such imprints, as others have, to garner clues about the structure of the trade. We must not forget, however, that the absence of provincial names does not mean that the book was only available in London, and the presence of provincial names is actually a deviation from the norms of a deeply conservative trade. They should always be treated as a warning that there is something slightly unusual about the book. This is illustrated in Figs. 3 and 4. Hoyle's book on whist is, as addicts will know, a key text in the history of that game; in it, Hoyle codified the rules. It was a popular book; this was the seventh edition of a book first published only five years earlier. Three major provincial sellers are named in the imprint and were, therefore, presumably involved in the distribution arrangements. Hildyard and Bryson were, in effect, regional distributors for the north of England, while Leake served the west, as well as a city in which card-playing was of more than usual importance. Why was the book singled out for this sort of attention? Perhaps because it was so popular that it was simply more convenient to ship copies in bulk to regional centres. A more sinister explanation may be that the use of two northern distributors was an attempt to pre-empt piratical incursions from Scotland or Ireland, an issue to which we shall return.

The book in Fig. 4 is of lesser interest in itself, but perfectly exemplifies the regional distribution patterns of the middle and late 18th Century. The author was a West Countryman, and his prestigious London publishers selected six western booksellers to act as regional distributors. The first of them, Goadby in Sherborne, was one of the key figures in the western book trade in the middle decades of the 18th Century. He was the owner of a widely distributed newspaper, *The Western Flying Post*. It has been argued that Goadby was, as it were, the lead distributor of this book, making use of the network of newspaper agents – all of whom were booksellers – which he had developed from Dorset to Land's End.[9]

In describing the Dillys, Vivian's London publishers, as 'prestigious', the word was chosen with some care. From fact and fiction alike we can document the prestige attached to London as opposed to provincial publication by 18th-Century, and no doubt 19th-Century, authors. Fig. 5 is an interesting example, since it contains a near-deception which implies that this is a 'London' book. In fact, read carefully – as most purchasers would not read it – the imprint means that the book was printed in London, but that the publisher, that is the owner of the copy and financial backer, was Hammond in Bath; it was 'printed for' him. Even Michael Johnson, justifiably renowned as one of the most learned of provincial booksellers, was not immune from such practices. In Fig. 6, the implication of the imprint is clear, namely that this book was published in London. In fact we know that Johnson was the publisher of Floyer's book, and the London booksellers were merely the distributors. It was indeed printed in London, but it is only by stretching the truth that we can really describe this as a 'London' book.

With Fig. 7, we come to the second category, or rather part of it, books printed in provincial towns intended for local or regional distribution only. Fig. 8 is a very clear example of the practice. This sermon preached by an obscure local clergyman can have been of little interest outside his immediate circle. This is really vanity publishing, and certainly the imprint implies that Pilborough was merely the agent of the unnamed persons at whose 'request' it was published. Those 'friends' almost certainly included the author himself. Certainly, there is a most unchristian air of deception about the whole title-page. A casual reader – or browser in a bookshop – could be forgiven for glancing at the lines printed in larger type, and concluding that this was the funeral sermon for the late Queen.

The book in Fig. 7 is more honest, and is of a book whose commercial prospects may have been a little brighter. The printer was William Bonny of Bristol, and he and three other regional booksellers acted as distributors. It is to be noted, however, that this is a very local book indeed, for none of the four distributors is more than a dozen miles from the author's home in Thornbury, just north of Bristol. Bonny was, at that time, the only reasonably accessible printer in that part of the country, and one interpretation of the imprint is that this too was a vanity production. In this case, however, the imprint is in any case imprecise. Strictly interpreted, it means that all four men printed the book, which is clearly wrong! It also serves therefore as a useful reminder that we must not be too mechanical in our interpretation of imprints, and that it was not until the 1730s that the familiar patterns of the middle and later 18th Century were almost universally adopted, especially in books printed outside London.

The second category is of books printed in Scotland, Ireland and Wales for distribution in those countries, or for sale outside them to places other than England and Wales. Eiluned Rees and Charles Benson deal with Welsh and Irish matters respectively in other papers in this book. Warren McDougall has added a Scottish dimension to what we already know of the importance of the Irish-American trade at the same period.[10]

The third category was of books printed in the provincial towns which were sold in London as well as elsewhere in the country, and the remaining illustrations all relate to this category, although in slightly different ways. The first example (Fig. 9) is really only one stage removed from a truly provincial book like Grove (Fig. 7). Again, the imprint seems to mean that the book was printed for the author, but we may assume that Pennington, who was reasonably well-established in the trade, used such contacts as he had to make the distribution arrangements. It has to be said, however, that he did not choose particularly important London distributors, for that is what Matthews and Hogg were intended to be. Their role in this book was, in effect, exactly the same as that of Hildyard, Bryson and Leake in my earlier example (Fig. 3), except that in this case we have a provincial book distributed in London, rather than a London book distributed in the provinces.

Samuel Rudder, printer, bookseller, antiquary and by the end of his life local celebrity and tourist attraction in Cirencester,[11] did a rather better job for Thomas

Huntley (Fig. 10). The Fletchers in Oxford were fairly large-scale operators, whose names are found in London imprints. The London distributor, Walker was an equally good choice. According to Nichols, whom there is no reason to disbelieve, he was a book wholesaler with a fairly large business.[12] Because of that, he could, of course, give Rudder access to the national distribution system radiating from London. This critical point is further illustrated by the last two examples. In both cases, they are explicitly printed at their respective authors' expense. Turner's book, however (Fig. 11), had some hopes of success. It is a mildly radical text – in so far as anything radical was deemed to be mild by the British government in 1793 – and the first named, and therefore principal, London distributor was Joseph Johnson, publisher of virtually every dissident writer at a very dangerous time.

The fourth category, books imported into England and Wales, brings us into very difficult territory. This is not the place to embark on an attempt to define what was and what was not a piracy in the 18th Century. I would, however, like to say a very little about imports. Some books were of course legally imported, and were distributed, in so far as they achieved wide distribution at all, through the normal mechanisms of the trade. These included the books in learned languages specifically exempted from the 1739 Act,[13] as well as books in modern European languages not otherwise published in this country. The Vaillant brothers and later John Nourse and his successors, for example, were major importers of French books, as well as publishing books in French for sale both in England and overseas. Although many of the imports were doubtless sold to the Huguenot community and other francophone groups in London, we do find them in advertisements which might have reached the provincial trade.[14]

At a more surreptitious level, there were books imported from Ireland, from Scotland, from the Low Countries, and to a much lesser extent from elsewhere, which, while they were perfectly legal in the countries in which they had been printed, could not legally be sold in England and Wales after 1710 because they were reprints of English texts first printed in England or Wales. Many of these books seem to have come in through the northern ports. Preston was a favourite port of entry for Irish books; it was there in 1733 or 1734 that Customs Officers siezed a consignment of Irish reprints which was to become a parliamentary *cause célèbre*.[15] Newcastle, Hull and York seem to have been the main ports of entry for Scottish reprints, at a time when coastal shipping was still the best means of freight transport between Scotland and England. The evidence is fragmentary, but I think it is reasonable to conclude that Irish and Scottish reprints were widely available in the north of England in the middle decades of the 18th Century. It has been argued elsewhere that one of the principal reasons for the London booksellers' efforts to improve their distribution arrangements in the 1750s was that they were losing the battle against the imported reprints among the booksellers in large parts of northern England.[16] The named provincial distributors of Hoyle's book (Fig. 3), which I mentioned earlier, may be part of that London reaction to the importers.

Whatever the details, and I suspect they will always remain obscure, it is clear that the Scottish and Irish imports, in particular, were a significant factor in the northern English book trade until well into the second half of the 18th Century. These books did not normally come into the trade through the London distributors, most of whom were far too committed to the defence of the stable mechanisms of legal publication and distribution whose establishment and maintenance had been the *raison d'être* of the 1710 and 1739 Acts. It follows, therefore, that there were regional distribution networks for these imported books. This was not, however, a separate trade, and therein lay the real danger to the London booksellers trying to defend the integrity of their investments in copies. Booksellers dealt indifferently in 'legitimate' and 'pirated' editions, a practice which was certainly not confined to obscure rustics who might have pleaded ignorance of the law and practices of the trade.

There can be little doubt that one of the carrots in the carrot and stick exercises which typified the Londoners' dealings with the major provincial booksellers in the 1740s and 1750s was to offer the regional distribution rights to recalcitrant importers who were prepared to abandon their wicked ways. John Hildyard, the York distributor of Hoyle's book, was the son of Francis, a long established and highly respectable bookseller in the city who had nevertheless been named to the House of Commons in 1734 as one of the recipients of the infamous parcels of books confiscated at Preston. The trade in Scottish and Irish reprints seems to have been largely provincial. It may be that when Donaldson established his deliberately provocative bookshop in London in the 1760s, he did so precisely because the Scottish reprints had never been generally available in the capital or indeed in much of southern Britain, whose inhabitants were, therefore, unable to benefit from Donaldson's allegedly altruistic attempts to reduce the price of books.[17]

The provincial trade was largely distributive, but that does not mean that it was insignificant. It was not. In commercial terms, the provincial market was very important to the London trade. Moreover, it probably increased at a greater rate than did the retail book trade in London itself for much of the 18th Century. The expenditure of tens of thousands of pounds by the London booksellers to establish their unchallenged access to the provincial bookshops was not the work of idealists seeking to uphold the law at their own expense. It was a hard-nosed investment to protect essential and rapidly developing markets. There was, however, a broader consequence, which was a wholly unintended result of the pursuit of commercial advantage and private profit. The efficient distribution mechanisms for books which had been developed by the middle of the 18th Century, and which were reinforced by the transportation revolution of the 1840s, were a critical link between metropolitan and provincial culture. At a time when print

was the unchallenged medium of mass communication, the book trade provided
the essential commercial channel through which that culture was disseminated.
The technical mechanisms of dissemination are merely the starting point for a real
study of the influence and importance of the printed word.

References

1. This paper was written in response to a request to chair and lead a discussion of the
    topics considered at the conference. It is, therefore, rather short, and offers sug-
    gestions rather than giving the results of new research. It is slightly rewritten from
    the verbal presentation.
2. For Collins, see C.Y. Ferdinand, 'Benjamin Collins, the *Salisbury Journal*, and the
    provincial book trade', *The Library*, 6th ser., 11 (1989), pp.116–38. For other exam-
    ples, see John Feather, *The Provincial Book Trade in Eighteenth-Century England* (Cam-
    bridge, 1985), pp.21–3, 104.
3. For the Cheney family, see Christopher R. Cheney, *John Cheney and His Descendants*
    (Banbury, 1936); see also Feather, *op. cit.*, pp.104–6.
4. Feather, *op. cit.*, pp.104–6.
5. Michael Perkin, 'William Eyres and the Warrington press'. In: Robin Myers and
    Michael Harris (eds.), *Aspects of Printing from 1600* (Oxford, 1987), pp.69–89.
6. For Johnson, see Leslie F. Chard, 'Bookseller to publisher: Joseph Johnson and the
    English book trade, 1760 to 1810', *The Library*, 5th ser., 32 (1977), pp.138–54.
7. For imprints in general, see Feather, *op. cit.*, pp.59–62.
8. See Philip Gaskell, *The First Editions of William Mason* (Cambridge Bibliographical
    Society, Monograph 1, 1951), pp.12–13.
9. Feather, *op. cit.*, pp.23, 61–2.
10. For the Irish-American trade, see Richard Cargill Cole, *Irish Booksellers and English
    Writers 1740–1800* (London, 1986), pp.40–61, 148–71.
11. For Rudder, see Roland Austin, 'Samuel Rudder', *The Library*, 3rd ser., 6 (1915),
    pp.235–51.
12. John Nichols, *Literary Anecdotes of the Eighteenth Century*, (London, 1812), vol.3,
    p.666.
13. 12 George II c. 36. See John Feather, 'The English book trade and the law 1695–
    1799', *Publishing History*, 12 (1982), pp.57–8.
14. For the import trade, see Giles Barber 'Book imports and exports in the 18th-
    Century'. In: Robin Myers and Michael Harris (eds.). *Sale and Distribution of Books
    from 1700* (Oxford, 1982), pp.77–105.
15. For this episode, see John Feather, 'The publishers and the pirates. British copyright
    law in theory and practice, 1710–1775', *Publishing History*, 22 (1987), pp.10–11.
16. Feather, *Provincial Book Trade*, pp.4–10.
17. For the Donaldson episode, see Gwyn Walters. 'The booksellers in 1759 and 1774:
    the battle for literary property', *The Library*, 5th ser., 29 (1974), pp.287–311.

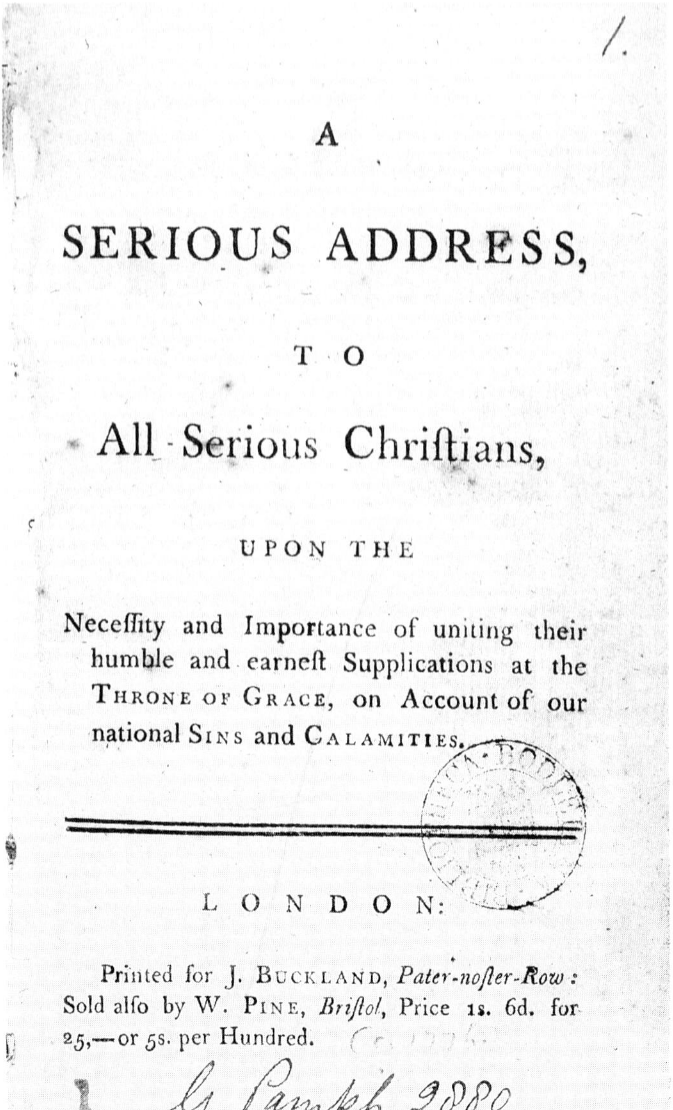

1.

A

SERIOUS ADDRESS,

T O

All Serious Chriſtians,

UPON THE

Neceſſity and Importance of uniting their humble and earneſt Supplications at the THRONE OF GRACE, on Account of our national SINS and CALAMITIES.

_____

L O N D O N:

Printed for J. BUCKLAND, *Pater-noſter-Row :*
Sold alfo by W. PINE, *Briſtol*, Price 1s. 6d. for
25,—or 5s. per Hundred.

G. Pamph. 2880.

Fig.1 *A serious address*, London [c.1776]
(Bodleian Library, Oxford: G. Pamph. 2880 (1))

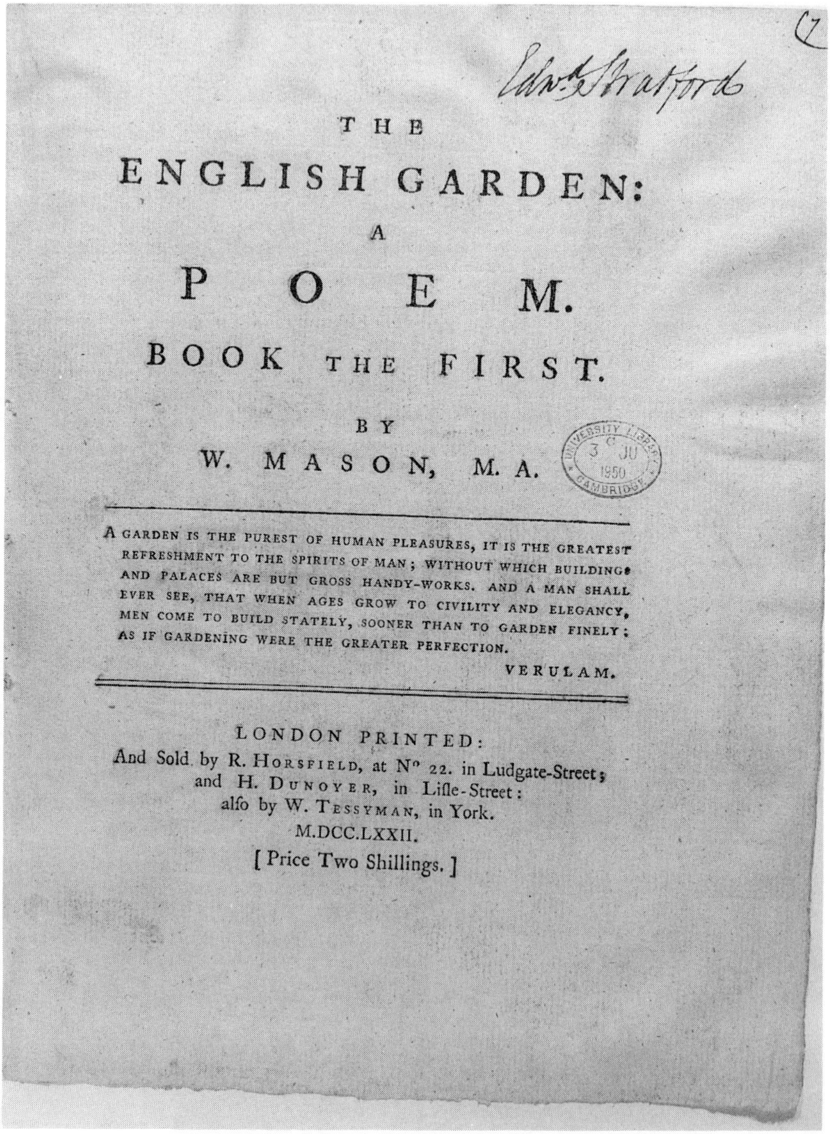

THE

ENGLISH GARDEN:

A

P O E M.

BOOK THE FIRST.

BY

W. MASON, M.A.

A GARDEN IS THE PUREST OF HUMAN PLEASURES, IT IS THE GREATEST
REFRESHMENT TO THE SPIRITS OF MAN; WITHOUT WHICH BUILDINGS
AND PALACES ARE BUT GROSS HANDY-WORKS. AND A MAN SHALL
EVER SEE, THAT WHEN AGES GROW TO CIVILITY AND ELEGANCY,
MEN COME TO BUILD STATELY, SOONER THAN TO GARDEN FINELY:
AS IF GARDENING WERE THE GREATER PERFECTION.

VERULAM.

LONDON PRINTED:
And Sold by R. HORSFIELD, at Nº 22. in Ludgate-Street;
and H. DUNOYER, in Lifle-Street:
alfo by W. TESSYMAN, in York.
M.DCC.LXXII.
[Price Two Shillings.]

Fig 2.   William Mason, *The English Garden*, London, 1772. (Cambridge
University Library: S718. c.76.1)

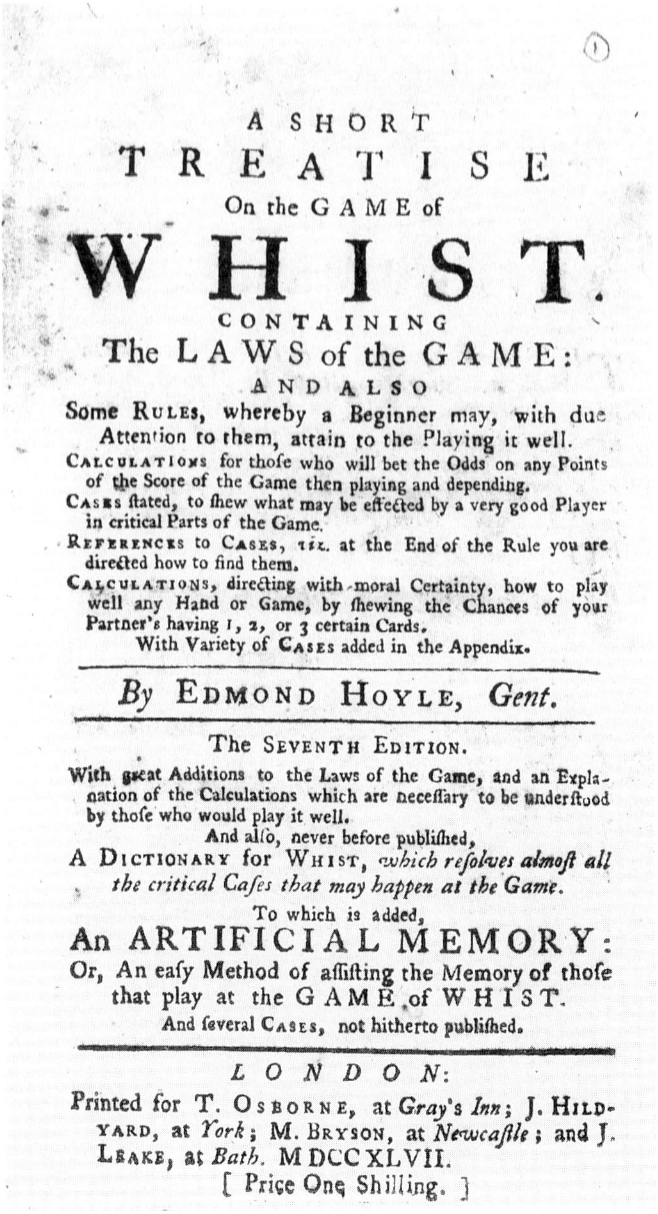

A SHORT

TREATISE

On the G A M E of

WHIST.

CONTAINING

The LAWS of the GAME:

AND ALSO

Some RULES, whereby a Beginner may, with due
Attention to them, attain to the Playing it well.

CALCULATIONS for thofe who will bet the Odds on any Points
of the Score of the Game then playing and depending.

CASES ftated, to fhew what may be effected by a very good Player
in critical Parts of the Game.

REFERENCES to CASES, *viz.* at the End of the Rule you are
directed how to find them.

CALCULATIONS, directing with-moral Certainty, how to play
well any Hand or Game, by fhewing the Chances of your
Partner's having 1, 2, or 3 certain Cards.

With Variety of CASES added in the Appendix.

By EDMOND HOYLE, *Gent.*

The SEVENTH EDITION.

With great Additions to the Laws of the Game, and an Explanation of the Calculations which are neceffary to be underftood
by thofe who would play it well.

And alfo, never before publifhed,

A DICTIONARY for WHIST, *which refolves almoft all
the critical Cafes that may happen at the Game.*

To which is added,

An ARTIFICIAL MEMORY:

Or, An eafy Method of affifting the Memory of thofe
that play at the GAME of WHIST.

And feveral CASES, not hitherto publifhed.

L O N D O N:

Printed for T. OSBORNE, at *Gray's Inn*; J. HILD-
YARD, at *York*; M. BRYSON, at *Newcaftle*; and J.
LEAKE, at *Bath.* MDCCXLVII.

[Price One Shilling.]

Fig 3. Edmond Hoyle, *A short treatise*, London, 1747. (Bodleian Library,
Oxford: Jessell f.548)

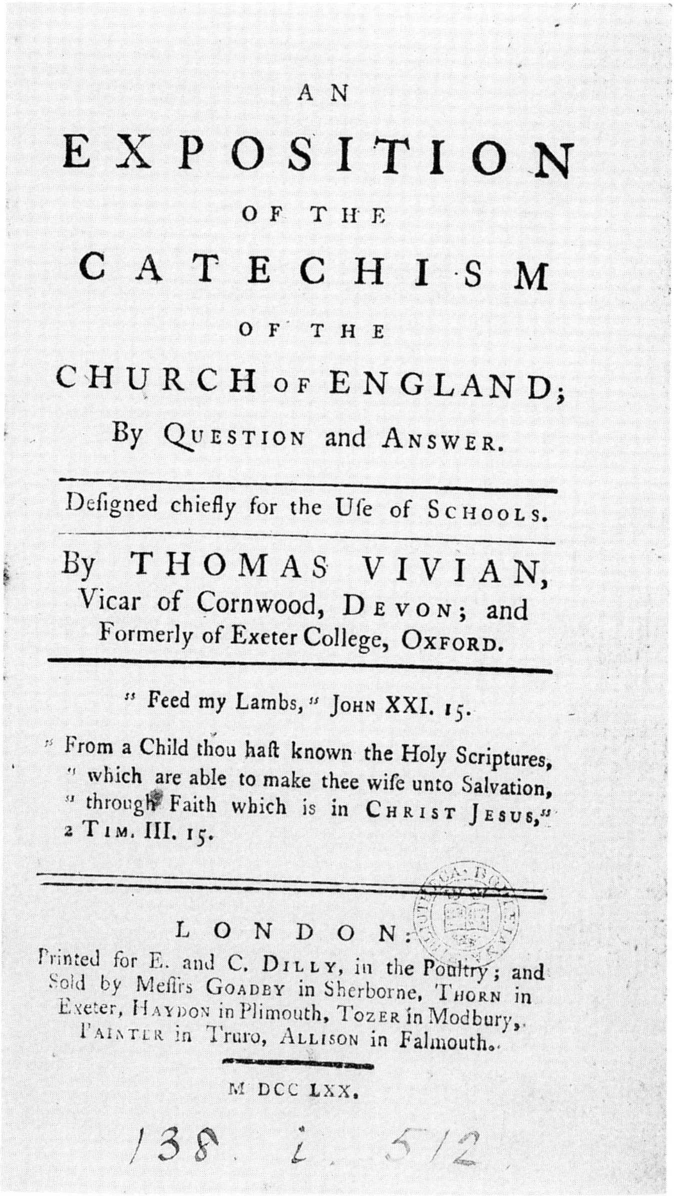

A N

EXPOSITION

OF THE

CATECHISM

OF THE

CHURCH OF ENGLAND;

By QUESTION and ANSWER.

Defigned chiefly for the Ufe of SCHOOLS.

By THOMAS VIVIAN,
Vicar of Cornwood, DEVON; and
Formerly of Exeter College, OXFORD.

" Feed my Lambs, " JOHN XXI. 15.

" From a Child thou haft known the Holy Scriptures,
" which are able to make thee wife unto Salvation,
" through Faith which is in CHRIST JESUS,"
2 TIM. III. 15.

LONDON:
Printed for E. and C. DILLY, in the Poultry; and
Sold by Mefirs GOADBY in Sherborne, THORN in
Exeter, HAYDON in Plimouth, TOZER in Modbury,
PAINTER in Truro, ALLISON in Falmouth.

M DCC LXX.

Fig 4.   Thomas Vivian, *An exposition*, London, 1770. (Bodleian Libary,
Oxford: 138 i. 512)

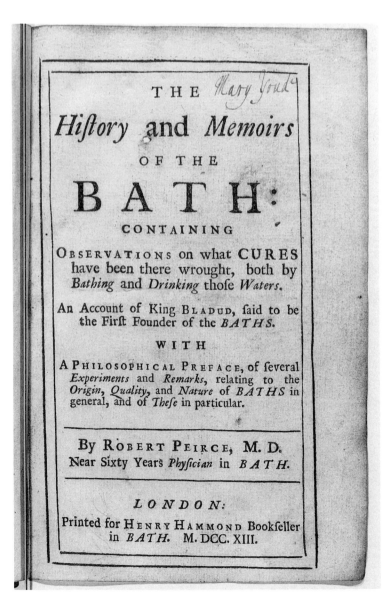

THE *Mary Youd*

Hiſtory and *Memoirs*

OF THE

BATH:

CONTAINING

OBSERVATIONS on what CURES
have been there wrought, both by
Bathing and *Drinking* thoſe *Waters*.

An Account of King BLADUD, ſaid to be
the Firſt Founder of the *BATHS*.

WITH

A PHILOSOPHICAL PREFACE, of ſeveral
Experiments and *Remarks*, relating to the
Origin, *Quality*, and *Nature* of *BATHS* in
general, and of *Theſe* in particular.

By ROBERT PEIRCE, M. D.
Near Sixty Years *Phyſician* in *BATH*.

LONDON:

Printed for HENRY HAMMOND Bookſeller
in *BATH*. M. DCC. XIII.

Fig 5.   Robert Peirce, *History and memoirs*, London, 1713. (Cambridge
University Library: S300. d.71.6)

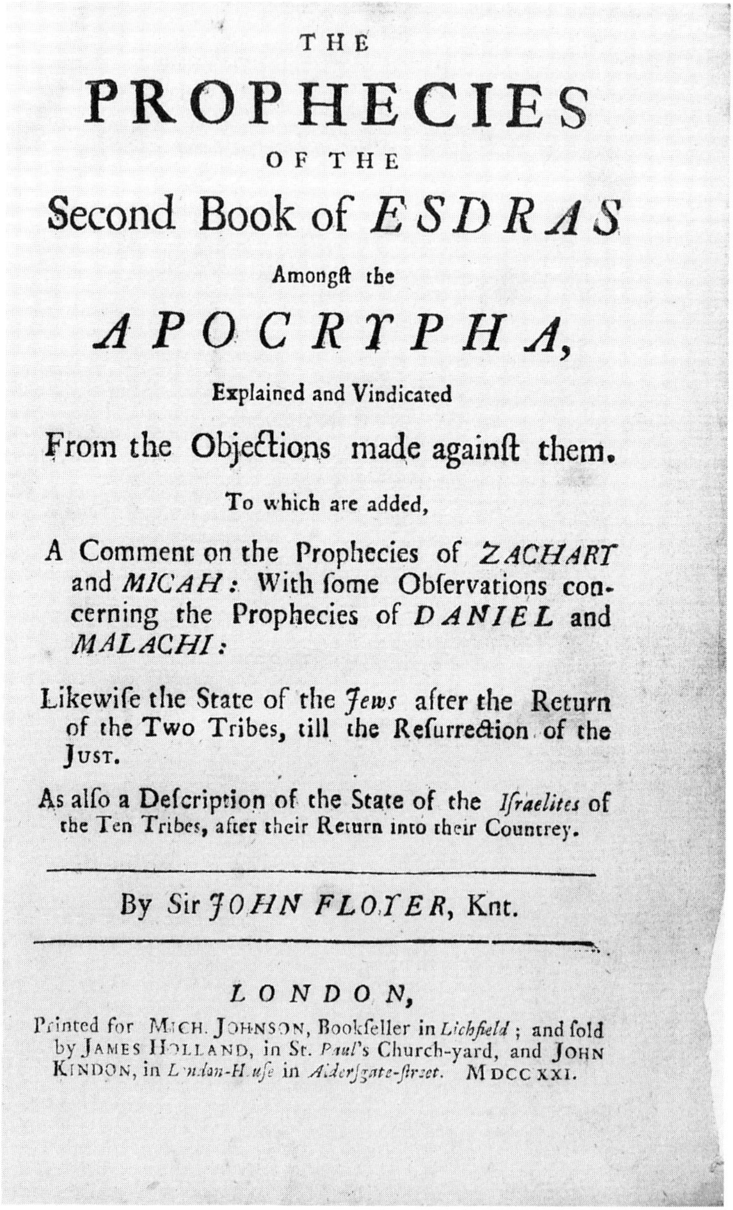

THE
PROPHECIES
OF THE
Second Book of *ESDRAS*
Amongſt the
A P O C R Y P H A,
Explained and Vindicated
From the Objeƈtions made againſt them.
To which are added,

A Comment on the Prophecies of *ZACHARY*
and *MICAH :* With ſome Obſervations concerning the Prophecies of *DANIEL* and
MALACHI :

Likewiſe the State of the *Jews* after the Return
of the Two Tribes, till the Reſurreƈtion of the
JUST.

As alſo a Deſcription of the State of the *Iſraelites* of
the Ten Tribes, after their Return into their Countrey.

By Sir *JOHN FLOYER*, Knt.

L O N D O N,
Printed for MICH. JOHNSON, Bookſeller in *Lichfield* ; and ſold
by JAMES HOLLAND, in St. *Paul's* Church-yard, and JOHN
KINDON, in *London-Houſe* in *Alderſgate-ſtreet.* MDCCXXI.

Fig 6. Sir John Floyer, *The prophecies*, London, 1721. (Cambridge University
Library: S100. c.72.8)

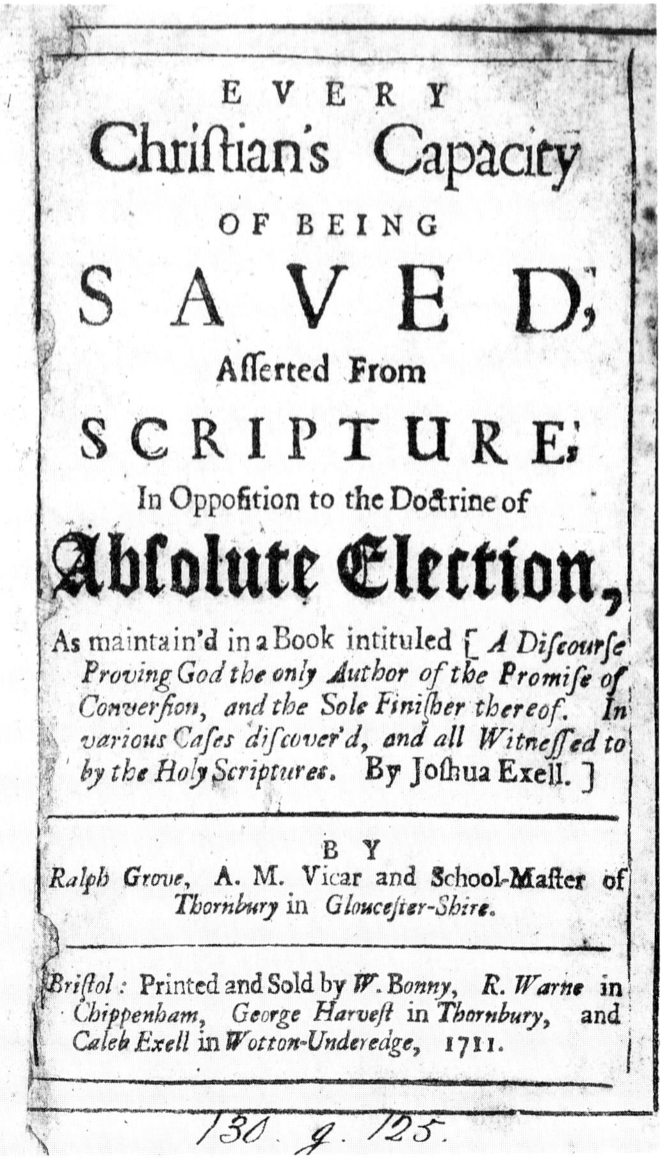

EVERY

Chriſtian's Capacity

OF BEING

SAVED,

Aſſerted From

SCRIPTURE,

In Oppoſition to the Doctrine of

Abſolute Election,

As maintain'd in a Book intituled [*A Diſcourſe
Proving God the only Author of the Promiſe of
Converſion, and the Sole Finiſher thereof. In
various Caſes diſcover'd, and all Witneſſed to
by the Holy Scriptures.* By Joſhua Exell.]

BY

Ralph Grove, A. M. Vicar and School-Maſter of
Thornbury in *Gloucester-Shire.*

Briſtol : Printed and Sold by *W. Bonny,* R. *Warne* in
Chippenham, George Harveſt in *Thornbury,* and
Caleb Exell in *Wotton-Underedge,* 1711.

130. g. 125.

Fig 7.   Ralph Grove, *Every Christian's capacity*, Bristol, 1711. (Bodleian Library,
Oxford: 130 g.25)

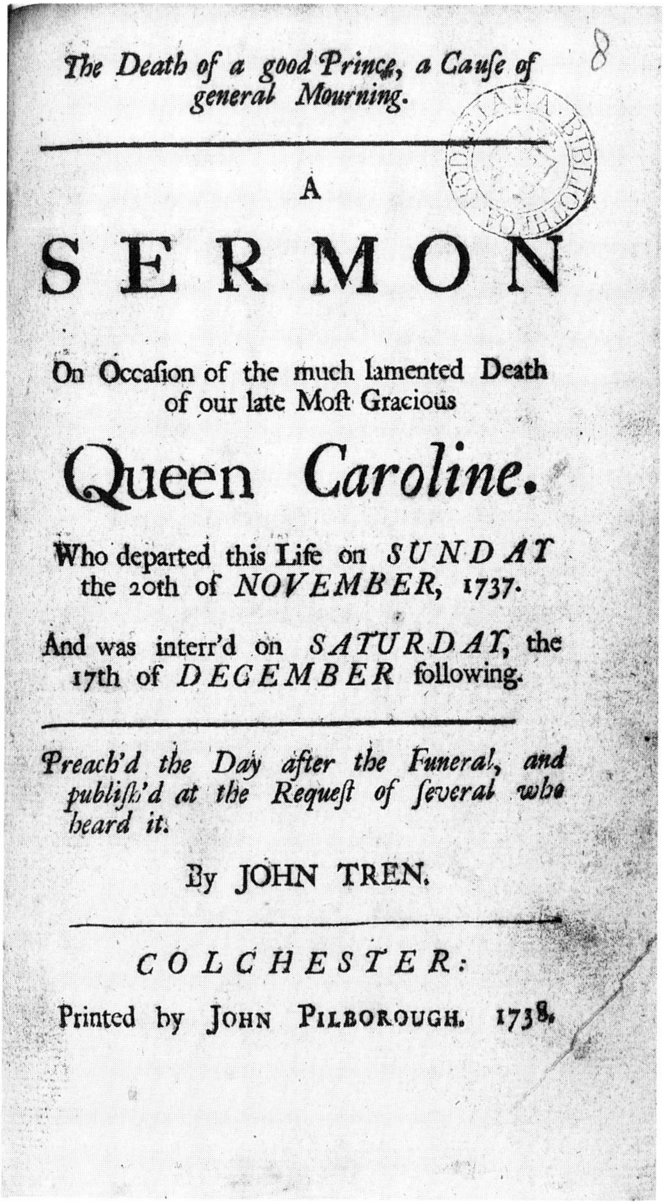

The Death of a good Prince, a Cause of
general Mourning.

A

SERMON

On Occasion of the much lamented Death
of our late Most Gracious

Queen *Caroline.*

Who departed this Life on *SUNDAY*
the 20th of *NOVEMBER,* 1737.

And was interr'd on *SATURDAY,* the
17th of *DECEMBER* following.

Preach'd the Day after the Funeral, and
publish'd at the Request of several who
heard it.

By JOHN TREN.

COLCHESTER:

Printed by JOHN PILBOROUGH. 1738,

Fig 8.   John Tren, *A sermon*, Colchester, 1738. (Bodleian Library, Oxford:
100q 69 (8))

THE

Writer's Time Redeemed,

AND

SPEAKER'S WORDS RECALLED,

By a Pen fhap'd both for oral Expedition, and the
moft legible Plainnefs and Punctuality:

OR

Annet's Short-hand Perfected,

Further enlarged and improved, in a Method ftrikingly
eafy, and engaging to the meameft Capacity.

IN TWO PARTS.

PART I. Contains the Characters claffed in their alphabetical
and derivative Order, together with the Rules of their Application, as far as neceffary for the Student, Letter-writer,
Merchant, &c. to take down their own Thoughts, or the
copying any Book or Manufcript, in as punctual and legible
a Manner as in common Writing; and upon Occafion, of
fufficient Expedition for the taking down a Sermon, Trial
at Law, &c. as delivered at the Pulpit, Bar, &c.

PART II. Contains Rules and Examples, with a fpecial View
to the following of a Speaker.——— Together with fufficient Copper-plate Specimens to both Parts.

*** This Short-hand will be of great Service to thofe
who have already learned BYROM as well as ANNET.

By THOMAS HERVEY,

of UNDERBARROW, near KENDAL.

Author of the *Englifh Climax*.

While panting Hearts indite,
Obedient Hands with equal ardour Write;
And diftant Friends, with Joy, know how to fpeak,
Wrapt in a Sheet, the Converfe of a Week.

KENDAL:

Printed by W. PENNINGTON,
And fold by J. SMITH, Bradford; J. MATTHEWS,
No. 18 in the Strand, and ALEXANDER HOGG,
in Pater-nofter-Row, London.

302. f. 12.

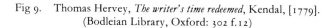

Fig 9.   Thomas Hervey, *The writer's time redeemed*, Kendal, [1779].
(Bodleian Library, Oxford: 302 f.12)

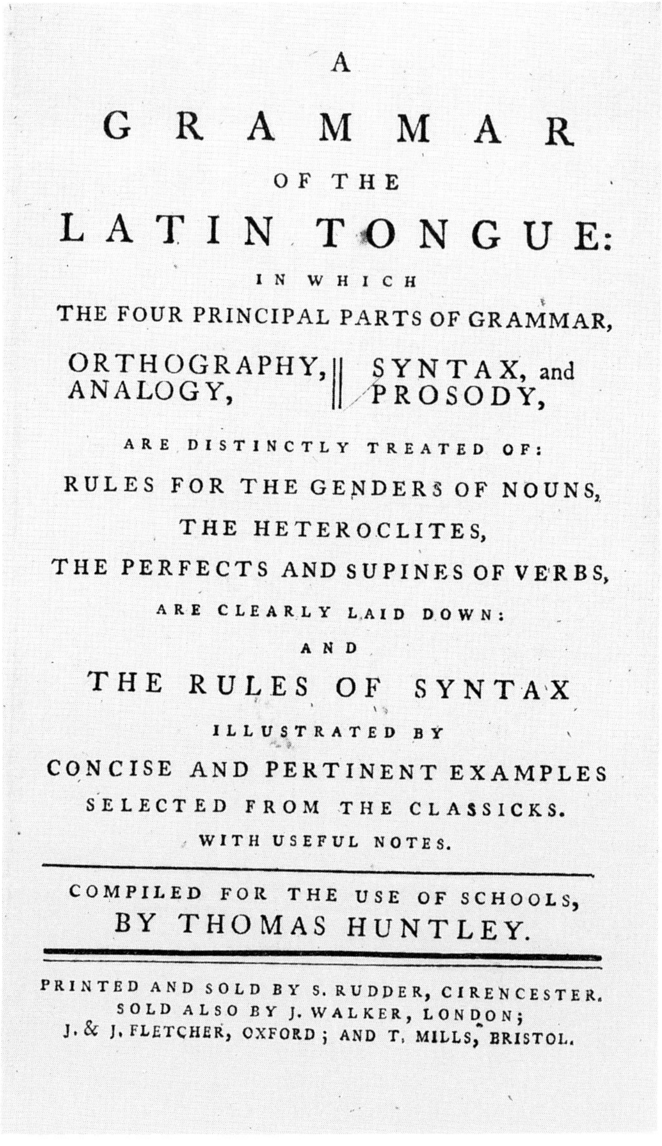

A

GRAMMAR

OF THE

LATIN TONGUE:

IN WHICH

THE FOUR PRINCIPAL PARTS OF GRAMMAR,

ORTHOGRAPHY, || SYNTAX, and
ANALOGY, || PROSODY,

ARE DISTINCTLY TREATED OF:

RULES FOR THE GENDERS OF NOUNS,

THE HETEROCLITES,

THE PERFECTS AND SUPINES OF VERBS,

ARE CLEARLY LAID DOWN:

AND

THE RULES OF SYNTAX

ILLUSTRATED BY

CONCISE AND PERTINENT EXAMPLES

SELECTED FROM THE CLASSICKS.

WITH USEFUL NOTES.

COMPILED FOR THE USE OF SCHOOLS,
BY THOMAS HUNTLEY.

PRINTED AND SOLD BY S. RUDDER, CIRENCESTER.
SOLD ALSO BY J. WALKER, LONDON;
J. & J. FLETCHER, OXFORD; AND T. MILLS, BRISTOL.

Fig 10. Thomas Huntley, *A grammar of the Latin tongue*, Cirencester, n.d.
(Bodleian Library, Oxford: 3058 f.46)

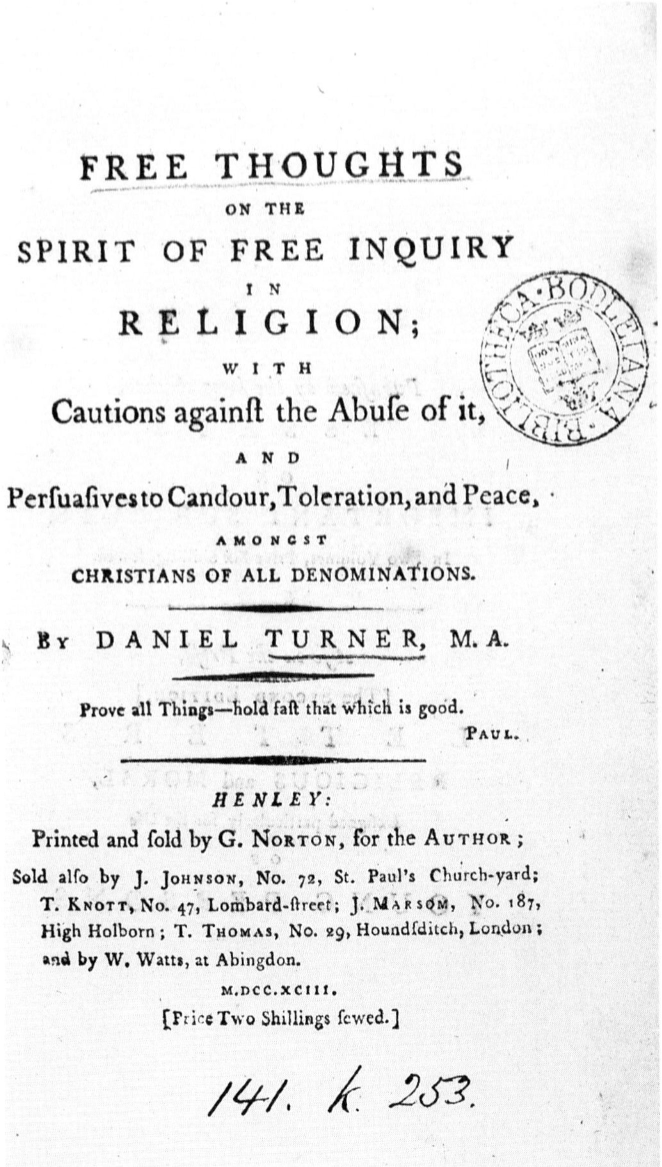

FREE THOUGHTS

ON THE

SPIRIT OF FREE INQUIRY

I N

RELIGION;

WITH

Cautions againſt the Abuſe of it,

A N D

Perſuaſives to Candour, Toleration, and Peace,

AMONGST

CHRISTIANS OF ALL DENOMINATIONS.

By DANIEL TURNER, M.A.

Prove all Things—hold faſt that which is good.
PAUL.

HENLEY:

Printed and ſold by G. Norton, for the Author;

Sold alſo by J. Johnson, No. 72, St. Paul's Church-yard;
T. Knott, No. 47, Lombard-ſtreet; J. Marsom, No. 187,
High Holborn; T. Thomas, No. 29, Houndſditch, London;
and by W. Watts, at Abingdon.

M.DCC.XCIII.

[Price Two Shillings ſewed.]

141. k. 253.

Fig 11.   Daniel Turner, *Free thoughts*, Henley, 1793. (Bodleian Library, Oxford:
141 K253)

APPENDIX

APPENDIX

A catalogue of Hamilton, Balfour and Neill publications
1750–1762

WARREN MCDOUGALL

THE PARTNERSHIP of Hamilton, Balfour and Neill began on Whitsunday 1750 and ended in August 1762. The Hamilton and Balfour bookselling partnership also finished then. For trade purposes, the dissolution was kept secret for a while, and John Balfour used the old firm's name on several publications in 1763 and 1764. I take 1750–1762 as the span of the company's productions, and append further Balfour titles.

This catalogue reflects the various activities of the three partners from 1750: the printing by Hamilton, Balfour and Neill for themselves and for others; publications of Hamilton and Balfour that were printed by Neill or by other printers; the imprints Hamilton and Balfour shared with other booksellers; some silent publishing by Neill – as when he took a share with William Strahan; and the firm's involvement in printing parts of books for Alexander Donaldson.

The layout of the catalogue is alphabetical by author within years. A shortened title is followed by imprint, format, edition size where known, publication and price (PP), copyright entry, and notes. Variants and other issues are shown.

BL	British Library
CM	*Caledonian Mercury*
EEC	*Edinburgh Evening Courant*
EUL	Edinburgh University Library
EU medical thesis	Thesis presented for the degree of M.D. at Edinburgh University
NLS	National Library of Scotland
SRO	Scottish Record Office
SM	*Scots Magazine*
Stationers' Register	*Records of the Worshipful Company of Stationers*
1746–73	1554–1920, ed Robin Myers (Cambridge, 1985, Part 1, microfilm reel 6, Entries of Copies 29 September 1746 to 30 December 1773.

University theses

The medical and law theses were printed on two types of paper, common and fine, and in some quantity. Walter Ruddiman printed 200 copies of a law thesis for the advocate George Wallace in 1754, 164 on ordinary paper, 36 on fine (EUL: ms. in La.II.694/2, with John Aitken's account for binding). There are several references to law theses in quantities of 200 in Patrick Neill's ledger, 1764–7 (NLS: Ms. Dep.196). Theses were presented, and distributed by booksellers. Patrick Neill gave a number of medical theses to a student from Thurso (letter of 18 June 1763 in NLS: Ms.Dep.196). Dr W. Cuming, physician at Dorchester, wrote to John Balfour 31 July 1771 asking for the medical theses of the last graduation, along with the law theses (NLS: Adv. Ms. 29.5.7, vol. 1, f.1).

1. DRUMMOND, Colin, *of Scotland*. [EU medical thesis] *Dissertatio medica inauguralis, de ictero.* Edinburgi: apud Hamilton, Balfour, et Neill. 4°.

2. EDINBURGH ENTERTAINER. *The Edinburgh Entertainer: containing historical and poetical collections. For the use of schools.* Edinburgh: printed for G. Hamilton & J. Balfour, J. Traill, J. Brown, J. Yair, and L. Hunter. 12°. PP: September 1750, *SM*; noticed also 10 June 1751, bound in calf and titled, 2*s.* 6*d. CM.*

3. FERGUSSON, Rev. Adam, *of Moulin. The leading characters of the Church of Rome. A Sermon upon Reformation and Revolution principles.* Edinburgh: printed by Hamilton, Balfour, and Neill. 8°. PP: September 1750, 6*d. SM.*

4. FORBES, Duncan, *of Culloden. Reflexions on the sources of incredulity with regard to religion.* Edinburgh: printed by Sands, Murray, and Cochran, for G. Hamilton and J. Balfour. 8°, 62 leaves. PP: 2 January 1750, 2*s.* bound. *CM.* Copyright: Entered at Stationers' Hall 6 February 1750, the whole share for Hamilton and Balfour (Stationers' Register, 1746–73, 74).

5. FORBES, Duncan, *of Culloden. Reflexions on the sources of incredulity with regard to religion. The second edition.* Edinburgh: printed by Sands, Murray, and Cochran, for G. Hamilton and J. Balfour. 8°, 46 leaves. PP: 5 March 1750, 1*s.* [stitched]. *CM.*

6. FORBES, Duncan, *of Culloden. Reflexions on the sources of incredulity with regard to religion. By the Right Honourable Duncan Forbes of Culloden, late Lord President of the Court of Session in Scotland.* Edinburgh: printed for G. Hamilton and J. Balfour. 8°, 63 leaves.

7. FORBES, Duncan, *of Culloden. Some thoughts concerning religion, natural and revealed. With Reflexions on the sources of incredulity with regard to religion.* Edinburgh: printed for G. Hamilton and J. Balfour. 8°. PP: September 1750, 3*s.* [bound.] *SM.*

8. HAMILTON and BALFOUR. [Catalogue of a collection of books, in most languages and faculties, to be auctioned in Writer's Court on January 4, 1750.] Notes. *Not seen.* The catalogues were to be had of Hamilton and Balfour at their shop. *CM* 19 December 1749.

9. LANGLANDS, Robert, *of Scotland*. [EU medical thesis]. *Dissertatio medica inauguralis, de hydrope-anasarca.* Edinburgi: apud Hamilton, Balfour, et Neill. 4°.

10. MONRO, Prof. Alexander, the first, *of Edinburgh University. The anatomy of the human bones and nerves. With an account of the reciprocal motions of the heart, and a description of the human lacteal sac and duct. Corrected and enlarged in the fifth*

edition. Edinburgh: printed for G. Hamilton, and J. Balfour. Sold by them and other booksellers there. At London, by Mess. Innys, Knapton, Rivington, Longman, Hitch, Miller, Hodges, and Wilson. At Dublin, by R. Main. 12°. PP: September 1750, 3*s. SM.*

11.   MONTESQUIEU. *De l'esprit des loix. Tome premier [-Tome second]. Nouvelle edition, avec les dernieres corrections & illustrations de l'Auteur.* A Edinbourg, chez G. Hamilton & J. Balfour. 2 volumes, 8°. PP: 21 November 1749, 12*s.* bound or 10*s.* sewed. *CM.*

Notes: (i) Subscription proposals of 1 June 1749 called for Scottish support. 'As the Publishers of this Book are to spare neither Expence nor Pains, in having it elegantly printed, and carefully corrected from the Errors both of the *Geneva* and *London* Editions, and at as cheap, if not cheaper Price than either: It is hoped that all Lovers of Learning, and Well-wishers to their Country, will rather chuse to encourage this *first Attempt* of reprinting a valuable foreign Book among ourselves, than any other Edition, especially as many *open* and *secret Attempts* have of late been made, and are still carrying on to destroy this infant Branch of Manufacture, in this part of the World'. *CM.*

(ii) Montesquieu's corrections, sent over through the good offices of David Hume, arrived after a large part of the book had gone through the press. The publishers explain in the Preface that they cancelled a number of leaves requiring substantial correction [eight in all]. (For Hume, see John Hill Burton, *Life and Correspondence of David Hume* [Edinburgh, 1846], I, 457.)

12.   MONTESQUIEU. *Two chapters of a celebrated French work, intitled, De l'esprit des loix, translated into English. One, treating of the constitution of England; another, of the character and manners which result from this constitution.* Edinburgh: printed for Mess. Hamilton and Balfour, and sold by them and other booksellers in town. (Price four pence.) 8°. PP: April 1750, 4*d. SM.*

13.   SCOTT, John, *of Scotland.* [EU medical thesis] *Dissertatio medica inauguralis, de salivationis ad luem veneream curandum inutilitate.* Edinburgi: apud Hamilton, Balfour, et Neill. 4°.

14.   SIDNEY, Algernon. *Discourses concerning government... In two volumes.* Edinburgh: printed for G. Hamilton and J. Balfour; and Daniel Baxter, bookseller in Glasgow.

14.1   VARIANT title-page: set with different type; rules added, 'In two volumes' deleted from title of vol. 2. Imprint reads: Edinburgh: printed for G. Hamilton and J. Balfour. 2 volumes, 8°. PP: 21 May 1750, bound in calf 10*s. SM.*

15.   STEEL, Rev. William, *of Waygateshaw. Memorial shewing the reasonableness and necessity of an immediate application to the King and Parliament for augmenting the small stipends*

in Scotland. Edinburgh: printed by W. Sands, A. Murray, and J. Cochran; for G. Hamilton and J. Balfour. Sold by them, and by the other booksellers of Edinburgh and Glasgow. (Price six pence.) 8°. PP: March 1750, 6d. SM.

16. SYDENHAM, Thomas. *Processus integri in morbes ferè curandis.* Edinburgi: apud Hamilton, Balfour, & Neill. 8° PP: September 1750 2s. SM.

17. WILSON, Andrew, M.D. *The Creation the ground-work of revelation, and revelation the language of nature.* Edinburgh: printed in the year M D C C L. 8° PP: 21 May 1750, 1s. CM.

1751

18. BARROW, Isaac. *The sermons of the learned Dr Isaac Barrow, late Master of Trinity-College, in Cambridge. Published by Archbishop Tillotson.* Volume 1. [–VI.] [Titles of last two volumes add 'upon the Apostles Creed' after 'Cambridge'.] Edinburgh: printed for G. Hamilton & J. Balfour, J. Traill, W. Miller, L. Hunter, J. Brown, J. Yair, and C. Wright. 6 volumes, 12°. PP: First four volumes 16 May 1751, last two November 1751, 15s. for the set in boards, 18s. bound. CM.

19. BROWN, Isaac, *of England.* [EU medical thesis] *Disquisitio medica inauguralis, de sonorum modulatorum vi in corpora humana.* Edinburgi: apud Hamilton, Balfour, et Neill. 8°.

20. BUCHANAN, George. *Buchanan's History of Scotland. In twenty books...The fourth edition... In two volumes. Adorned with copper plates, and a map of Scotland.* Edinburgh: printed by Hamilton, Balfour, and Neill, for J. Wood, at the Cross, Edinburgh, and R. Taylor, Berwick. [vol. 2 title page deletes 'at the Cross' from imprint and is dated 1752.] 2 volumes, 8°, 9 plates, 1 fold-out map. PP: In numbers weekly from May, 1751, 5d. fine paper, 3d. coarse. The completed edition December 1751, 8s. 4d. fine paper, 5s. coarse, stitched. SM.

21. [CHALMERS (or Chambers), Rev. John, *of Ely*, and Rev. Harry Spens, *of Wemyss*.] *An inquiry concerning a plan of a literary correspondence.* Edinburgh: printed in the year M,DCC,LI. 8°. PP: June 1751, 6d. SM.

22. A COLLECTION. *A collection of all the papers published in relation to the scheme for augmenting the stipends of the established clergy in Scotland.* Edinburgh: printed by Hamilton, Balfour, and Neill. 4°.

Notes: New material, a letter, arrived after copies had been sent to the country and while the bookbinder was stitching the sheets of the remainder; this was printed as an Appendix and joined to the *Collection*. (Advertisement on leaf $^2A2$).

22.1   VARIANT. The copies issued in the less complete version. *Not seen.*

22.2   ISSUE of the Appendix by itself. To supplement the incomplete copies the firm issued the Appendix with new preliminary matter and renumbered pages as :
An impartial account of the rise, progress, and nature of the scheme for augmenting the livings of the Scots clergy. In a letter to the publisher of the printed collection of papers relative to that affair. Edinburgh: printed by Hamilton, Balfour, and Neill. 4°. PP: 28 February 1751, *A collection* 7s. 6d., the Appendix alone 2s. *CM.*

23.   CLAMPET, George, *of Ireland*, [EU medical thesis]   *Dissertatio medica inauguralis, de diabete.* Edinburgi: apud Hamilton, Balfour, et Neill.   4°.

24.   DALRYMPLE, Sir David, *Lord Hailes*, ed.   *Sacred Poems: or, a collection of translations and paraphrases, from the Holy Scriptures. By various authors.*   Edinburgh: printed by Hamilton, Balfour, and Neil.   8°.   Edition size: 50, according to a note in NLS copy L.C.28.   PP: October 1751, 1s. 6d. bound. *SM.*

25.   DOBBIN, James, *of Ireland*. [EU medical thesis]   *Dissertatio medica inauguralis, de erysipelate.* Edinburgi: apud Hamilton, Balfour, et Neill.   4°.

26.   GIFFORD, William, *of England*. [EU medical thesis]   *Dissertatio medica inauguralis, de peripneumonia notha.* Edinburgi: apud Hamilton, Balfour, et Neill.   4°.

27.   GREGORY, David. [Preface by Colin Maclaurin.]   *A treatise of practical geometry. In three parts...The second edition.*   Edinburgh: printed by Hamilton, Balfour, and Neill.   8°.   PP: January 1751, 2s. *SM.*

28.   HAMILTON and BALFOUR.   [Catalogue of a large collection of valuable books, in most languages and faculties, which are to be exposed by way of sale (the lowest price being marked at each book), at the shop of G. Hamilton and J. Balfour.] *Not seen.* Notes: To be published a few days after 12 December 1751. Terms of sale: ready money only; gentlemen who paid to the extent of £20 would be entitled to £5 per cent discount. *CM.*

29.   HIRD, William, *of England*. [EU medical thesis]   *Disquisitio medica inauguralis, de lactis natura et usu.*   Edinburgi: apud Hamilton, Balfour, et Neill.   8°.

30.   HOWE, Charles.   *Devout meditations: or, a collection of thoughts upon religious and philosophical subjects. By a person of honour.*   Edinburgh: printed by Hamilton, Balfour, and Neill.   12°.

30.1   VARIANT title page, on another issue: *Meditations, devout and philosophical: or, a collection of thoughts upon religious and philosphical subjects. By a person of honour.*   Edinburgh: printed by Hamilton, Balfour, and Neill.   12°.   PP: 'Devout meditations' 4 December 1750, 2s. bound, 2s. 6d. in boards. *CM.* Copyright: Entered at Stationers' Hall, under 'Meditations, devout' title, 22 January 1751, the whole share for Hamilton and Balfour (Stationers' Register, 1746–73, 92).

31.   JONES, Samuel, *of Wales*. [EU medical thesis]   *Dissertatio physiologico-medica inauguralis, de venis absorbentibus.* Edinburgi: apud Hamilton, Balfour, et Neill.   8°.

32.   KELLY, Edmund, *of Ireland*. [EU medical thesis]   *Dissertatio medica inauguralis, de paronychia.* Edinburgi: apud Hamilton, Balfour, et Neill.   4°.

33.   LIVIUS, Titus, ed. Thomas Ruddiman.   *Titi Livii patavini historiarum ab urbe condita libra qui supersunt, cum omnium epitomis, ac deperditorum fragmentis: ad optimas editones castigati, accurante Tho. Ruddimanno, A.M. Tomus I. [–IV.]*   Edinburgi, in aedibus T. and W. Ruddimanni, veneunt autem apud G. Hamilton, A. Kincaid, ac socios.   4 volumes, 8°, fine-paper issue, on foolscap.

33.1   ISSUE in another format, with another bookseller added to the imprint: Edinburgi, in aedibus T. and W. Ruddimanni, venuent autem apud G. Hamilton, A. Kincaid, ac socios, & J. Brown.   4 volumes, 12°, common-paper issue.   PP: Noted in January 1751 in *SM*. 28 March 1751, 14s. the set bound and lettered (presumably the common-paper duodecimo). *CM.*

34.   MONTESQUIEU.   *Considerations sur les causes de la grandeur des Romains, et de leur decadence. (Nouvelle edition, revue, corrigée & augmentée par l'auteur.)*   A Edinbourg, chez Hamilton, Balfour, & Neill.   8°.   PP: 11 April 1751, 5s. bound. 'A few' copies printed for the Curious, on a fine writing medium paper, price finely bound, gilt and marbled, 9s. The edition was also sold bound with *De l'esprit des loix*, 2 volumes 1750, [11] 'and these three Volumes compleat the Works of that celebrated Author'. *CM.*

35.   PASCAL, Blaise.   *Thoughts on religion, and other subjects; by Monsieur Pascal. Translated from the French.*   Edinburgh: printed by R. Fleming for W. Gray junior, and sold by G. Hamilton and J. Balfour, J. Brown and G. Crawford in Edinburgh; J. Barry and J. Gilmour in Glasgow; T. Glass in Dundee, and R. Morison in Perth.   12°.   PP. December 1750, 2s. *SM.*

36.   PHILELEUTHERUS.   *A letter to a friend, upon occasion of a late book, intitled, Essays upon morality and natural religion.*   Edinburgh: printed for G. Hamilton and J. Balfour.   8°.   PP: 25 June 1751, 1s. *CM.*
Notes: A comment on Henry Home's recent work.

37.   RIDPATH, Rev. George, *of Stitchel*.   *Christian liberty opposed to Popish tyranny and superstition. A sermon preached at Kelso . . . April 16 1751.*   Edinburgh: printed by Hamilton, Balfour, and Neill.   8°.   PP: May 1751, 6d. *SM.*

38.   ROGERS, Christopher, *of Ireland*. [EU medical thesis].   *Dissertatio medica inau-*

guralis, de paraphrenitide.   Edinburgi: apud Hamilton, Balfour, et Neill.   4°.

39.   SCANLAN, John, *of Ireland.* [EU medical thesis]   *Dissertatio medica inauguralis, de lienteria.* Edinburgi: apud Hamilton, Balfour, et Neill.   4°.

40.   SOCIETY OF THE FREE BRITISH FISHERY .   *His Majesty's royal charter granted on the eleventh day of October, 1750 . . . for incorporating the Society of the Free British Fishery, with power to make by-laws, &c. for the improvement of the British white herring fisheries, and better regulation of the trade thereof; and for preventing frauds and impositions in the management of the same.*   Edinburgh: printed in the year M DCC LI.   8°.   PP: 3 January 1751, 6d. *CM.*

41.   VOLUSENE, Florence.   *De animi tranquillitate dialogus. Florentio Voluseno, auctore.* Edinburgi: apud Hamilton, Balfour, et Neill.   8°, 173 leaves including an errata leaf.   PP: 26 March 1751, on writing foolscap bound and lettered, 4s., on writing treasury post bound and lettered, 6s. *CM.*

42.   WISHART, William, *Principal of Edinburgh University,* and others.   Caption title, p.1: *Reasons of dissent from the sentence of the General Assembly May 15 1751.*   Caption title, p.4: *Reasons of dissent, entered on the 15th of May 1751, from the sentence of the General Assembly, censuring the reverend members of the Presbytery of Linlithgow, for not executing the sentences of the former Assemblies, appointing them to ordain and admit Mr James Watson minister of the Parish of Torphichen.*   8°.   PP: May 1751, 1d. *SM.*
Notes: The pamphlet is reprinted in *SM* May 1751, pp.220–21, and in Nathaniel Morren, *Annals of the General Assembly of the Church of Scotland* (Edinburgh, 1838–40), I, pp.209–11.

43.   WHYTT, Prof Robert, *of Edinburgh University.*   An essay on the vital and other involuntary motions of animals.   Edinburgh: printed by Hamilton, Balfour, and Neill.   8°.   PP: 24 October 1751, 5s. bound. *CM.*   Copyright: Entered at Stationers' Hall 11 December 1751, the whole share for Hamilton, Balfour and Neill (Stationers' Register, 1746–73, 106).

1752

44.   ALSTON, Prof. Charles, *of Edinburgh University.*   *A dissertation on quick-lime and lime-water.*   Edinburgh: printed by W. Sands, A. Murray, and J. Cochran. Sold by G. Hamilton and J. Balfour.   8°.   PP: 26 October 1752, 2s. in boards. *EEC.*   Copyright: Entered at Stationers' Hall 8 March 1753, the whole share for Hamilton and Balfour (Stationers' Register, 1746–73, 122).

45.   ALSTON, Prof. Charles, *of Edinburgh University.*   *Index medicamentorum simplicium triplex.*   Edinburgi: typis W. Sands, A. Murray, & J. Cochran. Veneunt autem apud G. Hamilton & J. Balfour.   8°.   PP: June 1752, 2s. stitched.

SM. Copyright: Entered at Stationers' Hall September 1752, the whole share for Hamilton and Balfour (Stationers' Register, 1746–73, 117).

46. BOSTON, Thomas. *Human nature in its fourfold state of...* [contents]. *In several practical discourses. By Mr. Thomas Boston, late minister of the gospel at Etterick. The ninth edition.* Edinburgh: printed by Hamilton, Balfour and Neill, for William Gray junior, at the foot of Peebles Wynd; and sold by him and other booksellers. 8°.

47. BRODIE, Alexander, *of Scotland.* [EU medical thesis]. *Disquisitio medica, inauguralis, de rabie canina.* Edinburgi: apud Hamilton, Balfour, et Neill. 4°.

48. CLARKE, John. *An introduction to the making of Latin... The twentieth edition.* Edinburgh: printed by Hamilton, Balfour, and Neill. 12°. PP: November 1752, 2s. *SM.*

49. EDINBURGH PHILOSOPHICAL SOCIETY. *Medical essays and observations, published by a society in Edinburgh. Volume I. [–V. Part II.] The fourth edition, revised and enlarged by the authors.* Edinburgh: printed by Hamilton, Balfour, and Neill. Five volumes in six parts, 12°, 24 plates. PP: 21 November 1752, one guinea bound. *EEC.* Copyright: The third edition was entered at Stationers' Hall 5 March 1748, the whole share for Hamilton and Balfour (Stationers' Register, 1746–73, 41), but the partners said this was to prevent piracy of the edition, not to establish their ownership of the Society's literary property; they said the Edinburgh booksellers William Monro and William Drummond had done likewise for the first two editions (*A vindication of Hamilton and Balfour*, 1756).

50. EDINBURGH ROYAL INFIRMARY. *Pharmacopoeia pauperum, in usum Nosocomii Regii Edinburgensis.* Edinburgi: apud Hamilton, Balfour, et Neill, sumptibus Nosocomii. 8°. PP: 21 April 1752, 1s. 'For the Convenience of the Students of Physic, they may be supplied with Copies by the Clerks of the Infirmary.' *EEC.* Copyright: This is the second edition, published for the benefit of the Infirmary; the Ruddimans published the first in 1746. The Infirmary's copyright was entered 2 October 1746 (Stationers' Register, 1746–73, 1).

51. EUCLID. *Euclid's elements of geometry, the first six, the eleventh and twelfth books; translated into English, from Dr. Gregory's edition, with notes and additions. For the use of the British youth. By E. Stone.* London, printed for and sold by Tho. Payne, next the Mews Gate, in Castle-street, near St. Martin's Church; sold also by Mr. James Fletcher at Oxford, Mr. Thurlbourn at Cambridge, Mr. Hildyard at York, Mr. Newton at Manchester, and by Mess. Hamilton and Balfour at Edinburgh. 8°.

52. FORBES, Duncan, *of Culloden. Reflexions on the sources of incredulity with regard to religion.* Edinburgh: printed for G. Hamilton and J. Balfour. 8°. PP: By 2 November 1752, 2s. bound. *EEC.*

53. GREIVE, James, *of England.* [EU medical thesis] *Dissertatio medica inauguralis, de*

calculo vesicae urinariae. Edinburgi: apud Hamilton, Balfour, et Neill. 4°.

54. HAMILTON and BALFOUR. *A catalogue of books, in physic and surgery, that are to be disposed of, by way of sale . . . for ready money only, on Wednesday the first of November . . . Catalogues to be had at the shop of G. Hamilton and J. Balfour. The first speaker is always to be preferred.* 8°.

55. HAMILTON and BALFOUR. [A catalogue of valuable books, in most languages and faculties, which are to be exposed by way of sale, (the lowest price being marked at each book) at the shop of G. Hamilton and J. Balfour, upon Tuesday the 28th of November 1752.] *Not seen.* PP: 21 November 1752. *EEC.*

56. HAMILTON, Rev. Gilbert, *of Cramond. The disorders of a church, and their remedies. A sermon preached . . . May 5. 1752.* Edinburgh: printed by Hamilton, Balfour, and Neill. 8°. PP: 19 May 1752, 4*d.* stitched in blue paper. *EEC.*

57. HOWE, Charles. *Devout meditations: or, a collection of thoughts upon religious and philosophical subjects. By the Honble Charles How, Esq; The second edition.* Edinburgh: printed by Hamilton, Balfour, and Neill. 8°. PP: 9 November 1752, on writing paper [foolscap] 2*s.* bound and titled. 'That this excellent Performance (which is very proper to be read at this Time) may circulate extensively, there are some Copies printed on a coarser Paper [pot], which will be sold bound and titled for 1*s.* 4*d.*' *EEC.*

58. LOMMIUS, Jodocus. *Jodoci Lommii Burani, medicinalium observationum libri tres . . . Edinburgi, M,D,C,LII. Veneunt apud G. Hamilton and J. Balfour, socios.* 12°. PP: 10 March 1752, 3*s.* bound. 'This Book is allow'd by the best Judges to contain the most important Doctrine of Hippocrates, Celsus, and other ancient Physicians, concerning the Symptoms and Events of Diseases, and to be written in a Stile of most uncommon Purity and Elegance. Wherefore great Care has now been taken to print the whole of it correctly, as well as to supply, from former Editions, many gross Omissions in the later ones, which had obscur'd the Author's Meaning, and render'd this celebrated Performance in a manner imperfect'. *EEC.*

59. LOUTHIAN, John. *The form of process, before the Court of Justiciary in Scotland. In two books . . . The second edition, with additions and amendments.* Edinburgh: printed by Hamilton, Balfour, and Neill. 8°. PP: by 9 November 1752, 4*s.* 6*d.* bound in calf, 3*s.* 8*d.* in sheets. *EEC.*

60. MOORE, Charles, *of Pennsylvania.* [EU medical thesis] *Prolusio inauguralis, de usu vesicantium, quae cantharides recipiunt, in febribus.* Edinburgi: apud Hamilton, Balfour, et Neill. 4°.

61. PRIDEAUX, Humphrey. *The Old and New Testament connected, in the history of the Jews and neighbouring nations . . . The twelfth edition.* Edinburgh: printed by Hamilton, Balfour and Neill: for Hamilton and Balfour, Kincaid and Donaldson, and

C. Wright, booksellers in Edinburgh; and W. Gray, bookseller in Dalkeith. 4 volumes, 12°, plate. PP: 14 May 1752, 12*s.* for four volumes bound, the price to rise to 14*s.* after 1 August. *EEC.*

62. ROBERTSON, William, John Jardine, Hugh Blair, John Home, and others. *Reasons of dissent from the sentence and resolution of the Commission of the General Assembly, met at Edinburgh March 11. 1752, concerning the conduct of the Presbytery of Dunfermline. To which is prefixed, A short narrative of the said conduct of the Presbytery, &c.* Edinburgh: printed in the year M,dcc,lii. 8°. PP: 18 May 1752, 4*d.* *EEC.*

63. SEMPLE, William, *of Ireland.* [EU medical thesis] *Dissertatio medica inauguralis, de arteriotomia.* Edinburgi: apud Hamilton, Balfour, et Neill. 4°.

64. SHAFTON, Benjamin, *of Ireland.* [EU medical thesis] *Dissertatio medica inauguralis, de lochiorum suppressione.* Edinburgi: apud Hamilton, Balfour, et Neill. 8°.

65. SIMSON, Prof. Thomas, *of St. Andrews University.* *An inquiry how far the vital and animal actions of the more perfect animals can be accounted for independent of the brain.* Edinburgh: printed by Hamilton, Balfour, and Neill. 8°, 2 plates. PP: 17 March 1752, 4*s.* bound. *EEC.*

66. SMITH, Henry, *of England.* [EU medical thesis] *Dissertatio inauguralis, de magnesia alba.* Edinburgi: apud Hamilton, Balfour, et Neill. 4°.

67. SWIFT, Jonathan. *Works.*
Series title: *The works of D. Jonathan Swift... The seventh edition.* Edinburgh: printed by Hamilton, Balfour and Neill. 9 volumes, 12°. [10 volumes including the *Supplement* of 1753].
Various imprints: Volumes 2–4: Dublin printed, and Edinburgh reprinted, for G. Hamilton & J. Balfour, and L. Hunter, at Edinburgh; and A. Stalker, at Glasgow, and sold by them and other booksellers.
Volumes 5–8: Dublin printed; and Glasgow reprinted, for A. Stalker, at Glasgow; and G. Hamilton and J. Balfour, and L. Hunter, at Edinburgh; and sold by them and other booksellers. [vol. 8 substitutes 'also' for 'sold'].
Volume 9: Edinburgh: printed for G. Hamilton and J. Balfour, and L. Hunter, at Edinburgh; and A. Stalker at Glasgow; and sold by them and other booksellers. PP: 30 April 1752, nine volumes, 18*s.* in sheets, £1. 2*s.* 6*d.* bound and titled; the booksellers said this price made it cheaper than any previous edition. *EEC.*
Notes: Teerink-Scouten 90.

68. SWIFT, Jonathan. *A tale of a tub... The thirteenth edition.* Edinburgh: printed for G. Hamilton & J. Balfour, and L. Hunter, at Edinburgh; and A. Stalker, at Glasgow; and sold by them and other booksellers. 12°.
Notes: Teerink-Scouten 240: A separate issue, with new title-page, of vol. 9 of the *Works* of 1752.

69.   SWIFT, Jonathan.   *Travels into several remote nations of the world.*   Edinburgh:
        printed by Hamilton, Balfour, and Neill, for W. Gray junior.   12°.
        Notes: Teerink-Scouten 307A.

70.   SWINHOW, Francis, *of England.* [EU medical thesis]   *Dissertatio inauguralis, de*
        thermarum antiquitate, contentis et usu.   Edinburgi: apud Hamilton, Balfour, et
        Neill.   8°.

71.   VOLTAIRE.   *Le siecle de Louis XIV . . . Tome premier.* [Tome second.] *Suivant la copie*
        de Berlin.   A Edimbourg: chez Hamilton, Balfour, and Neill.   2 volumes,
        12°.   PP: 20 August 1752, 5s. stitched in marble paper, 6s. bound and titled; 'a
        few are thrown off on a very fine Writing Paper for the Curious'. *EEC.*

72.   WHYTT, Prof. Robert, *of Edinburgh University.*   *An essay on the virtues of lime-water in*
        the cure of the stone . . . With an appendix, containing the case of the Honourable Horatio
        Walpole, Esquire, written by himself.   Edinburgh: printed by Hamilton, Balfour,
        and Neill.   12°.   PP: 26 October 1752, 1s.6d. stitched, 2s. bound. *EEC.*

1753

73.   AINSLIE, Alexander, *of Scotland.* [EU medical thesis]   *Dissertatio medica inuaguralis,*
        de vomitu idiopathico.   Edinburgi: apud Hamilton, Balfour, et Neill.   4°.

74.   ALSTON, Prof. Charles, *of Edinburgh University.*   *Tirocinium botanicum Edinburgense.*
        Conscriptum a Carolo Alston.   Edinburgi: typis W. Sands, A. Murray, & J.
        Cochran. Veneunt autem apud G. Hamilton and J. Balfour.   8°.   PP: in Ha-
        milton and Balfour's shop by 8 November 1753 [no price] *CM.*

75.   BALFOUR, James, *of Pilrig.*   *A delineation of the nature and obligation of morality. With*
        reflexions upon Mr. Hume's book, intitled, An inquiry concerning the principles of mo-
        rals.   Edinburgh: printed by Hamilton, Balfour and Neill.   12°.   PP: by 12
        March 1753, 2s. in boards, 2s. 6d. bound. *CM.*

76.   BLACKWELL, Thomas, *the younger.*   *Memoirs of the Court of Augustus. By Thomas*
        Blackwell, J.U.D. Principal of Marishal College in the University of
        Aberdeen.   Edinburgh: printed by Hamilton, Balfour and Neill.   [volume 2 has
        the date M,DCC,LV (for 1756) in the imprint.]   2 volumes, 4°, 17 plates.   Edi-
        tion size: vol. 1, 750–500 demy and 250 on printing medium (transcription of the
        Neill printing account in a copy of vol. 1 formerly at Neill and Company,
        Edinburgh).   PP: 2 guineas in boards for the 2 volumes [on demy paper], 2
        guineas for 'large Imperial paper' [printing medium]. Volume 1, 19 April 1753.
        EEC. Volume 2, 9 March 1756. *CM.*   Copyright: Entered at Stationers' Hall
        26 April 1753, the whole share for Thomas Blackwell (Stationers' Register,
        1746–73, 125.)

Note: volume 3, completed by John Mills, was published at London in 1763, printed for Andrew Millar.

77. BURNET, Gilbert. *Bishop Burnet's History of his own time. Volume I. [–VI.] Carefully corrected, and revised by the Folio copy.* Edinburgh: printed by Hamilton, Balfour, and Neill. 6 volumes, 12°. PP: volume 1, 30 January 1753, the others at intervals until the set was complete in June, 1s. 6d. a volume in sheets for the coarse paper, 2s. a volume in sheets for 'a very fine paper'. *CM, SM.*
Notes: in an advertisement within the edition, Hamilton and Balfour denounce the appearance of the Dutch piracy of Burnet (Kincaid and Donaldson were selling the Thomas Johnson edition), as well as the octavo published by Andrew Millar.

78. COURT of SESSION. [The decisions of the Court of Session, from the 4th of February 1752 to the 11th of March 1753; collected by Mr. Thomas Millar, Mr. Robert Bruce, Mr. John Swinton junior, and Sir David Dalrymple, advocates. By appointment of the Faculty of Advocates]. 2°. *Not seen.* PP: 6 December 1753, 5s. *CM.*
Notes: This marks the start of the Faculty of Advocates' official collection of court rulings. Hamilton, Balfour and Neill printed the *Decisions 1752–56* in parts over the next few years then in 1760 brought them together as Volume 1 of the series.

79. CROOKE, Clemens, *of St Christopher.* [EU medical thesis] *Dissertatio medica inauguralis, de pleuritide.* Edinburgi: apud Hamilton, Balfour, et Neill. 4°.

80. DOUGLAS, Sir Robert. An engraving with the caption title: *An historical, genealogical tree of the Royal family of Scotland, and name of Stewart for 1000 years back, to the present generation M D C C L. Humbly dedicated to the most illustrious prince, James Duke of Hamilton & Brandon, &c. &c. &c. by his Grace's most devoted, and most obedient servant, Robert Douglas.* 108 × 78 cm – two sheets pasted on linen (A. Baillie sculpsit Edinburgi). PP: August 1753, 5s. *SM.*

81. D'URBAN, John, *of Britain.* [EU medical thesis] *Dissertatio medica inauguralis, de haemorrhagia uterina.* Edinburgi: apud Hamilton, Balfour, et Neill. 8°.

82. FORBES, Duncan, *of Culloden. The whole works of the Right Honourable Duncan Forbes, late Lord President of the Court of Session. Now first collected . . . Vol I [–II.].* Printed for G. Hamilton and J. Balfour, in Edinburgh; and D. Wilson and T. Durham, in London. 2 volumes, 8°, 1 plate. PP: 8 May 1753 in Edinburgh, 5s. bound. *EEC.*

83. GRAINGER, James, *of Scotland.* [EU medical thesis] *Dissertatio medica inauguralis, de modo excitandi ptyalismum, et morbis inde pendentibus.* Edinburgi: apud Hamilton, Balfour, et Neill. 8°.

RE-ISSUED with the following:

84.   GRAINGER, James. *Historia febris anomalae Batavae, annorum 1746, 1747, 1748, &c. Accedunt monita siphylica. Auctore Jacobo Grainger, M.D.* Edinburgi, excudebant Hamilton, Balfour, et Neill.   8°.   PP: September 1753, 3s. in boards. *SM.*

85.   INNES, Robert, *of Scotland.* [EU medical thesis]   *Dissertatio medica inauguralis, de ileo.* Edinburgi: apud Hamilton, Balfour, et Neill.   8°.

86.   JAY, James, *of New York.* [EU medical thesis]   *Dissertatio medica inauguralis, de fluore albo.* Edinburgi: apud Hamilton, Balfour, et Neill.   4°.

87.   MAITLAND, William. *A history of Edinburgh.* Proof sheets.   2°.   131½ corrected sheets, worked on between April 1752 and February 1753, trimmed and bound into a volume; ms. in Edinburgh University Library, Dh.6.73.

88.   MAITLAND, William   *The history of Edinburgh, from its foundation to the present time . . . The whole illustrated with a plan of the town, and a great variety of other fine cuts of the principal buildings within the city and surburbs.* Edinburgh: printed by Hamilton, Balfour and Neill, for the Author.   2°, with Edgar's Plan of Edinburgh and 20 other plates.   Edition size: 762 (mss. at Edinburgh Public Library, Edinburgh Room). PP: 19 February 1753, £1. 1s. to subscribers, £1.4s. to others. *EEC, CM.*
Note: The Plan of Edinburgh was sold separately for 2s. 6d. retail, 2s. to book-sellers; the author's trade price for a set of plates was 5s. [EEC, and Maitland's receipts to Kincaid and Donaldson, 1754, in EUL mss. La.II.508].

89.   MERRIMAN, Samuel, *of England.* [EU medical thesis]   *Dissertatio physiologico-medica inauguralis, de conceptu.* Edinburgi: apud Hamilton, Balfour, et Neill.   4°.

90.   Monro, Donald, *of Scotland.* [EU medical thesis]   *Dissertatio medica inauguralis, de hydrope.* Edinburgi: apud Hamilton, Balfour, et Neill.   8°.

91.   OGILVIE, Rev. John. *The day of Judgement. A poem.* Edinburgh: printed by Hamilton, Balfour, and Neill.   8°.   PP: 24 May 1753, 8d. stitched in blue paper, 1s. bound. 'The Poem is printed on a Writing Paper [foolscap], and with a beautiful letter, in the same manner as [Sir David Dalrymple's] late Collection of Sacred Poems'. *EEC.* See (24) above.

92.   ROZEA, Jassintour. *The gift of Comus. Or, practical cookery. By Jassintour Rozea, principal cook to the late Charles Seymour Duke of Somerset. Number I. [–Numb. II.]* Edinburgh: printed by Hamilton, Balfour, and Neill.   8°.   PP: The work was to consist of 12 monthly numbers, but apparently only two appeared. Number 1, 9 January 1753, 'five sheets, on a fine Demy Paper and in a new Letter', 1s., sold for the author by George Rig, grocer, and Thomas Trotter, merchant. On 13

February copies were available also from Hamilton and Balfour and other book-sellers, 1s. stitched in blue paper. *EEC*, *CM*. Number 2, 22 March 1753, five sheets on a fine demy paper, 1s. *EEC*.

93. SCOTT, John, *excise officer in Biggar.* *An epitome of arithmetic. Containing, the common rules, and general method of operation, particularly in questions containing sums of diverse denominations* ... Edinburgh: printed by Hamilton, Balfour and Neill. 8°, 2 plates. PP: June 1753, 4s. *SM*.

94. SHAKESPEARE. *Works.* General title in volume 1: *The Works of Shakespear. In which the beauties observed by Pope, Warburton, and Dodds, are pointed out. Together with the author's life; a glossary; copious idexes; and, a list of the various readings. In eight volumes.*
Edinburgh: printed by Sands, Murray, and Cochran. for W. Sands, Hamilton and Balfour, Kincaid & Donaldson, L. Hunter, J. Yair, W. Gordon, and J. Brown. 8 volumes, 12°.
Imprints of volumes 1 and 2, and 5 to 8 are as above. Hamilton and Balfour are missing from the imprints of volumes 3 and 4: Edinburgh: printed by Sands, Murray and Cochran. For W. Sands, Kincaid & Donaldson, L. Hunter, J. Yair, W. Gordon, and J. Brown. PP: 31 July 1753, £1. 4s. bound in calf and titled. *CM*.
Notes: Edited by John Reid, corrector of the press for the printer, rather than by Hugh Blair. (See my paper, 'Copyright Litigation in the Court of Session, 1738–1749, and the Rise of the Scottish Book Trade', *Edinburgh Bibliographical Society Transactions*, vol. V part 5 (1988), p.14.)

95. STEWART, Gilbert, *of Scotland.* [EU medical thesis] *Dissertatio medica inauguralis, de morbis ab aetatum mutationibus.* Edinburgi: apud Hamilton, Balfour, et Neill. 8°.

96. STEWART, James, *of Aucharn* *The trial of James Stewart in Aucharn in Duror of Appin, for the murder of Colin Campbell of Glenure, Esq; factor for His Majesty on the forfeited estate of Ardsheil* ... Edinburgh: printed for G. Hamilton and J. Bal-four. 8°, 1 plate (map). PP: February 1753, 5s. in boards (*SM*); noted in *CM* 12 March.

97. SWIFT, Jonathan. *A supplement to Dr. Swift's Works, containing, I. Miscellanies, by Dr. Arbuthnot. II. Several pieces, by Dr. Swift and Mr. Pope. III. Poems on several occasions.* Edinburgh: printed for G. Hamilton and J. Balfour. 12°. PP: by 12 March 1753, 2s. 6d. *CM*. See 67.
Notes: Teerink-Scouten, 93, found this volume issued with a different title and the names of Tonson and Midwinter in the imprint. This points to recirculation by Londoners of seized Scottish reprints ('Copyright litigation ... and the Rise of the Scottish Book Trade,' pp.29–30).

98. WALLACE, Robert. *A dissertation on the numbers of mankind.* Proof sheets. The proofs bear the writing of Wallace and Patrick Neill; David Hume also wrote in a

few corrections. (EUL ms., La.II.96/2.)

99.   WALLACE, Robert.   , *A dissertation on the numbers of mankind in antient and modern times; in which the superior populousness of antiquity is maintained. With an appendix . . . and some remarks on Mr. Hume's Political discourse, of the populousness of ancient nations.*   Edinburgh: printed for G. Hamilton and J. Balfour.   8°.   PP: 6 February 1753, 4*s.* 6*d.* bound, 4*s.* in boards. *CM.*   Copyright: Entered at Stationers' Hall 8 March 1753, the whole share for Hamilton and Balfour (Stationers' Register, 1746–73, 122).

100.   WAYNE, Francis, *of England.* [EU medical thesis]   *Dissertatio medica, inauguralis de variolarum insitione.*   Edinburgi: apud Hamilton, Balfour, et Neill.   4°.

101.   WISHART, William, *the younger, Principal of Edinburgh University.*   *Discourses on several subjects.*   London: printed by W. Strahan; and sold by A. Millar in the Strand, and Mess. Hamilton and Balfour at Edinburgh.   12°.   Edition size: 1,589 common paper, 16 fine [Royal paper] (William Strahan printing account: BL, Add.Mss.48803A, f.16, Messrs. Millar and Strahan).

101.1   ISSUE of the first part: *An essay on the indispensible necessity of a holy and good life to the happiness of Heaven.*   London: printed by W. Strahan; and sold by A. Millar in the Strand, and Mess. Hamilton and Balfour at Edinburgh.   12°.   Edition size: 1,000 (Strahan printing account).   PP: 26 April 1753 in Edinburgh, the *Discourses* 2*s.* 6*d.* bound; the *Essay* was available separately, 8*d.* stitched, with an allowance to anyone buying in dozens to give away. *EEC.*

102.   WRIGHT, Edward, *of Scotland.* [EU medical thesis]   *Dissertatio medica inauguralis, de ferri historia naturali, praeparatis, et usu medico.*   Edinburgi: apud Hamilton, Balfour, et Neill.   8°.

1754

103.   AINSLIE, James, *of Scotland.* [EU medical thesis]   *Dissertatio medica inauguralis, de ictero.*   Edinburgi: apud Hamilton, Balfour, et Neill.   8°.

104.   ALSTON, Prof. Charles, *of Edinburgh University.*   *A dissertation on quick-lime and lime-water. The second edition, with additions.*   Edinburgh: printed by W. Sands, A. Murray, and J. Cochran. Sold by G. Hamilton and J. Balfour.   8°.   PP: June 1754, 1*s. SM.*

105.   ANACREON, with Sappho and Erinna. *Greek and Latin.*   AI TOY ANAKPEON-ΤΟΣ ΟΔΑI, Κὰ τὰ ΣΑΠΨΟΥΣ, ΚΑi EPPINNAΣ AEIΨANA.   Edinburgi, apud Hamilton, Balfour, & Neill.   32°.   Edition size: 500

Notes: '1754 April 23, Messrs Hamilton & Balfour D[rs], to printing a Greek, with Latin Translation of Anacreon, Sappho, & Erinna &c, at 18s. for 2½ sheets, 500 copies, £4. 10s. To a very great Number of Alterations by Professor [Robert] Hunter, and resetting 5 pages, 10s.' (Transcription of the Neill printing account in a copy formerly at Neill and Company, Edinburgh.)

105.1   ISSUE of the Greek section printed on silk.

106.   BLACK, Joseph. [EU medical thesis]   *Dissertatio medica inauguralis, de humore acido a cibis orto, et magnesia alba.*   Edinburgi: apud G. Hamilton et J. Balfour, Academiae Typographos.   8°.

107.   BLACKLOCK, Thomas.   *Poems on several occasions.*   Edinburgh: printed by Hamilton, Balfour and Neill.   8°.   PP: 12 February 1754, 3s. in blue boards. *CM.* Notes: printed for the author, who made 100 guineas from it, according to his friend David Hume (*The Letters of David Hume*, ed. J.Y.T. Greig [Oxford, 1932], I, p.184).

108.   BUTTER, William.   *A method of cure for the stone chiefly by injections. With descriptions and delineations of the instruments contrived for those purposes.*   Edinburgh: printed by Hamilton, Balfour, & Neill.   12°, 1 plate.   PP: 28 March 1754, 1s. *CM.*

109.   DIAPER, John, *of England.* [EU medical thesis]   *Dissertatio medica inauguralis, de clystere.*   Edinburgi: apud Hamilton, Balfour, et Neill.   8°.

110.   EDINBURGH PHILOSOPHICAL SOCIETY   *Essays and observations, physical and literary. Read before a society in Edinburgh, and published by them.* Volume I. [–II.]   Edinburgh: printed by G. Hamilton and G. Balfour, Printers to the University.   Volume 1, 8°, 8 plates.   Volume 2 [1756], 8°, 7 plates.   PP: Volume 1, at Edinburgh 2 May 1754, 6s. in boards including the copper plates by Ravenet (*CM.*, *SM.* for April); at London, 20 May, sold by Wilson and Durham, Millar, Nourse, J. and P. Knapton, Hitch and Hawes, and R. and J. Dodsley (*Public Advertiser*). Volume 2, at Edinburgh, 20 April 1756, 5s. in boards. *CM.*   Copyright: Entered at Stationers' Hall 20 May 1754, the whole share for Hamilton and Balfour (Stationers' Register, 1746–73, 143).
Notes: Volume 3 was published at Edinburgh, printed for John Balfour, in 1771.

111.   EDINBURGH ROYAL EXCHANGE   *Contract of agreement, for building an Exchange, in the City of Edinburgh, between the magistrates and town-council, and the tradesmen.*   Edinburgh: printed by Hamilton, Balfour, and Neill.   8°, 1 plate.   PP: 25 July 1754, 1s. 6d., the copper-plate by itself ['The south front of a new design'd square', J. Fergus delin., A. Bell sculp.], 4d. *CM.*

112.   ERSKINE, David, *Lord Dun. Lord Dun's friendly and familiar advices, adapted to the various stations and conditions of life, and the mutual relations to be observed amongst them.*   Edinburgh: printed for G. Hamilton and Balfour. [*sic*]   12°.   PP: 15

January 1754, the fine paper bound 2*s*., the coarse or common paper 1*s*. 2*d*. in boards. *CM, SM* for December 1753.

Notes: The author's assertion that the King must be obeyed in all circumstances drew pamphlets from Alexander Pitcairn [125] and Robert Wallace [130].

113.   ERSKINE, John.   *The principles of the law of Scotland: in the order of Sir George Macken-zie's Institutes of that law.*   Volume I [–II.]   Edinburgh: printed by Hamilton, Balfour and Neill.   2 Volumes, 8°.

113.1   VARIANT in one volume octavo, in the ordinary-paper state.   *Not seen.*   PP: 30 May 1754, in one large octavo, 7*s*. bound; 'There are a few Copies printed on a very fine paper', bound in two volumes, 10*s*. *CM*.

114.   FORBES, *Theodore, of Scotland* [EU medical thesis] *Dissertatio medica inauguralis, de tussi convulsiva.*   Edinburgi: apud Hamilton, Balfour, et Neill.   8°.

115.   GORDON, Alexander, *of Scotland.* [EU medical thesis]   *Dissertatio medica inau-guralis, de variolis.*   Edinburgi: apud Hamilton, Balfour, et Neill.   8°.

116.   GRAEME, Hugh.   *A letter to a gentleman in Edinburgh, concerning Mr. Graeme of Argomery's improvements of moss, and the benefits of these improvements to the nation.*   Edinburgh: printed for Hamilton & Balfour, and sold by them and other booksellers; and by the booksellers in Perth, Glasgow, & Stirling. M, DCC,LIV. (price four pence.)   8°.

116.1   VARIANT title-page, on the ordinary paper state, presumably with 'Price three pence'.   *Not seen.*   PP: 14 May 1754, fine paper 4d., coarse paper 3d. *CM*.

117.   HAMILTON and BALFOUR.   [A?] *catalogue of a very curious and valuable collection of books, in most languages and faculties, which are to be exposed by way of sale (the lowest price being marked to each book) at the shop of G. Hamilton and J. Balfour, upon Thursday the 21st of November 1754. Among which are . . . The books are generally in fine condition, and will be sold only for ready money. The person who commissions or demands a book first, is always preferred.*   8°.   PP: by 21 November 1754, *(Title-page.)*

118.   HART, Samuel.   *Herminius and Espasia: a tragedy. As it was acted at the theatre in Edinburgh.*   Edinburgh: printed for the author; and sold by G. Hamilton & J. Balfour.   8°.   PP: 12 March 1754. 1*s*. 6*d*. *CM, SM* for February.   Copyright: Entered at Stationers' Hall 23 April 1754, the whole share for Samuel Hart (Stationers' Register, 1746–73, 141).

119.   HORSBURGH, William, M.D.   *Experiments and observations upon the Hartfell Spaw: and an account of its medicinal virtues, so far as they have hitherto been discovered from experience.*   8°.   PP: June 1754, 1*s*. *SM*.

Notes: Horsburgh's account also appears pp. 341–71 in the Edinburgh Philos-phical Society's *Essays and Observations* [110], published in May.

120. HUME, David   *The history of Great Britain, Vol. I. Containing the reigns of James I. and Charles I. By David Hume, Esq;* Edinburgh: printed by Hamilton, Balfour, and Neill.   4°.   Edition size: 2,000 (*The Letters of David Hume,* ed. Greig, I, 193).   PP: 12 November, 1754, in both Edinburgh and London, according to *CM.* Advertised in the *London Gazette* of November 19–23, the book to be had from Gavin Hamilton, the publisher, as well as from Knapton, Longman, Hitch and Hawes, Millar, Dodsley, Rivington, T. Payne, and Wilson and Durham. The retail price was 14*s.* in boards; there were 'a few' large-paper copies, one guinea in boards.   Copyright: Gavin Hamilton entered the book at Stationers' Hall 11 November 1754, the whole share for David Hulme (Stationers' Register, 1746–73, 147).

121. HUNTER, Thomas, *of England.* [EU medical thesis]   *Dissertatio medica inauguralis, de chlorosi.* Edinburgi: cum Typis Academicis.   8°.

122. KENNEDY, Hugo Alexander, *of Ireland.* [EU medical thesis]   *Dissertatio medica inauguralis, de rhabarbaro.*   Edinburgi: cum Typis Academicis.   8°.

123. MURDOCH, Robert, *of Ireland.* [EU medical thesis]   *Dissertatio medica inauguralis, de gonorrhoea.* Edinburgi: apud G. Hamilton et J. Balfour Academiae Typographos.

124. PEYTON, Valentine, *of Virginia.* [EU medical thesis]   *Dissertatio medica inauguralis, de abortu.*   Edinburgi: apud Hamilton, Balfour, et Neill.   8°.

125. PITCAIRN, Alexander.   *Dissertation proving the absurdities of that enslaving and tyrannical doctrine of passive obedience and non-resistance, in all cases, to sovereignty; in opposition to Lord Dun's sentiments in...Friendly and Familiar Advices...*   Edinburgh, printed and sold by G. Hamilton, A. Kincaid, and W. Gordon, booksellers.   8°.   PP: May 1754, 1*s.* 6*d. SM.*

126. PLENDERLEATH, Rev. David, *of Dalkeith.   Religion a treasure to men, and the strength and glory of a nation. A sermon preached in the High-Church of Edinburgh, January 7. 1754. before the Society in Scotland for propagating Christian Knowledge ... To which is annexed, an account of the present state of the schools and missions supported by the Society...*   Edinburgh: Printed by Hamilton, Balfour, & Neill.   8°, with a whole sheet containing list of schools.   Edition size: 500, 300 of which were to be sent to London (SRO: SSPCK Minutes, GD95/1/4, pp.526, 542; GD/95/2/7, p.221).   PP: May 1754, 1*s. SM.*

127. ROSS, Alexander, *of Irleand.* [EU medical thesis]   *Dissertatio medica inauguralis, de amaurosi.*   Edinburgi: apud Hamilton, Balfour, et Neill.   8°.

128. TEMPLE, Sir William.   *The Works of Sir William Temple, Bar*ᵗ*. In four volumes, Volume* I. [–IV] *To which is prefixed, the life and character of the author.*   Edinburgh: printed for G. Hamilton & J. Balfour, A. Kincaid & A. Donaldson, L. Hunter,

W. Gordon, J. Yair, and C. Wright; and for A. Stalker, at Glasgow.   4 volumes, 8°.   PP: 28 May, 1754, £1 bound. *CM.*

129.   THOMSON, Alexander, *of Scotland.* [EU medical thesis]   *Tentamen de effectis pathematum in corpus.*   Edinburgi: apud G. Hamilton et. J. Balfour Academiae Typographos.   8°.

130.   WALLACE, Robert.   *The doctrine of passive obedience and non-resistance considered. With some observations on the necessity and advantages of the revolution in the year 1688 ... Published on occasion of Lord Dun's Friendly and familiar advices.*   Edinburgh: printed by Hamilton, Balfour, and Neill.   8°.   PP: February 1754, 6d. *SM.*

1755

131.   ASTON, Prof. Charles, *of Edinburgh University.*   A second dissertation on quick-lime and lime-water.   Edinburgh: printed by W. Sands, A. Murray, and J. Cochran. Sold by G. Hamilton & J. Balfour.   8°.   PP: July 1755, 1s. *SM.*

132.   ANDERSON, Walter   *The history of Croesus King of Lydia, in IV. parts.*   Edinburgh: printed by Hamilton, Balfour, & Neill.   12°.   table of currency and measure.   PP: 27 November 1755. 2s. 6 d. bound. *CM.* Trade price: on 28 November Alexander Donaldson paid the author 9s. for six copies (EUL ms., in La.II.58).

BLACKWELL, Thomas, *Memoirs of the Court of Augustus*, vol. 2. See (76).

133.   BROUGHTON, William, *of Ireland.* [EU medical thesis]   *Dissertatio medica inauguralis, de ulcere uteri.*   Edinburgi: apud G. Hamilton and J. Balfour Academiae Typographos.   8°.

134.   BROWN, Charles, *of England.* [EU medical thesis]   *Dissertatio medica inauguralis, de morbillis.*   Edinburgi: apud G. Hamilton et J. Balfour Academiae Typographos.   8°.

135.   CABELL, John, *of England.* [EU medical thesis]   *Prolusio medica inauguralis, de animi pathematibus quatenus morborum causis.*   Edinburgi: apud G. Hamilton & J. Balfour Academiae Typographos.   8°.

136.   COURT OF SESSION.   [Decisions of the Court of Session. From the sixteenth of June 1753, to the ninth of March 1754. Collected by Mr. Thomas Millar, Mr. Robert Bruce, Mr. John Swinton junior, Sir David Dalrymple, advocates. By appointment of the Faculty of Advocates.]   2 °. *Not seen.*   PP: This part of the

volume in progress appeared on 1 April 1755, 2s. stitched. *CM.*

137. DUGUET, J.J., translated by Thomas Lally *The principles of the Christian faith. In two volumes. Newly translated from the French. Vol. I.* [Vol.II.] Edinburgh: printed for G. Hamilton & J. Balfour, J. Traill, W. Miller, and J. Brown. 2 volumes, 12°.PP: 2 January 1755, 6s. bound and lettered. 'This excellent Performance was translated by Mr. Lally in 3 Vols. at the Price of 15s., which we have reduced so low as 6s. that it may in the Power of a greater Number to purchase a Book of so General Use'. *CM.* The reference is to the three-volume edition printed at London in 1749 for John Nourse.

138. ECROYD, Richard, *of England.* [EU medical thesis] *Dissertatio medica inauguralis, de rachitide.* Edinburgi: apud G. Hamilton & J. Balfour Academiae Typographos. 8°.

139. EDINBURGH REVIEW. [Alexander Wedderburn, William Robertson, Hugh Blair, John Jardine, Dr. James Russell, Adam Smith]
No. 1: *The Edinburgh Review. Numb. 1. (To be published every six months.) Containing an account of all the books and pamphlets that have been published in Scotland from the first of January to the first of July 1755. To each number will be added an appendix, giving an account of the books published in England and other countries, that are worthy of notice. This number contains...* Edinburgh: printed for G. Hamilton and J. Balfour 1755. Price 1s. 8°. PP: In the press by 17 July 1755, with publication expected in the beginning of August. Published 26 August, 1s. *CM.*
No. 2: Separate title-page not seen. It was probably in the style of the Hamilton and Balfour publication advertisement: [*The Edinburgh Review No. II. (To be published every six months.) Containing an account of all the books and pamphlets that have been published in Scotland from the first of July 1755 to the first of January 1756; with an account of such published in England and other countries as are most worthy of notice. This number contains...*] 8°. PP: 30 March 1756, 1s. *CM.*

140. FARR, William, *of England.* [EU medical thesis] *Dissertatio medica inauguralis, de usu mathematices et philosophiae naturalis in medicinae studio.* Edinburgi: apud G. Hamilton & J. Balfour Academiae Typographos. 8°.

141. FERGUSSON, Adam. [Faculty of Advocates thesis] *Disputatio juridica, ad tit. I. lib. XXII. Pand. De usuris, et fructibus, et causis, et omnibus accessionibus, et mora.* Edinburgi: in aedibus Hamilton, Balfour, & Neill. 4°.

142. FORREST, George, *of Scotland.* [EU medical thesis] *Dissertatio medica inauguralis, de ventriculi concoctione laesa.* Edinburgi: apud G. Hamilton & J. Balfour Academiae Typographos. 8°.

143. GOOLD, Simon, *of Ireland.* [EU medical thesis] *Dissertatio medica inauguralis, de ventriculi imbecillitate.* Edinburgi: apud G. Hamilton & J. Balfour Academiae Typographos. 8°

144.   HALL, John, *of England*. [EU medical thesis]   *Dissertatio medica inauguralis, de febre acuta puerperis superveniente.*   Edinburgi: apud G. Hamilton et J. Balfour Academiae Typographos.

145.   LOUIS XIV   One volume made up as two: *Lettres de Louis XIV. aux princes de l'Europe, à ses généraux, ses ministres, &c. Recueillies par Mr. Rose. sécrétaire du cabinet; avec des remarques historiques, par M. Morelly. Tome* [blank].   *[–Tome II.]*   A   Edinbourg: chez Hamilton, Balfour, & Neill.   12°.   PP: November, 1755, 3*s*. *SM*.

146.   McDONNELL, John, *of Ireland*. [EU medical thesis]   *Dissertatio medica inauguralis, de calculo.*   Edinburgi: apud G. Hamilton & J. Balfour Academiae Typographos.   8°.

147.   McFARLAN, John, *of Scotland*. [EU medical thesis]   *Dissertatio medica inauguralis, de dysenteria.*   Edinburgi: apud G. Hamilton & J. Balfour Academiae Typographos.   8°.

148.   MacLEANE, Lauchlin, *of Ireland*. [EU medical thesis]   *Dissertatio medica inauguralis, de erysipelate.*   Edinburgi: apud G. Hamilton & J. Balfour Academiae Typographos.   8°.

149.   MAXWELL, Walter, *of Scotland*. [EU medical thesis]   *Tentamen medicum inaugurale, de emeticorum usu.*   Edinburgi: apud G. Hamilton & J. Balfour Academiae Typographos.   8°.

150.   MONRO, Alexander, *the second*. [EU medical thesis]   *Dissertatio medica inauguralis, de testibus et de semine in variis animalibus.*   Edinburgi: apud G. Hamilton and J. Balfour Academiae Typographos.   8°.

151.   OWEN, John, [ed. Adam Gib]   *Salus electorum, sanguis Jesu: or the death of death in the death of Christ . . . Carefully revised and corrected.*   Edinburgh: printed by Hamilton, Balfour, and Neill, for James Young bookbinder in Edinburgh.   8°.

152.   ROBERTSON, William   *The situation of the world at the time of Christ's appearance, and its connexion with the success of his religion, considered. A sermon preached before the Society in Scotland for propagating Christian Knowledge, at their anniversary meeting, in the High Church of Edinburgh, on Monday, January 6. 1755 . . .*   Edinburgh: printed by Hamilton, Balfour, and Neill.   8°.   Edition size: 300 copies, 200 of which were sent to London. (SRO: SSPCK minutes, GD95/1/4, pp.556–7.)   PP. March 1755, 6*d*. *SM*.

153.   SALLUST   *Caii Crispi Sallustii belli Catalinarii et Jugurthini historiae.   Edinburgi: apud G. Hamilton et J. Balfour, Academiae Typographos.*   8°.   PP: Not noticed until December 1756 in *SM* and 4 January 1757 in *EEC.*, 3*s*. bound, paper advertised as finest writing treasury post.

154.   A Select Collection of English Plays   The 24 plays in the Collection were printed separately, and brought together in six volumes, with two tragedies and two comedies to a volume. Individual title-pages, and imprints, were retained. The general title page of each volume is in this style: *A select collection of English plays. In six volumes. Vol.I. [–VI]Containing* . . . [four titles in two lines separated by two vertical rules]   Edinburgh: printed for G. Hamilton & J. Balfour.   6 volumes, 8°.

154.1   Issued in another format?   The newspaper advertisement said the plays were 'calculated to be bound up in 6 volumes 12mo'. (*CM*. 29 May). *Not seen.*

155.   Vol. 1:   Rowe, Nicholas.   *The tragedy of Lady Jane Gray, written by Nicholas Rowe, Esq*;   Edinburgh: printed for G. Hamilton and J. Balfour.   8°.

156.   Vol. 1:   Rowe, Nicholas.   *The tragedy of Jane Shore, written by Nicholas Rowe, Esq*; Edinburgh: printed for G. Hamilton, and J. Balfour.   8°.

157.   Vol. 1:   Steele, Sir Richard.   *The conscious lovers. A comedy. Written by Sir Richard Steele.*   Edinburgh: printed for G. Hamilton, and J. Balfour.   8°.

158.   Vol. 1:   Congreve, William.   *Love for love. A comedy. Written by Mr. Congreve.*   Edinburgh: printed for G. Hamilton and J. Balfour.   8°.

159.   Vol. 2:   Congreve, William.   *The mourning bride: a tragedy. Wirtten* [sic] *by Mr. Congreve.*   Edinburgh: printed for G. Hamilton, and J. Balfour.   8°.

160.   Vol. 2:   Hill, Aaron.   *Alzira. Or Spanish insult repented: a tragedy. As it is acted at the Theatre-Royal in Drury-Lane.*   Edinburgh: printed for G. Hamilton, and J. Balfour.   8°.

161.   Vol. 2:   Farquhar, George.   *The beaux stratagem: a comedy. As it is acted at the Theatre-Royal in Drury Lane, by his Majesty's Servants.*   Edinburgh; printed for G. Hamilton and J. Balfour.   8°.

162.   Vol. 2:   Hoadly, Benjamin.   *The suspicious husband, a comedy. As it is acted at the Theatre-Royal in Drury-Lane. Written by Dr. Hoadly.*   Edinburgh: printed for G. Hamilton and J. Balfour.   8°.

163.   Vol. 3:   Philips, Ambrose.   *The distress'd mother. A tragedy. Written by Mr. Philips.*   Edinburgh: printed for G. Hamilton and J. Balfour.   8°.

164.   Vol. 3:   Rowe, Nicholas.   *The fair penitent, a tragedy. Written by Nicholas Rowe, Esq*;   Edinburgh: printed for G. Hamilton, and J. Balfour.   8°.

165.   Vol. 3:   Cibber, Colley, and Sir John Vanburgh.   *The provok'd husband, or, a journey to London. As it is acted at the Theatre-Royal by His Majesty's Servants. Written by the late John Vanburgh, and Mr. Cibber.*   Edinburgh: printed for G. Hamilton and J. Balfour.   8°.

166.   Vol. 3: CIBBER, Colley. *The careless husband. A comedy. Written by C. Cibber.* Edinburgh: printed for G. Hamilton and J. Balfour.   8°.

167.   Vol. 4: ADDISON, Joseph. *Cato, a tragedy, by Mr. Addison.* Edinburgh: printed for G. Hamilton, and J. Balfour.   8°.

168.   Vol. 4: OTWAY, Thomas. *The orphan, or, the unhappy marriage, a tragedy. Written by Tho. Otway.* Edinburgh: printed for G. Hamilton, and J. Balfour.   8°.

169.   Vol. 4: STEELE, Sir Richard. *The funeral, or grief a-la-mode, a comedy. As it is acted at the Theatre-Royal in Drury-Lane, by His Majesty's Servants. Written by Sir Richard Steele.* Edinburgh: printed for G. Hamilton, and J. Balfour.   8°.

170.   Vol. 4: VILLIERS, George, *2nd Duke of Buckingham. The rehearsal; as it is acted at the Theatre-Royal. Written by His Grace, George Villiers, late Duke of Buckingham. With notes . . .* Edinburgh: printed for G. Hamilton and J. Balfour.   8°.

171.   Vol. 5: THOMSON, James. *Tancred and Sigismunda; a tragedy. As it is acted at the Theatre-Royal, in Drury Lane, by His Majesty's Servants. Written by James Thomson.* Edinburgh: printed for G. Hamilton and J. Balfour.   8°.

172.   Vol. 5: MASON, William. *Elfrida, a dramatic poem. Written on the model of the ancient Green tragedy. By Mr. Mason.* Edinburgh: printed for G. Hamilton and J. Balfour.   8°.

173.   Vol. 5: CONGREVE, William. *The way of the world: a comedy. Written by Mr. Congreve.* Edinburgh: printed for G. Hamilton and J. Balfour.   8°.

174.   Vol. 5: GAY, John. *The beggar's opera. As it is acted at the Theatre-Royal, in Lincoln's-Inn-Fields. Written by Mr. Gay.* Edinburgh: printed for G. Hamilton and J. Balfour.   8°.

175.   Vol. 6: OTWAY, Thomas. *Venice preserv'd: or, a plot discovered. A tragedy. Written by Mr Thomas Otway.* Edinburgh: printed for G. Hamilton & J. Balfour.   8°.

176.   Vol. 6: ROWE, Nicholas. *Tamerlane: a tragedy. Written by N. Rowe, Esq;* Edinburgh: printed for G. Hamilton & J. Balfour.   8°.

177.   Vol. 6: RAMSAY, Allan. *The gentle shepherd. A Scots pastoral comedy, written by Allan Ramsay.* Edinburgh: printed for G. Hamilton & J. Balfour.   8°.

178.   Vol. 6: ADDISON, Joseph. *The drummer: or, the haunted house. A comedy. By Mr. Addison.* Edinburgh: printed for G. Hamilton & J. Balfour.   8°.
PP: the first 4 volumes by 29 May 1755. The price for 6 volumes, bound and lettered, was to be 12s.; some copies on a fine writing paper, bound and lettered, 15s. the set. [Individual, unbound copies, would therefore have probably sold for less than 6d.] 'The Publishers have been careful to give a Place to all good Plays

that are in use to be represented in any of the British Theatres, Shakespear's excepted, none of which are included, as the Works of this Author are presumed to be in every Body's hands.' *CM., EEC.*

179. SMITH, Hugh, *of England*. [EU medical thesis] *Dissertatio medica inauguralis, de sanguinis missione.* Edinburgi: apud G. Hamilton et J. Balfour Acadamiae Typographos. 8°.

180. VIRGIL. *P. Virgilii Maronis Bucolica, Georgica, at Ænis, ad optimorum exemplarium fidem recensita. Vol. I.* [–*II.*] Edinburgi: apud G. Hamilton & J Balfour, Academiae typographos. 2 volumes, 8°. Edition size: 1,250–500 on coarse pot, 500 on foolscap, 250 on treasury post (from a printing ledger transcription, in a copy of the book formerly at Neill & Co., Edinburgh.) PP: December, 1754, 1s. 6d., 4s., or 6s. *SM.*

181. WAINWRIGHT, James, *of Ireland*. [EU medical thesis] *Dissertatio medica inauguralis, de hydrocephalo.* Edinburgi: apud G. Hamilton & J. Balfour Academiae Typographos. 8°.

182. WALLACE, Robert. A half-sheet of proofs of an unpublished work: *Irenicum: or, an essay to promote peace and union in ecclesiastical affairs.* Edinburgh: printed by Hamilton, Balfour & Neill. 12°, 6 leaves, pp.13–154 in ms. (EUL: La.II.97/3)

183. WATSON'S, HOSPITAL. *The statutes and rules of George Watson's Hospital. Revised, amended and improven*... Edinburgh: printed by Hamilton Balfour and Neill. 12°.

184. WHYTT, Prof. Robert, *of Edinburgh University*. *An essay on the virtues of lime-water in the cure of the stone. The second edition corrected, with additions.* Edinburgh: printed by Hamilton, Balfour, and Neill. 12°. PP: 2 December 1754, 2s. 6d. CM.

185. WHYTT, Prof. Robert, *of Edinburgh University*. *Physiological essays, containing, I. An inquiry into the causes which promote the circulation of the fluids in the very small vessels of animals. II. Observations on the sensibility and irritability of the parts of men and other animals*... Edinburgh: printed by Hamilton, Balfour, and Neill. 12°. PP: 2 December 1755, 2s. 6d. bound. *CM.*

186. WISDOM of Solomon, and of Ecclesiasticus [ed. Sir David Dalrymple]. *The wisdom of Solomon.* Edinburgh: printed by Hamilton, Balfour, & Neill. Second title-page, p.[67]: *The wisdom of Jesus the son of Sirach; or, Ecclesiasticus.* Edinburgh: printed by Hamilton, Balfour, & Neill. 18°. PP: April 1755, 1s. 6d. stitched. *SM.*

1756

187. BARRY, David, *of Ireland*. [EU medical thesis] *Dissertatio medica inauguralis, de haemorrhoidibus.* Edinburgi: apud G. Hamilton & J. Balfour Academiae Typographos. 8°.

188. BUXTON, George, *of England*. [EU medical thesis] *Dissertatio medica inauguralis, de amaurosi.* Edinburgi: apud G. Hamilton and J. Balfour Academiae Typographos. 8°.

189. CLAUDE, Jean. *Self-examination, in order to a due preparation for the worthy receiving of the sacrament of the Lord's Supper. Written originally in French by M. Claude.* Edinburgh: printed by Hamilton, Balfour, & Neill. 8°. PP: April 1756, 10*d*. SM.

190. COURT OF SESSION. [Decisions of the Court of Session, from June 1754 to August 1755.] *Not Seen.* PP: August 1756, 3*s.* 6*d. SM.*

191. BRITISH SONGS [ed. Sir David Dalrymple]. *British songs. Sacred to love and virtue.* Edinburgh: printed by Hamilton, Balfour, & Neill. 16°. Edition size: 50, for private circulation, according to note by David Laing in NLS copy H.31. f.15.

192. DECKER, Sir Matthew. *An essay on the causes of the decline of the foreign trade, consequently of the value of the lands of Britain, and on the means to restore both.* Edinburgh: M,DCC,LVI. 12°. PP: 24 August 1756, 2*s.* 6*d.* bound, 'published by' Hamilton and Balfour. *CM.*

193. DOBSON, Matthew, *of England*. [EU medical thesis] *Dissertatio medica inauguralis, de menstruis.* Edinburgh: apud G. Hamilton & J. Balfour Academiae Typographos. 8°.

EDINBURGH PHILOSOPHICAL SOCIETY, *Essays and observations*, vol. 2. See (110).

EDINBURGH REVIEW, vol. 2. See (139).

194. EDINBURGH, Royal College of Physicians. *Pharmacopoeia Collegii Regii Medicorum Edinburgensis.* Edinburgi, apud Hamilton, Balfour, et Neill. 12°. PP: 6 April 2*s.* 6*d.* bound. *CM.*

195. GRAEME, Hugh. *Memorial anent the moss-culture by Mr. Craeme. Some reasons for carrying it on. With an apology for giving it up....* Edinburgh: printed by Hamilton, Balfour and Neill. 8°. PP: April 1756, 3*d. SM.*

196. HALDAN, Rev. Bernard, *of Glenholm*. *The foundations of religion and morality. A sermon preached in the Tron Church of Edinburgh... May 11. 1756 .* Edinburgh: printed by Hamilton, Balfour, and Neill. 8°. PP: May 1756, 6*d. SM.*

197. HAMILTON and BALFOUR. [A catalogue of a very curious and valuable collection of books, consisting of upwards of 7,000 volumes in most languages and faculties; which are to be exposed, by way of sale, (the lowest price being marked at each book) at the shop of G. Hamilton and J. Balfour, upon Thursday the first of January 1756. *Not seen.* PP: Published 18 December 1755. *CM.*

198. HAMILTON and BALFOUR. *A vindication of Hamilton & Balfour booksellers in Edinburgh, from the charge brought against them in A memorial concerning the property of the Edinburgh Medical Essays.* Edinburgh: printed for Mess. Hamilton & Balfour. 8°.
Notes: Answers claims made by the widow of the printer William Drummond. See (49), note.

199. HEINECCIUS, Johann Gottlieb. *J. Gotl. Heineccii, jurisconsulti et antecessoris, elementa philosophiae rationalis...* Edinburgi: apud G. Hamilton & J. Balfour. Academiae Typographos. 8°. PP: August 1756, 2s. *SM.*

200. OGILBY, Robert, *of Ireland.* [EU medical thesis] *Dissertatio medica inauguralis, de fonticulorum setaceorumque usu.* Edinburgi: apud G. Hamilton & J. Balfour Academiae Typographos. 8°.

201. PLATO. *The idea of beauty, according to the doctrine of Plato.* Edinburgh: printed in the year M,DCC,LVI. 8°. PP: May 1756. *SM.*

202. PSALMS, of David in metre. [The Psalms of David, according to the version approved by the Church of Scotland, and appointed to be used in worship. Edinburgh: Hamilton, Balfour, and Neill.] *Not collated.* Copy in New York Public Library. PP: 25 May 1756, 2s. on fine writing paper or 2s. 6d. with the church tunes; on coarser paper, bound, 1s. 2d., or 1s. 6d. with the church tunes. *CM.*

203. RUTHVEN, John, *Earl of Gowrie* [ed. Sir David Dalrymple]. *A discourse of the unnatural and vile conspiracie attempted by John Earl of Gowrye and his brother, against his Majestie's person at Saint Johnstoune, upon the 5th of August 1600.* 12°. Edition size: 24, according to pencilled note in NLS copy: 'A copy of this which belongs to Dr. Woodward... bore this inscription "There are only 24 Coppys of the Account published by authority. David Darlymple (Lord Hailes)." ' PP: 8 January 1756, 1s. *CM.*
Notes: Publisher's note leaf π2: 'All Persons who are possessed of any Papers which may tend to illustrate this obscure passage of the Scottish History, are entreated to communicate them to Mess. Hamilton and Balfour...'

204. SMITH, John, *of Queen's College, Cambridge* [ed. Sir David Dalrymple]. *Select discourses: treating...* [contents] Edinburgh: printed by Hamilton, Balfour, & Neill. 12°. PP: announced for 22 July 1756, 3s. bound. *CM.*

205. STANYAN, Abraham. *An account of Switzerland. Written in the year 1714.* Edinburgh: printed by Hamilton, Balfour, and Neill. 12°. PP: 11 March 1756, 2s. 6d. bound. *CM.*

206. STEWART, Prof. Matthew, *of Edinburgh University. A solution of Kepler's problem.* Edinburgh: printed by Hamilton, Balfour, & Neill. 8°, 1 plate.

207. TURNER, William, *of England.* [EU medical thesis] *Dissertatio medica inauguralis, de morbo hypochondriaco.* Edinburgi: apud G. Hamilton & J. Balfour Academiae Typographos. 8°.

208. VAUGHAN, William, *of England.* [EU medical thesis] *Dissertatio medica inauguralis, de rheumatismo.* Edinburgi: apud G. Hamilton & J. Balfour Academiae Typographos. 8°.

209. WADE, Brian, *of Ireland.* [EU medical thesis] *Dissertatio medica inauguralis, de inflammatione.* Edinburgi: apud G. Hamilton & J. Balfour Academiae Typographos. 8°.

1757

210. ALSTON, Prof. Charles, *of Edinburgh University.* A third dissertation on quicklime and lime-water. Edinburgh: printed by Sands, Donaldson, Murray, and Cochran. Sold by G. Hamilton and J. Balfour. 8°. PP: 12 January 1758, 9d. stitched. *CM.*

211. ANDREWS, Rev. Robert, *of Bridgenorth. Eidyllia: or, miscellaneous poems.* Edinburgh: printed by Hamilton, Balfour, and Neill. 4°. PP: by 9 March 1758, 1s. 6d. *CM.*

212. BAYLY, John, *of England.* [EU medical thesis] *Dissertatio medica inauguralis, de frigore quatenus morborum caussa.* Edinburgi: apud Hamilton, Balfour, & Neill, Academiae Typographos. 8°.

213. BULFINCH, Thomas, *of New England.* [EU medical thesis] *Dissertatio medica inauguralis, de crisibus.* Edinburgi: apud Hamilton, Balfour, & Neill, Academiae Typographos. 8°.

214. CARMICHAEL, Alexander, and John Brownlie, *masons. The Edinburgh smoke-doctor. Containing part I. An exact method of carrying up vents in new buildings, to prevent smoke*... Edinburgh: printed by Hamilton, Balfour, & Neill. 8°, 11 plates.

215. COURT OF SESSION *Decisions of the Court of Session, from the month of November M,DCC,XXXV.* Edinburgh: printed by G. Hamilton and J. Balfour. 2°. PP: 4 January 1757, 9s. *EEC.*

216.   ERSKINE, John.   *The principles of the law of Scotland: in the order of Sir George Macken-*
        zie's Institutions of that law. Vol. I. [II.] The second edition, revised by the author.
        Edinburgh: printed by Hamilton, Balfour, and Neill.   2 volumes, 8°.   PP: 2
        May 1757. *EEC.*

217.   GRAY, John, *teacher of mathematics in Greenock. The art of land-measuring explained. In*
        five parts . . .   Glasgow: printed by Robert and Andrew Foulis for the author.
        Sold by D. Wilson and J. Durham, in the Strand, London; G. Hamilton and J.
        Balfour, Edinburgh; and R. and A. Foulis, Glasgow.   8°, 9 plates.   PP: by 15
        September 1757, 6s. *EEC., SM.*   Copyright: Entered at Stationers' Hall 25
        November 1757, the whole share for the author (Stationers' Register, 1746–73,
        117).
        Notes: Gaskell 336.

218.   HAMILTON and BALFOUR   [A catalogue of a curious and valuable collection of
        books, that are to be disposed by way of sale, (the lowest price being marked at
        each book,) at the shop of G. Hamilton and J. Balfour on Saturday the first of
        January next, and to continue till all are sold off . . .]   *Not seen.*   PP: 21 Decem-
        ber 1756. *CM.*

219.   HAMILTON and BALFOUR.   [A catalogue of curious and valuable books, being
        the library of Mr James Armour, Clerk to the Signet, lately deceased, which will
        begin to be sold by auction, at the auction-house of Yair and Fleming, on Monday
        the 31st of January 1757 . . .]   *Not seen.*   PP: 18 January 1757. *EEC.*

220.   HAMILTON and BALFOUR.   [A catalogue of books in physick, surgery, botany,
        anatomy, and chemistry, which are to be sold by way of auction on Tuesday next,
        being the 8th of November, at the auction house of Yair and Fleming. Time of the
        auction from 5 to 8 o'clock at night . . .]   *Not seen.*   PP: 3 November 1757.
        EEC.

221.   HENRY,   Matthew.   *An   exposition   of   the   New   Testament.   In   two   vol-*
        umes . . .   Edinburgh: printed by Hamilton, Balfour, & Neill; for the publisher,
        J. Wood. Sold by most booksellers in Scotland; and at Newcastle, by W. Charnley
        & J. Fleming; at Alnwick, by A. Graham; at Berwick upon Tweed, by R. Taylor;
        at Belfast in Ireland, by J. Hay and R. Johnston.   2 volumes, 2°.

222.   HOG, Sir Roger, *of Harcarse. Decisions of the Court of Session* . . . *From 1681 to*
        1691.   Edinburgh: printed for G. Hamilton and J. Balfour.   2°.   PP: 2 May
        1757, 15s. *EEC., SM.* Hamilton and Balfour advertised for subscriptions as early
        as 14 December 1752, saying they proposed to begin printing in January 1753.
        EEC.

223.   HOME,   Francis,   M.D.   The   principles   of   agriculture   and   vegetation.
        Edinburgh: printed for G. Hamilton & J. Balfour.

223.1   ISSUED with a variant title-page, bearing another imprint and an altered date: Edinburgh: printed by Sands, Donaldson, Murray, and Cochran, for A. Kincaid and A. Donaldson.   8°.   Edition size: 500 ('Copyright Litigation . . . and the Rise of the Scottish Book Trade', 28–29).   PP: 4 January 1757, 'published by G. Hamilton and J. Balfour', 3s. EEC.

224.   HOME, John.   *Douglas: a tragedy. As it is acted at the Theatre-Royal in Covent-Garden.*   Edinburgh: printed for G. Hamilton & J. Balfour, W. Gray & W. Peter.   8°.   PP: 29 March 1757, 1s. 6. EEC. The price is also on the title-page.

225.   ANOTHER EDITION.   *Douglas: a tragedy. As it is acted at the Theatre-Royal in Covent-garden.*   Edinburgh: printed for G. Hamilton and J. Balfour.   8°.   PP: 19 May 1757, 6d. EEC.

226.   MASSON, Arthur, *teacher of languages in Edinburgh.*   *An English spelling book, for the use of schools. In three parts. . . . The second edition, with large improvements.*   Edinburgh: printed for the author, by Hamilton, Balfour, & Neill.   8°.   Edition size: 2,000 + ?   PP: 9 June 1757, 1s. EEC., SM. Masson advertised: 'The first edition of this book, which consisted of two thousand copies, being quite spent, the author has been encouraged to print this edition with large improvements, which have swelled it to a much bigger size, containing no less than 160 pages in Octavo. The price of the book, however, is not raised by this addition: only there are some copies printed on a finer paper which will be sold at 1s. 6d. Great allowance will be given to school-masters in the country. To be had at the shop of Messrs. Hamilton and Balfour, booksellers; and at Mr. Masson's lodgings, now in the third turnpike within the head of Niddry's wynd, east side.' EEC. 9 June.
Notes: The firm printed the third edition in 1761 [312]. In 1765, the author had Patrick Neill print another edition – 6,000 copies of the whole book, 2,000 additional copies of the first part (NLS: in MS.Dep.196, Patrick Neill's Ledger, p.28).

227.   MAXWELL, Robert, *of Arkland.*   *The practical husbandman: being a collection of miscellaneous papers on husbandry, &c.*   Edinburgh: printed by C. Wright and Company, for the Author: sold by him; J. Paton, Hamilton and Balfour, Kincaid and Donaldson, W. Sands, W. Miller, G. Crawfurd, W. Gordon, Yair and Fleming, J. Brown, C. Wright, L. Hunter, Gray and Peters, booksellers, Edinburgh: A. Stalker, D. Baxter, J. Gilmour, booksellers, Glasgow: F. Douglas, Aberdeen: J. More, Dundee; and E. Wilson, Dumfries.   8°, 1 plate.   Copyright: Entered for the author 1 April 1758 (Stationers' Register, 1746–73, 185). The verso of the title-page has a printed note signed by the author: 'This Book is entered in Stationers' Hall; and further to prevent pirating, I have signed each genuine Copy on the Back of the Title-page. Rt. Maxwell.'

228.   OWEN, Pryce, *of Wales.* [EU medical thesis]   *Dissertatio medica inauguralis, de*

mercurio. Edinburgi: apud Hamilton, Balfour, & Neill. Academiae Typographos. 8°.

229. PHAEDRUS. *Phaedri Augusti liberti Fabularum Æsopiarum libri quinque. Ex recensione Alexandri Cuningamii, Scoti. Accedunt Publii Syri, et aliorum veterum, sententiae.* Edinburgi: apud G. Hamilton & J. Balfour, Academiae Typographos. 8°. PP: 4 January 1757, on finest writing treasury post paper, 2*s.* bound. *EEC.*

230. RAMSAY, Robert, *of Scotland.* [EU medical thesis] *Dissertatio medica inauguralis, de bile.* Edinburgi: apud Hamilton, Balfour, & Neill, Academiae Typographos. 8°.

231. ROLLESTON, James, *of England.* [EU medical thesis] *Dissertatio medica inauguralis, de variolis.* Edinburgi: apud Hamilton, Balfour, & Neill. Academiae Typographos. 8°.

232. SWIFT, Jonathan. *Works.*
Series title: *The works of Dr. Jonathan Swift, Dean of St Patrick's Dublin . . . More complete than any preceding edition. In eight volumes.* Edinburgh: printed for G. Hamilton, J. Balfour, & L. Hunter.
Volume titles: *The works of Dr. Jonathan Swift, Dean of St Patrick's, Dublin. Vol. I.* [–VIII.] Edinburgh: printed for G. Hamilton, J. Balfour, & L. Hunter. 8 volumes, 12°.
PP: Proposals advertised 13 May 1756; in the press by 25 November 1756; published 8 December 1757, 12*s.* in sheets to subscribers and as 'ready money' up to 1 January 1758. *CM., EEC.*
Notes: Teerink-Scouten 94.

233. WILKIE, William. *The Epigoniad. A poem in nine books.* Edinburgh: printed by Hamilton, Balfour, & Neill. 8°. Edition size: 750 – 200 of which were sent to London (*The Letters of David Hume,* ed. Greig, I, 266). PP: 26 May 1757, 6*s.* for copies on treasury post, bound, 4*s.* for foolscap, bound. *EEC.* Copyright: Entered at Stationers' Hall 24 June 1757, the whole share for Hamilton, Balfour, and Neill (Stationers' Register, 1746–73, 171.)
Notes: The second edition was published by Millar, Kincaid & Bell with a London imprint in 1759.

234. WYNN, John, *of England.* [EU medical thesis] *Dissertatio medica inauguralis, de cantharidum viribus et usu.* Edinburgi: apud Hamilton, Balfour, & Neill. Academiae Typographos. 8°.

1758

235. BETHUNE, John. *Four short discourses on funeral occasions, by a minister of the Church of*

Scotland. Edinburgh: printed by Hamilton, Balfour, & Neill.   8°.   PP: May 1758, 6*d. SM.*

236.   BUCKHAM, James, *of Scotland.* [EU medical thesis]   *Dissertatio medica inauguralis, de ventriculi inflammatione.* Edinburgi: apud Hamilton, Balfour, & Neill, Academiae Typographos.   8°.

237.   CLAYTON, Thomas, *of Virginia.* [EU medical thesis]   *Dissertatio medica inauguralis, de parca et simplici medicina.* Edinburgi: apud Hamilton, Balfour, & Neill, Academiae Typographos.   8°.

238.   COURT of SESSION.   [Decisions of the Court of Session from November 1755 to March 1756.]   2°.   *Not seen.*   PP: March 1758, 2*s. SM.*

239.   CROOKS, Alexander, *of Scotland.* [EU medical thesis]   *Dissertatio medica inauguralis, de arthritide.* Edinburgi: apud Hamilton, Balfour, & Neill, Academiae Typographos.   8°.

240.   DALRYMPLE, Sir Hew.   *Decisions of the Court of Session, from M,DC,XCVIII, to M,DCC,XVIII. Collected by the Right Honourable Sir Hew Dalrymple of North Berwick, President of that court.* Edinburgh: printed for Gavin Hamilton & John Balfour.   2°.   PP: 3 August 1758, 12*s.* bound for the ordinary copies on foolscap, 16*s.* bound 'for a few copies on a fine Writing Demy paper'. *CM.*

241.   DAVIES, Robert, *of Ireland.* [EU medical thesis]   *Dissertatio medica inauguralis, de chlorosi.* Edinburgi: apud Hamilton, Balfour, & Neill, Academiae Typographos.   8°.

242.   DICK, Rev. Robert.   *The simplicity and popularity of the divine revelations, and their suitableness to the circumstances of mankind. A sermon preached in the High Church of Edinburgh, November 8. 1757*   Edinburgh: printed by Hamilton, Balfour, & Neill.   8°.   PP: November 1758, 6*d. SM.*

243.   EDINBURGH ROYAL INFIRMARY.   *Pharmacopoeia pauperum, in usum Nosocomii Regii Edinburgensis. Editio tertia.* Edinburgi: apud Hamilton, Balfour, et Neill, sumptibus Nosocomii.   8°.   PP: by 16 February 1758, 1*s.*; sold also by the clerks of the Infirmary. *CM.*

244.   FALLON, John, *of Ireland.* [EU medical thesis]   *Dissertatio medica inauguralis, de strumis.* Edinburgi: apud Hamilton, Balfour, & Neill. Academiae Typographos.   8°.

245.   FORDYCE, George, *of Scotland.* [EU medical thesis]   *Dissertatio medica inauguralis, de catarrho.* Edinburgi: apud Hamilton, Balfour, & Neill, Academiae Typographos.   8°.

246.   GARDINER, John, *of Scotland.* [EU medical thesis]   *Dissertatio medica inauguralis, de*

vino. Edinburgi: apud Hamilton, Balfour, & Neill. Academiae Typographos. 8°.

247. HAMILTON and BALFOUR. [A catalogue of valuable books, which begin to be sold by auction on Monday the 16th of January 1758.] *Not seen.* PP: by 22 December 1757. *EEC.*

248. HAMILTON and BALFOUR. [A catalogue of books, to be disposed of by way of sale (the lowest price being marked at each book in the catalogue) beginning on Monday the 23rd [of January] instant.] *Not seen.* PP: by 12 January 1758. *CM.*

249. HAMILTON and BALFOUR. [A catalogue of a large library of books.] *Not seen* PP: to be available at the shop three weeks before an auction beginning 20 November 1758. (*CM.* 5 September 1758).

250. HOME, Francis, M.D. *Principia medicinae. Auctore Francisco Home, Collegii Medicorum Edinburgi Socio.* Edinburgi: apud G. Hamilton, J. Balfour, & P. Neill, Academiae Typographos. 8°. PP: 9 March 1759, 4*s.* in boards. *CM.*

251. HOME, John. *Agis: a tragedy. As it is acted at the Theatre-Royal in Drury-Lane.* Edinburgh: printed for G. Hamilton and J. Balfour. 8°. PP: 14 March 1758, 1*s.* 6*d. CM.*

252. LANDER, John, *of Ireland.* [EU medical thesis] *Dissertatio medica inauguralis, de cataracta.* Edinburgi: apud Hamilton, Balfour, & Neill. Academiae Typographos. 8°.

253. LEECHMAN, Prof. William, *of Glasgow University. The wisdom of God in the gospel revelation. A sermon, preached at the opening of the General Assembly of the Church of Scotland, in May 1758.* Edinburgh: printed by Hamilton, Balfour and Neill. 8°. PP: 3 June 1758, 1*s. CM.* Copyright: Entered at Stationers' Hall 8 July 1758, the whole share for Hamilton, Balfour and Neill (Stationers' Register, 1746–73, 188).
Notes: Reprinted by William Bradford of Philadelphia in 1759.

254. MACARTHUR, Samuel. *Urania: a poem.* Edinburgh. Printed by Hamilton, Balfour, & Neill. 8°. PP: May 1758, 8*d. SM.*

255. MICHAELSON, Thomas, *of England.* [EU medical thesis] *Dissertatio medica inauguralis, de gonorrhoea virulenta.* Edinburgi: apud Hamilton, Balfour, & Neill. Academiae Typographos. 8°.

256. MONRO, Prof. Alexander, the first. *The anatomy of the human bones and nerves. With an account of the reciprocal motions of the heart, and a description of the human lacteal sac and duct. Corrected and enlarged in the sixth edition . . .* Edinburgh: printed for G. Hamilton, and J. Balfour. Sold by them and other booksellers there. At London, by

Mess. Hitch and Hawes, and A. Millar, J. Nourse, R. Baldwin, Rivington and Fletcher, and Wilson and Durham. At Dublin, by J. Smith.   12°.   PP: 16 February 1758, 3s. bound. *CM.*

257.   MONRO, Prof. Alexander, the second.   *Observations, anatomical and physical, wherein Dr. Hunter's claim to some discoveries is examined. With figures.*   Edinburgh: printed by Hamilton, Balfour, & Neill, August M,DCC, LVII.   8°,2 plates.   PP: August 1758, 2s. (*SM.* and title-page.)
Notes: This pamphlet and the following one relate to the controversy between Monro and Dr William Hunter over who was the first to discover the nature of the lymphatic vessels; Mark Akenside also became involved in the dispute.

258.   MONRO, Prof, Alexander, the second.   *Answer to the Notes on the postscript to Observations anatomical and physiological...*   Edinbrgh [sic]: printed in the year M,DCC,LVIII.   8°.   PP: 7 December 1758, 4d. (*CM.*), and a response to the October publication in London of Mark Akenside's *Notes on the postscript.*

259.   MURRAY, Patrick, *Lord Elibank.   Thoughts on money, circulation, and paper currency.*   Edinburgh: printed by Hamilton, Balfour and Neill.   8°.   PP: by 3 June 1758, 6d. *CM.*

260.   PLUTARCH
Series title: *Plutarch's Lives, in six volumes. Translated from the Greek. To which is prefixed the Life of Plutarch, written by Mr. Dryden.*   Edinburgh: printed by Hamilton, Balfour, & Neill.
Volume titles: *Plutarch's Lives, Volume I. [-VI.]Containing...* Edinburgh: printed by Hamilton, Balfour, & Neill. M,DCC,LVII.[-M,DCC,LVIII.]   6 volumes, 12°.   PP: Proposals for an eight-volume edition of *Plutarch's Lives* were advertised in *EEC.* 21 May 1757 by Gordon, Donaldson, Fleming, Wright, Crawford and J. Brown. Hamilton and Balfour responded by advertising that they had had an edition in the press for more than 12 months. Several 'unforeseen incidents' had delayed publication but gentlemen who wished could have three volumes immediately; no money was required until the whole edition was finished (*EEC.* 24 May 1757). The six-volume edition was published by Hamilton and Balfour 28 September 1758. 18s. bound and lettered. *CM.*

261.   RICHARDSON, Edward. [EU medical thesis]   *Dissertatio medica inauguralis, de epilepsia.*   Edinburgi: apud Hamilton, Balfour, & Neill, Academiae Typographos.   8°.

262.   ROBERTSON, Prof. James, *of Edinburgh University.   Grammatica linguæ Habrææ ... In usum Juventutis Academicae.* Edinburgi: apud Hamilton, Balfour, & Neill, Academicae Typographos. Prostant venales apud Hamilton & Balfour, et Gul. Miller,

Edinburgi; Wilson & Durham, Londoni... 8°. PP: by 8 June 1758, 5s. CM.

263. ROLLIN, Charles. *The ancient history of the Egyptians, Carthaginians, Assyrians, Babylonians, Medes and Persians, Macedonians, and Grecians.* Edinburgh: printed for Hamilton and Balfour, Kincaid and Donaldson, and W. Gray. 10 volumes, 12°, 10 plates. PP: 11 November 1758, 10 volumes with 10 copper plates, £1.5s. bound in calf leather and titled. *CM.*

264. SMITH, Charles. *A short essay on the corn trade, and the corn laws.* Edinburgh: printed in the year M,DCC,LVIII. 8°. PP: by 11 March 1758, 1s. CM. SM. for February notes that it was reprinted from a London pamphlet.

265. TERENCE. *Terentii comoediae, ad fidem optimarum editionum expresae.* Edinburgi, apud Hamilton, Balfour, et Neill, Academiae Typographos. 8°. 141 leaves.

265.1 VARIANT, with 145 leaves:
The firm's outstanding apprentice, William Smellie, who composed and corrected the edition by himself, expanded the preliminaries by reimposing the type and by adding new headings. Edition size: at least 250. Hamilton, Balfour, and Neill won an Edinburgh Society silver medal for the edition (*CM.* 4 February 1758), and this was the minimum number to be printed under the terms of the competition. PP: March 1758, 4s. 6d. SM.

266. WILLISON, Rev. John, *of Dundee. The Mother's Catechism*, English and Gaelic.
English title-page: *The mother's catechism for the young child: or, a preparatory help for the young and ignorant, in order to their more easy understanding the catechisms of a larger size.* Edinburgh: printed by Hamilton, Balfour, & Neill. 8°. PP: The SSPCK agreed on 1 June 1758 to have the edition printed, and to pay the translator £100 Scots (SRO GD 95/1/4, pp. 625-6).
Notes: The pages are laid out in two columns, with English in one and Gaelic in the other.

267. WILSON, Andrew, M.D.
General title: *Human nature surveyed by philosophy and revelation. In two essays. I. Philosophical reflections on an important question. II. Essay on the dignity of human nature...* London: sold by Mess. Whiston and White in Fleetstreet, Mess. Rivington and Fletcher, in Paternoster-row; and by Mess. Hamilton & Balfour, and A. Kincaid & J. Bell, at Edinburgh. 8°.

267.1 SEPARATE ISSUE of the second essay: *An essay on the dignity of human nature, being a sequel to the Philosophical reflections...* London: sold by Mess. Whiston and White in Fleetstreet, Mess. Rivington and Fletcher, in Paternoster-row; and by Mess. Hamilton & Balfour, and A. Kincaid & J. Bell, at Edinburgh. 8°, 63 leaves. PP: 3 June 1758, 2s. for the whole work in boards, the *Essay on the dignity of human nature*, 1s. 6d. CM.

1759

268.   CAMPBELL, Prof. Archibald, *of St. Andrews University. The authenticity of the gospel-history justified: and the truth of the Christian revelation demonstrated, from the laws and constitution of human nature. In two volumes.* Edinburgh: printed by Hamilton, Balfour, and Neill.   2 volumes, 8°.   PP: 24 February 1759, 10s. in boards. *CM.* Price later reduced to 8s., because it contained fewer sheets than advertised in the subscription proposals. *Edinburgh Chronicle,* 26 May 1759.

269.   DALRYMPLE, James, *Viscount Stair,* ed. John Gordon and William Johnstone. *The institutions of the law of Scotland, deduced from its originals, and collated with the civil, and feudal-laws, and with the customs of neighbouring nations ... The third edition, corrected, and enlarged, with notes.* Edinburgh: printed for G. Hamilton and J. Balfour.   2°.   PP: 19 July 1759, £2. 2s. in boards, £2. 5s. bound; 'a few copies thrown off on a very fine and large paper', £3. 3s. in boards, £3. 6s. bound (*Edinburgh Chronicle*). Publication of this definitive edition was projected at first for February 1750 (*CM.* 8 August 1749). The first 85 pages were edited by Gordon; the printing stopped, then the work was completed by Johnstone (advertisement within the book).

270.   THE EDINBURGH CHRONICLE.
Volume 1: 22 March to 15 September 1759.   Volume 2: 18 September 1759 to 15 March 1760.   Volume 3: 17 March 1760 to March 1761.
Series titles, each with a two-page index, were given retrospectively for volumes 1 and 2:
The Edinburgh Chronicle; or, Universal Intelligencer. For the year 1759. [For the year 1759–60.] Containing, besides a full collection of news, foreign and domestic, a variety of useful and entertaining essays, both in prose and poetry. Volume I. From March 22. to September 15. [Volume II. From September 18.1759. to March 15.1760.] Edinburgh: printed for Patrick Neill and John Reid; and sold at the first laigh shop below the entry to the Exchange, and at the printing office in the College.
Colophons:
Printed for G. Hamilton, J. Balfour and P. Neill, and sold at the shop of William Gray bookseller, east wing of the New Exchange. Price two-pence halfpenny each.
On 1 September 1759 changed to:
Edinburgh: printed by Gavin Hamilton, John Balfour, Patrick Neill, and John Reid; for the said P. Neill and J. Reid; and sold at the printing-office in the College, and by William Gray in the Exchange, where advertisements are taken in.
On 26 April 1760 changed to:
Edinburgh: printed by Gavin Hamilton, John Balfour, and Patrick Neill; for the

said P. Neill and Company, and sold by William Gray, bookseller, at his shop, in the New Exchange, where, and at the printing-office in the College, commissions and advertisements are taken in.

4°, eight pages per number, three columns to a page.

PP: 22 March to 15 September 1759, twice a week; 17 September 1759 to 30 April 1760, three times a week; from May 1760, once a week. The price of 2½d, was lowered to 2d. at the start of volume 2.

271.   EDINBURGH ROYAL INFIRMARY.   *Pharmacopeia pauperum, in usum Nosocomii Regii Edinburgensis.*   Edinburgi: apud Hamilton, Balfour, et Neill, sumptibus Nosocomii.   8°.

272.   LAUDER, Sir John, *Lord Fountainhall.   The decisions of the Lords of Council and Session, from June 6th, 1678, to July 30th, 1712 ... Volume I. [–Volume II.]*   Edinburgh: printed for G. Hamilton and H. Balfour.   2 volumes, 2°.   PP: volume 1, 4 August 1759, £1. 5s. in sheets until 12 November, when this subscription rate would be raised. *Edinburgh Chronicle.* Volume 2 publication announced for 3 December 1761, £1. 6s. in boards. *CM.* 31 November 1761.

273.   MACQUEEN, Rev. Daniel, *of Edinburgh.   A sermon on Colos. i.23. Preached before the Society in Scotland for propagating Christian Knowledge, at their Anniversary meeting, in the High Church of Edinburgh, on Monday, January 1.1759, (published at their desire) by Daniel MacQueen ...*   Edinburgh: printed by Hamilton, Balfour, and Neill.   8°.   Edition size: 500, 200 of which were sent to London. A few were put into the bookseller's shop, to be sold at 6d., while the remainder were taken by the SSPCK for distribution to members (SRO: GD 95/1/4, p.640).   PP: 26 May 1759, 6d. *Edinburgh Chronicle.*

274.   PORTERFIELD, William, M.D.   *A treatise on the eye, the manner and phaenomena of vision.* In two volumes.   Edinburgh: printed for A. Miller [*sic*] at London, and for G. Hamilton and J. Balfour at Edinburgh.   2 volumes, 8°, 8 plates.   PP: 24 February 1759, 12s. bound. *CM.*

275.   ROBERTSON, William.   *The situation of the world at the time of Christ's appearance, and its connexion with the success of his religion, considered ... The third edition.*   Edinburgh: printed for Hamilton & Balfour, and sold by them, and Mr. Millar, London.   8°.   PP: 26 May 1759, 6d. *Edinburgh Chronicle.*

276.   RUSSELL, Balfour, *of Scotland.* [EU medical thesis]   *Dissertatio medica inauguralis, de cupro.*   Edinburgi: apud Hamilton, Balfour, & Neill. Academiae Typographos.   8°.

277.   SKELTON, Frances, *of Ireland.* [EU medical thesis]   *Dissertatio medica inauguralis, de ophthalmia.*   Edinburgi: apud Hamilton, Balfour, & Neill, Academiae Typographos.   8°.

278.   TOWNSEND, Richard, *of Ireland*. [EU medical thesis]   *Dissertatio medica inauguralis, de rheumatismo*.   Edinburgi: apud Hamilton, Balfour, & Neill, Academiae Typographos.   8°.

1760

279.   ADDISON, Joseph.   *The Spectator . . .Carefully corrected*. Edinburgh: printed by Hamilton, Balfour, & Neill.   8 volumes?   12°.   *Volumes 2–8 not seen*.

280.   BUDD, William, *of Ireland*. [EU medical thesis]   *Dissertatio medica inauguralis, de ischuria vera*.   Edinburgi: apud Hamilton, Balfour, et Neill.

281.   CARLYLE, Alexander.   *The question relating to a Scots militia considered*. Edinburgh: printed for Gavin Hamilton and John Balfour.   8°.   PP: January 1760, 6*d. SM*.

282.   COURT OF SESSION.   *Decisions of the Court of Session, from the beginning of February 1752, to the end of the year 1756. Collected by Mr Thomas Millar, Mr Robert Bruce, Mr. John Swinton junior, Sir David Dalrymple, Mr John Dalrymple, Mr Walter Steuart, advocates*.   Edinburgh: printed for Gavin Hamilton and John Balfour.   2°.   PP: constitutes volume 1 of Faculty of Advocates' official collection. Complete edition announced for 29 January 1760, 18*s*. bound. Parts published since 1752 also sold separately: 1752, 5*s*.; 1753, 2*s*.; 1754, 3*s*. 6*d*.; 1755, 2*s*.; 1756, 3*s*. *CM*. 26 January 1760.

283.   DEMPSTER, George.   *Reasons for extending the militia acts to the disarmed counties of Scotland*.   Edinburgh: printed for Gavin Hamilton and John Balfour.   8°. PP: March 1760, 3*d. SM*.

284.   DONALDSON, Alexander.   [Hamilton, Balfour and Neill printing of an auction catalogue for Donaldson]   8°.   *Not seen*.   Edition size: 750.
Notes: 'To Alexander Donaldson. 1759, Dec. 21. To printing his Auct[ion] Catalogue, 1 sheet 8vo long primer 750 Copys coarse Crown, the paper ours, £1.11. 0*d*' (SRO West, in CS.231, Currie Mack Misc. Bundle 1 no.20.).

EDINBURGH CHRONICLE, 1760.   See (270).

285.   ELLIOT, William, *of Scotland*. [EU medical thesis]   *Tentamen medicum inaugurale, de medicamentis stimulantibus in genere*.   Edinburgi: apud Hamilton, Balfour, et Neill, Academiae Typographos.   8°.

286.   FLEURY, John Charles, *of Ireland*. [EU medical thesis]   *Tentamen medicum inaugurale, de natura febris intermittentis in genere*.   Edinburgi: apud Hamilton, Balfour, et Neill.   8°.

287.   FORDYCE, James.   *The folly, infamy, and misery of unlawful pleasure. A sermon preached*

before the General Assembly of the Church of Scotland, May 25. 1760. Edinburgh: printed for G. Hamilton and J. Balfour. M D C C L X. (Price eight pence.) 8°. 34 leaves. PP: 9 June 1760, 8*d*. (*CM.*) 'This sermon was preached before the grandest audience in Scotland, was delivered with all the graces of oratory, and is bought up with the greatest avidity, especially by the beau-monde, which last circumstance is very uncommon with regard to sermons' (*SM.* for May 1760, p.280).

288. FORDYCE, James. *The folly, infamy, and misery of unlawful pleasure.* [second edition] Edinburgh; printed for G. Hamilton and J. Balfour. 8°, 25 leaves. PP: announced for the last week of August 1760 (*CM.* 23 August), although not noted in *SM.* until October; 6*s*.

289. GOGUET, Antoine Yves. [Hamilton, Balfour and Neill printing of Subscription proposals for *The origin of laws, arts, and sciences*, which was published at Edinburgh, 3 volumes, 1761, Alex. Donaldson and John Reid, for the translator.] Folio page. *Not seen.*
Notes: 'To Alexander Donaldson. 1760, May 26. To subscription for ye Origin of Laws a small fol. page Eng[li]sh 2½ q[uires] writing foolscap, the paper his, 3*s*. 6*d*.' (SRO West: in CS.231, Currie Mack. Misc. Bundle 1 no.20).

290. GROOT, Hugo de. *Hugonis Grotii de jure belli ac pacis librorum III. Compendium. In usuem studiosae juventutis Academiae Edinensis.* Edinburgi: apud Hamilton et Balfour, Academiae Typographos. 12°.

291. HALL, Henry, *of England.* [EU medical thesis] *Tentamen medicum inaugurale, de urinis.* Edinburgi: apud Hamilton, Balfour, et Socios. 8°.

292. HAMILTON and BALFOUR. *A catalogue of books, in most languages and faculties, the libraries of several gentlemen deceased. Which are to be exposed to sale by auction . . . on Monday the 24th of November 1760.* Edinburgh [1760]. 8°. PP: by 1 November 1760. *CM.*

293. HENRY, Matthew. [Hamilton, Balfour and Neill printing for Alexander Donaldson of part of volume 4, *Henry's exposition of the Old and New Testament*, which was published at Edinburgh, sixth edition, 6 volumes, 1760, by Alexander Donaldson and John Reid.] 2°. Edition size: 1,000.
Notes: 'To Alexander Donaldson. 1760, May 28. To last 18 sheets of ye 4th Vol of Henrys Exposition of the Bible 1000 Copys at, £1. 5. 8 per sheet, £23.2.0*d*.' (SRO West: in CS.231, Currie Mack, Misc. Bundle 1 no.20).

294. MACPHERSON, James. *Fragments of ancient poetry, collected in the Highlands of Scotland, and translated from the Galic or Erse language.* Edinburgh: printed for G. Hamilton and J. Balfour. 8°. PP: 14 June 1760, 1*s*. *CM.* Copyright: Entered at Stationers' Hall 28 June 1760, the whole share for Hamilton and Balfour (Stationers' Register, 1746–73, 203).

295.   MACPHERSON, James.   *Fragments of ancient poetry, collected in the Highlands of Scotland, and translated from the Galic or Erse language. The second edition.*   Edinburgh printed for G. Hamilton and J. Balfour.   8°.   PP: 23 August 1760, 1s.

296.   RATHO, CLUB, of Edinburgh.   *Considerations addressed to the nobility and gentlemen of the landed interest, to engage them to use their influence to have the prohibition of the distillery of malt spirits taken off in Scotland.*   Edinburgh: printed by Hamilton, Balfour, Neill, and Reid, for William Gray. M D C C L X. (price three pence.)   8°.   PP: 3d. (title-page).

297.   SULLY, Duke of.   [Hamilton, Balfour and Neill printing for Alexander Donaldson of parts of volumes 4 and 5 of *Memoirs of Maximilian de Bethune, Duke of Sully, prime minister of Henry the Great,* which was published at Edinburgh in October 1760, 5 volumes, printed for A. Donaldson.]   12°.   Edition size: 1,000.
Notes: 'To Alexander Donaldson. 1760, Aug[u]st 9. To 9 sheets being letter B-T of the 4th vol. of Sullys Memoirs, 12mo small pica, 1000 copys at £1.6.8. pr Sheet, £12. To 6½ sheets being letter B-O of ye 5th vol. of Sully, £8.13.4. To foot notes on both these vols, £1.4.8. To paper for proofs, & tympan sheets for Swift [i.e. the *Works* published in 1761] & Sully, 9s. 7d.'. (SRO West: in CS.231, Currie Mack. Misc. Bundle 1 no.20).

298.   WALLACE, George.   *A system of the principles of the law of Scotland. By George Wallace, advocate. Vol. 1.*   Edinburgh: printed for A. Millar, D. Wilson and T. Durham in the Strand, London; and G. Hamilton and J. Balfour, Edinburgh.   2°.   Edition size: 500 (EUL: in La.II.694/6).   PP: announced for 27 March 1760, £1.5 s. in boards. *CM.* March 24.   Copyright: Entered at Stationers' Hall 18 March 1760, the whole share for George Wallace (Stationers' Register, 1746–73, 201).

1761

299.   ADDISON, Joseph.   *The Spectator ... Carefully corrected.*   Edinburgh: printed by Hamilton, Balfour & Neill, for John Wood.   8 volumes. 12°.

300.   BLACKLOCK, Thomas.   *Faith, hope, and charity, compared. A Sermon on I Corinth. xiii.13. Preached in Lady Yester's, Edinburgh, April 19. 1761.*   Edinburgh: printed by Hamilton, Balfour, & Neill.   8°.   PP: May 1761, 6d. *SM.*

301.   BOOTH, James, *of England.* [EU medical thesis]   *Dissertatio medica inauguralis, de ileo.*   Edinburgi: apud Hamilton, Balfour, et Neill, Academiae Typographos.   8°.

302.   BUCHAN, William, *of Scotland.* [EU medical thesis]   *Dissertatio medica inauguralis, de infantum vita conservanda.*   Edinburgi: apud Hamilton, Balfour, et Neill, Academiae Typographos.   8°.

303. BUTTER, William, *of Scotland*. [EU medical thesis] *Dissertatio medica et chirurgica, de arteriotomia*. Edinburgi: apud Hamilton, Balfour, et Neill, Academiae Typographos. 8°.

303.1 VARIANT: The letters 'A.M.' inserted after the athor's name on title-page; errata inserted on leaf E4 verso.

304. DALRYMPLE, Sir David. *A plan for cleaning the streets of the City of Edinburgh*. Edinburgh; printed in the year M,DCC,LXI. 8°: PP: 14 October 1761, 6*d. CM.

EDINBURGH CHRONICLE, 1761. See (270)

305. FERGUSON, Adam. *The history of the proceedings in the case of Maragret, commonly called Peg, only lawful sister to John Bull, Esq*; London: printed for W. Owen, near Temple Bar. 8°. Edition size: 1,000. (*See* (306) notes) PP: in Edinburgh, 3 January 1761, 2*s*.6*d*. on a fine writing paper, sold by W. Gray and all the other booksellers of Edinburgh, and D. Home, bookseller in Glasgow. *EEC*.

306. FERGUSON, Adam. *The history of the proceedings in the case of Margaret, commonly called Peg, only lawful sister to John Bull, Esq; The second edition*. Printed for W. Owen, near Temple Bar. 8°. Edition size; 750. PP: in Edinburgh, 11 February 1761, 1*s*.; same booksellers as before, with the addition of F. Douglas, Aberdeen. *CM*. Notes: Printed by William Strahan, with Patrick Neill participating in the publication costs and sales of the first and second editions (Strahan printing account: British Library, Add.Mss.48803A, f.43.).

307. HAMILTON and BALFOUR. [A large collection of medical and botanical books, being the library of the late Dr. Charles Alston, Professor of Botany in the University of Edinburgh.] *Not seen*. PP: by 24 January, 1761, for auction on 2 February. *CM*.

308. HAMILTON and BALFOUR. [A very valuable collection of books, consisting of about 6,000 volumes in most languages and faculties, particularly, the largest collection of English law, that ever was exposed to sale in this country, being the library of the late Mr. Baron Edlin.] *Not seen*. PP: by 24 January 1761 for an auction to begin 9 February from 5 to 8 p.m. and to continue nightly, in the auction house in the New Exchange. 'The room is very large and commodious, and gentleman will be furnished with seats and tables'. *CM*.

309. HAMILTON and BALFOUR. [A very valuable collection of books in most languages and faculties.] *Not seen*. PP: 18 November 1761 for auction beginning 30 November. *CM*.

310. HAMILTON, Thomas, *Earl of Haddington*. *A treatise on the manner of raising forest trees, &c*. Edinburgh: printed for G. Hamilton and J. Balfour. 12°, 1 plate. PP: by 12 September 1761, 1*s*. 8*d*. in boards. *CM*.

311.   HOWE, Charles. *Devout meditations: or, a collection of thoughts upon religious and philosophical subjects . . . The third edition.* Edinburgh: printed for G. Hamilton and J. Balfour; and for D. Wilson at Plato's Head, and T. Durham at the Golden-Ball in the Strand, London.   12°.   PP: by 12 September 1761, 2s. bound. *CM.*

LAUDER, Sir John, *Lord Fountainhall. Decisions of the Lords of Council and Session, vol. 2. See* (272).

312.   MASSON, Arthur, *teacher of languages in Edinburgh.   An English spelling book, for the use of schools . . . The third edition improved.* Edinburgh: printed for the author. By Hamilton, Balfour, & Neill.   12°.   PP: by 14 October 1761, 1s. *CM.* Copyright: Entered at Stationers' Hall 11 June 1761, the whole share for Arthur Masson (Stationers' Register, 1746–73, 213).
Note: *See* (226).

313.   POPE, Alexander.   *The Iliad of Homer. Translated by Alexander Pope, Esq;* Edinburgh: printed by Hamilton, Balfour, & Neill.   12°, 1 plate.   PP: 3 December 1760, along with the *Odyssey,* in 2 volumes 12mo, sold by Hamilton and Balfour, A. Donaldson, G. Crawfurd, J. Wood, and E. and J. Robertson; 7s. 6d. for the 2 volumes bound in calf, or 4s. for the *Iliad,* 3s. 6d. for the *Odyssey.* (Announced in *CM.* 26 November.)

314.   POPE, Alexander.   *The Odyssey of Homer.   (Not seen with a Hamilton, Balfour and Neill imprint.)* PP: as (313).

315.   RATTRAY, David, *of Scotland.* [EU medical thesis]   *Dissertatio medica inauguralis, de aquae communis viribus medicatis.*   Edinburgi: apud Hamilton, Balfour, et Neill, Academiae Typographos.   8°.

316.   REFLECTIONS.   *Reflections upon the tax of two pennies Scots per pint, on all ale and beer; first granted anno 1693, by the Parliament of Scotland, to the City of Edinburgh, and since continued to Edinburgh, and granted by the British Parliament to many other towns in Scotland.* Edinburgh: printed in the year MDCCLXI.   8°.   PP: 18 March 1761, 4d. *CM.*

317.   SHIPPEN, William, *of Pennsylvania.* [EU medical thesis]   *Dissertatio anatomicomedica, de placentae cum utero nexu.*   Edinburgi: apud Hamilton, Balfour, et Neill, Academiae Typographos.   8°.

318.   SWIFT, Jonathan.   [Hamilton, Balfour and Neill printing of part of volume 2 of *The Works of Dr. Jonathan Swift, Dean of St Patrick's, Dublin,* which was published at Edinburgh, 8 volumes, 1761, printed for A. Donaldson at Pope's Head.]   12°.   Edition size: 1000.

Notes: 'To Alexander Donaldson. 1760, May 29. To 7½ sheets being letter A-P of ye *2d* vol. of Swift's works 12mo long primer 1000 Copys on Demy paper at £1. 10*s*. pr sheet, £11. 5*s*. To Brevier foot notes . . . 1*s*.7*d*. (SRO West: in CS.231. Currie Mack. Misc. Bundle 1 no.20).

319. WHYTT, Prof. Robert, *of Edinburgh University.* *An essay on the virtue of lime-water and soap in the cure of the stone. The third edition corrected, and enlarged with an appendix . . .* Edinburgh: printed by Hamilton, Balfour and Neill. 12°, 1 plate. PP: 12 September 1761, 2*s*. 6*d*. CM.

320. WHYTT, Prof. Robert, *of Edinburgh University.* *Physiological essays, containing . . . The second edition, corrected and enlarged. With an appendix, containing answer to M. de Haller's remarks in the 4th volume of the Memoires sur les parties sensibles et irritables.* Edinburgh: printed by Hamilton, Balfour and Neill. 12°.

320.1 SEPARATE ISSUE OF THE APPENDIX: *A review of the controversy concerning the sensibility and moving power of the parts of men and other animals; in answer to M. de Haller's late remarks on these subjects in the Memoires sur les parties sensibles et irritables, tom. iv.* Edinburgh: printed by Hamilton, Balfour and Neill. 12°. PP: 12 September 1761, *Physiological Essays*, 3*s*., the Appendix, 1*s*. CM.

321. YOUNG, Thomas. [EU medical thesis] *Dissertatio medica inauguralis, de lacte.* Edinburgi: apud Hamilton, Balfour, et Neill, Academiae Typographos. 8°.

1762

322. BERKELEY, John, *of England.* [EU medical thesis] *Dissertatio medica inauguralis, de haemoptoe.* Edinburgi: apud Hamilton, Balfour, et Neill, Academiae Typographos. 8°.

323. CARLYLE, Alexander. *The question relating to a Scots militia considered. In a letter to the lords and gentlemen who have concerted the form of a law for that establishment. By a freeholder. The fourth edition.* Edinburgh: printed for Gavin Hamilton and John Balfour. 8°. PP: 24 February 1762, 3*d*. CM.

324. COURT OF SESSION. *The decisions of the English judges, during the usurpation, from the year 1655, to his Majesty's Restoration, and the sitting down of the Session in June 1661.* Edinburgh: printed for G. Hamilton and J. Balfour. 2°. PP: 23 February 1762, 10*s*. for fine paper, 8*s*. for common. *CM.* 20 February.

325. HARRIS, Richard, *of Ireland.* [EU medical thesis] *Dissertatio medica inauguralis, de abortu.* Edinburgi: apud Hamilton, Balfour, & Neill, Academiae Typographos. 8°.

326. HAMILTON AND BALFOUR. [Book catalogue.] *Not seen.* PP: by 30 October 1762 for auction beginning 6 December; contained 'many thousand' volumes, including history, law, divinity, Elzivir and other editions of the classics. *CM.* 30 October, 4 December.

327. HOWE, Charles. *Devout meditations; or, a collection of thoughts upon religious and philosophical subjects. By a person of honour.* Edinburgh: printed for G. Hamilton and J. Balfour. 12°.

328. LAW, John, *of Ireland.* [EU medical thesis] *Dissertatio medica inauguralis, de asthmate recidivo spasmodico.* Edinburgi: apud Hamilton, Balfour, et Neill, Academiae Typographos. 8°.

329. MACCHIAVELLI, N. *The Works of Nicholas Machiavel, Secretary of State to the Republic of Florence. Newly translated ... By Ellis Farnsworth, M.A. Vicar of Rosthern in Cheshire ... In two volumes.* London: printed for Thomas Davies ... Thomas Waller ... R. and J. Dodsley ... James Fletcher ...; Mess. Balfour and Hamilton, at Edinburgh; and Mr James Hoey, junior, at Dublin. 2 volumes, 4°, 6 half-sheets and 1 sheet of plans, 1 plate. PP: in Edinburgh 27 November 1762, £1. 6s. bound, £1. 12s. in boards.*CM.*

330. MADDOCKS, James, *of England.* [EU medical thesis] *Dissertatio medica inauguralis, de lavatione frigida.* Edinburgi: apud Hamilton, Balfour, & Neill, Academiae Typographos. 8°.

331. MONRO, Prof. Alexander, the first. *The anatomy of the human bones, nerves, and lacteal sac and duct. Corrected and enlarged in the seventh edition ...* Edinburgh: printed for G. Hamilton, and J. Balfour. Sold by them and other booksellers there. At London, by A. Millar, Mess. Hawes and Company, J. Nourse, R. Baldwin, S. Richardson, E. Dilly, D. Wilson, and T. Becket. M,DCC,LXIII. 12°. PP: 17 November 1762, 3s. bound.
Notes: [1762] dated 1763.

332. MONRO, Prof. Alexander, the first. *An expostulatory epistle, to William Hunter, M.D.* Edinburgh: printed for G. Hamilton and J. Balfour. 12°. PP: by 8 December 1762, 'printed so as it may be bound up with the *Anatomy*', 7th edition [331]. *CM.*
Notes: Monro's name is printed at the end; he is defending his son Alexander against remarks made in Hunter's *Medical Commentaries.*

333. NOBLE, Charles Frederick *A voyage to the East Indies in 1747 and 1748. Containing ... ; and illustrated with copper-plates.* London: printed for T. Becket and P.A. Dehondt, at Tully's Head; and T. Durham ... 8°, 11 plates. Edition size; 1,000. PP: at London and Edinburgh 10 November 1761, 5s. bound. 'Booksellers in Scotland may have this book upon the same terms as from the London

booksellers, by directing their commissions, to Patrick Neill, Printer in the College of Edinburgh, he having a number of copies for that purpose'. *CM.*

333.1   RE-ISSUED IN 1765 with a new title page: *A voyage to the East Indies in 1747 and 1748. Containing . . . and illustrated with copper-plates. By Charles-Frederick Noble, Esq; late Lieut-Governor of Marlbro' Port.*   London: printed, and sold by all the booksellers.
Notes: This was a joint publishing venture by Neill and William Strahan, printed at London by Strahan (Strahan's printing account: BL, Add.Mss.48803A, f.100 verso.).

334.   RICCALTOUN, Robert   *An inquiry into the spirit and tendency of Letters on Theron and Aspasio. With a view of the law of nature, and an inquiry into Letters on the Law of Nature. Entered at Stationers Hall.*   Edinburgh, printed for Hamilton, Balfour and Neill.   12°.

334.1   ANOTHER ISSUE: The imprint reads,   Glasgow. Printed for John Orr in the Salt-market. MDCCLXII.

334.2   ANOTHER ISSUE: The imprint reads,   London. Printed for E. Dilly in the Poultry. MDCCLXII.
PP: in Edinburgh and London, 30 November 1761, 2s. *CM.*   Copyright: Entered at Stationers' Hall 8 January 1762 for 'Patrick & Neal', an error for 'Patrick Neill' (Stationers' Register, 1746–73, 220).

335.   SELECT POEMS.   *The select poems of Dr Akenside, Mr Gray, Mr Mason, W. Shenstone Esq; Mess. Wartons, Ld Lyttleton, Mr Dyer, Mr Beattie, Mr Blacklock, Mr Scott, etc.*   Edinburgh: printed by G. Martin & J. Wotherspoon; for W. Russel. Sold by Kincaid & Bell, Hamilton & Balfour, W. Gordon, and W. Gray.   12°.

336.   SMIBERT, Williams, *of Massachusetts.* [EU medical thesis]   *Dissertatio medica inauguralis, de menstruis retentis.*   Edinburgi: apud Hamilton, Balfour, & Neill, Acadamiae Typographos.   8°.

337.   STENHOUSE, James, *of Scotland.* [EU medical thesis]   *Dissertatio medica inauguralis, de peripneumonia vera.*   Edinburgi: apud Hamilton, Balfour, et Neill, Academiae Typographos.   8°.

338.   STEUART, Sir James, *of Goodtrees.   Direlton's doubts and questions in the law of Scotland, resolved and answered . . . The second edition.*   Edinburgh: printed for G. Hamilton & J. Balfour, and A. Kincaid & J. Bell.   8°.

339.   STEVENSON, William, *of Ireland* [EU medical thesis]   *Dissertatio medica inauguralis, de diabete.*   Edinburgi: apud Hamilton, Balfour, et Neill, Academiae Typographos.   8°.

340.   VAUGHAN, James, *of England* [EU medical thesis]   *Dissertatio medica inauguralis, de*

polypo cordis. Edinburgi: apud Hamilton, Balfour, et Neill, Academiae Typographos. 8°.

341.   WITHERSPOON, John   *Seasonable advice to young persons: a sermon on Psalm i.I.*
Preached in the Laigh Church of Paisley, on Sabbath, Feb. 21st, 1762.   Glasgow: printed
by Robert Urie. Sold by Daniel Baxter, and John Barry, booksellers in Glasgow;
G. Hamilton & J. Balfour; A. Kincaid & J. Bell; and W. Gray, junior, booksellers in Edinburgh; R. Banks, bookseller in Stirling; J. Bisset, bookseller in Perth;
J. More, bookseller in Dundee; J. Meuros, bookseller in Kilmarnock; E. Wilson
and L. McLachlan, booksellers in Dumfries; C. Hutcheson, bookseller in Greenock; and G. Knox, bookseller in Ayr.   8°.   PP: 6*d.* (title-page).

1763

(Following the dissolution of the partnership, Balfour used the old firm's name for some
time, for trade purposes.)

342.   BALFOUR, James, *of Pilrig.*   *A delineation of the nature and obligation of morality. With
reflexions on Mr. Hume's book, intitled, An inquiry concerning the principles of morals. The
second edition.*   Edinburgh: printed for Hamilton, and Balfour.   12°.

343.   BLAND, Theodore, *of Virginia* [EU medical thesis]   *Dissertatio medica inauguralis,
de coctione alimentorum in ventriculo.*   Edinburgi: apud Hamilton, Balfour, & Neill,
Academiae Typographos.   8°.

344.   EDINBURGH ROYAL INFIRMARY   *Pharmocopoeia pauperum, in usum Nosocomii Regii
Edinburgensis.*   Edinburgi: apud Hamilton, Balfour, et Neill.

345.   GREGORY, David. [Preface by Colin Maclaurin]   *A treatise of practical geometry. In
three parts . . . The fifth edition.*   Edinburgh: printed by Hamilton, Balfour, and
Neill.   8°, 5 plates.

MONRO, Prof. Alexander, the first.   *The anatomy of the human bones,* 7th edition.   *See* (331).

1764

346.   HAMILTON and BALFOUR   *A catalogue of exceeding curious and valuable books, in most
languages and faculties, lately imported from France and Holland, consisting of several
thousand volumes, which are to be sold at the shop of Gavin Hamilton and John Balfour, for
ready money only . . .*   Edinburgh: printed in the year M,DCC,LXIV.   8°.

Index

[Numbers in *italics* refer to illustrations.]